Teacher Book

fusion

Science 11–14

1

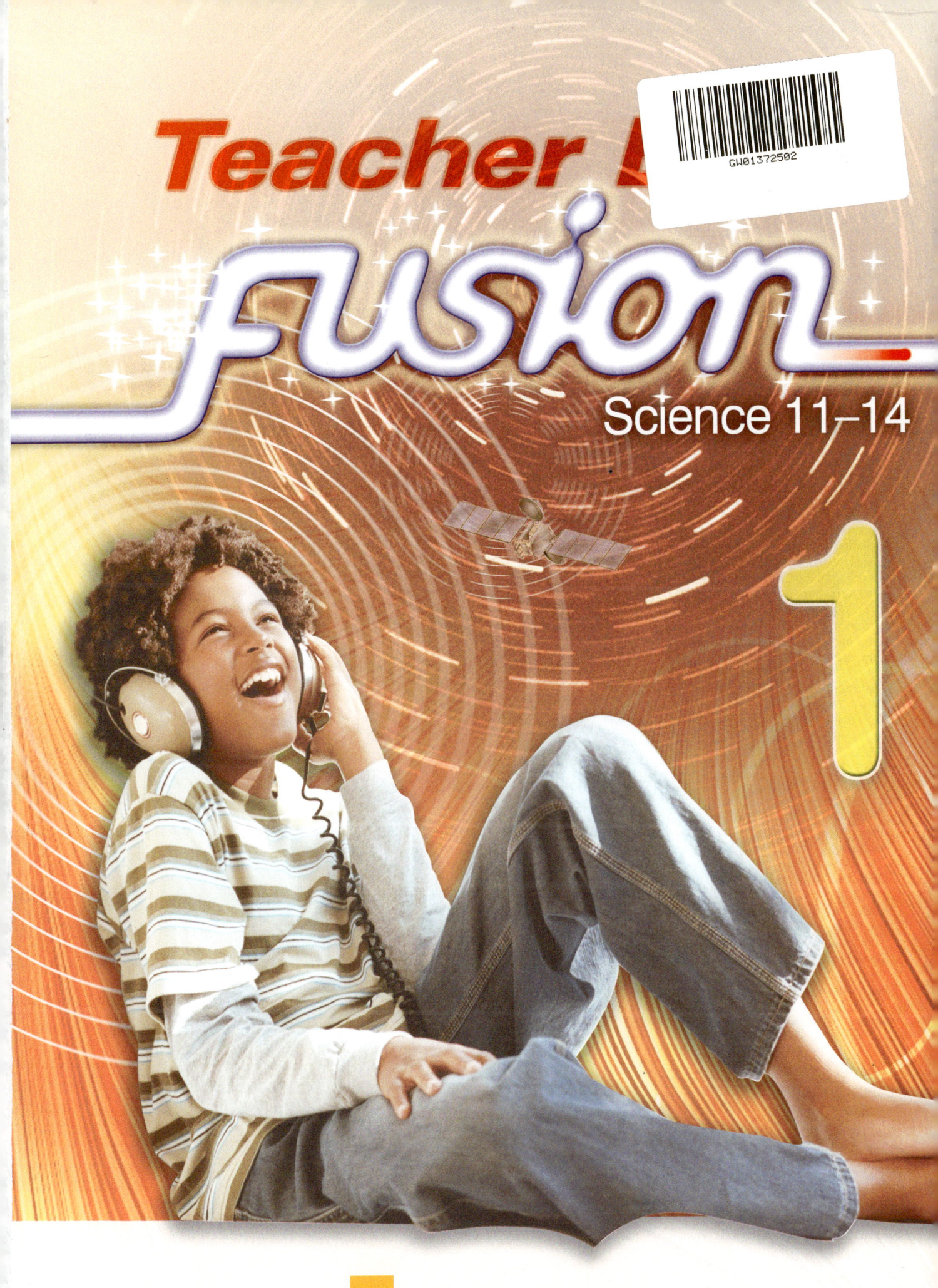

Nelson Thornes

Acknowledgements:

The authors wish to express their special thanks to the following people:

Neil Roscoe	David Sang
John Payne	Sam Holyman
Sarah Ryan	Phil Routledge
Amanda Wilson	Geoff Carr
Annie Hamblin	Paddy Carr
Hazel Banfield	Harry Carr
Ruth Miller	Pip Carr
Jane Taylor	Wilf Carr
Judy Ryan	Enid Carr
Paul Lister	

Text © Lawrie Ryan, Phil Routledge, Sam Holyman, David Sang, 2008

Original illustrations © Nelson Thornes Ltd 2008

The right of Lawrie Ryan, Phil Routledge, Sam Holyman, David Sang to be identified as authors of this work has been asserted by them in accordance with the Copyright, Designs and Patents Act 1988.

All rights reserved. No part of this publication may be reproduced or transmitted in any form or by any means, electronic or mechanical, including photocopy, recording or any information storage and retrieval system, without permission in writing from the publisher or under licence from the Copyright Licensing Agency Limited, of Saffron House, 6–10 Kirby Street, London EC1N 8TS.

Any person who commits any unauthorised act in relation to this publication may be liable to criminal prosecution and civil claims for damages.

Published in 2008 by:
Nelson Thornes Ltd
Delta Place
27 Bath Road
CHELTENHAM
GL53 7TH
United Kingdom

08 09 10 11 12 / 10 9 8 7 6 5 4 3 2 1

A catalogue record for this book is available from the British Library

ISBN 978 0 7487 9834 6

Illustrations by GreenGate Publishing, Barking Dog Art, Harry Venning and Roger Penwill

Cover photograph: Photo Library

Page make-up by GreenGate Publishing Services, Tonbridge, Kent

Printed and bound in the Netherlands by Wilco

Contents

Introduction ... iv

B1 Cells, Tissues and Organs ... 2
- B1.1 Cells, Tissues and Organs ... 2
- B1.2 Using a Microscope ... 4
- B1.3 Looking at Animal Cells ... 6
- B1.4 Looking at Plant Cells ... 8
- B1.5 Special Cells ... 10
- B1.6 Cells, Tissues, Organs and Systems ... 12
- B1.7 The Skeleton ... 14
- B1.8 Joints and Muscles ... 16
- B1.9 Microbes ... 18
- B1.10 Growing Microbes ... 20
- B1.11 Useful Microbes ... 22
- B1.12 Harmful Microbes ... 24
- Answers to End of Topic Questions ... 26

B2 Reproduction ... 28
- B2.1 Fertilisation ... 28
- B2.2 Sex Organs ... 30
- B2.3 Fertilisation in Humans ... 32
- B2.4 Pregnancy ... 34
- B2.5 Birth ... 36
- B2.6 Growing up ... 38
- B2.7 Periods ... 40
- B2.8 In Control ... 42
- B2.9 Reproduction in Plants ... 44
- B2.10 Flowers and Pollination ... 46
- B2.11 Fertilisation in Plants ... 48
- B2.12 Spreading the Seeds ... 50
- Answers to End of Topic Questions ... 52

C1 Reversible and Irreversible Changes ... 54
- C1.1 What is Happening Around Us? ... 54
- C1.2 What are Reversible and Irreversible Changes? ... 56
- C1.3 Are All Acids Dangerous? ... 58
- C1.4 Are All Alkalis Dangerous? ... 60
- C1.5 Indicators ... 62
- C1.6 Acid Reactions: Neutralisation ... 64
- C1.7 Acid Reactions: Metals ... 66
- C1.8 Acid Reactions: Metal Carbonates ... 68
- C1.9 Is It a Metal? ... 70
- C1.10 Burning ... 72
- C1.11 Fuels and Oxygen ... 74
- C1.12 Making Oxygen ... 76
- Answers to End of Topic Questions ... 78

C2 Particles in Action ... 80
- C2.1 What is Matter? ... 80
- C2.2 Solids ... 82
- C2.3 Liquids ... 84
- C2.4 Gases ... 86
- C2.5 Gases in Action ... 88
- C2.6 Changing State ... 90
- C2.7 Mixtures ... 92
- C2.8 Separating Mixtures: Sieving and Filtering ... 94
- C2.9 Separating Mixtures: Chromatography ... 96
- C2.10 Separating Mixtures: Distillation and Evaporation ... 98
- C2.11 Grouping Chemicals ... 100
- Answers to End of Topic Questions ... 102

P1 Electricity and Magnetism ... 104
- P1.1 Strike a Light! ... 104
- P1.2 Complete Circuits ... 106
- P1.3 Electric Current ... 108
- P1.4 Cells and Batteries ... 110
- P1.5 Shocking Stuff! ... 112
- P1.6 Series and Parallel ... 114
- P1.7 Magnetic Forces ... 116
- P1.8 Making Magnets ... 118
- P1.9 A Field of Force ... 120
- P1.10 Electromagnets ... 122
- P1.11 Electromagnets at Work ... 124
- Answers to End of Topic Questions ... 126

P2 Forces and Energy ... 128
- P2.1 Getting Stronger ... 128
- P2.2 Measuring Forces ... 130
- P2.3 Bending, Stretching ... 132
- P2.4 Friction ... 134
- P2.5 Floating and Sinking ... 136
- P2.6 A Matter of Density ... 138
- P2.7 Fuels Alight ... 140
- P2.8 Burning the Past, Wrecking the Future? ... 142
- P2.9 Renewables – Cleaning up our Act ... 144
- P2.10 Making More of Energy ... 146
- P2.11 How Much Energy? ... 148
- Answers to End of Topic Questions ... 150

How Science Works ... 152
- Finding the answers to questions (1) ... 152
- Finding the answers to questions (2) ... 154
- The skills of investigation (1) ... 156
- The skills of investigation (2) ... 158
- The skills of investigation (3) ... 160

Glossary ... 162

Acknowledgements ... 167

Welcome to Fusion

About the course

Motivate, Improve, Progress …

Fusion has been written specifically to help you to deliver the new Programme of Study for Key Stage 3 Science from 2008. With its fully blended approach including the Pupil Book, Teacher Book and online electronic resources, you have the tools in place to deliver your science lessons in a stimulating and engaging way, with differentiation included throughout. The electronic resources are located in our online environment, Nelson Thornes learning space, and provide you with the facility to assign differentiated resources to individual pupils making **personalising learning** easy. **Assessment for learning** is built in throughout the course.

The Pupil Book

Fusion Pupil Book is structured into six teaching topics per year each with How Science Works (HSW) integrated throughout. Each topic has an Introduction lesson enabling you to establish prior learning, usually through the means of a practical activity. The Introduction lesson is also used to experiment and formulate ideas about the forthcoming topic. All this is done in a context that pupils are familiar with, either in their everyday lives or that they have previously visited relevant topics in science lessons.

The topic itself has a very practical approach to motivate and engage pupils. Context-led throughout, the text is highly accessible to ensure that there are no barriers to learning and understanding about science.

At the end of each topic is a spread of questions – one page assesses knowledge and understanding of the range and content whilst the other page assesses application of ideas and the How Science Works approach.

In addition to How Science Works being integrated throughout, there is also additional support for How Science Works at the back of the Pupil Book and Teacher Book. This additional section incorporates a skills-based approach and can be used separately or integrated within the teaching of the rest of the topics.

How to use the Teacher Book

This Teacher Book is designed to help you to plan and deliver motivating and engaging science lessons. It contains a reduced size replica of the Pupil Book page, and the curriculum references, objectives, opportunities to incorporate How Science Works, Functional Skills, Teaching Notes, Practical Support Notes, Support for SEN and Extension and potential homeworks to support the delivery of the lesson.

Questions: In-text questions support the learning from the page and build confidence. The Summary Questions reflect the Learning Objectives for the spread and are listed hierarchically. Answers are provided in the Teacher Book to support the teacher.

Functional skills: Opportunities have been identified to help you to deliver Functional skills throughout your teaching of science. Functional skills are practical skills in English, mathematics, and ICT. These equip individuals to work confidently, effectively and independently in their every day lives, be it in school, at home or in the workplace. Other opportunities for linking up to other subjects are explored in both the Teacher Book and Pupil Book.

Introduction double-page spread: These two pages provide the information to help you teach the topic ahead. It provides details of how the new Programme of Study will be covered by the topic. It also covers Level Descriptors for the topic as well as Learning Objectives and learning outcomes for the Introduction lesson including How Science Works opportunities.

The Lesson: Every page of the Pupil Book and Teacher Book has electronic support located in the online environment, Nelson Thornes learning space. With two starter and two plenary suggestions tailored to the teaching time, the lesson has a suggested route through with lots of teaching ideas based around each Pupil Book double-page spread. For every practical within the Pupil Book you will find the corresponding Practical Support feature in the Teacher Book that gives a list of the equipment needed, safety references and further guidance to carry out the practical. Differentiated Practical Support sheets, Teacher Notes and Technician Notes are located in the Nelson Thornes online learning environment.

Differentiation: Ideas to support pupils with SEN and to extend those who have successfully completed other activities in the lesson are provided to help you tailor your lessons to individuals.

Homework suggestions: Based around the lesson, potential stimuli for homework are identified, and there is additional support for homework activities in the online resources.

Online Resources

Animations, simulations, interactive activities and non-interactive worksheets are located in the Nelson Thornes learning space to fully support the delivery of the Fusion course. These are linked to the Pupil Book and help deliver the ideas suggested within the Teacher Book as indicated by icons.

A wealth of resources is included in the online environment including differentiated practical support sheets, Teacher Notes and Technician Notes, differentiated Level Assessed Tasks, Webquests, resources to support starters and plenaries, interactive activities to support teaching and learning, Lesson Objectives (including WALT and WILF objectives), Revision Quizzes, Progress Checks, differentiated homeworks and much more!

To help you identify the electronic resources that have been created to specifically support the lesson, icons have been placed in the Teacher Book next to the area that they support. All topics additionally have Revision Quizzes and Progress Checks in both an interactive and non-interactive format, a Level Assessed Task and a Webquest. The assessment resources provide you with an opportunity to monitor and record pupil progress and tailor your lessons accordingly.

To help you to determine the type of electronic resources available to support the lesson, the following icons have been used:

Video – Exciting and relevant video taken from a variety of sources to enhance the learning of certain topics

Worksheets – to include practicals, Teacher Notes, Technician Notes, some homeworks and specific materials to support lower attainers and extend higher attainers.

Interactives – simulations, animations, Webquests, interactive activities and PowerPoints.

Assessment – Revision Quizzes, Progress Checks, Level Assessed Tasks, End of Year Tests

Learning Objectives PowerPoint – for each lesson to include WALT (We Are Learning To) and WILF (What I am Looking For)

We hope that this course will provide you with everything you need to engage your pupils in their science lessons and that its flexible approach will help you to motivate all pupils to progress and achieve their best. Good luck!

B1.1 Cells, Tissues and Organs

NC links for the topic
- Organisms, behaviour and health
- Life processes are supported by the organisation of cells into tissues, organs and body systems.
- … growth, development, behaviour and health can be affected by diet, drugs and disease.
- Key processes: use a range of scientific methods and techniques to develop and test ideas and explanations.
- Key processes: assess risk and work safely in the laboratory, field and workplace.
- Key processes: carry out practical and investigative activities, both individually and in groups.

Level descriptors for the topic
- **AT2 level 4:** They describe some processes and phenomena related to organisms, their behaviour and the environment.

  They recognise that evidence can refute or support scientific ideas.

  They recognise some applications and implications of science.
- **AT2 level 5:** They describe some processes and phenomena related to organisms, their behaviour and the environment, drawing on abstract ideas and using appropriate terminology, e.g. functions of organs.

  They explain processes and phenomena … such as the main stages of the life cycles of humans and flowering plants.
- **AT2 level 6:** They explain the importance of some applications and implications of science such as control of fertility.
- **AT2 level 7:** They describe a wide range of processes and phenomena related to organisms, their behaviour and the environment, using abstract ideas and appropriate terminology and sequencing a number of points.
- **AT2 level 8:** Pupils demonstrate extensive knowledge and understanding related to organisms, their behaviour and the environment. They use and apply this effectively in their descriptions and explanations, identifying links between topics, for example relating cellular structure of organs to their associated life processes.
- **AT2 exceptional performance:** Pupils demonstrate both breadth and depth of knowledge and understanding of organisms, their behaviour and the environment. They apply this effectively in their descriptions and explanations, identifying links and patterns within and between topics, for example linking internal and external cell structures to life processes.

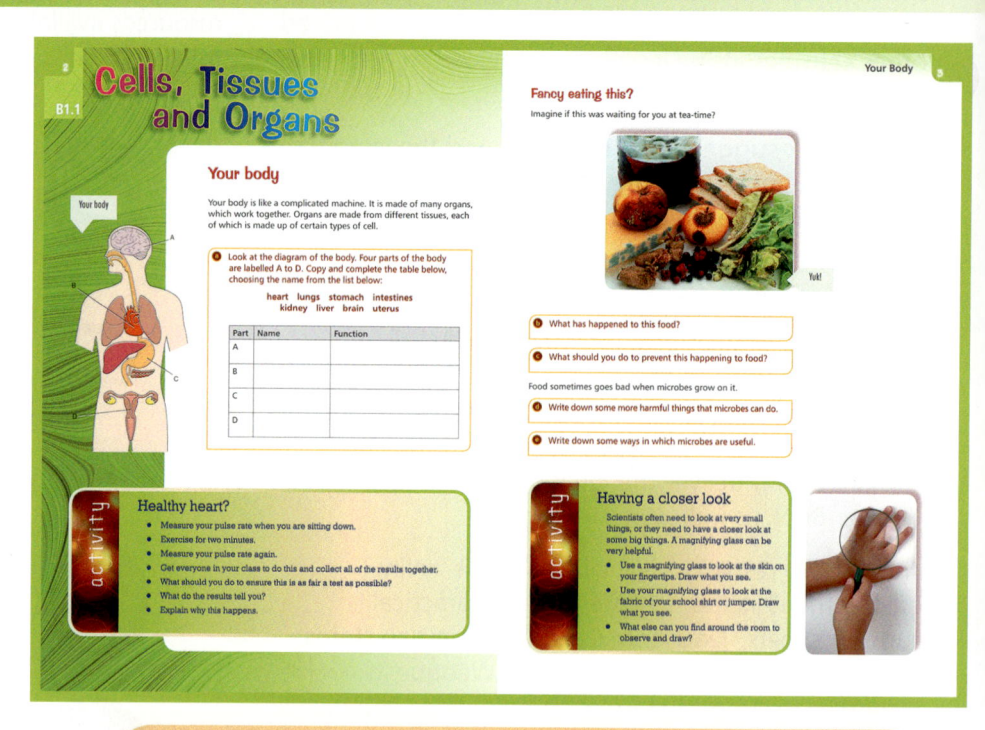

Learning Objectives
Pupils should learn:
- Where our major body organs are and what they do.
- To describe ways in which microbes can be harmful and helpful.
- To use a magnifying glass.

Learning Outcomes
- All pupils should be able to locate the major organs on a diagram, know that microbes can help or harm us.
- Most pupils should be able to locate the major organs, describe their functions, state some of the uses and hazards of microbes and use a magnifying glass.
- Some pupils should also be able to do the above with increased depth and detail.

How Science Works
- Describe and record observations and evidence systematically. (1.2d)

Answers to in-text questions

a

Part	Name	Function
A	Brain	Controls the body, memory, learning, etc.
B	Heart	Pumps blood around the body
C	Stomach	Digestion of food.
D	Uterus	Where the fetus develops.

b Gone off / gone bad / rotted / decomposed

c Keep it in a fridge/cool place.

d Make us ill.

e Making foods, e.g. cheese/yoghurt, making useful products, e.g. medicines, etc.

The Lesson

Starter Suggestions

Let's get organised
Give the pupils a set of cards which contains the names of some organs and their functions. Get the pupils to sort out the organ cards and place them to one side. Pupils are then to match the organs with function cards. Have a set of blank cards available for pupils to complete themselves as extensions. (5–10 mins)

System down!
Imagine the body has a control room (possibly inside the brain) inhabited by little creatures monitoring all the body systems. In small groups draw out tables of body parts and failure symptoms for each one (a template will help lower attaining groups). Share these once complete. (10–15 mins)

Main Lesson

- Discuss the starter activity 'Let's get organised'. Draw out from the pupils their current level of knowledge of the major organs of the body and tailor the rest of the lesson accordingly. Using PowerPoint describe the functions of the brain (in terms of controlling the rest of the functions of the body), the stomach and intestines (in terms of the dissolving and absorption of food and excretion of waste) the lungs (in terms of gas exchange with carbon dioxide going out and oxygen coming in) and the heart (in terms of pumping blood around the body). Copy and complete the table from the pupil book (in-text q.1) regarding parts, names and functions.

- Discuss the role of the heart in particular. Get the pupils to squeeze their fists in the air, hard, every second for a minute. Discuss how amazing heart muscle is that it can do that for a lifetime without getting tired. Hold an open discussion on why we need a heart. Get beyond 'to keep us alive' into details of transport of gases, food, waste, heat, water and hormones.

Healthy heart
- Give the pupils a worksheet on measuring their heart rate. Show the pupils how to measure their pulse at the wrist (place index and second fingers just above the tendons on the thumb side of the lower wrist about 2 cm down from the start of the palm); for those who find this difficult show how to measure it at the neck. Digital readouts can be available from data-loggers and specialist heart monitors for use in sports. Check these out in advance, as some can be intermittent in function.

- Discuss what will be needed to ensure a fair test. Draw out duration and severity of exercise, method and duration of measurement. Discuss methods of ensuring these are the same for everybody.

- Working in pairs get the pupils to take each other's resting heart rates. Record these first and place onto an Excel spreadsheet set to calculate the class average automatically.

- Get one from each pair to carry out some exercise. Stepping onto and off a gym bench is easy to arrange. Alternatively running on the spot or, if in a suitable place, a short circular run will do. Make sure pupils are fit and happy to do this.

- At the end of the exercise get the pupil to take their own pulse while their partner times 15 seconds. Multiply this by four to get beats per minute and record it.

- Swap roles and repeat.

- Collect all the post-exercise data together and again enter it onto an average calculating spreadsheet.

- From a bar chart of the class average results before and after exercise draw out a conclusion regarding the effect of exercise on heart rate. Lead a discussion about reasons for this.

Fancy eating this?
Look at the photo of the rotten food in the pupil book. Alternatively arrange for some rotten food, such as a mouldy tomato, to be in a bowl covered in cling film and hand this around ensuring it is not opened. Discuss ways in which microbes can be helpful. Pupils to answer the in-text questions, possibly completing as homework.

Having a closer look
Count-out magnifying glasses, one between two. Ask the pupils to use them to examine skin on fingertips, fabric on uniforms and other objects around the room. Ask if they can see any microbes. Warn about looking at the Sun or light sources through magnifying glasses. Remind them of the character 'Sid' in the film *Toy Story* and what he did to Woody's forehead with a magnifying glass.

Plenary Suggestions

Small is beautiful
Describe in as much detail as possible one view through your magnifying glass. Use poetic language and imagination to encourage others to see the world a different way. Read out a number of examples from the group. (5–10 mins)

Body-bit bingo
Give each pupil a bingo card with the names of the major organs and their functions on it. Picking these at random, e.g. from strips of paper in a hat, read them out. Play for a line, two lines and full house. (10–15 mins)

Practical Support

Healthy heart?

Equipment and materials required
Per pair: Stop-watch. If available, data-logger and heart rate monitor or sports monitor.

Safety
Ensure that the exercise the pupils carry out is appropriate. If necessary pupils with disabilities can carry out appropriate activities such as arm movements for wheelchair users. Ensure that no exercise causes undue stress.
CLEAPPS: Handbook/ CD-ROM section 14.5.

Fancy eating this?

Equipment and materials required
bowl with half a mouldy tomato inside, in plastic bag or sealed in clingfilm.

Safety
Ensure that the pupils do not open this.

Having a closer look

Equipment and materials required
Magnifying glasses. Frensel lenses of the type used in car or bus back windows can also be useful here.

Safety
Ensure that the pupils do not look at light sources or focus sunlight on inappropriate objects

B1.2 Using a Microscope

NC links for the lesson
- Organisms, behaviour and health
- Life processes are supported by the organisation of cells into tissues, organs and body systems.
- Practical enquiry skills: carry out practical and investigative activities, both individually and in groups.

Learning Objectives
Pupils should learn:
- How to focus a microscope.
- To calculate by how much a microscope magnifies.
- To record what they see through a microscope.

Learning Outcomes
- All pupils should be able to use a microscope effectively and safely and label some parts.
- Most pupils should be able to perform simple calculations regarding magnification.
- Some pupils should also be able to link the structure of microscopes with that of early models.

How Science Works
- Describe and record observations and evidence systematically. (1.2d)

Functional Skills Link-up

Mathematics
- Use simple formulae expressed in words for one or two-step operations (level 1).

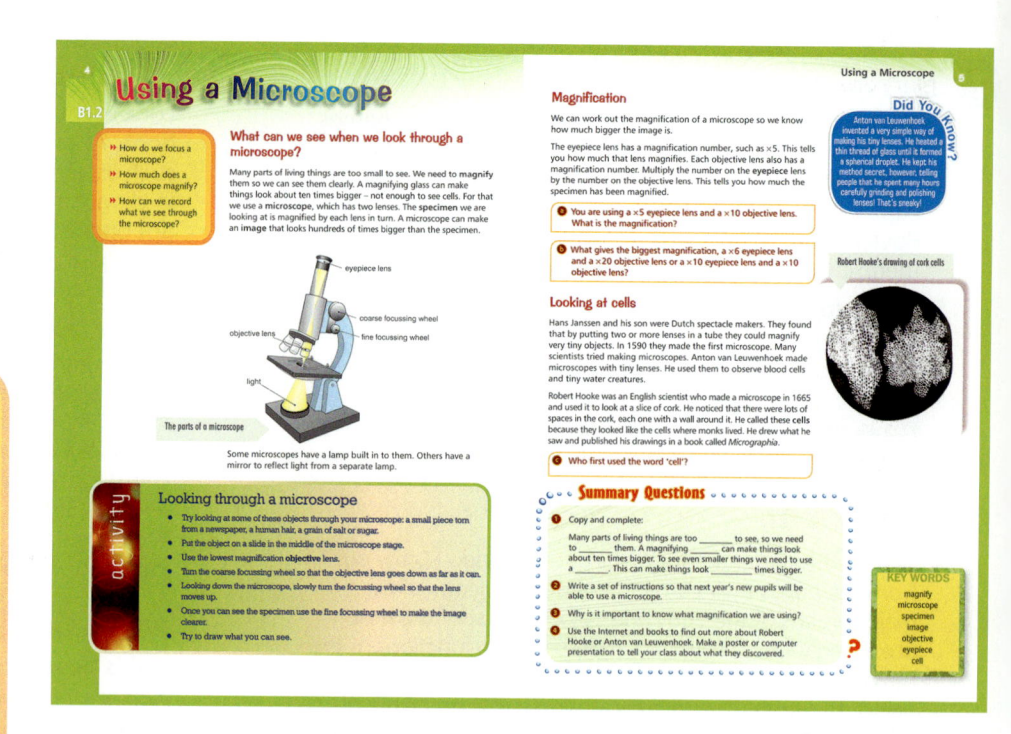

Learning Styles
Visual: Looking at microscope slides and projected images.
Auditory: Listening to exposition.
Kinaesthetic: Interacting with microscope and specimens.
Interpersonal: Working as part of a group to set up slides for observation.
Intrapersonal: Imagining the miniaturisation journey as in the starter 'That shrinking feeling'.

Answers to summary questions

1. Many parts of living things are too **small** to see, so we need to **magnify** them. A magnifying **glass** can make things look about ten times bigger. To see even smaller things we need to use a **microscope**. This can make things look **hundreds of** times bigger.

2. Put the object on a slide in the middle of the microscope stage. Use the lowest magnification objective lens. Turn the coarse focussing wheel so that the objective lens goes down as far as it can. Looking down the microscope, slowly turn the focussing wheel so that the lens moves up. Once you can see the specimen use the fine focussing wheel to make the image clearer.

3. So we can work out the size of the specimen.

4. Research.

The Lesson

Starter Suggestions

Cells sentences

Pupils should write down a sentence which contains the word 'cells'. They then discuss their sentences, drawing out the common meanings of the word and separate this from the scientific meaning. (5 mins)

That shrinking feeling

Ask the pupils if they have seen any films or cartoons where people have shrunk (see if any pupils are familiar with and can talk about the 'Parasites Lost' episode in the animation *Futurama*, where the cast are miniaturised and go inside Fry to kill his worm infestation Alternatively the film *Inner space* has appropriate footage. Pupils should imagine themselves miniaturised to a microscopic scale. Ask them to write what they think various objects would look like as they took a journey around the classroom. Discuss this with the class. (10 mins)

Main Lesson

- Start off by projecting a number of interesting images of insects, pollen and other such engaging material. Discuss this hidden world and how impossible it was, until fairly recently, to know what these things looked like. A good starting point is www.cellsalive.com.

- **Looking through a microscope**
  Show the pupils a microscope. If possible use a Flexicam and digital projector to display details. Name each part in turn, explaining the name and giving ways of remembering them. The eyepiece is the piece next to the eye. Use questioning – what is the name for the thing we are looking at? (an object); so the lens next to that is the 'objective'. What is the name for the part on a tank which rotates? (the turret); the same goes for the bit which rotates on the microscope. Ask the pupils when they last saw a theatre performance or a band. Ask them what the name is for the raised platform that people stand on to be looked at (the stage); the same goes for the microscope. Get the pupils to imagine sliding down a sheet of glass to help remember the word 'slide'.

- Show the pupils how to carry a microscope correctly. Warn pupils against focussing down too far and breaking the slide.

- Describe the functions of the focussing wheels and demonstrate this using a Flexicam down an eyepiece. Use a PowerPoint sequence to describe the safe use of the microscope in terms of focussing up to an object after looking from the side, and adjusting the height of the objective lens to just above the specimen. Check by questioning.

- Pupils are to fill in a worksheet to label the parts of the microscope and match the parts with their descriptions on a paired sheet.

- Explain the magnification system in terms of eyepiece power × objective power. Carry out a simple exercise on the board or on a PowerPoint to reinforce this.

Plenary Suggestions

Drag and drop labels

Pupils are to drag and drop the correct labels onto the correct places on a projected microscope diagram. To add competition the exercise can be timed. (5–10 mins)

Hooke video

Show a video extract from the work of Robert Hooke. (10–15 mins)

Practical Support

Looking through a microscope

Details

Pupils are to use microscopes to examine a wide range of common objects such as salt crystals, hair, needle tips (care that these are not used inappropriately and are sterile). If available, have a number of prepared slides of interesting specimens to look at such as fly's wings, insect mouthparts, bees' legs and stings. If time allows, pupils may make diagrams of what they see and state the magnification.

Support

During the practical, circulate and ensure that all pupils are able to focus their microscopes. If inexperienced, practise this yourself beforehand. Many pupils have difficulty in using a microscope for the first time. Try getting them to look with both eyes open and focus their slide yourself, ask them to look at it and then defocus it either down or up and ask them to put it back into focus. Tell the pupils not to put fingers on lenses.

Safety

Demonstrate safe handling using body and base.

Differentiation

SEN

A series of 'Can you tell what it is yet?' cards showing small details of larger objects could be made. Alternatively, a sheet with a small round hole in it could be placed over a series of photographs and the pupils have to work out what it is by looking at a small part. This could be geared to the ability of the pupils by changing the nature of the photograph.

Extension

Pupils should be given an opportunity to look at the range of miniature sculptures made from grains of rice and sugar recently sold for £11.2 million, by the sculptor Willard Wigan, as reported by the BBC on 11 May 2007. A report could be drawn up of how he made his sculptures.

Answers to in-text questions

a × 50

b × 6 eyepiece lens and a × 20 objective lens

c Robert Hooke

B1.3 Looking at Animal Cells

NC links for the lesson
- Organisms, behaviour and health
- Life processes are supported by the organisation of cells into tissues, organs and body systems.

Learning Objectives
Pupils should learn:
- The parts of an animal cell we can see through a microscope.
- The jobs of the parts of an animal cell.

Learning Outcomes
- All pupils will be able to examine cheek cells and with help label an animal cell.
- Most pupils will be able to label an animal cell and describe the functions of the parts and state which parts are only in animal cells.
- Some pupils will also be able to draw links between the structures of cell organelles and their functions.

How Science Works
- Describe and record observations and evidence systematically. (1.2d)

Learning Styles
Visual: Observing cells.
Auditory: Discussing the features.
Kinaesthetic: Carrying out the practical.
Interpersonal: Group involvement in setting up the practical.
Intrapersonal: Contemplating the large number of cells we are made up of.

Answers to in-text questions
(a) Length of cell in mm/2000 = actual size (exact answer will depend on the measurement taken by the pupil).
(b) It makes it easier to see the specimen.

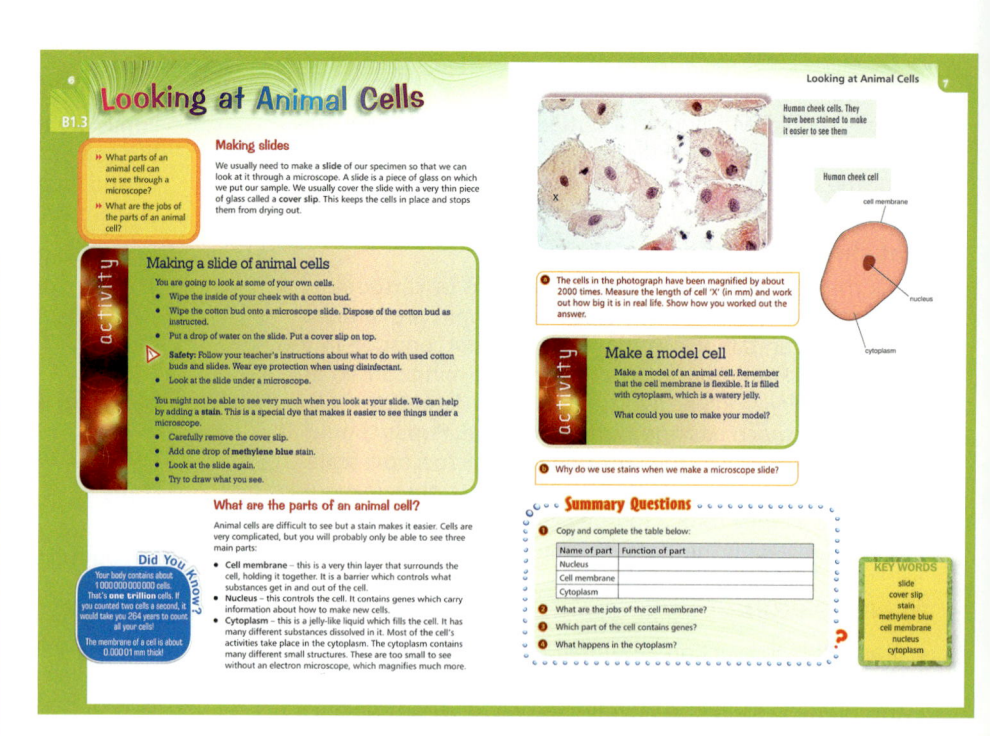

The Lesson

Starter Suggestions

Microscope quiz
Run a quick quiz on microscopes from last time. Allocate a microscope part to each pupil as they come into the room ('you are a slide', 'you are an eyepiece', etc.). Write up or project some functions. 'If you think that you are that part stand up'. Get a volunteer from among the group to explain what the part does. (5–10 mins)

Cell parts functions
Show the class a small piece of paper and tell them you have a set of plans on how to build a new organism. Roll it up and place it inside a plastic film container, or washing-up powder ball, or similar small receptacle. Place it inside an un-inflated wide necked balloon, preferably pink. Partially fill the balloon with gooey liquid (glycerol or similar) through a funnel and tie off the top. Tell the class that the liquid contains the substances needed for life. Ask them to make a rough drawing of this and to write down what each bit does – the plans, the container, the life sustaining goo and the balloon. This will visually reinforce the idea of each part of the cell having a discrete job. (10–15 mins)

Main Lesson
- Show a PowerPoint slide of the structure of an animal cell. Talk through the functions of each part and link them to the model just made (if 'Cell parts functions' is not used as a separate starter demonstrate it first). Get pupils to either drag and drop labels on from a commercial package or use laminated key word cards. When teaching the word 'cytoplasm', remind the pupils of the Hitchcock film *Psycho* (they should know the word) then point to your toe. Emphasise that it is cytoplasm not psychoplasm as this is a common mispronunciation. Tell pupils that 'cyto' means 'cell'.
- Take the pupils through the practical technique for 'Making a slide of animal cells' in stages, demonstrating each one, ensuring good hygiene practice at all times. Each pupil should have half a cotton bud. They should be instructed to wipe the inside of their mouth, then wipe the bud onto the slide, then immediately place the bud into a beaker of disinfectant. The slides should be placed in a beaker of disinfectant on completion of the practical. The demonstration could be done using a digital video camera in advance, or using PowerPoint slides. Divide into groups of no more than three.

Looking at Animal Cells

Plenary Suggestions

Counting the cells

Get a pupil to count to ten at a normal pace. This should take about five seconds. Hand out calculators and get the pupils to calculate at this rate how long it would take to count all the cells in a human body. Refer to 'Did you know', there are 1 000 000 000 000 and counting constantly this would take about 260 years. Discuss what we need all these cells for and what parts they have to help them carry out these functions, relating to 'Cell parts functions' if used at the start. (5–10 mins)

Pin the label on the cell

Fill in a worksheet relating parts to functions. Many may be able to copy and complete the table in Summary question 1. Blindfold a pupil and, with a helper to stop them from bumping into things, play a game of 'Pin the label on the cell' using key word cards and a big drawing on the board. (10–15 mins)

Practical Support

Making a slide of animal cells

Equipment and materials required

Cotton buds (cut in half), microscope slides, cover slips, seeker (or pencil), small pots of disinfectant (sodium chlorate(I)), microscopes, dilute methylene blue, digital micrsoscope and Flexicam (if available).

Details

Demonstrate how to wipe the inside of your cheek with a cotton bud. This is a good time to discuss with pupils the collection of DNA evidence for screening after crimes.

Demonstrate how to wipe the bud on the slide giving an even cover.

Demonstrate disposal into disinfectant solution in pots spaced around the room in advance. Emphasise the importance of safe disposal.

Demonstrate the use of a plastic pipette to place a small drop of water in the centre of the slide. Emphasise the importance of not washing the cells off and of not touching the place on the slide where the cells are.

Demonstrate how to lower a cover slip onto the slide (see below).

Observe under the microscopes using correct technique from last time. Use low magnification first (x40) then step up to x100 and, if available, x400. Display what can be seen using each power using a Flexicam or similar to project the image.

Discuss the difficulty of seeing detail and through questioning elicit the need for a stain. Demonstrate the introduction of a small amount of dilute methylene blue (take care – this will permanently stain skin and eye tissues). As an alternative to removing and replacing the cover slip the stain may be run along the side of the cover slip without disturbing it, and will diffuse throughout the specimen at varied dilution making the probability of finding a good visible cell more likely.

Show the pupils what the stained cells look like either by displaying a slide or projecting from the eyepiece. Refer to the picture in the pupil book.

Show pupils drawings of the cells and then ask them to carry out the practical and draw and label the cells.

Question the pupils to ascertain their understanding, refer them to the prompts in the text and carry out the practical, circulating among the groups while keeping a general eye on proceedings.

Support

Dropping a cover slip on needs some skill, so practise it first. Hold the cover slip between thumb and index finger of the left hand (right hand if left handed). Rest it onto the slide and adjust the height until the slip is at about 45 degrees. Place your left second finger behind the slide to stop it slipping and with your right hand place the tip or a seeker or pencil under the right edge of the slip. You can now let go of the slip with your left index finger and thumb, lowering the slip down over the specimen slowly to avoid air bubbles. These are often mistaken for cells as they appear as distinct black circles or black edged patches under magnification.

If the field of view looks bright blue, the methylene blue dye will need to be further diluted. It should look very pale blue with only the cells and especially their nuclei standing out.

Safety

Eye protection should be worn at all times. According to your local authority guidelines, you may wish the pupils to wear disposable gloves.

Take care with dilute methylene blue as it will permanently stain skin and eye tissues.

Follow CLEAPSS guidance in handbook/CD-ROM section 14.4.2.

Sodium chlorate(I): CLEAPSS Hazcard 89, Recipe card 62, handbook/CD-ROM 15.12.3.

Dilute methylene blue: CLEAPSS Hazcard 32.

Differentiation

SEN

Play snap using cards with arrowed diagrams of the parts of animal cells, descriptions of their functions and their names.

Extension

Provide computer access and ask the pupils to find out more about the structure of the cell membrane, the cytoplasm and the contents of the nucleus, linking this to function.

Ask: 'Given the cell dimensions in "Did you know?" how many cells would it take piled on top of each other to be as thick as your little finger?'

Answers to summary questions

1

Name of part	Function of part
Nucleus	Controls the cell, contains DNA/genes/chromosomes/genetic information
Cell membrane	Controls what enters and leaves the cell
Cytoplasm	Where chemical reactions take place in the cell

2 Controls what enters and leaves the cell; holds contents of the cell together.

3 Nucleus.

4 Chemical reactions take place.

B1.4 Looking at Plant Cells

NC links for the lesson
- Organisms, behaviour and health
- Life processes are supported by the organisation of cells into tissues, organs and body systems.

Learning Objectives

Pupils should learn:

- The parts of a plant cell they can see through a microscope.
- How to make a slide of a plant cell.
- The differences between animal and plant cells.

Learning Outcomes

- All pupils will be able to set up a slide and with help label a plant cell.
- Most pupils will be able to set up a slide well, label a plant cell and describe the functions of the parts.
- Some pupils will also be able to draw links between the structures of the cell organelles and their functions.

How Science Works

- Describe and record observations and evidence systematically. (1.2d)

Answers to summary questions

1. Nucleus – contains genetic information/controls the cell
   Cell membrane – controls what enters and leaves the cell
   Cytoplasm – where chemical reactions take place.
2. Chloroplast – where photosynthesis takes place
   Cell wall – keeps shape of cell
   Vacuole – stores substances.
3. Cell wall is thicker, stronger, fully permeable, made of cellulose.
4. No, because light does not reach the roots therefore photosynthesis does not occur.
5. Cell wall.
6. Ask pupils to critique their models.

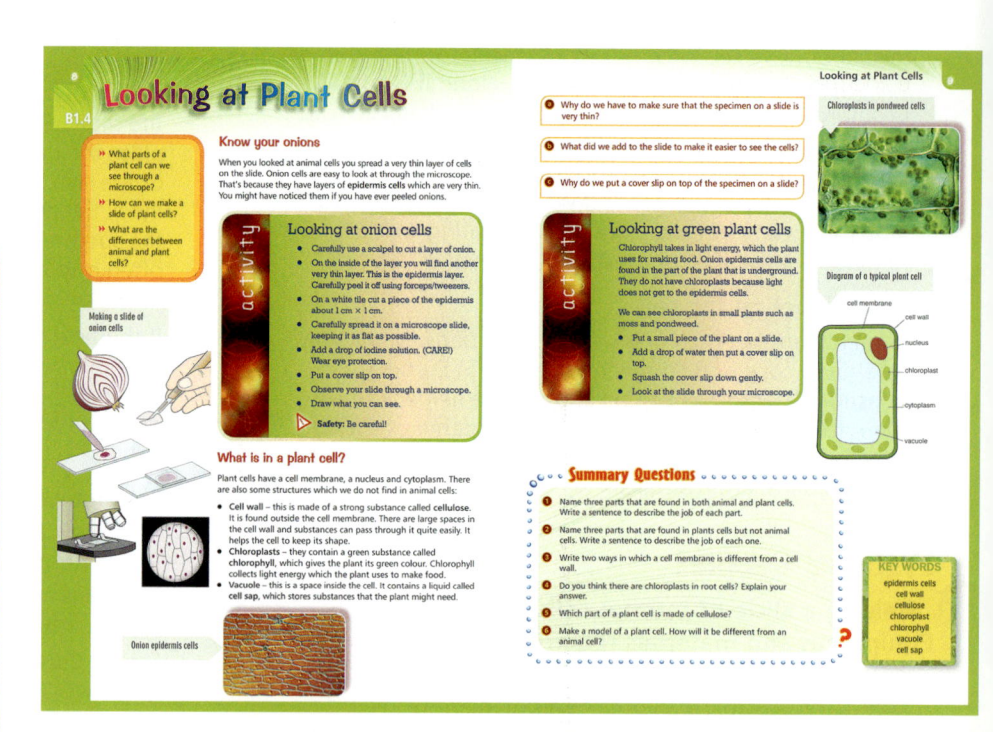

The Lesson

Starter Suggestions

Football cell
Show the pupils a deflated football. Remind them of 'Wilson', the pet football in the Tom Hanks film *Castaway*. Get a volunteer to pump up the ball. Ask them what is happening. Show a broken football with the bladder inside. Have gooey stuff such as glycerine or wallpaper paste inside the bladder along with a balloon full of liquid, some green jelly beans and a container such as a film canister with a rolled-up piece of paper inside representing plans for a new plant. Tell them that you are all going to look at plant cells and see if anyone can guess what any of the bits represent. (5–10 mins)

Boneless Bertie
Bring in an herbaceous (non-woody) plant such a geranium, about the same height as the length of a pupil's forearm (20 to 30cm). Hold it next to a volunteer with their arm held upright. Ask the pupils what would happen if you took all of the bones out of the volunteer's forearm. Ask them to discuss, in pairs, why this does not happen to the plant and to write their ideas down. Share ideas from around the class in a discussion. (10–15 mins)

Main Lesson

- Use PowerPoint and an exposition to describe the structure and function of each of the parts. Use laminated key word cards to help class involvement in this, such as by writing a simple cloze passage on the board and having volunteers or victims come and place the labels on the correct parts.
- As a demonstration of the function of the cell wall, have a balloon completely wrapped in parcel tape. This should be able to support the weight of several pupils on a board balanced on top if all the rubber is completely covered.

Learning Styles

Visual: Looking at plant cells.
Auditory: Listening to exposition and discussing with peers.
Kinaesthetic: Making the slide.
Interpersonal: Working as part of a group.
Intrapersonal: Developing confidence in use of microscopes.

Looking at Plant Cells

- Pupils should complete a worksheet drawing lines between parts and functions on a diagram of a typical plant cell.

Looking at onion cells

- Demonstrate each of the stages in preparing an onion epidermal cell slide, asking pupils to recap each stage to check and to reinforce learning. How to remove the epidermal layer using a large slice of onion. Cut a section of onion about 1 cm square and repeat the peel. Place the section of epidermis onto a small drop of water in the centre of the slide using forceps. Add a drop of iodine and place the cover slip on using the method described under 'Practical Support' on the previous page. Take care not to get iodine on the skin or the clothes as it stains them. Mop up any excess fluid using the paper towel. Mount on the stage of a microscope and reinforce the correct method for focussing, i.e. view from the side while winding the lenses down towards the specimen then focus back upwards. Remember to use low power first. Using a video camera attached to the projector helps all to see the detail of each stage.
- A PowerPoint summary of these stages before the practical can remind the pupils and be left on display during the practical. If possible, project an image of what they should see and label the parts.
- If time allows, get the pupils to draw a half A4 size plain paper drawing of what they see. A good example of a past pupil's work displayed will help them to get an idea of how much detail to put in, as it is easy to do too little or too much. Don't let them forget to write down the magnification.
- At the end of the practical, through questioning check that pupils have seen each of the features and can identify them

Looking at green plant cells

- As a demonstration of chloroplasts and chlorophyll, talk about grass stains on PE kits. Have a bottle of chlorophyll extract to hold to the light (or extract some in front of the class by grinding grass in alcohol in a pestle and mortar with a little sand then filtering). (**Safety**: make sure there are no naked flames.) To observe chloroplasts, filamentous algae from a pond can be used, either as a projected demonstration or as an extension activity once the main slide activity is complete.

Plenary Suggestions

P or B?

If the 'Football cell' starter is used, get it out again and ask pupils to write or record a short passage on what is represented by what. Formalise this after discussion by using 'show me' boards to write down the key word answers to questions on each part. Identify which parts are in plants but not in animal cells, again using 'Show me' boards with either P on for just plants or B for both, in response to called-out parts. (10–15 mins)

What a flop!

If the 'Boneless Bertie' starter was used, show a wilted plant and ask the pupils again in pairs to discuss and explain why this happens. Have a list of key words on the board for them to tick off in their answers. Carry out a class discussion of their answers to finish. (5–10 mins)

Practical Support

Looking at onion cells

Carry out the preparation and mounting of the onion epidermis slide as described above in 'Main Lesson'.

Equipment and materials required

Class set of scalpels, white tiles, forceps, slides, cover slips, seekers or mounted needles, iodine solution, pipettes, paper towels, onion, beakers of water.

Support

Circulate around the class assisting with focussing and lighting if not using lamps. Have beakers of water set up around the room for disposal of the slides and bins for the onion debris at the end of the lesson.

Red onion can be used in addition to the white variety. If a section is picked which has a mixture of red pigmented and un-pigmented cells the contrast is striking.

One of the major difficulties is that the pupils get the layer of epidermis folded over on itself. Share this with the pupils beforehand and tell them or show what it looks like. Use a seeker to disentangle layers while holding one end down with forceps. Again enable the pupils to identify air bubbles.

Safety

Take care that pupils wear eye protection while handling iodine and show caution when handling the fragile glass cover slips and scalpels.

Looking at green plant cells

Safety

Ethanol (alcohol) is highly flammable and harmful, make sure there are no naked flames: CLEAPSS Hazcard 40A.

Differentiation

SEN

Physical assistance may be needed for the practical.

Give the pupils laminated large A4 diagrams with sets of labels of each part to place on repeatedly for reinforcement.

Extension

Get the pupils to draw out a list of job descriptions for each of the plant parts. Make them humorous and inventive and as detailed as possible.

They could also dehydrate some red onion in salt solution to show plasmolysis.

Homework Suggestion

Show the pupils some model cells or photographs of them. Ask them to make one for display.

Answers to in-text questions

a So that light can pass through it.

b Stain/dye/iodine.

c Stops it drying out, keeps it flat.

B1.5 Special Cells

NC links for the lesson
- Organisms, behaviour and health
- Life processes are supported by the organisation of cells into tissues, organs and body systems.

Learning Objectives
Pupils should learn:
- That different cells have different functions.
- How the structure of the specialised cells relates to their function.

Learning Outcomes
- All pupils will be able to describe at least one specialised animal cell and one specialised plant cell.
- Most pupils will be able to describe a range of specialised cells and relate their structure to function.
- Some pupils will also be able to describe a wide range of specialised cells and in detail relate their structure to function.

Learning Styles
Visual: Observing slides and PowerPoint.
Auditory: Listening to exposition.
Kinaesthetic: Playing the floor dominoes plenary game.
Interpersonal: Playing the 20 questions plenary game.
Intrapersonal: Considering the very small size, very great number and complexity of the cells of the body.

Answers to in-text questions
a. So they can swim.
b. So lots of them can fit closely together and absorb light.
c. It absorbs water and minerals from the soil because it has a large surface area.

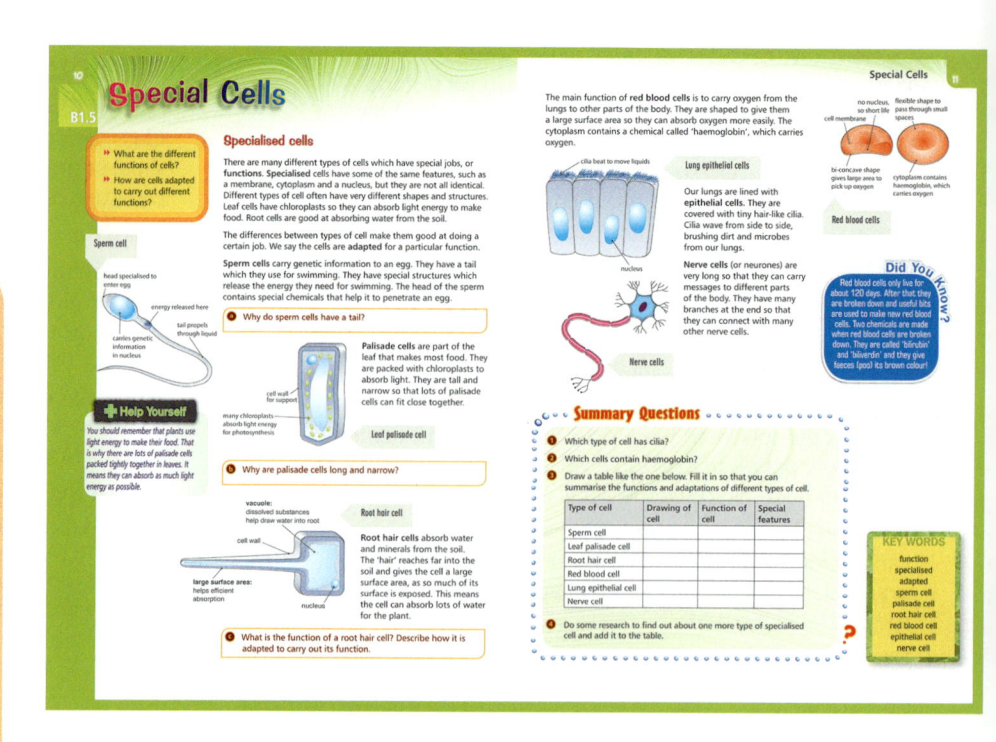

Answers to summary questions
1. Lining of lung (also others, e.g. lining of oviduct).
2. Red blood cells.
3.

Type of cell	Drawing of cell	Function of cell	Special features
Sperm cell		Fertilises egg	Tail, able to release lots of energy, chemicals in head to help penetration of membrane of egg
Leaf palisade cell		Site of photosynthesis	Tall thin shape, lots of chloroplasts
Root hair cell		Absorbs water and minerals	Large surface area
Red blood cell		Carries oxygen	Large surface area, contains haemoglobin
Lung epithelium cell		Removes mucus with dirt and microbes	Has cilia
Nerve cell		Carries electrical impulses between parts of the body	Long, has branched ends

Special Cells

The Lesson

Starter Suggestions

Pencil case feature spotting
Recap structure of animal and plant cells through board diagrams and questioning. Get the pupils to empty out their pencil cases. For each type of object in there they should give its name, its features or characteristics and how they help it to do its job. Carry this out through questioning. Lead into learning objectives. (5–10 mins)

Footwear features
Pupils are given one minute in pairs to write down as many types of footwear as they can, including sports and industrial footwear. Get a list from the pupils by questioning, choose suitable examples to write on the board, e.g. football boot, Wellington, roller skate, etc. Get the pupils to write down a feature of each type of footwear that suits it for its purpose. Use the vocabulary to be used later regarding cells (characteristic, adaptation, specialised). (10–15 mins)

Main Lesson

- Show the pupils a PowerPoint slide of cell adaptations. Talk through each one, showing it first then asking the pupils to guess, comment, describe and ask questions before delivering information to fill in any gaps not raised during discussion. Specialised cells to be covered should include:
- **Root hairs cells** (long thin projections providing large surface area for absorption of water).
- **Palisade cells** (regular shape for packing close together for maximum light collection, chloroplasts).
- **Sperm cell** (head containing genes, motor area, tail for swimming). You may like to relate the size and number to that of egg cells.
- **Nerve cell** (many extensions for connecting to other cells, long for carrying nerve impulses around the body, insulating coating gets laid down onto mature nerve cells to speed up the rate of transmission. This occurs during teenage years – tell them it is happening inside their heads right now).
- **Red blood cell** (flexible shape for squeezing through small capillaries). Demonstrate their shape by showing suitable biconcave shaped mints. Mention them changing colour from red when carrying oxygen to purple when they release the oxygen. Examine the inside of each other's lower lip to see both oxygenated and deoxygenated blood in vessels near the surface. Wash hands before and after.
- **Lung epithelial cell** (epithelial cells are hair-like projections for moving a layer of mucus to clean airways or move an egg down the oviduct). Talk about how people do crowd surfing in a mosh pit, showing video of people doing this at concerts/festivals. If the crowd were all moving their arms in the same direction any people or objects falling onto them would be moved away. Draw a parallel with the self-cleaning function and warn about smoking destroying this system.
- Introduce the practical and tell the pupils which features to look out for on each slide or specimen. The specimens and slides can be arranged in a circle of previously focused microscopes and the pupils can circulate around them. Alternatively the specimens and slides can be placed at convenient points around the lab for collection and return.
- **Video reinforcement:** if available show a video of the different cell types and remind the pupils of the vocabulary and adaptations which goes with each.

Extensions on xylem, phloem, guard cells, and glandular cells could be useful here.

- **Worksheet on monster cells:** this could be within the lesson if fast progress is made or could be introduced and completed as homework. Imagine a monster which has strange and wonderful adaptations. What sort of specialised cells might it have? What would the functions of their special features be? Pupils should report their imagined findings in any way they choose.

Plenary Suggestions

20 questions
A pupil leaves the room. The others decide which type of specialised cell they are. The pupil is called back in and have to guess which type of cell they are by asking questions about the features of the cell. With lower attaining classes it may be necessary to write these features out on the board or on a prompt card. Repeat with different pupils and different cell types. (5–10 mins)

Floor dominoes
Play a game of floor dominoes using A4 sheets with pictures of the specialised cells on one end and descriptions of their adaptations on the other end. A playing card size version might also be of use. Have a small prize for the winning team. (10–15 mins)

Practical Support

Using microscopes, specimens and prepared slides examine root hair cells. Specimens could include root hairs (these look particularly good if binocular microscopes are available), nettle stinging cells (warn regarding abuse of these). Commercial slides could include sperm, eggs, nerve cells (giant axons are good), leaf palisade cells, red blood cells. Diagrams may be drawn if time allows but are not essential.

Support

Set up mung beans or cress to germinate in small Petri dishes with damp cotton wool in the bottom several days before the practical so as to give them time to develop root hairs. Cover them with cling film to keep the moisture in. Do not touch the root hairs or they will be damaged. If slides are not available the Internet has suitable images.

Differentiation

SEN

Draw out some specialised cell pictures with their names beside them. Place them into a cardboard frame with five flip-up sections on one end, covering the name of the cell type. Pupils get six points for getting the name right without lifting any of the flaps and loose one point for each section they have to flip up to reveal part of the name.

They could also make a model of a specialised cell using for example, Plasticine.

Extension

Provide the pupils with Internet access and point them at suitable interactive websites so as to carry out their own research on specialised cells and test themselves.

B1.6 Cells, Tissues, Organs and Systems

NC links for the lesson
- Organisms, behaviour and health
- Life processes are supported by the organisation of cells into tissues, organs and body systems.

Learning Objectives
Pupils should learn:
- What tissues are and be able to name some.
- How tissues group together to form organs.
- What is meant by an organ system.

Learning Outcomes
- All pupils will be able to name some tissues, some organs and some systems.
- Most pupils will be able to put cells, tissues, organs and systems into hierarchical order.
- Some pupils will also be able to give detailed ways of how to distinguish between layers of the hierarchy and give details of system functions.

Answers to summary questions

1
a) The function of the respiratory system is to take in oxygen and get rid of carbon dioxide.
b) The main parts of the circulatory system are heart and blood vessels/arteries, veins and capillaries.
c) The reproductive system of a woman … [any sensible answer].
d) The nervous system is important because … [any sensible answer].

2 Heart, lungs, liver, cornea, kidney.

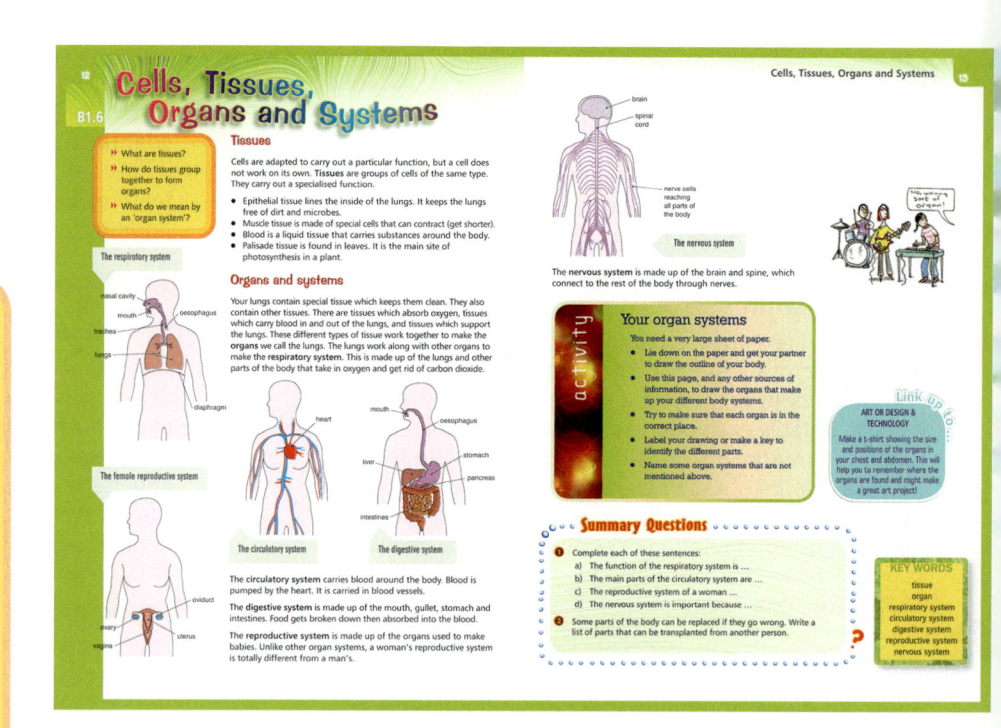

Learning Styles
Visual: Observing the PowerPoint slide show of the heirarchical arrangement.
Auditory: Discussing words involved in either of the starter activities.
Kinaesthetic: Interacting with torso models or layered cut and stick organ diagrams.
Interpersonal: Discussing the heirachy with others in the group.
Intrapersonal: Identifying the positions of organs within their own body.

Cells, Tissues, Organs and Systems

The Lesson

Starter Suggestions

What do we need tree

Draw the word 'live' in the top centre of the board. Below it draw a series of lines coming down from the centre and ask the pupils what we need to live. Write down their suggestions as the next layer down, pick one and do the same again, e.g. if they say 'breathe' draw lines out beneath saying what we need to breathe. Once the upside-down tree pattern has been established, get the pupils to draw out their own version. After a few minutes get some examples and establish the idea of a hierarchy of organisation. (5–10 mins)

Word meanings

Display the words 'cell', 'tissue', 'organ', 'system' on the board. Ask the pupils to write a sentence containing each word, emphasising that it doesn't matter whether they are science sentences or everyday sentences. Apply a short time limit. Get some pupils to read out their sentences and, on the board, build up a picture of the common usage of these words and their everyday meanings (e.g. systems in football, organs in churches, tissues to blow your nose on, and cells in a prison). Dismantle these examples to show that systems are a lot of different things working together (like strikers, midfield, and goalkeeper); organs contain different things such as pipes, keyboard, etc. but have one job, making the organ sound (in this model an orchestra would be the system). Tissues are all made out of the same stuff, display one or whip them repeatedly from a box for a humorous effect. Cells are identical single units. (10–15 mins)

Main Lesson

- Show the pupils a PowerPoint slide of the various levels of organisation within the human body. Starting from cells of the same type working together forming a tissue, progress to various tissues working together to make something happen in an organ. Finish off by describing how a number of organs working together form an organ system. Allow plenty of discussion time to get the concepts bedded in and use key word cards repeatedly to reinforce the vocabulary. While talking about organs you may hand around some organ donor cards. These can be obtained by searching the Internet for a current URL. For further discussion opportunities describe to the pupils the spoof reality TV show that was carried out by the makers of *Big Brother*, where a dying woman was supposed to choose from between several would-be recipients who would get her kidneys and therefore survive (also clarify that you can survive with one kidney).
- Using a torso model if available, or layered OHP diagrams, show the major organ systems: respiratory, circulatory, digestive, reproductive, nervous.
- See 'Practical support'.
- Get the pupils to complete a worksheet on which they should match the pictures of organs to their names and their functions, and similarly for diagrams of systems, their names and their functions. As an extension, provide a list of additional words they can classify as belonging to cells, tissues, organs or systems. You could also mention plants – that a leaf is an organ, etc.

- A video summary, if available, may be of use to summarise the main learning points of the lesson without demanding a teacher-centred focus for the class.

Plenary Suggestions

Drag and drop example sorter

Using a class set of laptops (if available) or a digital projector, carry out a drag and drop containers exercise. This will enable the pupils to carry out a sorting exercise to file examples into cells, tissues, organs and systems boxes. (5–10 mins)

Hierarchy voting

Describe examples of cells, organs, tissues or systems. Pupils have to vote for which classification they belong to, using either 'show me' boards, paper or a gesture-based voting system. Share class views and correct any misconceptions. (5–10 mins)

Practical Support

If time allows it would be stimulating to show the pupils examples of some organs, e.g. heart, lungs, liver, kidneys. It may not be appropriate to do dissection at this stage, but to bring in some fresh organs from a butcher would be beneficial. Allowing the pupils to touch the organs adds zest, but can only be used if local authority and school health and safety allow. Also the pupils need to be co-operative and well controlled, washing their hands with soap immediately after. It would also be good to show pupils examples of a plant organ, e.g. leaf, stem, flower.

If you ask at a butchers shop for a fresh lamb's pluck, they may be able to get in a heart and lungs still joined. Find out on which day the animal is slaughtered and use the same day if possible.

Safety

Risk assess and carry out hygienically, being careful with disposal. See information in CLEAPSS handbook/CD-ROM section 14.7.2.

Differentiation

SEN

Felt tabards can be bought which come with sets of fabric organs. These attach be means of Velcro and provide an enjoyable physical interactive learning experience. They are referred to as 'inside-out organs tunics'.

Extension

Provide the pupils with computer and Internet access and allow them to look for websites which display appropriate information about organs.

B1.7 The Skeleton

NC links for the lesson
- Organisms, behaviour and health
- Life processes are supported by the organisation of cells into tissues, organs and body systems.

Learning Objectives

Pupils should learn:
- The four functions of the skeleton.
- What makes bones strong.

Learning Outcomes
- All pupils will be able to name the four functions of bones and that they contain calcium.
- Most pupils will be able to name the four functions of bones and link this to protein and calcium content, including the importance of vitamin D and know that hollow shapes are strongest.
- Some pupils will also be able to relate the diameter of a rod to strength for a given amount of material.

How Science Works
- Describe an appropriate approach to answer a scientific question using a limited range of information and making relevant observations. (1.2a)

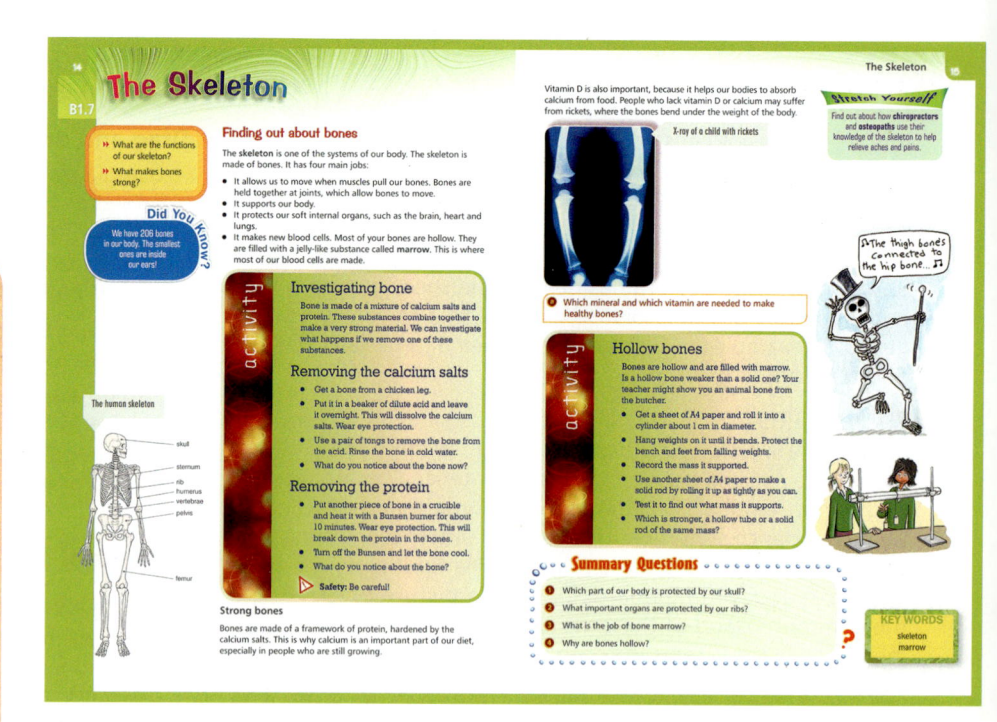

The Lesson

Starter Suggestions

Skeleton fight

Show the pupils a large scale model skeleton. Remind the pupils of the section in the film *Pirates of the Caribbean – The Black Pearl* where the skeletons of the crew are fighting. Imagine they are a really picky viewer writing a snotty text to the producer criticising the film for being unrealistic. What would they say about bones without bodies? Get them to write the texts. Ask a pupil to choose another one to read out their text. (5–10 mins)

Bone thief disease

Ask pupils to write a short piece from a horror story where the touch of an infected person spreads an unknown and deadly disease dissolving your

Learning Styles

Visual: Observing demonstrations.
Auditory: Listening to discussions.
Kinaesthetic: Carrying out the practical.
Interpersonal: Group work for the practical.
Intrapersonal: Imagining a boneless body.

Answers to summary questions

1. Brain.
2. Heart and lungs.
3. Makes red blood cells.
4. So they are lighter.

Answers to in-text questions

a. Calcium (and phosphorus), vitamin D.

bones as it goes. Volunteers are to read their stories. (10–15 mins)

Main Lesson

- Drawing from the starter, whichever is chosen, discuss the functions of the skeleton.
- To show protection, ask the pupils to push the centre of their brow with a finger. Ask what would happen if the bone vanished. Similarly ask a boy to push in the centre of his sternum, again asking the class what would happen if the bone vanished. If animal skulls are available in the department pass them around. (Wire shut any jaws with teeth still in.)
- Ask the pupils if they have ever been hit in the head. From the emerging stories draw out that some parts of the skull are thick and strong because they are more likely to be hit.
- To show support, get the pupils to put their hands up in the air and imagine what would happen if their bones disappeared. Show the pupils a bone and ask what you need for strong healthy bones. Discuss what is in milk that helps make healthy bones (protein and calcium). Ask if anyone has been sick recently. Ask what it tasted like. Draw out that stomachs contain acid. Ask if anyone has seen a dog eating bones. Draw out that although dogs eat bones their excreta don't contain bones. Draw out that the bones must be broken down by acid in the stomach.
- Show pictures of a child with rickets. Explain that it is caused by lack of vitamin D which helps your body to absorb calcium.

Plenary Suggestions

Skeleton diagram
Provide the pupils with a skeleton diagram to colour code the areas that are used for each function. (5–10 mins)

Interactive skeleton
Complete the interactive activity by labelling the bones on the skeleton.

On the Internet, either individually or as a class, search the web for interactive skeleton building activities and related information. (10–15 mins)

Practical Support

Investigating bone: removing the calcium salts
Equipment and materials required
For each group: 250 ml beaker, a small piece of bone such as sections of ribs (to fit beaker), a bottle of dilute (1 mol/dm^3) hydrochloric acid, labels, forceps or tongs, paper towels, seeker. Optional: electronic balance.

Details
Divide into groups of about three. Explain that we are going to remove the calcium salts from the bone.

Wearing eye protection, pupils to place the bone in the bottom of the beaker and pour in sufficient dilute acid to cover it.

Label the beaker and leave until the next lesson. Alternatively get the pupils to set this up for another group and give them a set of bones which have already been submerged for at least 24 hours.

Pupils to remove the steeped bone from the acid using forceps or tongs. They then rinse it in cold water, examine it and prod it gently using a seeker, recording any observations.

Safety
1 mol/dm^3 hydrochloric acid is an irritant: CLEAPSS Hazcard 47A.

Investigating bone: removing the protein
Equipment and materials required
Crucible with lid, pipe-clay triangle, tongs, Bunsen burner, small piece of bone, forceps, paper towels, seeker.

Details
Explain that we are going to remove the protein from the bone by burning it. Pupils should examine a small piece of bone and place it into a crucible. Cover with a lid and place in a pipe-clay triangle. Wear eye protection.

Heat strongly for at least 10 minutes. Do not remove the lid during heating as the bones can shatter. Switch off the Bunsen and allow the crucible to cool. Pupils should examine the bone using the seeker and/or the forceps.

Hollow bones demonstration
While the bones are heating in the crucibles show the following demonstration:

Roll a piece of A4 paper around a clamp stand rod with the long axis on the paper parallel to the rod. Secure it with three short strips of tape at each end and the centre. Mark the centre.

Do the same with another piece of A4, but this time roll it as tight as you can to try to make a solid rod. In practice this will mean narrow folds.

In advance, set up two clamps side by side arranged so that when a 100 g mass hanger is hung from the centre of the paper rod, its base rests just above a pair of contacts connected to a battery and buzzer.

Cover the base of the mass hanger with aluminium foil to improve conductivity.

Place one of the rods in the tester. Do not tighten the clamps, they should just touch the rod and have about a centimetre overlap to allow for bending.

Add the hanger, then more 100 g masses one at a time until the hanger touches the contacts and sounds the buzzer.

Repeat with the other rod. Summarise results.

State that bones are actually full of marrow which makes red blood cells.

Differentiation

SEN
Make an A3 or larger size skeleton diagram with pre-determined colour codes for functions and a key. Cut the bones into several major sections and put Velcro tabs at the correct places to join it back together. Pupils should assemble the skeleton and state which function different parts have as they are pointed to. Alternatively assemble a digital skeleton from a suitable Internet site.

Extension
Repeat the rod strength test practical with tubes of various diameters and work out a formula to relate diameter to strength. Higher attaining groups may weigh the bones before and after immersion and burning. They could calculate percentage weight loss.

B1.8 Joints and Muscles

NC links for the lesson
- Organisms, behaviour and health
- Life processes are supported by the organisation of cells into tissues, organs and body systems.

Learning Objectives
Pupils should learn:
- How our skeletons move.
- How our joints work.

Learning Outcomes
- All pupils will be able to state that muscles can only pull bones.
- Most pupils will be able to describe how a pair of antagonistic muscles work.
- Some pupils will also be able to describe how a pair of antagonistic muscles work in detail and relate joint structure to function.

Functional Skills Link-up
English
- Write clearly and coherently including an appropriate level of detail. (Level 1)

Learning Styles
Visual: Observing PowerPoint and animations.
Auditory: Listening to discussions.
Kinaesthetic: Getting involved in the dissection.
Interpersonal: Plenary rotary quiz activity, 'Joint questions'.
Intrapersonal: Writing individual questions.

Answers to in-text questions

a Cartilage is very smooth and the space between the bones is filled with synovial fluid.

b Soreness in the joints; difficulty moving joints; swelling in joints.

c Hinge, ball and socket.

d So that the skull can squeeze through the vagina.

e The arm bends.

f The arm straightens.

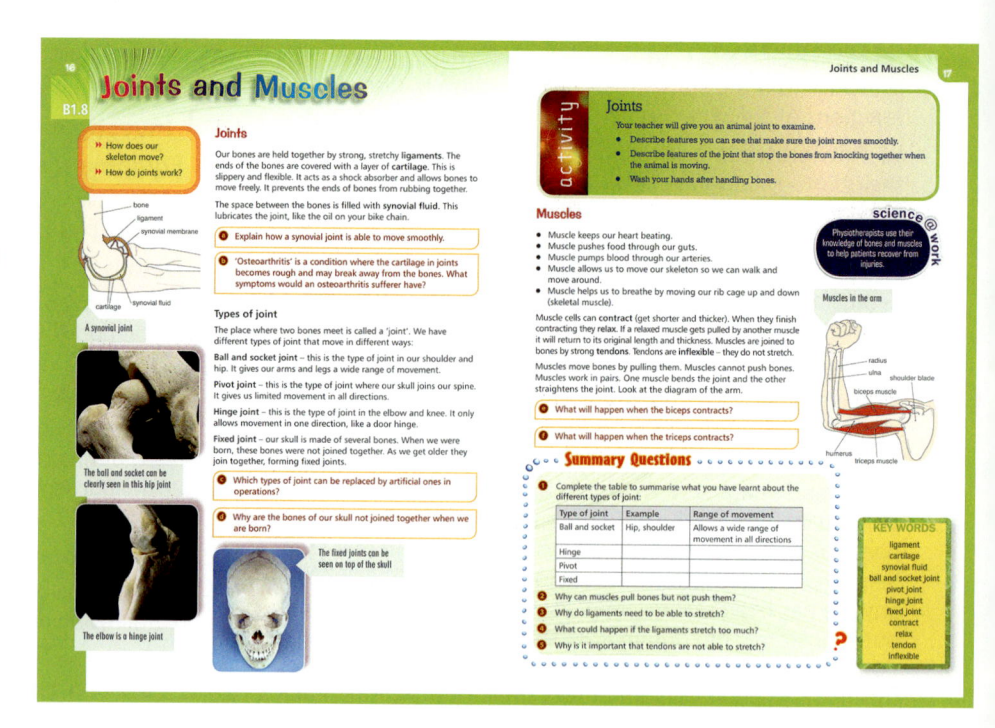

The Lesson

Starter Suggestions

Joint names
Show the pupils a model skeleton and question them about the names of the joints. Get a series of volunteers to show the rest of the class how each joint moves. (5–10 mins)

Name that joint
Provide two fly swats of different colours. Draw a big button on the board. Get a pair of volunteers to come forward and stand on either side of the board. When you say the names of two body parts with a joint between them (e.g. lower arm and upper arm) they have to get their swat onto the button first if they know the name of the joint (e.g. elbow). Play best out of three, winner chooses the next contestant. Limit the joints to shoulder, elbow, wrist, hip, knee, ankle and knuckles. (10–15 mins)

Answers to summary questions

1

Type of joint	Example	Range of movement
Ball and socket	Hip, shoulder	Allows a wide range of movement in all directions
Hinge	Knee, elbow	Allows movement in one direction
Pivot	Neck	Rotation and some back and forth and side to side
Fixed	Skull	Nil

2 Because muscles can only contract.

3 So that bones can move at joints.

4 Bones pull apart at joints and cause dislocation.

5 So that bones move when muscles contract.

Joints and Muscles

Main Lesson

- Show a PowerPoint slide, if you have one, of the types of joint throughout this session.
- Describe each type of joint in turn. Start with the fixed joints. Show a skull if one is available. Ask if any pupils in the class have baby brothers or sisters. Ask about the tops of their heads and you may be lucky and get a description of the fontanelle (soft spot). If you have a large skeleton model available, pass an orange through the pelvis and talk over why it is important that skull bones are not joined before birth.
- Introduce the term 'synovial joints' which refers to the moving joints (all the rest apart from fixed). Show a diagram of a synovial joint gleaned from the Internet.
- Discuss the parts and their functions.
- **Cartilage** is to stop the bones from grinding into each other. Ask if anyone has a relative with arthritis. Ask them to describe the symptoms. If two real bones are available, grind them together until they make a noise.
- **Ligaments** join bones to bones (remind the pupils of Michael Owen's horrific knee injury which kept him out of the World Cup in 2006).
- **Synovial fluid** acts as a lubricant. It is a better lubricant than engine oil! With the same bones used for grinding together before, add some glycerine to act as a lubricant and the noise should stop.
- Describe a **ball and socket joint**. If a model or a hip replacement set is available, allow the pupils to handle this. Show the 3D movement by getting the pupils to touch their hands together behind their backs. Put the names of ball and socket joints onto a table on the board.
- Describe a **hinge joint**. Ask if anyone in the class is double jointed. Using a large door hinge, ask a volunteer to try to open it sideways. Put the names of hinge joints onto a table on the board. A model hinge joint should be made.
- Describe a **pivot joint**. If available, a camera tripod has a good pivot joint on the top. Show the movement of the skull on the top of the vertebral column on a skeleton model. Write the skull/neck as a pivot joint onto a table on the board.
- Describe **muscles** as only pulling by contracting, and that there are three types: smooth in the guts, cardiac in the heart and skeletal which is all the rest.
- Describe **tendons** as joining muscles to bones. Tell the story of Achilles being dipped in invincibility liquid covering all but his heel, which proved his undoing as he was killed by a poisoned arrow in his weak spot. Get the pupils to feel their own tendons in their tensed forearms. In medieval battles, prisoners often had the lower biceps tendon cut to prevent them from lifting a sword.
- Dissect a chicken's leg (optional).
- Get a volunteer to roll up their shirt sleeves and raise and lower a small weight. Impersonate an angry person shouting 'Don't antagonise me!' Introduce the concept of an antagonistic pair as working against each other, one contracting as the other relaxes. Show an animation of an antagonistic pair of muscles in action. If available, use a model to reinforce this. Identify where other antagonistic pairs are.
- Pupils should copy down the board notes and fill in the labels on a blank diagram of an antagonistic muscle pair (biceps and triceps).

Plenary Suggestions

Muscle pair animations

The pupils should observe animated antagonistic pairs of muscles from an appropriate Internet site. Then they explain to one another how this happens, gaining a point for each of the key words from the pupil's book. (5–10 mins)

Joint questions

Split the class into groups of three or four. Within each group get each pupil to write one question about joint types, one about synovial joints and one about antagonistic muscle pairs onto a sheet of paper. When all have finished pass the pieces around the room. Have a small prize for the best question set as voted for at the end. (10–15 mins)

Practical Support

Demonstration dissection of a chicken's leg

Equipment and materials required

Large wooden dissecting board, half a fresh chicken (preferably with claws on), scalpel, dissecting scissors, seeker, bag for disposal. A Flexicam and projector will help pupils to see.

Details

Get a half bird fresh from a reputable butcher. Remove the skin and using scissors and scalpel expose the outside of the hip and knee joints. Demonstrate the movement range of each. There is a good 'yuk factor' if you take the knee joint past the point at which it breaks. Be careful of bone splinters. Dissect the joints looking out for the synovial fluid as it comes out. A volunteer could place some between their fingers to comment on how slippy it is. Expose the cartilage. Identify the ligaments. Dissect a muscle. Show how the muscle sheath becomes the tendon. Pull on some tendons to move the leg introducing the word inflexible (this is best if the claws are still attached being careful to clean the claws beforehand as they can be contaminated with excreta). At the end of the dissection (not before) allow the pupils to feel the surface of the cartilage and then tell them to wash their hands thoroughly.

Differentiation

SEN

Provide the pupils with sets of coloured cards, one colour for each joint type, one letter per card. The pupils are to shuffle the pack and spell out the type names. Timing and repeating giving achievable targets and rewards will be motivating.

Extension

Pupils to research into hydrostatic skeletons and endoskeletons. Focus on how size and complexity of the body plan restricts skeleton type suitability. Link to why we don't get giant insects

B1.9 Microbes

NC links for the lesson
- Organisms, behaviour and health
- Life processes are supported by the organisation of cells into tissues, organs and body systems.
- …health can be affected by diet, drugs and disease.

Learning Objectives

Pupils should learn:
- The four types of microbe.
- How we can see microbes.
- What microbes look like.

Learning Outcomes
- All pupils will be able to name the four types of microbe.
- Most pupils will be able to name the four types of microbe and give examples and features of each.
- Some pupils will also be able to name the four types of microbe and give several examples and detailed features of each, including similarities and differences.

How Science Works
- Describe and record observations and evidence systematically. (1.2d)

Answers to summary questions

1. Smaller, no cell membrane, cannot reproduce outside living cells.
2. Viruses, bacteria, protozoa, fungi.
3. Bacteria and fungi.
4. [Look for clarity of presentation of information, accuracy, etc.]

The Lesson

Starter Suggestions

How many diseases?
Ask the pupils to list as many diseases as they can in pairs in two minutes. (Pupils will come up with some diseases that are not infections, e.g. cancer. This may need some extra explaining.) Ask some of the pupils to read out their lists. Collect the names of the diseases on the board, writing them in groups in different coloured pens according to their causal agent. Do not at first tell the pupils you are doing this. When enough have been gathered, ask the pupils why you have put them into several different groups. This should lead into a discussion on types of microbe. (5–10 mins)

Warding it off
Show the pupils an orange with cloves in it and hand around a container of pot pourri for them to sniff. Show them an image of a Middle Ages doctor's long-nosed face mask used to keep bad odours away. Show images of the tattoos on the ice mummy found in the Alps. Explain that these were to keep away diseases. Pupils are to write a message to these people to tell them why they were wrong and what really causes diseases. (10–15 mins)

Main Lesson
- Define 'microbes' as being another name for micro-organisms and explain that this means living things that are too small to see with the naked eye. Draw a gravestone on the board and write on it 'R.I.P. Germs', explaining that in this science topic 'germs' is a word we will not use. Draw out by

Learning Styles

Visual: Microscopic observation.
Auditory: Listening to exposition.
Kinaesthetic: Carrying out the practical.
Interpersonal: Group work setting up and observing through the microscopes.
Intrapersonal: Considering the scales involved.

Microbes

questioning from the pupils what they know about microbes so far and summarise this on the board. From the starters, disease causing organisms will be identified. Discuss that there are microbes which do not cause diseases and there are ones which can be useful to us.

- Show the pupils a PowerPoint slide show of the main types of microbe, discussing each one in turn.
- While discussing fungi, show the class a mushroom. Explain that the main part of the mushroom fungus consists of tiny threads which break things down. A film clip of speeded-up decay would be useful here.
- While discussing bacteria, show the pupils a jelly bean representing a bacterium. Get them to look at the millimetre gradations on their rulers. An average bacterium is about 2.5 μm across, so if we scaled up their rulers the millimetre marks would be 4 m apart. Measure out 4 m and show the pupils what it would look like. Some bacteria are smaller and some much larger, up to 0.75 mm, and are visible to the naked eye. Fluffy pet microbes are available from certain companies (and Internet search for giant microbes may be useful) and include *Salmonella*, complete with flagellae. For a demonstration of binary fission, give a pupil a small ball of Plasticine and ask them to show it to the class. Ask them to roll it in their hands and give them a little more Plasticine to add to the lump every few seconds until they have a lump twice as big as the first one. This can then be pulled apart and two new ones are started.
- While discussing protozoa, mention the malaria parasite *Plasmodium* and its life cycle. For a 'yuk factor' give details of how the mosquito sticks its face into your body and then is sick down its nose into your blood. It does this to put in anticoagulants to stop its tubes getting clogged up with blood clots, but there are living things in the vomit and they breed in your blood making you ill.
- While discussing viruses, show the powers of ten magnifier activity which is available on some Internet sites. State that if a virus were the same size as a jelly bean, the ruler millimetre marks at the same magnification would be 500 m apart (1 and 1/4 times around an athletics running track).

Plenary Suggestions

Microbes summary
Pupils should finish off the practical by filling in a worksheet, by labelling diagrams and filling in a grid. (5–10 mins)

Net search for microbes
In pairs pupils use the Internet to research types of microbe. Assign each group to one type, ensuring balanced overall coverage. Produce a PowerPoint slide for each type. E-mail home and complete for homework. (10–15 mins)

Answers to in-text questions

- **a** No, mushroom and toadstool are types of fungi.
- **b** Movement.
- **c** They engulf and digest smaller microbes.
- **d** Because they can only reproduce inside living cells.

Did You Know?
Thiomargarita namibiensis is the record holder for the largest microbe. Because the largest ones are 750 μm in diameter, they are quite visible to the naked eye. They are unusual in that they utilise sulfates and nitrates to get their energy. They live on the ocean floor off the coast of Namibia and store the nitrates they find after storms at sea.

Practical Support

Looking at microbes

Equipment and materials required

Microscopes, slides, hand lenses, Petri dishes of mouldy foods (lids taped in two places but not sealed), Petri dishes of *Micrococcus luteus* culture (lids taped in two places but not sealed).

Details

Examine the specimens mentioned below with hand lenses first. Set up microscopes (binocular if available) and view a previously prepared piece of mouldy bread or fruit or blue cheese in a Petri dish and observe the fungal threads (hyphae). Ensure that the pupils do not open the lids. Provide them with plain paper and ask them to draw what they see. Repeat this procedure with Petri dishes with visible colonies of a visible non-pathogenic bacterium such as *Micrococcus luteus* which is a bright yellow colour.

For the fungi plates, moisten a piece of bread and leave it out in the open air for a couple of hours then place it into a Petri dish and place a lid on. Secure but do not seal the lid (danger of anaerobic microbes establishing themselves). Leave in a warm place for several days in advance of the required lesson.

Cultures of *Micrococcus luteus* can be bought from biological supplies companies such as Blades Biological. Tape and warn pupils against opening, in case a pathogen has crept in. If the culture is supplied in a broth using aseptic techniques remove a small drop on a sterile wire loop and spread on a cooled fresh plate of agar gel in a standard plastic Petri dish. Allow to incubate for several days at 20 °C before the practical.

Safety
Dispose of the plates hygienically after the practical: CLEAPSS handbook/CD-ROM section 15.2.14.

Differentiation

SEN
Carry out a life skills exercise on ways of ensuring that microbes are not transferred from person to person (hand washing, good hygiene practices), modelling the practices and then pupils emulating this.

Extension
Pupils should extend the disease and causal organism list in the starter 'How many diseases'. Have a range of books on microbes from the library to refer to.

B1.10 Growing Microbes

NC links for the lesson
- Organisms, behaviour and health
- Life processes are supported by the organisation of cells into tissues, organs and body systems.

Learning Objectives
Pupils should learn:
- How we can grow bacteria.
- How to measure factors affecting the growth of yeast.

Learning Outcomes
- All pupils will be able to describe in simple terms how to grow bacteria.
- Most pupils will be able to describe how to grow bacteria and be able to measure factors affecting the growth of yeast.
- Some pupils will also be able to describe in detail how to grow bacteria and be able to measure factors affecting the growth of yeast with precision and accuracy.

How Science Works
- Recognise the range of variables involved in an investigation and decide which to control. (1.2b)

Learning Styles
Visual: Observing PowerPoint and demonstrations.
Auditory: Listening to exposition and discussion.
Kinaesthetic: Carrying out the practicals.
Interpersonal: Group work.
Intrapersonal: Reflecting on ideas learned.

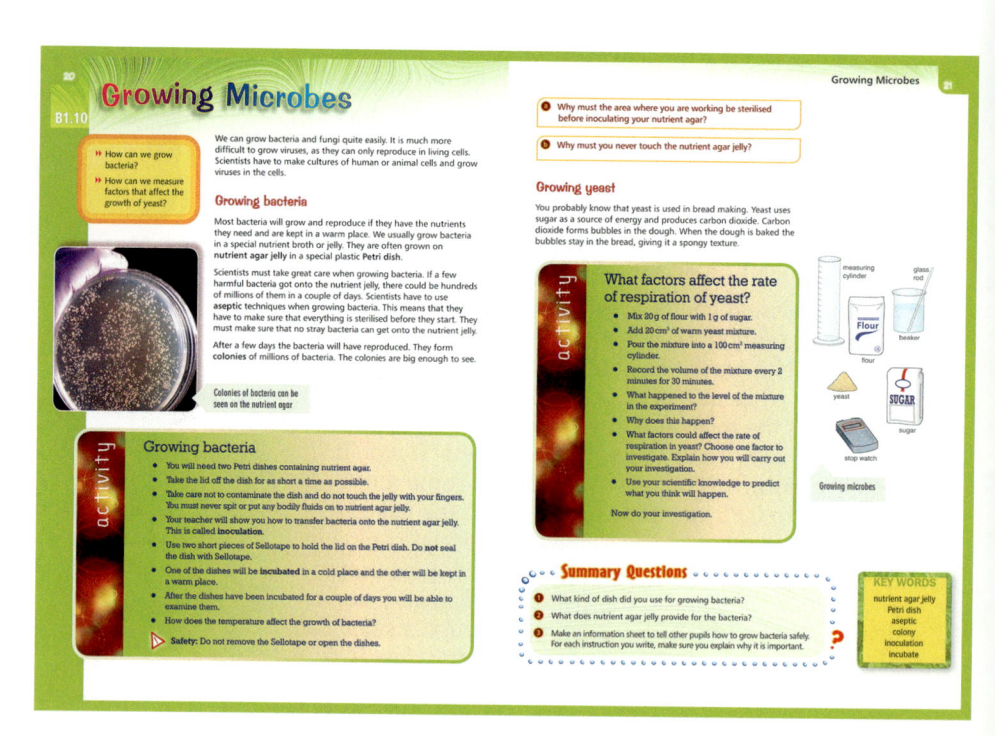

The Lesson

Starter Suggestions

Rice and chess and bacterial growth curves
Show a chessboard and a bag of rice. Tell the story of the Chinese warrior who fought very bravely for his emperor, who in reward asked him what he would like. The warrior asked for one rice grain on the first square of a chessboard, two on the second, four on the third, eight on the fourth and so on. The emperor agreed. With a large display calculator or projected display show how quickly this would accelerate. With a graphing program, such as Simple Data Handling, the graph will be drawn as you enter the data and an exponential growth curve will emerge. What happened to the Emperor? Relate this to bacterial growth in ideal conditions. (5–10 mins)

Rotten racers
Show the pupils, or ask them to imagine, two ripe peaches in perfect condition. If people were to race to see who could make the peach go rotten first, how could they go about doing this? Discuss and debate. Draw out ideal conditions for microbial growth. (10–15mins)

Main Lesson
- Set up a demonstration of the 'What factors affect the rate of respiration of yeast?' practical. Ask the pupils to predict what will happen if you put more sugar in or keep it in the cold. Have a water bath in the lab at 35°C and a tub of broken ice. Place a tube of mixture into each and leave one in the room. Set volunteers to measure and record them every two minutes

Answers to summary questions

1. A Petri dish.
2. Nutrients.
3. [Look for clear, ordered instructions, giving reasons for the importance of each precaution. A certificate could be given on successful completion of this task.]

Growing Microbes

during the rest of the practical. As an extension, or if it comes up in discussion, try one without the sugar.
- Use a PowerPoint presentation to go over the 'Growing bacteria' practical. Introduce the key terms and equipment. Pass around a Petri dish and ask the pupils to say the name out loud. Pass around one containing nutrient agar and allow the pupils to touch it, but not to scoop it out. When it comes back to the front ask who would like to lick it? When you get a 'yuk' reaction, ask why not? All the fingers will have had bacteria on them. Ask what would happen if we put this plate somewhere where the bacteria would grow fast. Ask if anyone in this class was in an incubator as a baby. Do they know of anyone who was? Have they seen how eggs are made to hatch? Introduce the term 'incubation'.
- Emphasise the importance of not contaminating the plates. Label the fingered plate and incubate at 20°C for examination in the next lesson.

Plenary Suggestions

Yeast feedback
Pupils who monitored of the yeast practical should provide feed back to the group. (5–10 mins)

Flow diagrams
Get the pupils to create a flow diagram showing what happens to the rate of growth under different conditions (warmer or colder, more or less sugar). An outline on the board will help this. Discuss the flow chart in the light of the results and summarise. (10–15 mins)

Practical Support

Growing bacteria

Equipment and materials required
For each group: two Petri dishes and lids – filled to 1/3 depth with nutrient agar and left to set, Chinagraph pencil or OHP pen, wire loop, Bunsen burner, bench mat, culture of *Micrococcus luteus* or other suitable microbe, alcohol or sterilising fluid, cotton wool, Sellotape strips.

Details
Demonstrate the aseptic techniques required. Swab down an area to work on using disinfectant or alcohol (**safety**: no naked flames while using this). Flame a wire loop until cherry red. Allow to air cool. Place a sterile nutrient agar filled Petri dish and lid at the base of a Bunsen burner. Introduce the term 'inoculation' and link to the jabs they will recently have had. If using a broth for inoculation, hold the culture bottle close to the flame of a Bunsen and remove the lid. Run the flame over the top of the bottle. Keeping the bottle near the flame and beneath it, place the cooled wire loop into the culture. Remove the loop and replace the lid. If using an agar culture remove the lid of the Petri dish in a similar way and scoop up a colony of bacteria with the sterilised wire loop.

Remove the lid of the Petri dish and run the wire loop over the surface of the agar in a zigzag pattern, turning the dish through 90° and then repeating. Place a lid on. Tape shut but do not seal airtight. Label with name, date, species (*Micrococcus luteus* or other suitable microbe), medium and incubation temperature (20°C) on the bottom of the dish using a Chinagraph pencil or OHP pen.

Place the plates bottom side up (to avoid condensation drops) in an incubator set to not more than 25°C and leave for several days.

After demonstration and warning regarding contamination, get the pupils to carry out the practical in groups of two or three. Set up two plates per group, labelling one 'fridge' and one 'incubator'. Get a volunteer with a thermometer to check the temperatures of these places, or as an extension set up a data-logger. Predict what will happen, giving reasons. Place the Petri dishes *in situ* and leave for several days before examining.

On examination, draw what the plates looked like and examine colonies with a hand lens. Do not open the Petri dishes. Dispose of them by totally immersing them in a suitable disinfectant solution.

Safety
Ethanol (alcohol) is highly flammable and harmful, make sure there are no naked flames: CLEAPSS Hazcard 40A. See CLEAPSS handbook/CD-ROM section 15.2. Autoclave before disposal.

What factors affect the rate of respiration of yeast?

Equipment and material required
Water bath, ice bath, 100 ml measuring cylinder, flour (20 g for each group), sugar (1 g for each group), yeast, stop-clock.

Details
A water bath preheated to 35°C and an ice bath, 100 ml measuring cylinders and stop-watches. Use fresh yeast and water at 35°C to start the culture. Try out first and if your yeast packet produces too much froth, cut down the sugar until it is contained within a measuring cylinder after 30 mins.

Differentiation

SEN
Demonstrate each stage of the practicals and ask the pupils to take digital photographs. Use these with prompt cards later on to make a display.

Extension
Pupils can set up a data-logger to record the temperature of the two incubation sites. Each day they record the temperature and the number of colonies or, if dense, the percentage coverage. They plot this against time for each site and work out how the growth rate is linked to temperature. They need to get a numerical value, such as how many percent more colonies/cover the warm one has. Does this change over time?

Answers to in-text questions
a. So that there are no microbes that could contaminate your nutrient agar.
b. So that you do not contaminate the jelly with microbes from your fingers or transfer microbes growing on the jelly onto your fingers.

B1.11 Useful Microbes

NC links for the lesson
- Organisms, behaviour and health
- Life processes are supported by the organisation of cells into tissues, organs and body systems.

Learning Objectives

Pupils should learn:
- How microbes can be used to make food and other products.

Learning Outcomes
- All pupils will be able to name some products made using microbes.
- Most pupils will be able to describe how a range of products are made using microbes.
- Some pupils will also be able to describe in detail how a wide range of products are made using microbes.

How Science Works
- Describe and record observations and evidence systematically. (1.2d)

Answers to summary questions

1. Use of different microbes, time left to mature, etc.
2. A protein molecule that controls chemical reactions in living things.
3. Production of fuels such as gasohol and biogas.
4. Poster.

The Lesson

Starter Suggestions

Anyone for microbes?

Remind the pupils of the yeast demonstration from the previous page. Ask if anyone knows what else yeast can be used for. Discuss products which can be made using microbes and collect suggestions on the board. (5–10 mins)

Wipe out!

Ask pupils to imagine that all the micro-organisms on the planet died due to a blast of cosmic radiation (anything visible to the naked eye was unaffected). What effect would this have? Discuss this and describe this situation in whatever way you prefer. Read out volunteers' work. As a backing track the Beachboys 'Wipe-out' could be used from the album *Still Cruisin*. (10–15 mins)

Main Lesson

- Bring in a loaf of bread, empty wine, beer and spirits bottles and a jar of Marmite (preferably the special edition Guinness Marmite in the black and white jar), some blue cheese, some mycoprotein such as Quorn, a pot of natural yoghurt and a bottle of Yakult or similar bacterial drink. Hand these around and discuss them, emphasising that eating in the laboratory is not permitted. Be aware of potential blue cheese allergies. Using PowerPoint explain the production of each of the examples above.
- Give the pupils a simple matching exercise where they have to join the substance being acted on with the substance produced by the yeast (e.g.

Learning Styles

Visual: Observing the PowerPoints slides.
Auditory: Discussing the types and uses of microbes.
Kinaesthetic: Carrying out the practicals.
Interpersonal: Group work during the practicals.
Intrapersonal: Appreciating the wide range of impacts microbes have on our lives.

Useful Microbes

wheat flour → bread, grapes → wine, apples → cider). This could be a two part list or a columns activity.

- Show the pupils a picture of a head of barley and give a description using PowerPoint slides of the process of malting. Ask the pupils if they have heard of the American drink malted milk?
- Extend this discussion to the production of beer. Ask if anyone has relatives who brew their own beer or wine and get them to discuss it.
- Remind the pupils of the process of anaerobic respiration (sugar → ethanol + carbon dioxide). Carry out the demonstration of making wine as described below.
- Show the pupils a pot of yoghurt. Get the pupils to read the names of the bacteria written on the side of the pot. Set up the yoghurt making practical described below, if possible in a domestic science room so that it may be permissible for the pupils to taste their products.

Plenary Suggestions

Wipe out remixed
If the pupils carried out the 'Wipe-out!' starter, they can add to their notes using knowledge gained during the lesson. (5–10 mins)

On your head be it
A chosen pupil can be provided with some pictures of bread, beer, wine, yoghurt, cheese and probiotic drinks. They take one face down from a shuffled pack and with their forefinger hold it to their foreheads facing outwards, without looking at it. They then have to ask questions about how they were made and guess what type of food or drink they are. A prompt list of questions will help lower attaining pupils. (10–15 mins)

Practical Support

Demonstration – making wine

Equipment and materials required
1 gallon demi-john, airlock and bung with a hole, sterilising solution (such as sodium metabisulfite), 500 ml grape juice concentrate (or 2 l of fruit juice plus 1 kg dissolved sugar), yeast nutrient, sachet of commercial wine yeast, sugar, 250 ml conical flask, cotton wool, labels.

Details
First mix the contents of a fresh packet wine yeast with a teaspoon of sugar and about 150 ml luke-warm water (about 30°C) in a sterilised 250 ml conical flask. Plug lightly with cotton wool and leave to stand until frothy. Take a 1 gallon demi-john and rinse it out with sterilising solution (such as sodium metabisulfite), then again with cold water, rinsing several times. Add 500 ml grape juice concentrate (or 2 l of fruit juice plus 1 kg dissolved sugar) and a teaspoonful of yeast nutrient. Mix with water to fill to within 5 cm of the shoulder. Pour out 80 ml into a measuring cylinder and, using a hydrometer, measure and record the specific gravity. Add the yeast starter culture. Seal with a sterilised airlock. Ask the pupils why it is necessary to sterilise everything. Label and leave in a warm place, transferring to a cool place once fermentation has stopped.

Safety
Sodium metabisulfite is harmful: CLEAPSS Hazcard 92.

Yoghurt

Equipment and materials required
Full-fat milk (150 ml per pupil), measuring cylinder (200 ml), optional dried milk powder, hot plate, live natural yoghurt (1 teaspoon per 250 ml), teaspoon, sterile yoghurt pots, cling film, universal indicator solution (flammable), pH probe and data-logger.

Details
Boil 150 ml of full-fat milk for each pupil, assuming that they will have a pot each. For extra creaminess dried milk power can be added at this stage.

Allow it to cool to below 40°C (so as to not denature the enzymes).

Add live natural yoghurt containing *Lactobacillus acidophilus* at the rate of one teaspoonful per 250 ml and stir well.

Pour the mixture into sterile yoghurt pots and seal with cling film. Test the pH of a small sample or place a pH probe attached to a data-logger into a sample pot (this one is not to be eaten).

Safety
If possible, make yoghurt in domestic science (home economics) room.

Differentiation

SEN
Pupils can carry out a simple card sort exercise to arrange the parts of the equation for anaerobic respiration. This can be carried out using laminated cards and can be scaled as appropriate.

Extension
Pupils may with to extend their understanding of the topic by looking in detail at the importance of keeping a pure strain of microbes for a particular food product, for example a particular yeast for brewing a beer.

You may like to get them to set up some barley to germinate, testing it for sugar at various points during the process.

They may also wish to look into the claims of probiotics through Internet searches.

Give the pupils the formula for glucose, ethanol and carbon dioxide and ask them to work out how many of each molecule are on each side of the equation.

Answers to in-text questions

a Germinate barley so it starts to grow → starch changes to sugar → add water and yeast

B1.12 Harmful Microbes

NC links for the lesson
- Organisms, behaviour and health
- Life processes are supported by the organisation of cells into tissues, organs and body systems.
- … growth, development, behaviour and health can be affected by diet, drugs and disease.

Learning Objectives

Pupils should learn:
- Which diseases are spread by microbes.
- How diseases are spread.
- How the body defends itself against disease.

Learning Outcomes
- All pupils will be able to name some diseases spread by microbes.
- Most pupils will be able to name a range of diseases spread by microbes and describe how they are spread and how the body defends itself.
- Some pupils will also be able to name a wide range of diseases spread by microbes and describe in detail how they are spread and how the body defends itself.

Functional Skills Link-up
English
- Read and understand texts (explanatory) in detail. (Level 1)

Answers to in-text questions

a Protozoa, virus

b Small hair-like structures on cells in the breathing system. They brush microbes and dirt out of our lungs.

c By causing blood to clot.

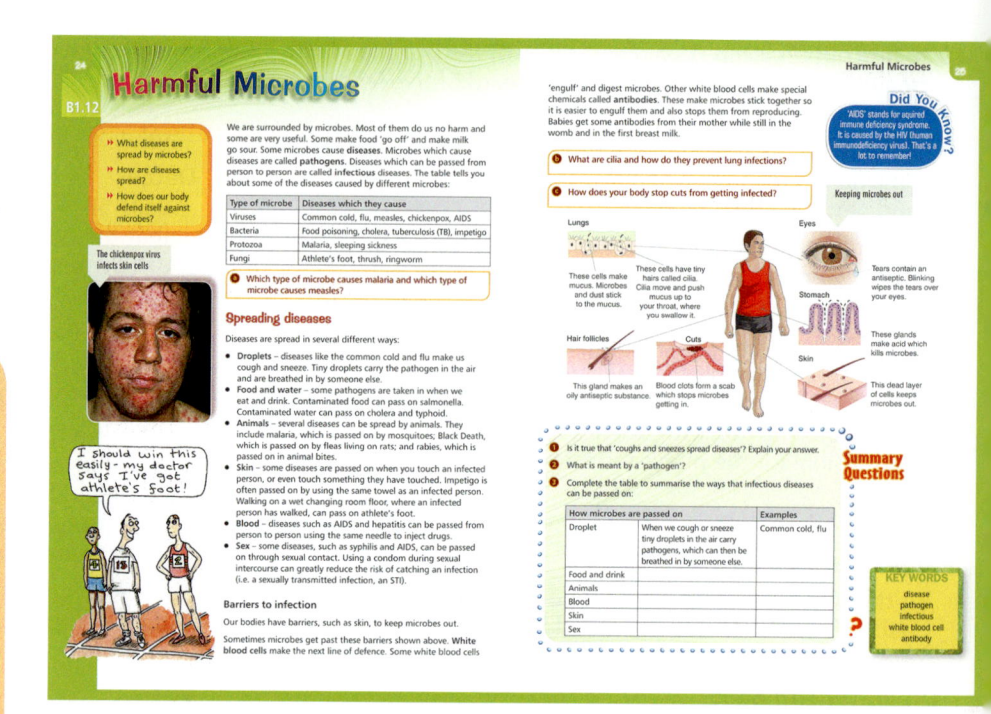

Learning Styles

Visual: Creating and decorating a concept map.
Auditory: Explaining the barriers to infection.
Kinaesthetic: Making and playing with the 'Chance' cards.
Interpersonal: Playing the 'Key words charades' plenary.
Intrapersonal: Considering the objectives and checking their own learning outcomes.

Answers to summary questions

1 Yes – the droplets of liquid from our mouth and nose contain microbes.

2 A microbe that causes diseases.

3

How microbes are passed on		Examples
Droplet	When you cough or sneeze tiny droplets in the air carry pathogens, which can then be breathed in by someone else	Common cold, flu
Food and drink	Microbes are swallowed in contaminated food and drink	Cholera, typhoid, salmonella
Animals	Microbes get into the blood in insect or animal bites	Malaria, rabies
Blood	Microbes are passed in contaminated blood, mainly when drugs are injected from dirty needles	HIV, hepatitis
Skin	Microbes pass from the skin of an infected person, or from something an infected person has touched	Impetigo, conjunctivitis, athlete's foot
Sex	Passed from one person to another by sexual contact	HIV, syphilis, chlamydia, gonorrhoea

Harmful Microbes

The Lesson

Starter Suggestions

Who's had what?
Give out a sheet with a list of common diseases. Pupils should work in pairs or threes and tick off between them which diseases they have had. Have a ghastly prize for the unhealthiest group. Make sure there are no controversial ones listed. Discuss with the class which diseases are caused by microbes and which ones have other causes. If the class is particularly healthy include family members. (5–10 mins)

Diseases – map of what I know…
Divide the class into groups of about four. Give each group a large A3 size sheet of paper. Ask them to start with the word 'diseases' in the centre of the page and draw out collectively a concept map of their knowledge of the topic showing the words involved and how they are linked together, labelling each link. Allow about eight minutes for drawing out, then five minutes circulating looking at other groups' material, then a brief summary from the front. (10–15 mins)

Main Lesson

- Discuss the main causes of disease with the pupils, illustrating this with a PowerPoint presentation. Introduce the terms 'pathogen' and 'infectious' (they are likely to know the latter but not the former) and reinforce the main types of microbe and the disease they may cause, limited to colds, 'flu, measles, chickenpox and AIDS for viruses; food poisoning, cholera, TB and impetigo for bacteria; malaria and sleeping sickness for protozoa; and athletes foot, thrush and ringworm for fungi. Elicit stories from the group regarding personal experience or close knowledge of the diseases involved and share knowledge – do this with caution, depending on the class group.

- Show a video clip on infectious diseases, such as that of the work of John Snow on cholera if one is available. A good cartoon reference is where Homer Simpson orders a Juicer from the Far East and the box contains Osaka 'flu microbes. Bart doesn't want to go to school and tells his immune system to give up the fight (Episode 9F20 – 'Marge in chains').

- Read through the section entitled 'Spreading diseases' in the pupil book. Divide into groups of about three. Give each group of the pupils a set of blank cards with the word 'Chance?' written on the back. Their task is to write up scenarios where people catch a disease and the circumstances under which this takes place. Emphasise that these must be realistic but not offensive. These cards can be shuffled and read out to the class. De-personalise this by having the chance cards apply to fictional characters.

- A video clip of a slowed-down sneeze will illustrate the dangers effectively. This, along with some useful accurate and amusing advice on how to cough and sneeze more hygienically, is available if an Internet search for 'cough safe' is carried out.

- Discuss barriers to infection. Give the pupils a drawing of a medieval castle and ask them to identify what is happening to cartoons of microbes trying to get in. Defence mechanisms could include a wall representing the skin; boiling oil representing heating food; throwing vats of acid over the invaders representing stomach acid; soldiers cutting up the invaders representing white cells; defenders with lassoes and flags causing the invaders to clump together representing the antibodies; microbes being passed hand over hand then thrown out representing the cilia.

- Show a PowerPoint slide of a new born calf suckling its mother. Explain the importance of the first milk (colostrum) for providing the offspring with antibodies.

- Ask the pupils to complete the table in Summary Question 3 showing how microbes are passed on. You should provide a pre-printed copy for lower attaining pupils.

- Ask the pupils to create a similar table showing the barriers to infection and how they work.

- Carry out an interactive whiteboard exercise with drag and drop category boxes for diseases, methods of infection, ways of spreading microbes and types of microbes. Each key word in turn appears in the centre of the screen and the pupil has to choose which bin to put it in. An option to colour code these could help when learning difficulties are more pronounced.

Plenary Suggestions

Key word role play
Pupils should write and carry out a role-play exercise where a mother or father is asking a doctor or a nurse about the best ways to protect their child from infections. Pick on two couples and appoint a judge to tick off when they make relevant questions and appropriate comments onto a scoreboard. (5–10 mins)

Key word charades
Provide a set of key word cards from the lesson, including all the key words in the pupil book, the methods of infection (do not allow sexually transmitted diseases for reasons of decency), the names of the diseases featured and the barriers to infection discussed. Place them face down on the front desk. Get a pair of volunteers to come to the front. They are to choose a card, look at it and place it face down to one side. They must then act out the key word together while others guess. Do not allow shouting out. (10–15 mins)

Differentiation

SEN
Pupils can carry out an interactive whiteboard exercise with drag and drop category boxes for diseases, methods of infection, ways of spreading microbes and types of microbe. Each key word in turn appears in the centre of the screen and the pupil has to choose which bin to put it in. An option to colour code these could help when learning difficulties are more pronounced.

Extension
With higher attaining pupils you should discuss some of the ethical issues surrounding infectious diseases. They could research the controversy over the claimed link between MMR jabs and autism, evaluating the evidence. They could look at the ethical issues regarding objection to the use of condoms and the consequences of unprotected sex leading to high HIV infection rates in sub-Saharan Africa, including looking at other means of prophylaxis.

Answers to Cells, Tissues and Organs – End of Topic Questions

Answers to know your stuff questions

1 **a** Bone. [1]

  b Any *one* from:
  A bone is broken;
  It is broken. [Accept 'fractured' or 'snapped'.] [1]

  c (i) A line to the elbow or shoulder within the areas circled below: [1]

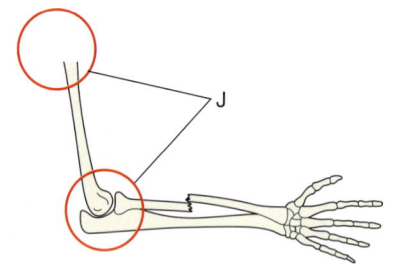

  [Accept a line which ends on a finger joint.]

  (ii) So that it can move *or* bend. [1]
  (iii) Muscles. [1]

2 **a** A: respiratory system [1]
  B: reproductive system [1]
  C: circulatory system [1]
  D: digestive system [1]
  E: skeleton [1]

  b Reproductive. [1]

3 **a** Cell wall, [Answers may be in either order.][1]
  chloroplast. [Accept 'vacuole'.] [1]

  b Nucleus. [1]

  c Chloroplast. [1]

  d Vacuole. [Accept 'sap'.] [1]

  e Near the upper surface of a leaf. [1]

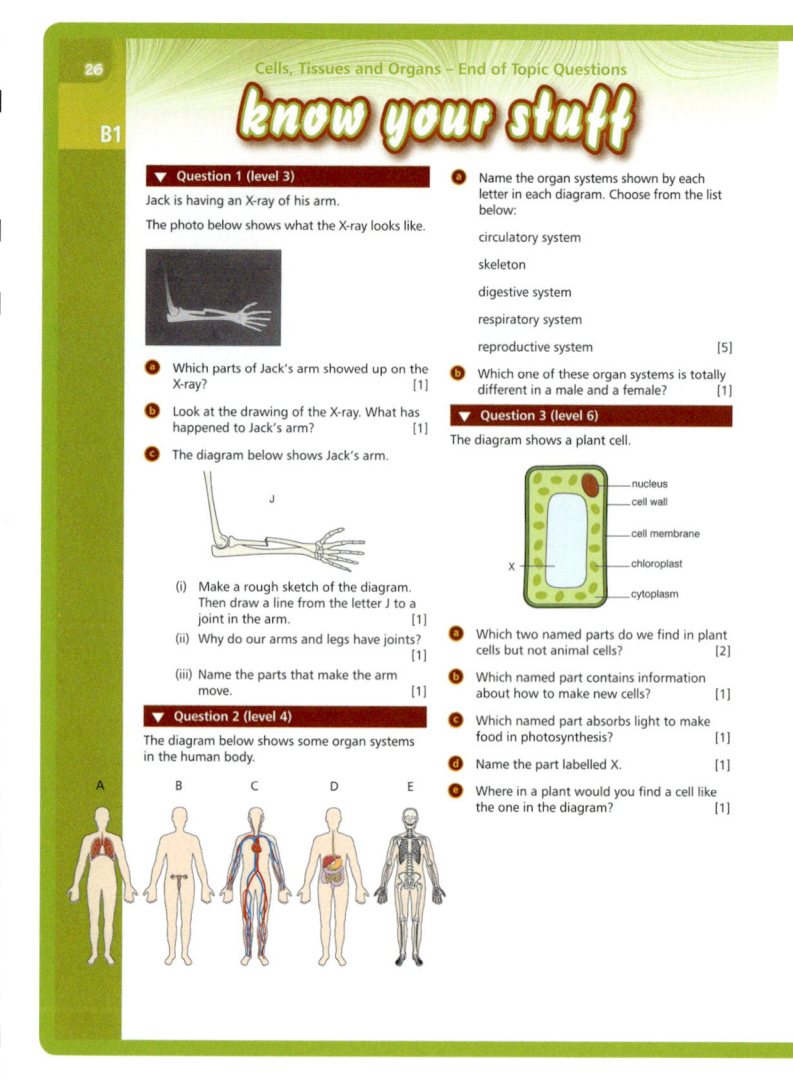

Cells, Tissues and Organs – End of Topic Questions

How Science Works

Question 1 (level 5)

Bacteria in the skin can cause spots. A scientist investigated the effect of spot cream on bacteria.

a He grew bacteria on the surface of jelly in a Petri dish.

At what temperature would the bacteria reproduce quickly?

Choose from the temperatures below:

90°C   10°C

35°C   −10°C   [1]

b The researcher placed two small circles of paper onto the surface of the jelly. One had been soaked in spot cream. The other had been soaked in water. The diagrams below show the jelly at the start of the experiment and two days later.

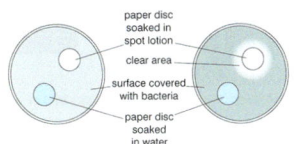

What happened to the bacteria in the clear area around the paper soaked in spot cream? [1]

c What was the control used in this experiment? [1]

d What safety precautions should the researcher take in this investigation? [2]

Question 2 (level 6)

One evening Sitel and Runi ate chicken salad which had been left in Runi's locker all day. The next day both girls were ill. Their doctor gave them antibiotics to take for eight days.

The graph shows the effect of antibiotics on the number of bacteria in the body.

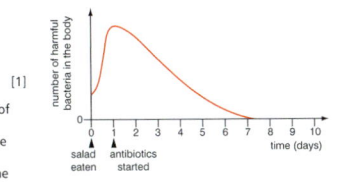

a Use the graph to explain why the girls did not become ill until the day after eating the salad. [1]

b After taking the antibiotics for eight days, Runi was completely better. Explain why she got better. [1]

c Sitel was told to take the antibiotics for eight days. She felt much better after five days so she stopped taking the antibiotics. The next day she felt very ill again. Use the graph to help you explain why Sitel became ill again. [2]

d Food will keep longer if you place it in a refrigerator at 4°C.

This does not kill bacteria.

What is the effect of low temperature on bacteria? [1]

Answers to How Science Works questions

1
 a 35°C [1]

 b The spot cream killed the bacteria. [Accept 'they died' or 'they were killed or destroyed'.] [1]

 c The paper disc soaked in water. [Accept 'the other disc'.] [1]

 d Any *two* from:
Keep the lid on the dish.
Seal *or* secure the dish.
Wear gloves.
Wear a mask *or* eye protection.
Use tweezers to add the paper disc. [2]

2
 a Any *one* from:
There were not enough bacteria in the food *or* body.
The bacteria multiplied by the next day. [1]

 b The antibiotic *or* medicine killed all the bacteria. [1]

 c Any *one* from:
Antibiotic *or* medicine had not killed all the bacteria.
There were still bacteria left alive.
The bacteria multiplied. [2]

 d Any *one* from:
It slows down reproduction.
It is too cold for the bacteria to divide *or* reproduce. [1]

B2.1 Reproduction

NC links for the topic
- Organisms, behaviour and health.
- The human reproductive cycle includes adolescence, fertilisation and fetal development.
- Conception, growth, development, behaviour and health can be affected by diet, drugs and disease.

Level descriptors for the topic
- **AT2 level 4:** Pupils describe some processes and phenomena related to organisms, their behaviour and the environment.
- **AT2 level 5:** The main functions of … animal organs and why these functions are necessary.
- **AT2 level 5:** The main stages in the life cycles of humans.
- **AT2 level 6:** The importance of some applications and implications of science.
- **AT2 level 7:** How evidence supports some accepted scientific ideas such as the structure and function of cells.
- **AT2 level 8:** Describe and explain the importance of a wide range of applications and implications of science.
- **AT2 exceptional performance:** demonstrate both breadth and depth of knowledge and understanding of organisms.

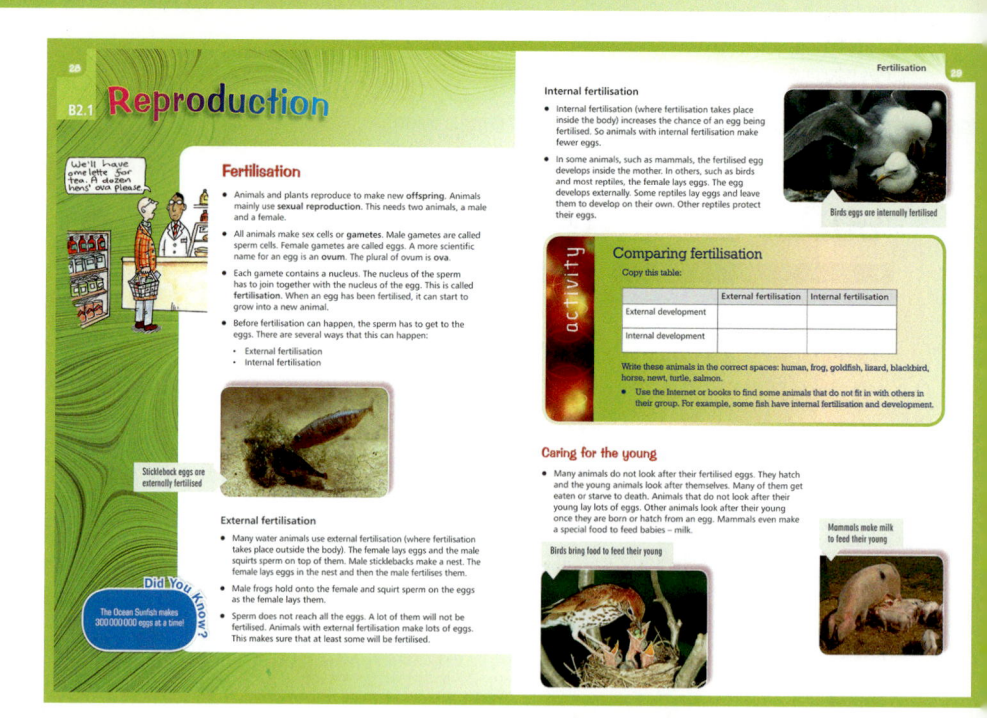

The Lesson

Starter Suggestions
Youngest you

Pupils should imagine that they have a device that will take them back in time. Unfortunately it is a prototype and your body does not stay the same as it is now, it gets younger as you go back in time. Ask: if you did this, when would you stop being you? Pupils should write down their idea and share it with the group. (5–10 mins)

Learning Objectives
Pupils should learn:
- What fertilisation means.
- Where fertilisation happens in animals.

Learning Outcomes
- All pupils should be able to define fertilisation as the joining of sex cells.
- Most pupils should be able to define fertilisation, provide examples and differentiate between internal and external fertilisation.
- Some pupils should also be able to evaluate the effectiveness of various fertilisation strategies and relate this to body structure and behaviour.

How Science Works
- Describe patterns and trends in secondary data … (if using the numbers of offspring extension). (1.2f)

Functional Skills Link-up
ICT skills
- Access, navigate and search internet sources of information purposefully and effectively. (Level 1)

Learning Styles
Visual: Observing PowerPoints and video clips.
Auditory: Describing different types of strategy.
Kinaesthetic: Dice throwing activity.
Interpersonal: Considering the timeline.
Intrapersonal: Group working on dice game.

Answers to activity
Comparing fertilisation

a

	External fertilisation	Internal fertilisation
External development	Goldfish, frog, salmon, newt	Lizard, blackbird, turtle
Internal development		Horse, human

Fertilisation

Getting started

As the pupils come into the room, tell each one that they are a different creature ('you are an elephant', 'you are a fish', 'you are a frog', etc.). Use enough animals to provide a suitable group size, e.g. six to eight of each type of animal. The pupils should get into groups of the same animal and discuss how they get started in life and write out their ideas clearly on an A3 sheet of paper. When all have written their ideas, or after a time limit, get the groups to leave their papers and circulate looking at the papers of the other groups. (10–15mins).

Main Lesson

- Discuss either starter activity and from it draw out the idea of sex cells joining together. Introduce the word 'gametes' and the term 'sexual reproduction'. Pupils can write down definitions for these in their exercise books.
- Show a PowerPoint display of sperm cells and ova, reminding the pupils of these terms from their earlier work on specialised cells. While describing ova it may be useful to have an egg to demonstrate with.
- Show the pupils a **'Life on Earth' timeline** on a till roll or similar, with the emergence of life, sexual reproduction, fish, amphibians, reptiles, mammals, birds and humans marked on it at suitable places (see 'Practical Support'). Remind, or inform, the pupils that all animal life originally came from the sea. Ask how the sperm might get to the eggs. Complete a section of a worksheet on this.
- Show a video clip of stickleback nest building and their fertilisation. Describe this on the worksheet.
- Remind, or inform, the pupils that the first land animals had to return to the water to breed and that their descendants are the amphibians, including frogs, toads and newts. Again reinforce with video and complete sections of a worksheet.
- Remind, or inform, the pupils that mammals and birds rely on internal fertilisation, as there is no surrounding water for the sperm to swim in. A moist area is needed. If available, show a video clip of sperm swimming to support this. Fill in a worksheet.
- Differentiate between birds and mammals, as male mammals have a penis whereas birds do not. Birds rely on placing their external genital openings (cloacae) next to each other.
- **Dice game:** Divide the class into groups of about four. Give each group a box of dice and a container to shake them into. Using a projected large calculator, show them the probability of throwing a six, two sixes in a row, etc. Show the pupils the probability of them surviving to a breeding age in a variety of animals. If they were a sunfish (one in 100 000 000); a frog (1 in 8000); a duck (1 in 6); a human (99 out of 100). Using several dice at once, try to throw eight sixes in a row. You would need to be this lucky to survive to breed as a sunfish. Try to throw five sixes in a row. You would have to be this lucky to survive as a frog. Try to throw a six to survive as a duck. To die as a human you have to throw three sixes in a row.
- Discuss the activity – who died and who survived? Link this with the degree of parental support each species gives to its offspring and complete the appropriate worksheet section.
- As an extension, draw out a graph using Simple Data Handling or Excel to show the relationship between the number of offspring and their survival rate.

Plenary Suggestions

In or out?
Pupils should complete the 'Comparing fertilisation' table. They then comment on it and discuss. (5–10 mins)

Am I bothered?
Divide the class into small groups. Each one is to take an animal's eye view and imagine a humanised version of one of the range of creatures discussed during the lesson. In character, the pupils are to comment on: the attitude taken towards the offspring regarding how many of them there are; what is to happen to them; how much concern they do or do not show. Ham it up and get the pupils to present their cameos to the rest of the group. (10–15 mins)

Practical Support

'Life on Earth' timeline

Equipment and materials required

Till roll timeline (adjust scaling factor to suit available space and materials. A suitable factor would be 1 m to 500 million years giving a till roll length of 7.4 m or about 25 feet).

Details

Life started 3700 million years ago.

Sexual reproduction started about 1200 million years ago.

First fish evolved 505 million years ago.

Amphibians evolved 363 million years ago.

Reptiles evolved 300 million years ago.

Mammals evolved 220 million years ago.

Birds evolved 133 million years ago.

Humans evolved 0.153 million years ago.

Dice game

Equipment and materials required

Boxes of dice and throwing trays, list of powers of 6 (6, 36, 216, 1296, 7776, 46 656, 279 936, 1 679 616).

Differentiation

SEN
Use Plasticine models of sperm and egg in conjunction with a torso model or large A3 diagram to show the process of fertilisation. With guidance they could produce a simple stop-motion animation of the process.

Extension
Give Internet references or library books so that pupils can look at more extreme methods of protecting offspring, such as: the mouth brooding fish (http://en.wikipedia.org/wiki/Mouthbrooder); the frog which looks after its offspring in cavities in the skin of its back or mouth, e.g. the marsupial frog genus *Gastrotheca*, the midwife toad genus *Alytes* or Darwin's frog *Rhinoderma darwinii*.

Homework Suggestion

The pupils could find out the numbers of offspring of a range of animals to create a collective collage display.

B2.2 Sex Organs

NC links for the lesson
- Organisms, behaviour and health
- The human reproductive cycle includes adolescence, fertilisation and fetal development.

Learning Objectives

Pupils should learn:
- The functions of women's sex organs.
- The functions of men's sex organs.

Learning Outcomes

- All pupils should be able to name some of the major parts of the male and female reproductive systems and describe their functions in simple terms.
- Most pupils should be able to name all of the parts of the male and female reproductive systems and describe their functions.
- Some pupils should also be able to describe the male and female reproductive systems in detail including alternative names and be able to give comprehensive descriptions of their functions.

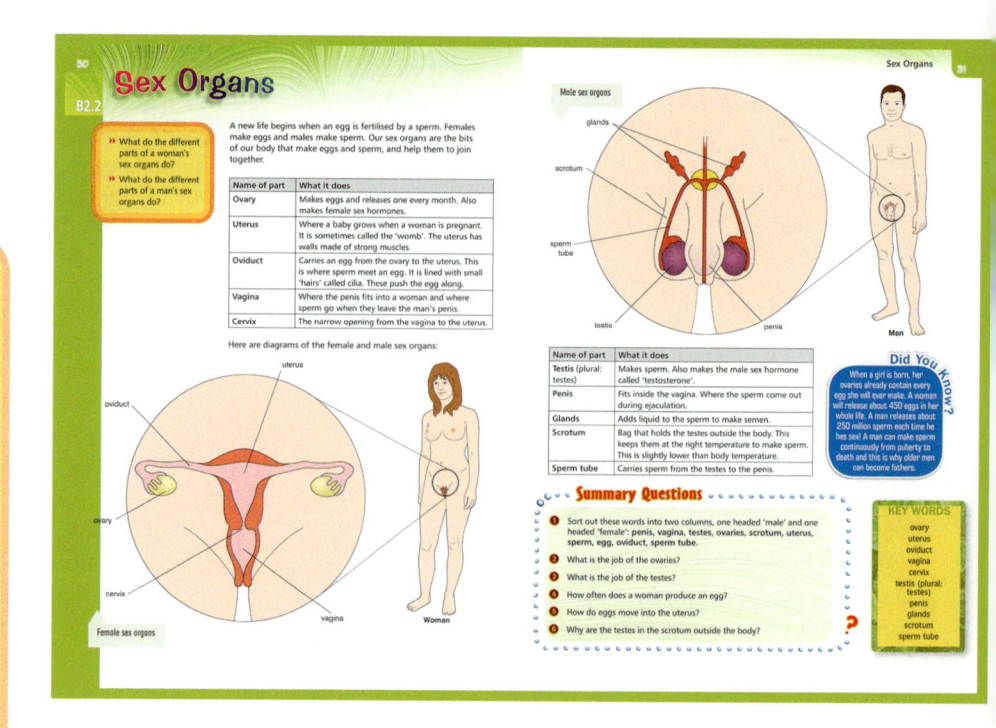

Functional Skills Link-up

ICT skills
- Select and use software applications to meet needs and solve problems (audio). (Level 2) See Extension work.

Learning Styles

Visual: Looking at the diagrams of the anatomical parts.
Auditory: Talking to peers about the meaning of words and phrases.
Kinaesthetic: Manipulating letter cards sets if the 'Mixed up bits' plenary is used.
Interpersonal: Group discussion about the meanings of the key words.
Intrapersonal: Evaluating own knowledge of sexual anatomy and improving it.

Answers to summary questions

1. **Male**: penis, testes, scrotum, sperm, sperm tube.
   Female: vagina, ovaries, uterus, egg, oviduct.
2. To make eggs (and hormones).
3. To make sperm (and hormones).
4. Every 28 days (once a month).
5. Moved by cilia in the oviduct.
6. They work best a bit below body temperature.

The Lesson

Starter Suggestions

Why have two sexes?

Discuss stereotyping on gender grounds. What are the significant differences between males and females and what importance do they have? (5–10 mins)

Heard the word

Put the key words from the pupil book onto the board as laminated flashcards. Ask the pupils if anyone recognises any of them and can tell what they mean. In a bubble next to each word write down any correct definitions. On completion, remove the cards but leave the bubbles and any unrecognised cards there for use later on. (10–15 mins)

Main Lesson

- Using PowerPoint diagrams go through the structure of the male reproductive system. Ask the pupils to fill in the labels on unlabelled diagrams as you go. Emphasise that sperm is not made in the penis (a common misconception).

- Go through the same process with the female system. Initially use front and side views of the system, annotating them as the terms are introduced. Draw out or project a from-below diagram of the female system viewed between the legs, emphasising that females have three orifices rather than the two, which men have, and showing the relative positions of the anus, vagina, urethra, clitoris and labia. As many girls are ignorant of the details and variety of the anatomy of their vulva it should be valuable. It is not expected that they should memorise all these terms but it is an appropriate time to mention them.

- While showing these diagrams it is important to emphasise that every set of genitals, either male or female, is unique so there is no 'normal' shape, size or colour. The arrangement is generally the same, but the individual parts will differ greatly in appearance.

- This is a good opportunity for pupils to ask questions that may be worrying them. Introduce ground rules, scientific terms only, no personal comments or references to known individuals. You can collect anonymous questions on slips of paper folded up and put into a box. You may have to filter out some silly ones, but genuine queries will arise – use professional judgement as to how to address these.

- Give the pupils a sheet summarising the functions and get them to fill in a table matching the functions to the parts.

- If available show a good quality sex education video (view first and check for suitability). Liaison with the PSHE department will be helpful, as will familiarity with the school's and local authority's policies on sex education.

- The Summary Questions can be completed at this stage.

- Use a drag and drop labelling exercise to reinforce the learning of the key words and phrases from the lesson.

Plenary Suggestions

Before either of these refer back to the 'Heard the word' starter if used and get the pupils to replace the word cards in the appropriate bubbles. Give definition bubbles to any previously undefined cards.

Mixed up bits

Ask the pupils to solve a list of anagrams of the names of parts that they have been studying such as the following: SPINE (penis) RUM COST (scrotum) SETSIT (testis) VIA NAG (vagina) REXVIC (cervix) SUTURE (uterus) CUTVOID (oviduct) VAYOR (ovary) SNAGLD (glands) PETERS BUM (sperm tube) As an extension, pupils can make up their own anagrams of the names of the parts. These could be on sets of cards if required, or as a digital anagram sorter. (5–10 mins)

Sex parts crossword

Give the pupils a crossword to complete with clues to the different parts of anatomy they have studied. As an extension, get them to create alternative clues and try them out on each other. (10–15 mins)

Differentiation

SEN

Use cut-and-stick labels onto a large A4 or even A3 diagram of each gender's sexual anatomy.

Extension

Pupils could use recording apparatus such as a dictaphone or a microphone into a PC or laptop to record a summary of the parts and their functions discussed in the lesson. They could extend the content based on a more advanced text such as the AQA GCSE Science series.

Homework Suggestion

Pupils could revise for a short slip test (a verbal test needing a number of single word answers, these usually written on slips of paper) on the parts and their functions.

They could be given a blank grid to fill in a word search for their peers to use.

B2.3 Fertilisation in Humans

NC links for the lesson
- Organisms, behaviour and health.
- The human reproductive cycle includes adolescence, fertilisation and fetal development.

Learning Objectives
Pupils should learn:
- How sex cells are adapted to their jobs.
- How a sperm and an egg get together.
- What happens in fertilisation.

Learning Outcomes
- All pupils should be able to describe some basic features of sperm and eggs and be able to outline the process of how fertilisation takes place in humans.
- Most pupils should be able to describe adaptations of sperm and eggs and be able to describe the process of how fertilisation takes place in humans.
- Some pupils should also be able to relate structure to function and be able to describe the processes which lead up to fertilisation in detail.

How Science Works
- Use key scientific vocabulary and terminology in discussions and written work. (1.1c)

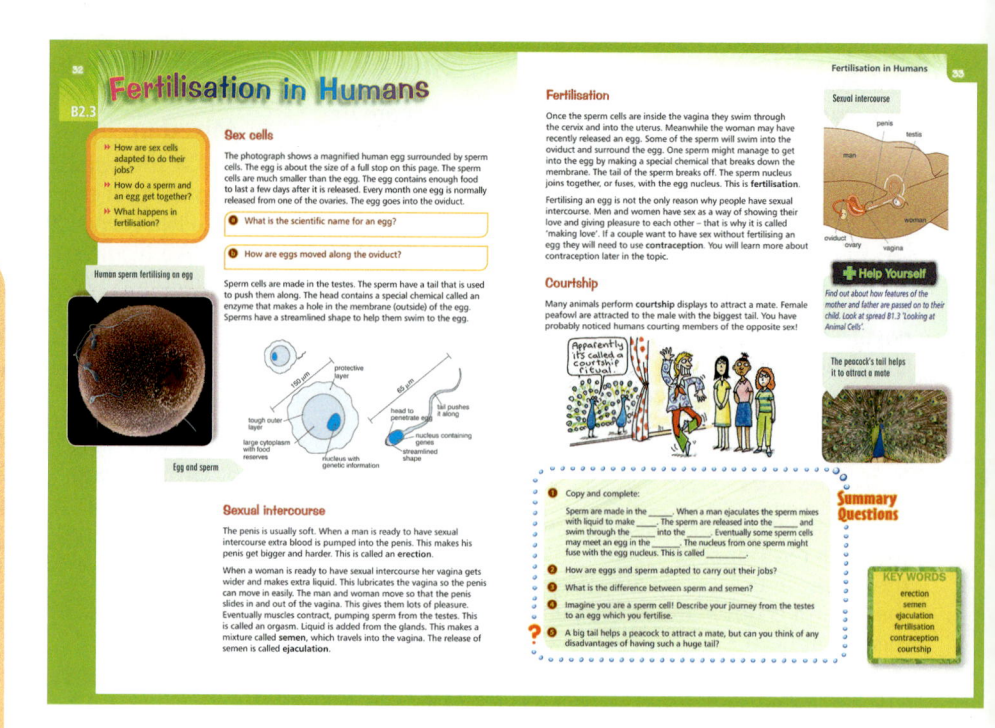

Learning Styles
Visual: Looking at PowerPoints.
Auditory: Listening to exposition.
Kinaesthetic: Role-play exercises
Interpersonal: Group conversations on the topic.
Intrapersonal: Reflecting on own understanding and re-evaluating.

Answers to summary questions

1. Sperm are made in the **testes**. When a man ejaculates the sperm mixes with liquid to make **semen**. The sperm are released into the **vagina** and swim through the **cervix** into the **uterus**. Eventually some sperm cells may meet an egg in the **oviduct**. The nucleus from one sperm might fuse with the egg nucleus. This is called **fertilisation**.

2. Eggs contain a food supply; sperms have tails for swimming, have a streamlined shape, produce lots of energy, make chemicals to make a hole in the membrane of the egg.

3. Sperm are the male sex cells (gametes); semen is the mixture of sperm and liquid.

4. testes   sperm tube   out of penis   vagina   cervix   uterus   oviduct   egg

5. Very heavy, especially when wet; it would make the bird vulnerable to predators.

Fertilisation in Humans

The Lesson

Starter Suggestions

Name the parts
Project unlabelled diagrams of the male and female reproductive systems and a sperm and an egg, together with a list of the relevant terms. Ask pupils to volunteer to attach the label to the appropriate part or organ. (10–15 mins)

Situations vacant
Have a brief discussion about the roles of the sperm and the egg, and then suggest to the pupils that they write a job description for each. Choose some pupils to read out their descriptions. (5–10 mins)

Main Lesson

- Following on from the starter suggestion 'Name the parts', discuss the detailed structure of a sperm and an egg. It could be instructive to provide paper scale models of a sperm and an egg. In humans, a sperm cell has a head measuring 5μm by 3μm and a tail 50μm long. A human ovum measures on average 145μm in diameter, so the diameter of the model egg needs to be about 30 times larger than the head length of the model sperm.
- Use a PowerPoint slide to illustrate and label the sperm and egg step-by-step, adding a function to each of the parts named.
- Show video footage of fertilisation taking place, talking over the role of the enzymes in helping the head of the sperm to penetrate the egg.
- Discuss the result of fertilisation. What is the fertilised egg now called? (zygote)
- Using diagrams of the male and female reproductive systems, discuss where eggs and sperm are formed, where fertilisation takes place and then consider how far each type of sex cell has to travel. This could reinforce the differences in structure, and the need for motility of sperm.
- Discuss the difference in numbers of sex cells produced – usually only one egg released per month, but millions of sperm produced in the testes. Get pupils to suggest reasons why there are such big differences in numbers.

Plenary Suggestions

Situations vacant – re-advertisement
Review the 'Situations vacant' starter if used, or use as a plenary. If used to start the lesson, ask the pupils if they would alter their job descriptions. (5–10 mins)

Mnemonic
Using M for male and F for female, get the pupils to think of descriptive terms for the sex cells beginning with these letters, e.g. for male – many, minute, motile; for female – fat, few, food. (10–15 mins)

Using Quia (www.quia.com)
Create a flashcard/matching pairs/wordsearch/concentration exercise based on the key words in the unit. Pupils should complete the exercises, print out the word list and stick them into their exercise books.

Differentiation

SEN
Model fertilisation using role play: represent the egg by having a circle of pupils with one in the centre. Have several others around the outside to represent the sperm, circling around the egg. The pupil representing the nucleus of the egg chooses one 'sperm' to get hold of the 'egg' and then the others lock arms tightly representing the membrane so that no more 'sperm' can get in. The pair in the centre can give the new child a name. Repeat this several times to reinforce the message and get the pupils to state what is happening at each stage.

Extension
Give the pupils a list of the key terms and get them to play a linking game, where they have to choose a minimum of two terms and a maximum of four and link them in a coherent sentence. Impose a strict time limit and give points for each correct link. If any single terms remain, give one point for a correct definition.

Alternatively, ask them to work out exactly how far a sperm has to travel in order to fertilise an egg. It should be possible to provide some approximate lengths for the different organs. Figures could be scaled up so that an equivalent of a person swimming the Channel could be made.

Homework Suggestion

Pupils to do the 'Using Quia' plenary if not done so far.
Alternatively, Summary Questions 1–4 from the pupil book.

Answers to in-text questions

a Ovum (plural ova).

b Moved by cilia.

B2.4 Pregnancy

NC links for the lesson
- Organisms, behaviour and health
- The human reproductive cycle includes adolescence, fertilisation and fetal development.

Learning Objectives
Pupils should learn:
- What the fetus needs and how it gets it.
- How the fetus is protected.
- How the fetus develops.
- What the mother needs to do to care for the fetus.

Learning Outcomes
- All pupils should be able to state in simple terms what a fetus needs, how it gets it, how it is protected and how it develops.
- Most pupils should be able to state the above clearly and fully.
- Some pupils should also be able to state the above in detail and relate this knowledge to anatomy and physiological systems.

How Science Works
- Recognise and explain the value of using models and analogies to clarify explanations. (1.1a1) (See Main Lesson – modelling placenta.)

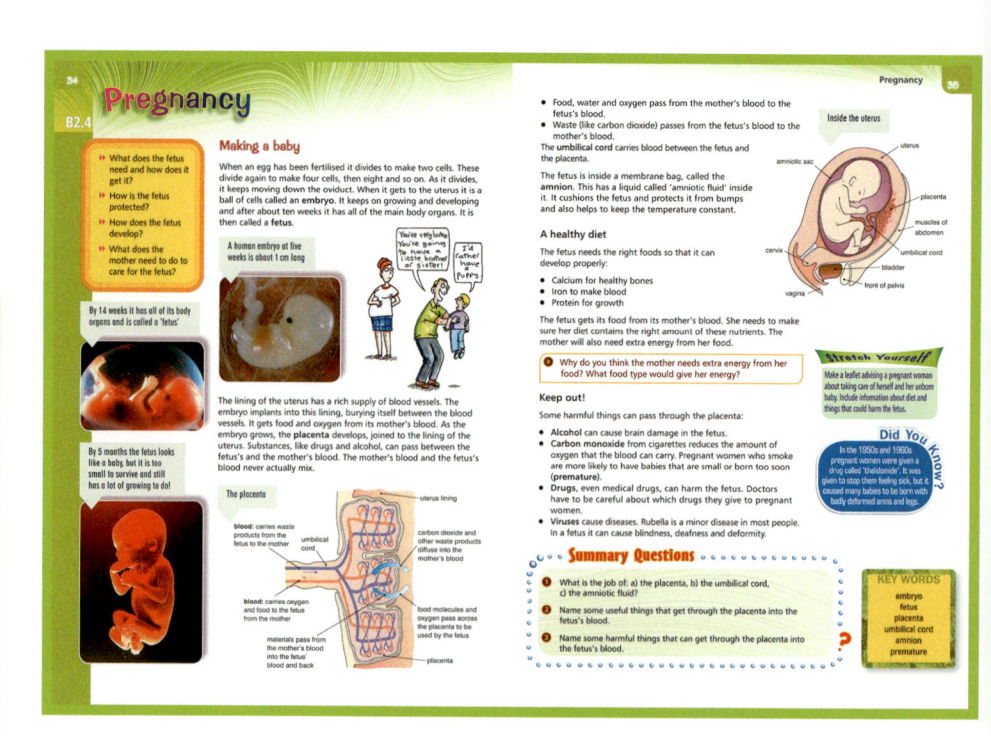

Learning Styles
Visual: Observing PowerPoint.
Auditory: Taking part in discussions.
Kinaesthetic: Carrying out practical activities.
Interpersonal: Role-play exercises.
Intrapersonal: Considering life before birth.

The Lesson

Starter Suggestions

Reproduction race
Give the pupils a class set of calculators. Tell them to: start by putting the number 1 into the calculator. Multiply this by 2 then multiply the answer by 2. Continue until you reach or pass one million. Ask: 'How many times did you have to double the number?' (20) The pupils should time how long it has taken them. A small reward could be given to the top group. (5–10 mins)

Before I was born
As they come into the lesson, give each pupil a photocopied tiny set of foot prints, about half a cm long. Ask them to consider that their feet were once that size. Ask them to consider what they feel about that fact, in silence for 30 seconds, then encourage them to share their thoughts with a small group, then with the class. Guide the discussion rather than lead it. (10–15 mins)

Answers to summary questions

1.
   a) Where useful things diffuse from mother's blood to fetus's blood; waste diffuses from fetus's blood to mother's blood.
   b) Carries blood between fetus and placenta.
   c) Acts as a shock absorber to avoid injury to fetus.
2. Oxygen, antibodies, sugar, amino acids, food.
3. Nicotine and other drugs, carbon dioxide, some viruses, e.g. HIV.

Pregnancy

Main Lesson

- Using PowerPoint describe how the pupils developed before their birth. Use individuals' names chosen from the teaching group as illustrative of each stage. Introduce and define the words 'embryo' (in humans from conception to about the eighth week of pregnancy) and 'fetus' (a developed embryo which has all the features of its adult form). Ask the pupils to complete a sentence: 'The difference between an embryo and a fetus is … ' Tell them you are going to select some pupils to read their sentences out, and do so. Give support to those who find the task difficult.
- Watch an appropriate video on development, such as the excellent 2005 video from National Geographic 'Life before Birth'. Alternatively, there are excellent resources on the website www.justthefacts.org. This has a pro-life viewpoint. It contains some high quality presentations of unbiased factual information on the development of the unborn child in the womb especially in the 'Your first nine months' section. View first to check suitability for your pupil group and with your schools sex education policy. Try to be aware of any appropriate social circumstances within the class.
- Pupils could complete a worksheet summarising the changes which occur from when the egg is fertilised until full term of pregnancy.
- Pupils should carry out a picture sorting exercise to match scale photographs of the developing fetus with age and descriptions on a worksheet, matching appropriate letters to the pictures.
- Some schools have pregnancy suits available, which will help pupils to appreciate the extent of the physical exertion involved in moving around while pregnant. Information on where to purchase these is available if you search on the Internet for 'empathy belly'.
- Ask the pupils to carry out a thought experiment, imagining dropping a tiny delicate waterproof computer onto the floor. Imagine it again with the computer suspended inside a bag of viscous fluids envisaging how this would protect it.
- If time allows for a practical, carry out a whole class placenta exchange demonstration. Split the class into two. Get one half to fill 15 cm sections of Visking tubing with a solution of food colouring. The coloured solution represents useful substances in the mother's blood. Tie off the ends. The other half of the class is to fill similar sections of Viking tubing with water. These represent the fetus's blood. When all are completed lay them alternately side-by-side in a shallow tray, so that they are in contact with each other, simulating the placenta. Allow sufficient time for diffusion (at least half an hour), then examine the contents of the transparent tubes to see if the colouring has passed across. Discuss the strengths and weaknesses of the simulation.
- Using PowerPoint, show slides of the types of food that pregnant woman need. Carry out a pairing exercise on a worksheet to join the food to the function.
- Draw out from the pupils, through discussion, the substances mentioned in the pupil book which can cross the placenta. Again, using PowerPoint, reinforce this and complete sections on the worksheet as a record and revision aid.

Plenary Suggestions

True or false
Divide the class into fours as far as possible. One pair is to set the other pair a series of five questions based on the lesson to which there can be true or false answers. Allow five minutes for construction of the questions, five minutes for asking each other, and five minutes for feedback of ways in which they have proved their knowledge. (15 mins)

Mummy don't do it
Write or record a plea from an unborn child to its mother asking for her to make conditions good within the womb. This could be monologue, rap or any method of communication, as long as it gets across the message of how to keep the unborn safe. Read out or role play a willing volunteer's work. (10–15mins)

Practical Support

Placenta exchange demonstration
Equipment and materials required

Per group: 2–25 cm Visking tubing, 250 cm^3 coloured glucose solution, strong thread or thin string, plastic tray, food colouring, beaker for water bath, Bunsen burner, tripod and gauze.

Differentiation

SEN
Use a model womb if available.

Lay out a set of laminated scale diagrams in order of age.

Extension
"Embryonic haiku"

Explain what a 'haiku' is (a short poem of three lines, these generally being of five syllables, seven syllables, then five syllables again). Give an example, e.g.

> A heron rises
> In the middle of the swamp
> Under the full moon.

Pupils to create a haiku poem based on consideration of the life of an embryo.

Homework Suggestion

Answer the Summary Questions from the pupil book.

Write a 'before I was born' story.

Answers to in-text questions

a Energy used by fetus, more effort (and therefore more energy) needed for movement of mother. Carbohydrates.

B2.5 Birth

NC links for the lesson
- Organisms, behaviour and health
- The human reproductive cycle includes adolescence, fertilisation and fetal development.

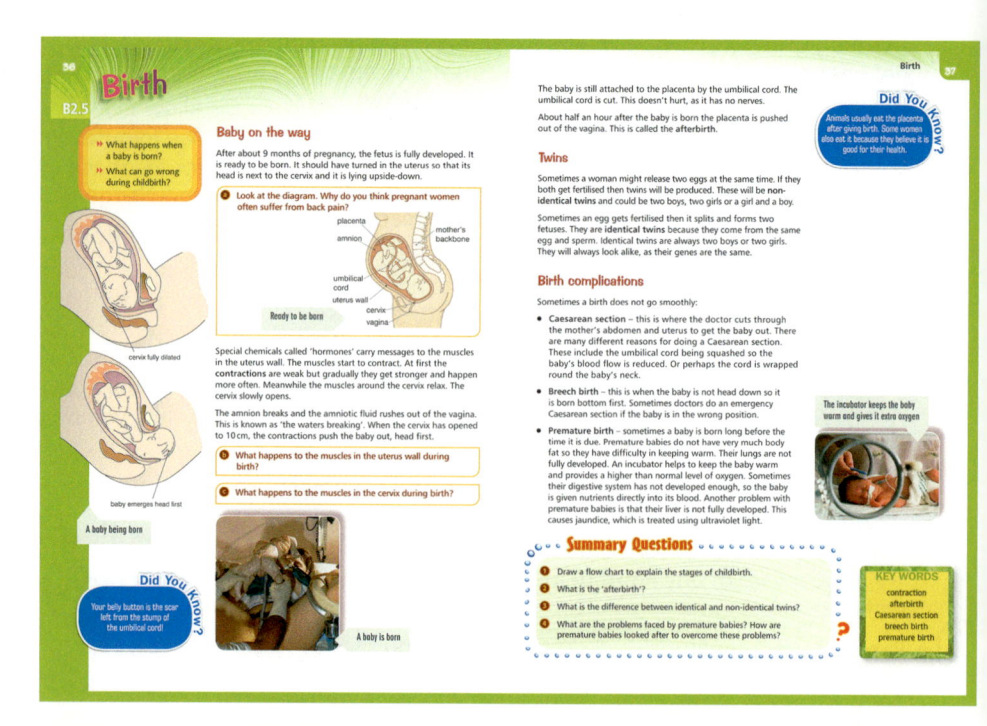

Learning Objectives
Pupils should learn:
- What happens when a baby is born.
- What can go wrong during childbirth.

Learning Outcomes
- All pupils should be able to describe in simple terms what happens during a normal birth and name a complication.
- Most pupils should be able to describe a normal birth and what may go wrong.
- Some pupils should also be able to describe in detail a normal birth and give full descriptions of what may go wrong using several examples.

How Science Works
- Use key scientific vocabulary and terminology in discussions and written work. (1.1c)
- Describe patterns and trends in secondary evidence … (1.2f) (See Extension activity.)

Learning Styles
Visual: Observing the photographs of various parts of the birth process.
Auditory: Listening to exposition.
Kinaesthetic: Using hands to simulate dilation of cervix.
Interpersonal: Discussion on twins and on birth difficulties.
Intrapersonal: Reviewing the knowledge covered in the unit so far.

Answers to summary questions

1. hormones produced   contractions start   muscles of cervix relax   cervix opens   waters break   more contractions   baby born
2. The placenta.
3. Identical twins come from the same egg and sperm and have identical genes; non-identical come from different eggs and sperm.
4. Little body fat so difficult to keep warm, lungs not fully developed. Incubator keeps baby warm and increases the amount of oxygen in the air they breathe.

Birth

The Lesson

Starter Suggestions

12 word birth
Pupils are to describe their understanding of how they were born in 12 words exactly. They are to work in silence individually at first, then to share and check with their neighbours. Ask for some examples to be read out. (5–10 mins)

The story so far
Review the process of reproduction as studied so far from gamete production to intercourse, to fertilisation and gestation. Place the key words which have been used in the unit so far on the board on laminated flash cards. Ask a volunteer pupil to state the meaning of one of the words and then remove that card. The pupil can then pick another pupil and get them to give a definition from the remaining cards. (10–15 mins)

Main Lesson

- Using a series of PowerPoint slides give an exposition on the sequence of stages in a normal birth. Encourage the pupils to predict what will happen in each stage. Pupils can complete the appropriate sections of a worksheet as they go along. Flag up any new key words and place printed laminated cards of the new key words onto the side of the board as they emerge during the discussion. If an anatomical model of a pregnant woman at full term is available, take a break from the PowerPoint and gather the pupils around the model, getting them to describe what the parts are, using the key words on the board.

- A useful clip to use at this point is the section from the 2005 film *A cock and bull story*, where the actor Steve Coogan playing Tristram Shandy is suspended upside down in a giant transparent plastic model uterus. Follow this with a discussion of the accuracy of the model and naming of the parts represented.

- When describing the cervix get the pupils to clench their fists and look at their curled little finger from beneath. This is a similar size to an un-dilated cervix. Ask the pupils to describe its function. Get the pupils to place their left and right hands together, index finger to index finger and thumb to thumb making as wide a circle as possible. Explain that this is the width that the cervix has to dilate in order to allow a baby's head to pass through it. Pupils can measure this gap to check it. It should be about 10 cm diameter.

- Show the pupils a suitable film showing the preparations for childbirth and an actual delivery. Be aware of any pupils who are particularly squeamish or faint at the sight of blood. Pupils can complete a simple series of questions on a worksheet accompanying the film. Cutting the umbilical cord usually sparks a discussion on the various styles of bellybutton ('inies', 'outies', etc.) and on how this happens in the wild. Rural pupils may well have experience of lambing, and some pupils may have seen their pets give birth.

- Using PowerPoint, show slides of various twins, asking the pupils to relate this to real-life examples known to them. There will be pairs of non-identical twins and probably some identical twins (monozygotic) in the school. Refer to the film *Twins* starring Danny DeVito and Arnold Schwarzenegger. The record for surviving multiple births in humans is 7, born by Caesarean section in Iowa, USA. The probability of having identical twins is about 3 in 1000. That for non-identical (di-zygotic) twins is between 5 and 20 in 1000.

- Write the word 'problems' on the board and encourage the pupils to tell what they know about birth problems. Try to draw out descriptions of breech birth, Caesarian section (make a link to *MacBeth* if they are studying it and to *Julius Caesar*) and premature births, again using PowerPoint to illustrate the knowledge covered.

- This is a good opportunity for an open discussion time, as the pupils will have stories about themselves or their relatives that they wish to share.

- Be aware that some issues may be sensitive for pupils who may have had an upsetting recent experience personally or in their family.

Plenary Suggestions

Broken birth sentences
Give the pupils a series of sentences summarising the birth process. Each one should be broken into several smaller phrases and mixed up. The pupils are to reassemble first each sentence and then the whole passage. This can be carried out in small groups. (10–15 mins)

Birthday drag and drop
Pupils can use a computer application or worksheet to complete a drag and drop exercise placing boxes containing information about the birth process, twins and birth complications into the correct area on a background frame. (5–10 mins)

Differentiation

SEN
Give the pupils a baby model, and film them using a video camera. Get them to show which position the baby is normally in before birth, where the cord can cause problems, where the cord is attached. Give them a second doll and ask them to state what two babies born at the same time are called and how they can come about. If both dolls are the same, get them to talk about identical twins. If they are different, non-identical twins can be discussed.

Extension
Using the Internet to locate the data, pupils should prepare a statistical report on the causes of multiple births and their probabilities and how these vary with time, age of the mother, genetic pre-disposition and geographical location. Pupils should use full scientific descriptions of the types of twin (e.g. mono-zygotic and di-zygotic).

Homework Suggestion

Complete the in-text questions and Summary Questions 1–4 from the pupil book.

Compile a list of 16 questions with single-word answers from which a crossword can be compiled.

Answers to in-text questions

a Weight and position of fetus puts strain on/bends the spine.

b They contract.

c They relax.

B2.6 Growing up

NC links for the lesson
- Organisms, behaviour and health
- The human reproductive cycle includes adolescence, fertilisation and fetal development.

Learning Objectives
Pupils should learn:
- What new babies need.
- How humans and other animals grow.
- The changes that take place at puberty and how they are controlled.

Learning Outcomes
- All pupils should be able to describe what new babies need, growth and puberty changes in simple terms.
- Most pupils should be able to do the above using full descriptions.
- Some pupils should also be able to state the reasons why the above are necessary and inter-relate the concepts involved.

How Science Works
- Identify a range of data and other evidence to back an argument and a counterclaim in less complex and/or familiar contexts, e.g. advantages and disadvantages of breastfeeding and using formula milk. (1.1a3)

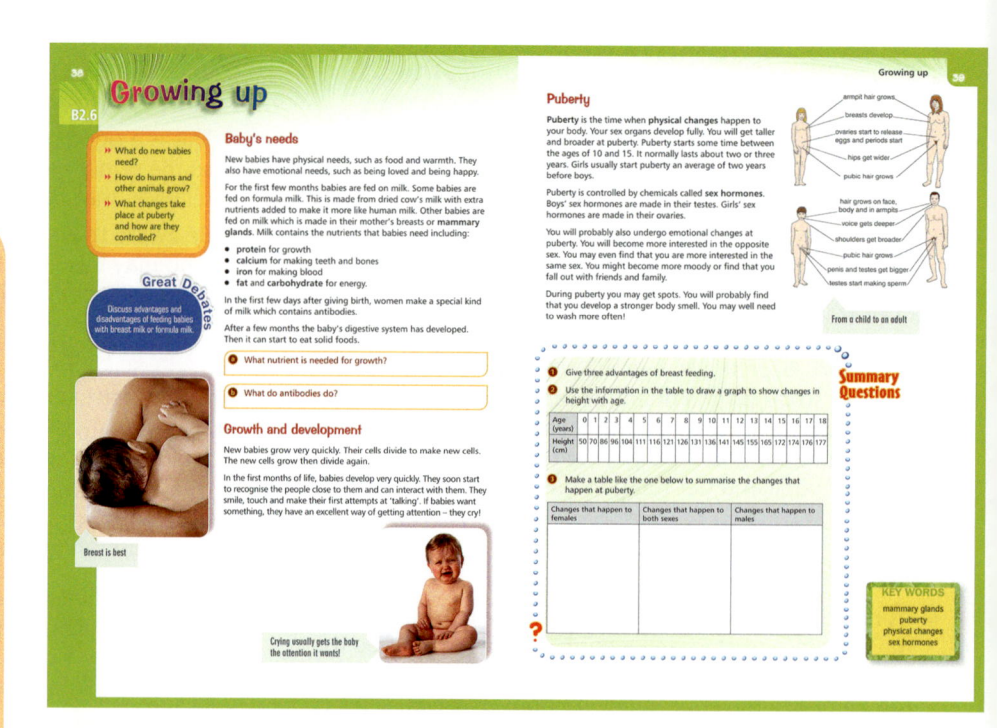

Functional Skills Link-up
ICT skills
- Create and develop charts and graphs to suit requirements, using suitable labels. (Level 1) See Summary Question 2.

Learning Styles
Visual: Observing the sections of video.
Auditory: Listening to the exposition and video clips of conversations.
Kinaesthetic: Playing the 'Needs cards' plenary.
Interpersonal: Taking part in the discussions.

Answers to summary questions

1. Exactly matches nutritional needs of the baby; gives the baby antibodies; helps bonding between baby and mother.

2. [Give 1 mark each for: choice of scale; labelling axes; accuracy of points; line of best fit.]

3.

Changes that happen to females	Changes that happen to both sexes	Changes that happen to males
Breasts get bigger	Pubic hair develops	Penis and testes get bigger
Hips widen	Underarm hair develops	Shoulders get broader
Start having periods	Emotional changes	Chest and facial hair start to grow

Growing up

The Lesson

Starter Suggestions

The story so far…
Going back to the moment of fertilisation, track the development of the individual through a series of photographs. Pick individuals in a 'hands down' exercise to describe what has been happening at each stage until birth has occurred. (5 mins)

Answers and questions
Provide the pupils with 10 words or short phrases based on the previous work on gamete formation, conception and birth. Pupils are to provide the questions to these answers. Ask some volunteers to share the resulting questions with the rest of the class. (10 mins)

Main Lesson

- Show video footage of a newborn baby. For identification and personalisation this could ideally be the named offspring of a member of staff, or of a sibling of a class member if one of suitable age is available and mother and father agree to allow it. Alternatively footage is available on many child development videos such as 'Child Observation No.1' from Siren Films. Ask the pupils to put the words '(name's) needs' in the centre of a sheet of paper and either draw or write down what they think the baby will need in its first few months. Discuss these needs and collect suggestions on the board, then ask the pupils to fill in the relevant parts of an accompanying worksheet.

- Discuss the need for food. Show a PowerPoint slide of the human mammary gland in section and describe its function.

- Is breast best? Discuss the reasons for breast feeding and some of the drawbacks. If available, an audio or video recording of some young mothers discussing their experiences of breast feeding would be useful, especially if they are known to the pupils. Pupils can make notes on the benefits and drawbacks of each type of infant feeding.

- Show the pupils a pot of formula milk. Ask a volunteer to make a demonstration batch up according to the instructions. Get them to examine the photocopied labels of the formula and to fill in an accompanying section of a worksheet to cover the role of protein, calcium, iron, carbohydrate and fat.

- Show the pupils an animation of what antibodies do in terms of the immune system. Emphasise that the antibodies are generated in response to the body's immune system encountering pathogens. Explain that as a baby has not encountered pathogens, it has no antibodies of its own and must acquire them from its mother. Ask the pupils to fill in the relevant worksheet section.

- Show the pupils a video of other pupils discussing the physical changes that they experienced as they went through puberty, discussing their thoughts, worries and expectations. Pupils are to fill in a summary table, such as that found in Summary Question 3 in the pupil book, covering the major changes during puberty in males, in females and those common to both. Explain these are caused by hormones, where these hormones are made and give essential personal hygiene advice.

- **PSHE link:** 'Baby think it over' virtual infant simulators may be available from the PSHE dept. Some of these are designed to mimic the attention needed by a young child. Looking after one for a weekend can be an illuminating experience, especially for anyone who may be contemplating starting a family early.

Plenary Suggestions

All change!
Ask the pupils to draw out a table of puberty changes with three columns labelled 'males', 'females' and 'both'. Pupils to fill this in, discussing it with a partner. Then review the class responses. (5–10 mins)

Needs cards
Pupils are to play a card game where one player lays down cards with the four nutrients from the pupil text and the other lays down cards showing the uses to which these nutrients are put. Players take turns to lay down the cards. When one player lays their card on top of the corresponding card layed by the other player they may take that pile. If they do not spot the correspondence and lay again on top of the pair then the other player can point this out and win the pile. The winner is the first person to gain all the cards. (10 mins)

Differentiation

SEN
Give the pupils cards with the words and/or pictures 'boys' and 'girls'. The teacher or the learning assistant describes a body change which occurs in puberty and the pupils have to hold up a boy card, a girl card or both (if applicable). Seek consensus and record the findings in an appropriate manner, such as stickers in the appropriate parts of the exercise book or worksheet.

Extension
Pupils use the information provided in Summary Question 2 regarding growth rates to work out the rate of growth in terms of percentage increase over every three year period (0–3, 3–6, etc.). They can then compare this with overall height increase in centimetres during each of these periods. They write a paragraph summarising the interpretations of the graphs and giving considered opinions on any differences seen between the sets of figures.

Answers to in-text questions

a Protein.

b Help fight disease.

B2.7 Periods

NC links for the lesson
- Organisms, behaviour and health
- The human reproductive cycle includes adolescence, fertilisation and fetal development.

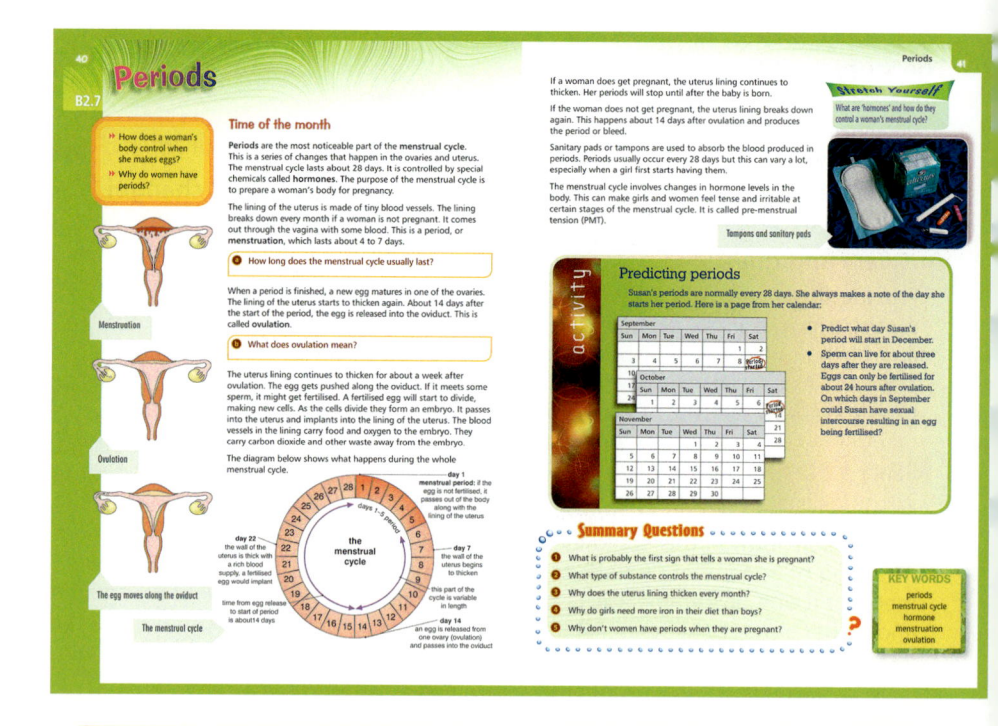

Functional Skills Link-up
English
- Understand texts in detail. (Level 1)

Learning Objectives
Pupils should learn:
- How a woman's body controls the time when eggs are released.
- Why women have periods.

Learning Outcomes
- All pupils should know the meanings of the words 'menstruation', 'ovulation' and 'periods'.
- Most pupils should be able to describe these processes.
- Some pupils should also be able to describe these processes in detail and be able to link them to specific hormones.

Learning Styles
Visual: Looking at Lennart Nilssen's photographs.
Auditory: Participating in discussions.
Kinaesthetic: Carrying out the card sequencing exercise.
Interpersonal: Group discussions.
Intrapersonal: Consideration of the issues involved, either for themselves if female or for their girl peers if male.

Answers to summary questions

1. She misses a period.
2. Hormones.
3. So there is a rich blood supply which will supply food and oxygen to an embryo.
4. They lose iron in menstrual blood.
5. The uterus continues to thicken as the fetus develops.

The Lesson

Starter Suggestions

Reasons for periods discussion

Most pupils know vaguely that something called periods occurs when girls start to mature. Without giving any information yourself, lead a discussion on why periods happen. If the class needs support in carrying out discussions, get a cheap microphone (it doesn't need to be plugged into anything) and make it a rule that only the person holding the microphone can speak. Ask a volunteer to move around the class giving the microphone to prospective speakers. (5–10 mins)

Periods brainstorm

Divide the pupils into groups of about four. Get them to put the word 'periods' in the centre of a large sheet of paper and, using free association, write down around the word any connected words or phrases or bits of information that they know. Share the outcomes of this exercise with the other groups by passing the sheets around the room, and then use a summary session to introduce the main lesson material. (10–15 mins)

Main Lesson

- Using PowerPoint, proceed with the main section of the lesson, going over the stages of the menstrual cycle. Ensure that the whole class has an involvement by asking pupils to pick on other ones to answer questions at each stage of the exposition.
- Using an inflatable plastic beach ball, get the pupils to pass it from arm to arm simulating a fertilised egg being wafted along through the oviduct by the action of cilia and implanting into the uterus wall (a target group of pupils at the far side of the room from where the ball starts off).
- Some excellent images to illustrate this process are also available on the web.
- Use an animation of the menstrual cycle as reinforcement. The pupils can answer questions.
- Show some tampons and sanitary towels. As a link with PSHE it may be suitable to discuss hygiene and to go over some of the problems which can be associated with unwise use of tampons, such as toxic shock syndrome caused by *Staphylococcus aureus*.
- Give the pupils a sequencing exercise with short statements summarising each of the stages of the menstrual cycle to put into the correct order. This can be done either electronically, or as a set of statements to cut up, place into the correct order and stick in to their exercise books.
- Get the pupils to carry out the 'Producing Periods' activity in The Pupil Book. Explain the reasons for the limited dates in a woman's cycle when she can get pregnant (approximately days 11–15). Ask the pupils to write down the title 'Could she get pregnant?' into their exercise books and to copy down a list of girls' names (get the pupils to choose these) from the board. If preferred, this exercise can be carried out in groups with each group being allocated a girl's name. Carry out an exercise where two dates are identified, the first one being for the date during the month of September when the woman starts her period and the second one being for the date when she has sexual intercourse without using contraceptives. Refer the pupils to the calendar sections of the pupil book. The number generation can be done by drawing numbers from 1 to 30 from a hat (Internet-based random number generators could be used for this). If the date number generated for the date of sexual intercourse is greater than the date generated for that of the period, then assume it refers to a date in October. Assume that sperm can live inside a woman for an average of 3 days. Continue generating pairs of dates until all the girls on the board are pregnant. If the pupils are working in groups, tick off their girls' names as the pregnancies occur. Warn the pupils that variation can occur in ovulation dates and reliance on having sex only during unfertile dates is not a very reliable method of birth control.
- Information available on how long sperm can survive inside a woman is variable and could be anything from 48 hours to 7 days. This reinforces that it is difficult to be sure when a woman can get pregnant.

Plenary Suggestions

Which word?

Place all the key words on laminated cards on the board. Using the reveal function on an interactive whiteboard if available, or otherwise using a standard board and pen or an OHP, slowly unveil (or write up) a clue as to which word is being referred to. This can be played as a competitive exercise, with points given for being the first group to spot the word and a small motivating prize can be given at the end. (5–10 mins)

Spot the blot

Give the pupils a short passage of text describing the menstrual cycle. This will have a number of errors in it. Pupils are to highlight or circle these, number them and write in the corrections below. Ask the pupils to share which ones they have found and carry out a peer marking exercise on the sheets. (10–15 mins)

Differentiation

SEN

Give the pupils an exercise to draw lines between words and their simple meanings.

Extension

Pupils can use the Internet to look up ectopic pregnancy and be prepared to talk about it if required.

Homework Suggestion

Pupils can answer the in-text questions and Summary Questions from the pupil book.

Pupils can produce a public information leaflet entitled 'The facts about menstruation' aimed at pre-menstrual girls as a discussion aid.

Answers to in-text questions

a 28 days.

b Release of an egg from the ovary.

B2.8 In Control

NC links for the lesson
- Organisms, behaviour and health
- The human reproductive cycle includes adolescence, fertilisation and fetal development.
- Conception, growth, development, behaviour and health can be affected by diet, drugs and disease.

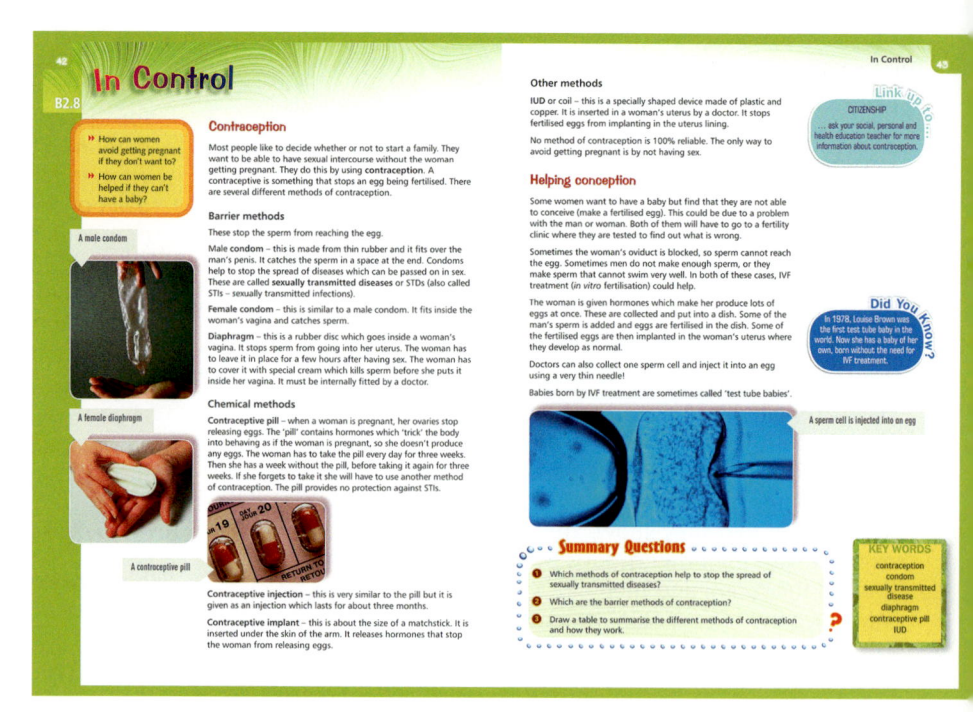

How Science Works
- Identify a range of scientific data and evidence to back an argument and the counterclaim in less complex and/or familiar contexts, e.g. IVF or contraception. (1.1a3)

Learning Objectives
Pupils should learn:
- How women can avoid getting pregnant if they don't want to.
- How women can be helped to have a baby.

Learning Outcomes
- All pupils should be able to describe at least two methods of birth control and know what IVF means in simple terms.
- Most pupils should be able to describe fully male and female condoms and their use; contraceptive pills, injections and implants; IUDs and know some reasons why conception may be difficult and the meaning of IVF. Most should also understand which methods give protection from STDs/STIs and which don't.
- Some pupils should also be able to do the above in detail and be aware of the ethical controversies involved and be able to take a reasoned and balanced view.

Learning Styles
Visual: Observing PowerPoint.
Auditory: Taking part in class debate.
Kinaesthetic: Game creation.
Interpersonal: Group work on the game designing activity.
Intrapersonal: Reflecting on the effectiveness of different methods of contaception.

Answers to summary questions

1. Male and female condoms.
2. Male and female condoms, diaphragm.
3.

Method	How it works
Male condom	Stops sperm from meeting egg
Female condom	Stops sperm from meeting egg
Diaphragm	Stops sperm from meeting egg
Contraceptive pill, injection, implant	Stops woman producing an egg
IUD	Stops fertilised egg from implanting

The Lesson

Starter Suggestions

True or false?
Give the pupils a list of five or six statements about conception and contraception which contain some true ones and some common myths or misunderstandings.

e.g. 'You can't get pregnant if you have a shower after having sex.' [false]

'Birth control pills help you lose weight.' [false]

'Birth control pills stop you being moody before periods.' [false]

'You can't get pregnant when you are breast feeding.' [false]

'You can't catch STDs/STIs if you are on the pill.' [false]

'You can get contraceptive pills for men.' [true]

Discuss the responses with the rest of the class. (5–10 mins)

Post–it… what I know so far
Give each of the pupils a self-adhesive note (Post-it or similar). They are to write down descriptions of how a woman can avoid getting pregnant if she doesn't want to and stick them to the board at the front. Ask a volunteer to read some of them out (vetting them for inappropriate content if necessary) and another volunteer to summarise the methods on another section of the board or, if projecting, as a word document. (10–15 mins)

Main Lesson

- Divide the class into pairs and give each pair of pupils an information sheet summarising the content to be learned and a set of highlighters. Looking at the first half of the sheet they are to highlight in one colour the words 'Barrier methods of contraception' and the names of any types which are mentioned. They are to do the same in another colour for chemical methods of contraception. When completed, they can compare their sheets with their nearest neighbours. Mention chemical spermicides which can increase the percentage reliability of these methods. As a point of interest you could mention that the ancient Egyptians used to use crocodile dung as a spermicide, and the Romans used wine or lemon juice. None of these are effective and can be dangerous!

- Ask the pupils if anyone knows what STDs are and draw out the existing knowledge from the group. Using discussion and exposition to build on this to establish the importance of the alternative use of condoms as a prophylactic device.

- Discuss the sheet they have just filled in. Find out if there were things that they didn't know. Using PowerPoint illustrate the use of male and female condoms, diaphragms, contraceptive pills, injections and implants. You may like to have specimens of some of these methods to show the class. These are usually available from family planning clinics for demonstrations in schools.

- Although not in the pupil book it would be useful to discuss long term surgical methods of contraception, such as vasectomy and tubal ligation (tying the oviducts to stop eggs from descending to the uterus) and to answer some of the pupils' queries regarding these topics. Anonymous questions on slips of paper may again be of benefit.

- A short discussion on the morning after pill could be held. Sound out the classes opinions and hold a snap ballot to poll whether they think these should be freely available without prescription or not, and what the role of parents might be.

- Ask the pupils to complete a summary of the different types of contraceptive, either on a worksheet or copied into their books.

- Ask the pupils to look back at their information sheets and read the second half, looking for information regarding the problems which potential parents can face and about IVF and information on how it works. Get them to highlight these again in different colour.

- Show the pupils a video or an animation of a couple who want to have a child but are unable to. Discuss the possible problems which may have occurred and some ways of overcoming them. Emphasise that fertility problems are quite common and nothing to be ashamed of, and that about 1 in every 6 couples will experience difficulty in starting a family.

- The pupils are to carry out a game designing activity. Divide the class into groups of about four and give each group a large sheet of paper and sets of coloured pens. Using the title 'Inconceivable' ask the pupils to design a board game using the key words from the lesson. These should be displayed prominently and the pupils should check these off as they use them to ensure full coverage of the learning objectives. Give a time limit of about 10 minutes and then the groups can circulate to look at each other's work and check the key word coverage. Marks could be given for each one used and for originality, humour and attractive style. If time allows, have some dice available so that the best games can be played.

Plenary Suggestions

Drag and drop contraception and fertility
Ask the pupils to carry out a drag and drop exercise where words or short phrases appear in the centre of the screen and must be placed into one of four boxes, these being: chemical contraceptives, barrier contraceptives, fertility problems and fertility treatments. (5 mins)

Contraception blockbusters
Divide the class into two large groups (this could be boys and girls). Using a 'Blockbusters' style game format, get the pupils to play a game using questions drawn from this lesson and the previous ones. Provide a small prize for the winning group. (10 mins)

Differentiation

SEN
Pupils to use a hangman style exercise to identify the key words. Some of the letters could be placed in advance and a list of the key words provided to choose from.

Extension
With a higher attaining group, a point of controversy could be whether the use of the morning after pill and IUDs are ethically sound and tie this in with and the debate on when a life starts.

Homework Suggestion

Pupils imagine they are a doctor. They are to write a letter giving advice to a young couple who want to start a family in a few years, but not just yet.

B2.9 Reproduction in Plants

NC links for the lesson
- Organisms, behaviour and health
- Life processes are supported by … body systems.

Learning Objectives

Pupils should learn:
- The meaning of the phrase 'asexual reproduction'.
- The advantages and disadvantages of asexual reproduction.

Learning Outcomes

- All pupils should be able to define asexual reproduction and give an example from plants.
- Most pupils should be able to define asexual reproduction and state its advantages and disadvantages.
- Some pupils should also be able to do the above and demonstrate some knowledge of mitosis.

Functional Skills Link-up

English
- Present information in a logical sequence. (Level 1)

Learning Styles

Visual: Observing the videos and PowerPoint.
Auditory: Taking part in discussions.
Kinaesthetic: Practical on cuttings.
Interpersonal: Group work.
Intrapersonal: Consideration for other organisms.

The Lesson

Starter Suggestions

New plants – how does it happen?
Pupils are to describe to each other how plants make copies of themselves. They then share this with the class through discussion. (5–10 mins)

Green fingers
Get the pupils to close their eyes and be quiet. Ask them to imagine a scene in a garden. Smell the wet grass and the flowers. You are cutting flowers from a plant with a pair of secateurs. (Show the pupils a pair previously if

Answers to summary questions

1. A swollen root containing stored food, from which a plant can grow.

2.

Advantages of asexual reproduction for the plant	Disadvantages of asexual reproduction for the plant
New plants produced quickly	All plants are susceptible to the same diseases
New plants exactly suited to environment	New plants will all be at a disadvantage if there is environmental change

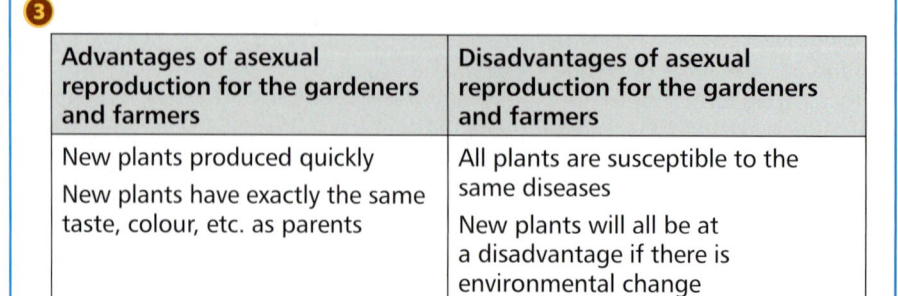

3.

Advantages of asexual reproduction for the gardeners and farmers	Disadvantages of asexual reproduction for the gardeners and farmers
New plants produced quickly	All plants are susceptible to the same diseases
New plants have exactly the same taste, colour, etc. as parents	New plants will all be at a disadvantage if there is environmental change

Reproduction in Plants

they are unlikely to know what they are.) Imagine that you accidentally cut off the end of your index finger. Instead of picking it up and running to the doctor, you push the severed finger into the ground. The finger slowly grows a hand, the hand grows an arm, the arm grows a body and a head and eventually an identical copy of you rises from the ground, smiles at you, shakes your hand and says 'Thanks mate!'. Bring the class back from imagining and discuss the scene. Explain that we cannot do this, but some animals and most plants can and do carry out this sort of thing! (5–10 mins)

Main Lesson

- Get the best four or five artists in the class to draw a flower each onto one sheet of A4 paper. Arrange with the reprographics staff beforehand and ask a volunteer take the sheet down to them to duplicate one copy for each pupil (reduced if necessary to save paper). Relate this to the self-duplication process which happens in asexual reproduction in plants.
- Show the pupils a range of plants which reproduce by asexual means, such as strawberries, daffodils, potatoes, ginger, duck weed and couch grass. Arrange these in a circus around the room. Get the pupils to observe each one in turn and write down a comment on how they think it reproduces.
- Show the pupils a PowerPoint slide show covering the types of asexual reproduction mentioned in the pupil book, namely bulbs, runners and tubers.
- **Taking cuttings:** use mature well-grown geranium or zonal pelargonium plants. Other suitable species include Wandering Sailors of the family *Tradescantia* and the vigorously asexually *Bryophyllum diagremontiana* or *Bryophyllum tubifolium*. Demonstrate the method first. (See 'Practical Support'.)
- The class should try to take at least one cutting each and able members should be capable of taking several. As a motivator, ensure that the pupils can take these cuttings home once rooted.
- Discuss, with illustrations, the advantages which humans get from adapting plants to suit their needs, e.g. non-toxic potatoes. (Many of the *Solanacea* family to which potatoes belong are fairly deadly.)

Plenary Suggestions

Which method?
Give pupils a sheet which has the pictures of the plants studied during this session. Fill in the description sections for each explaining how it reproduces. (5–10 mins)

Asexuals rule!
In pairs, pupils to prepare a short monologue to promote the benefits of a sex-free life and reproduction pattern. These can be recorded on audio, video or on mobile phones if the pupils have these. Share the best examples with the rest of the class. (10–15 mins)

Answers to in-text questions

a See table in Summary Question 2; one advantage and one disadvantage needed.

Practical Support

Cuttings

Equipment and materials required

Suitable stock plants: geraniums or zonal pelargoniums, *Tradescantia*, *Bryophyllum* and any other plants which are available and suitable for asexual reproduction.

Per group: scalpel, white ceramic tile, rooting powder, dibber or similar implement, label, cutting compost (50% peat or peat substitute, 50% Perlite or Vermiculite), pot approx 10 cm diameter, plastic bag, elastic band, newspaper for covering the benches.

Details

Make sure in advance that you have plenty of cutting material.

Pick a strong growing young shoot. Using a scalpel cut it just below a node (where a leaf joins) to give a cutting about 10 cm long. Place it onto a white tile and remove the lower leaves leaving only the top two or top one if it is large. If it is very large the top leaf may be cut in half. These procedures are to reduce the water loss through evaporation, as the cutting will have no roots and will be short of water. Do not disrupt the tip of the plant. Place the end of the cutting in commercial rooting powder. Explain that this contains hormones to help the cutting to grow new roots and an anti-fungal agent to prevent infection. (In practice, rooting powders make very little difference to the success rate in classroom practicals, so it is best not to try to expand this into an investigation.) Place newspaper on the benches to aid in clearing up.

Fill a 7 cm square plastic pot to the brim with cutting compost made from 50% peat and 50% Perlite or Vermiculite (beware of breathing in the dust from these materials). This should be firmed down and moistened. Using a dibber or the end of a pen make a small hole in the compost about 5 cm deep. Place the cutting into the hole and firm the compost around it using your index and second fingers of both hands placed tip to tip. This forms a diamond-shaped hole which can go around the stem. Label the cutting with name, date, species and, if known, variety. Place a small plastic bag over the top of the pot and secure with a rubber band. Place in a warm bright environment and water when required.

Safety
Take care with scalpels.

Do not allow rooting powder to be inhaled or to touch the skin for fear of allergic reactions. Also contains fungicide.

Differentiation

SEN
Make a mint! Pupils to take cuttings from mint plants and sell them to staff once rooted. Arrange with the school canteen to allow mint from the practical to be used as a garnish or to make sauce.

Extension
Pupils to look up the process of mitosis on the Internet or in textbooks. Summarise the process using diagrams or audio recording.

Homework Suggestion

Pupils to write out crossword clues for the key words used in this lesson for use during the starter of the next one.

B2.10 Flowers and Pollination

NC links for the lesson
- Organisms, behaviour and health
- Life processes are supported by … body systems.

Learning Objectives
Pupils should learn:
- The advantages and disadvantages of sexual reproduction in plants.
- How plants reproduce sexually.
- How pollen gets from one plant to another.

Learning Outcomes
- All pupils should be able to state that flowers are for sexual reproduction in plants and that pollen is often transferred between flowers.
- Most pupils should be able to list advantages and disadvantages of sexual reproduction, to describe the function of flowers and to define and describe pollination.
- Some pupils should also be able to do the above and link structure to function for each of the parts.

Functional Skills Link-up
English
- Read and understand texts and take appropriate action. (Level 1)

Learning Styles
Visual: Inspecting pollen pictures.
Auditory: Discussing pollination.
Kinaesthetic: Flower dissection.
Interpersonal: Group work.
Intrapersonal: Use of imagination.

Answers to in-text questions
a. Stamen made of the anther and filament.
b. Carpel made of stigma, style and ovary.
c. To get nectar.
d. Moths mainly fly at night so the flowers attract them by smell rather than by bright colours.

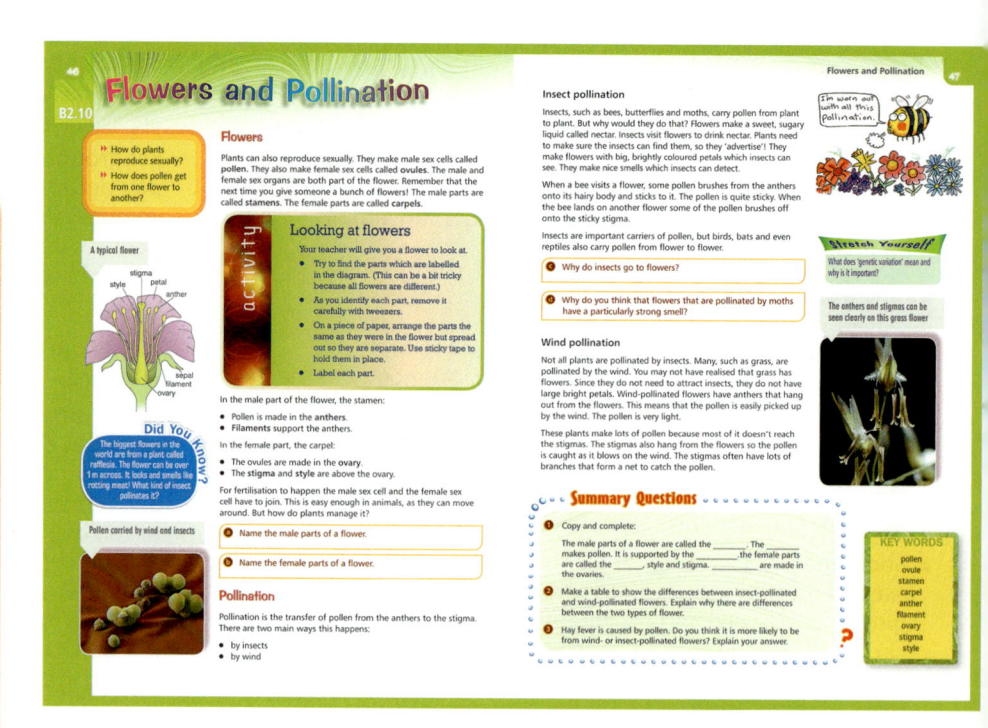

The Lesson

Starter Suggestions

What are flowers for?
Show the pupils some beautiful slides of flowers and pass around, or have on display, some examples in the classroom. Ask the pupils to write down, in a single sentence, what flowers are for. Get volunteers to read out some of their responses. Conclude by summarising the job of flower as being 'seed factories'. (5–10 mins)

Asexual crossword
If the homework set last lesson on making crossword clues was carried out, use these to create an interactive crossword using a program such as Hot Potatoes (available as a free download from http://hotpot.uvic.ca). This can be saved to the school intranet for access during revision or for completion as another homework. (10–15 mins)

Answers to summary questions

1. The male parts of a flower are called the **stamen**. The **anther** makes pollen. It is supported by the **filament**. The female parts are called the **carpel**, style and stigma. **Ovules** are made in the ovaries.

2.

Wind-pollinated	Insect-pollinated
Light pollen grains so easily carried on the wind	Sticky pollen so it sticks to insects
No nectar	Make nectar so that insects visit flowers
Dull colours and no petals	Bright coloured petals to attract insects
No smell	Smell to attract insects
Anthers hang outside flower so that wind blows pollen off	Anthers inside flower
Feathery stigmas to catch pollen	Sticky stigma

3. Wind-pollinated pollen because it is more easily carried in the air.

Flowers and Pollination

Main Lesson

- Remind the pupils of the word 'gametes'. Draw out, through questioning, that the male sex cells in animals are called 'sperm' and the female ones are called 'ova'. Ask if anyone in the room suffers from hay fever and ask what causes hay fever. Explain that it is caused by 'gametes up the nose', as pollen are the male sex cells of plants. Show some beautiful PowerPoint slides of the surface of pollen as show by electron microscopy.
- Reviewing last lesson, draw out that asexually reproduced offspring are identical and explain that this can have drawbacks in terms of responding to environmental changes and vulnerability to pests and disease. Show a slide of a batch of different coloured puppies and introduce the idea that sexual reproduction is an important source of variation.
- Break open a ripe ovary of a daffodil flower and show the ovules inside using a Flexicam if available. If not, use a PowerPoint slide. Explain that these are the female sex cells called 'ovules' and that the function of the flower is to bring the male and female sex cells together so that a seed can be formed.
- Using PowerPoint, explain the structure of a typical flower. Ask the pupils to say the names of the parts out loud as they encounter them, and reinforce the words by Blu-tacking up laminated flash cards with the words on as they are introduced. Some of the following memory aids may be useful :
- St*amens* are the male parts, they have the word 'men' within them.
- Anthers: get the pupils to imagine a stag with big antlers with pollen cascading from them.
- Filament: the pupils may have met this in terms of the wire inside a light bulb. Ask them to imagine a stag on the top of a giant light bulb.
- Stigma: get the pupils to touch a stigma and describe what it feels like. They will come up with 'sticky'; work through assonance with the pupils repeating out loud 'sticky stigma'.
- Style: use imagination again with the pupils imagining a very tall slim model walking down a catwalk with great elegance. Link to the common usage of the word 'style'. To tie in with stigma, get the pupils to imagine pouring a tin of golden syrup on the top of the model's head.
- Ovary: link this to the previous work on human anatomy. Ask if anyone in the class has ever eaten an ovary, stating that you yourself have and betting that others have too. At this point show the pupils an apple cut in half. Don't pass it around, as the temptation to eat it will be very strong. Explain that the flesh of the apple is the swollen ovary with the seeds inside.
- *Ovule*: use a pun, '*you'll* remember what this is called'.
- Carpel: if you hold a drawing of a carpel sideways and draw some eyes and fins on it looks like a fish and you can bridge to the word 'carp'.
- Show time lapse footage of fruit developing, if available. If this series of lessons is during the spring or early summer, show the pupils stems of wallflowers or of broad beans. The youngest flowers at the top will still be in full petal and, as you go down the stem, the sequence of development becomes clear as you look at progressively older flowers dropping their petals and turning into seed pods.
- Carry out the 'Looking at flowers' dissection. Use daffodils and demonstrate it first using a Flexicam to display, if available.
- Ask why the flowers are coloured and scented. Using PowerPoint show the process of insect pollination. Pupils are to complete a table of features in a worksheet summarising pollination.
- Show the pupils a grass flower. Ask why it is not coloured or scented. Draw out the details of wind pollination and show slides of the main features. Complete the wind pollination features table in a summary worksheet.

Plenary Suggestions

Wind or insect?
Show the pupils a series of slides of flowers. Using 'show me' boards ask the pupils to write either W or I to show if they think the flowers are wind- or insect-pollinated. (5 mins)

Drag and drop flower parts
Using an interactive diagram of a typical insect-pollinated flower, pupils are to drag and drop labels for all the parts into the appropriate places. This can be repeated several times, timed and carried out as a competition. Various web-based versions can be found if searched for. (10–15 mins)

Practical Support

Looking at flowers

Equipment and materials required

For each pupil:

One daffodil flower (have a few spares), white ceramic tile, scalpel, scissors, seeker or mounted needle, lots of strips of clear adhesive tape (these are best stuck to the edge of the bench), hand lens.

Details

Remove each part and arrange them in sets on a plain piece of A4 then stick them down and label them.

The following order works:

sepals

petals and corolla (explain that this is made from fused petals)

stamens (six – don't separate into anthers and filaments, just label them)

carpel – using a scalpel with care, cut it vertically. Label stigma, ovary and ovules.

Safety

Beware of severe pollen allergies. Care with scalpels/scissors/mounted needles.

Differentiation

SEN
Pupils to make a giant paper flower for a wall display.

Extension
Using the Internet, texts or library resources, pupils can look up meiosis and find out how variation is introduced by sexual reproduction. This is preparatory work for eventual full coverage at GCSE level.

Homework Suggestion

Revise flower parts for a short slip test.

Complete in-text and Summary Questions from pupil book.

B2.11 Fertilisation in Plants

NC links for the lesson
- Organisms, behaviour and health
- Life processes are supported by … body systems.

Learning Objectives
Pupils should learn:
- How fertilisation takes place in flowers.
- Which factors affect the growth of pollen tubes.

Learning Outcomes
- All pupils should be able to describe in simple terms what a pollen tube is.
- Most pupils should be able to describe the process of fertilisation in plants and name several factors which affect pollen tube growth.
- Some pupils should also be able to describe the process of fertilisation in plants in detail and explain the science underlying the factors that affect pollen tube growth.

How Science Works
- Recognise that the presentation of experimental results through the routine use of tables … and simple graphs makes it easier to see patterns and trends. (1.2d)

Functional Skills Link-up
Mathematics
- Use simple formulae expressed in words for one- to two-step operations. (Magnification.) (Level 1)

Learning Styles
Visual: Observing pollen growth.
Auditory: Discussing how the pollen nucleus can descend to the ovule.
Kinaesthetic: Carrying out the practical.

Answers to in-text questions
a. Pollen.
b. Ovules.
c. So that pollen stays there.

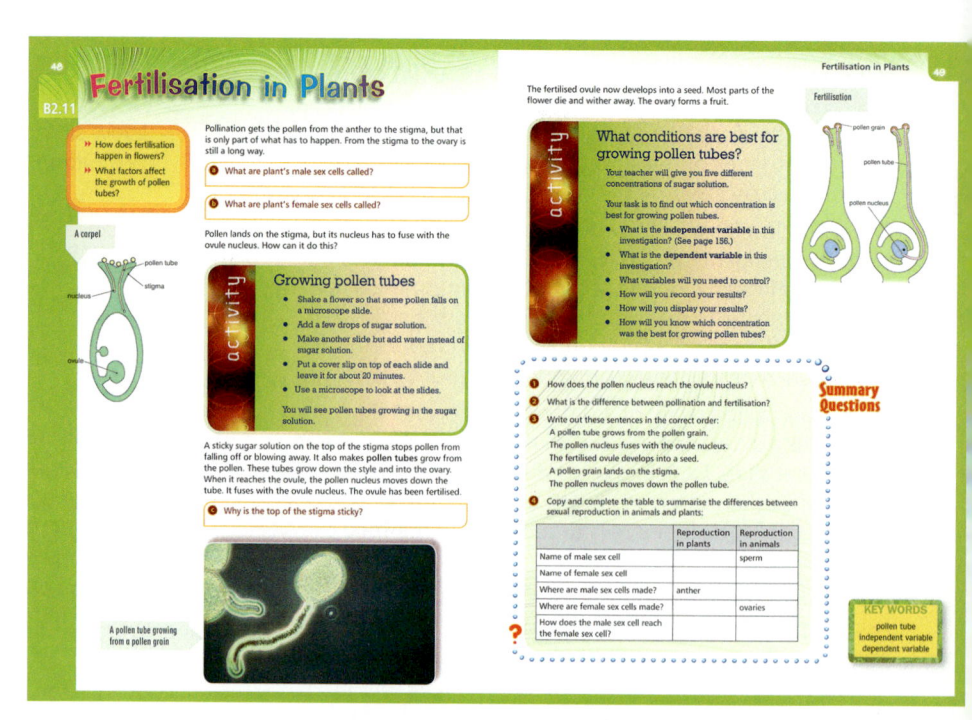

The Lesson

Starter Suggestions

Slip test – flower parts
If the pupils have revised flower parts and pollination for homework following the last lesson, give them a short slip test using single word answers to assess their recall and understanding. Adjust the level of difficulty to suit the particular teaching group. (5–10 mins)

How does that happen?
Ask the pupils to summarise from last time the process of pollination. Ask what has happened when pollination is complete. Establish that this is

Answers to summary questions

1. Along a pollen tube which grows from the pollen grain down the style to the ovary.

2. Pollination is transfer of pollen from anther to stigma; fertilisation is joining of pollen and ovule nuclei.

3. A pollen grain lands on the stigma.
   A pollen tube grows from the pollen grain.
   The pollen nucleus moves down the pollen tube.
   The pollen nucleus fuses with the ovule nucleus.
   The fertilised ovule develops into a seed.

4.

	Reproduction in plants	Reproduction in animals
Name of male sex cell	Pollen	Sperm
Name of female sex cell	Ovule	Egg (ovum)
Where are male sex cells made?	Anther	Testes
Where are female sex cells made?	Ovary	Ovary
How does the male sex cell reach the female sex cell?	Carried by wind or insects	Swims

Fertilisation in Plants

when the pollen is stuck to the stigma. Ask the pupils to discuss in pairs how the nucleus inside the pollen grain might get to the ovule which is deep inside the ovary. Get them to write down, or draw out their ideas, then share these with others around them. Collect the thoughts of the class on the board and discuss them. (10–15 mins)

Main Lesson

- Using PowerPoint show the stages in the process of fertilisation, including the pollen grain landing on and sticking to the stigma, the grain germinating (be careful that the pupils do not confuse this with seed germination) the pollen tube growing down the style and into the ovary, the pollen nucleus descending down the tube and eventually joining with the nucleus of the ovule. Do not go into details of the many nuclei actually involved; only mention those which eventually fuse.
- Show the pupils a video clip of pollen tubes growing. Ask volunteers to say what is happening at each stage. Pose the question: 'Where does the tube get the materials from to build its walls?'
- Link to existing knowledge with stills of the video game 'Lemmings', where small creatures have to tunnel their way through obstacles. Draw a parallel with what the pollen nucleus has to do.
- If one is available, show the pupils a head of sweet corn complete with the 'silks', which are the individual styles down which each pollen nucleus has to travel to reach an ovule. An interesting addition to this illustration is if some sweet corn cobs with varied colouration such as 'Indian Summer' F1 are used. As each individual kernel has been fertilised by one male gamete, the different colouration makes clear the different genetic content of each nucleus.
- Practicals: 'Growing pollen tubes'; 'What conditions are best for growing pollen tubes?'
- Discuss with the class what might be in the sticky stuff at the top of the stigma. Remind the pupils that making the pollen tube will need energy. Ask the pupils what they eat when they want quick energy? After having established that there is sugar in the liquid at the top of the stigma and that this helps the pollen to start growing, ask the pupils to devise a plan to find out which concentration of sugar would work best.
- Divide the class into six groups. Allocate each of the first five groups a concentration of sugar to work with. Choose from the following: 0%, 5%, 10%, 15%, and 20%. Ask the sixth group to carry out the experiment using onion epidermis following the practical directions.
- Observe the slides during the rest of the lesson, and arrange a rota to allow one from each group to come and examine them after appropriate intervals to suit the schools arrangements over the next two days. Pupils are to record growth of pollen tubes and collectively report back next lesson.
- Collect results from the class when they arise. If a good set of tubes grows within the lesson, project a view of it using a Flexicam with microscope attachment.
- Discuss the events following fertilisation if not carrying out the 'What's next?' plenary.

Plenary Suggestions

What's next?
Give the pupils a set of cards to put into the correct order describing the sequence of events once fertilisation has taken place. (5–10 mins)

The great escape
Ask the pupils to imagine they are a prisoner in a cell. If they can successfully make a tunnel from their cell floor to a secret hidden chamber and find the secret of new life, they will live again and grow to new heights. Ask the pupils to write down what the prisoner is (the pollen nucleus) where it is held (the grain), what the cell floor and ground below is (the stigma and style), what the secret chamber is (the ovule) and how they will attain new life (through the growth of the seed). (10–15 mins)

Practical Support

Growing pollen tubes; What conditions are best for growing pollen tubes?

Equipment and materials required
100 cm³ sugar solution, either 0, 5, 10, 15 or 20 g sucrose (granulated sugar), 0.01 g yeast extract, e.g. Marmite, one small crystal of boric acid, 1 g agar, distilled water to make up to 100 cm³.
Ripe anthers on various plants, Petri dish and lid, microscope and slides.

Safety
Wear eye protection.

Onion epidermis practical

Equipment and materials required
One large mild Spanish onion, scalpel, white tile, Petri dish and lid, forceps, ripe anthers, damp paper towels, microscope and slides.

Details
Peel some epidermal tissue from between the layers of an onion. Place a layer of this onto a slide with the side that was towards the outside of the onion uppermost. Dust with ripe pollen and place in a closed Petri dish with a piece of moist paper towel. For details see the SAPS website.

Safety
Take care with scalpels.

Differentiation

SEN
Pupils to sequence a series of pictures showing the stages in the growth of a pollen tube.
Pupils to make models using modelling balloons and peas.

Extension
Pupils to calculate rates of growth using scale factors.
Ask the pupils to imagine a scale model of a pollen tube large enough to get a golf ball down to represent the pollen nucleus. Assume a golf ball to be 4 cm across and a real pollen tube to be 16 μm in diameter. What would the scale be? If the real distance from the stigma to the ovule is 1.5 cm, how long would the golf ball model one have to be? If it was big enough for a person to crawl down, how long would it be?

Homework Suggestion

Complete the questions from the pupil book.
Make a scale model of a stigma, style and ovary with a tube down which a model nucleus can pass.

B2.12 Spreading the Seeds

NC links for the lesson
- Organisms, behaviour and health
- Life processes are supported by … body systems.

Learning Objectives
Pupils should learn:
- How seeds are dispersed from the parent plant.
- The conditions necessary for seed germination.

Learning Outcomes
- All pupils should know what the words 'dispersal' and 'germination' mean.
- Most pupils should be able to describe several mechanisms which aid seed dispersal and name the three conditions required for germination.
- Some pupils should also be able to describe in detail and link the structural details of the mechanisms to their function and show awareness of the diversity of germination conditions which different species of plants exhibit.

How Science Works
- Describe and suggest how planning and implementation could be improved. (1.2e)

Functional Skills Link-up
ICT skills
- Create and develop charts and graphs to suit requirements, using suitable labels. (Level 1)

Learning Styles
Visual: Observing the video clips and specimens.
Auditory: Jointly planning the investigation with their peers.
Kinaesthetic: Carrying out the practical investigation.
Interpersonal: Group work on the practical.
Intrapersonal: Considering the necessity for dispersal.

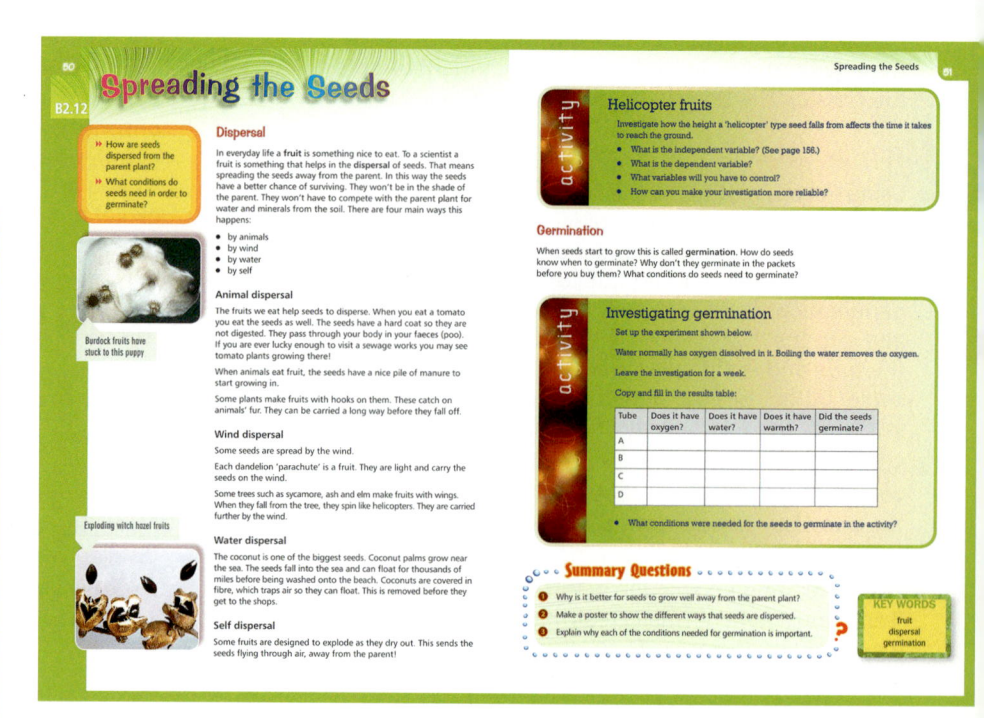

The Lesson

Starter Suggestions

The story so far…
Give the pupils a set of statements relating to the formation of gametes within a flower, pollination, fertilisation and seed formation. Ask them to number the sequence in order of the occurrence of the events. Check this out with the rest of the class. (5–10 mins)

School's out for ever
Ask the pupils to think about what would happen to the school field if the school was closed forever, just locked up and left (possible backing track *School's out* by Alice Cooper). Working in pairs, get the pupils to think about and write down ways in which seeds might get transported to the school field. Share the results with other pairs and then with the rest of the class. (10–15 mins)

Main Lesson
- Show the pupils a family tree (this could be your own). Ask a volunteer pupil to describe their family tree. Ask where all members of the family live (be sensitive here as not all pupils will be comfortable with sharing this information). Ask the pupils to think about what it would be like if all their family came to stay. Where would they all sleep? What problems would there be? On the board, summarise the problems which would occur due to overcrowding. Ask what would really happen and draw out that they would move elsewhere. Emphasise that plants can't move, so don't have

Answers to summary questions

1. So they do not have to compete for water, minerals and sunlight.
2. [Poster should include various types of wind, water, 'explosive' and animal dispersal. Give marks for clear explanations, especially if accompanied by diagrams.]
3. Air/oxygen needed so seeds can get energy; warmth so they can grow quickly; water because reactions take place in water.

Spreading the Seeds

this option. Relate this to plants, asking what would happen if all the seeds from a plant just fell to the ground directly below the parent plant?

- Set up a circus display of seeds of various types around the room. Have a range of examples representative of the different methods (see 'Practical support'). Use actual specimens or attractive laminated colour photographs. Photographs of Coco de mar (*Lodoicea maldivensis*) always amuse. Label each station with a letter. Give the pupils a worksheet with a blank table on it with columns for letter, name of seed, name of mechanism and how it works. Fill in the sheet and then go over the findings, summarising them on the board or on a PowerPoint slide.
- Show the pupils a short section of video footage or animation on each of the types of mechanism and how they work. Discuss this and check pupils' understanding through questioning as you proceed.
- Ask if there will be any relationship between how tall a tree is and how far its winged seeds will fly. In small groups, pupils plan an investigation examining the effect of height on flight distance. A writing frame will be beneficial. Carry out the practical. One method is to use a blanket with concentric circles at 20 cm intervals and drop 25 seeds from various heights, converting number to percentage in each section. A graph or bar chart can be produced for each height and these can be over layed and compared.
- Show a germinating seed (either a specimen or on PowerPoint). Discuss the question of what seeds need in order to germinate and demonstrate how to set up the practical 'Investigating germination'. Have an example prepared. Carry out the practical and leave it set up for the next lesson.

Plenary Suggestions

Which method quiz

Carry out an interactive quiz on the lesson content. Use programs such as Hot Potatoes or Quia (both are available either free or at low cost through Internet searches). Adjust the difficulty level according to your experience of the class, so that about two-thirds of the class can get about two-thirds of the questions correct. (5–10 mins)

Dispersal concept map

Give the pupils a concept map with the links between the boxes which will contain the key words labelled. Have a list of the key words in a box at the bottom of the page. For differentiation down, you can fill in the vowels in advance. For differentiation up, challenge the pupils to add new key words or new links between existing key words. (10–15 mins)

Practical Support

Seed display

Equipment and materials required

Burdock, dandelion, sycamore, acorns, lupins, coconut (in husk), poppy, apple.

Helicopter fruits

Equipment and materials required

Several hundred dry sycamore or field maple seeds. Dustpans and brushes. Metre rules, tape measures, litter pickers. Optional – several sheets, one for each group, with concentric rings drawn on them like a target at 20 cm intervals. Pre-printed tables to record the findings will help many pupils.

Details

Pupils either should design their own experiment or carry out the optional method described below.

Each group is to take a plastic or paper cup with 25 dry winged seeds in and invert it over the centre of the target on the sheet, recording the number of seeds which fall into each distance category, and multiplying it by four to get a percentage. Do this for 0.5, 1.0, 1.5 and 2.0 m.

Safety

Do not allow the pupils to stand on benches. Use litter pickers to hold the cups at the higher heights.

Investigating germination

Equipment and materials required

For each group: four test tubes, labels, test-tube rack, bungs, 20 small seeds (e.g. mustard, cress, mung beans), boiled water, cotton wool or Vermiculite (care regarding dust) oil, pipette.

Details

Set up four tubes each with five seeds: one with no water (dry cotton wool only – keep in the classroom); one with no oxygen (cover the seed with boiled water and pour in some oil with a pipette to form a seal on the top); one with no warmth (with moist medium placed in the fridge); and one with all of these (moist, medium, kept at room temperature). Leave for a week. Give criteria for germination, e.g. split testa, visible plumule and radicle, and count and calculate percentage germination rate at each temperature.

Differentiation

SEN

Hold a competition to see whose seed goes furthest. Provide a small prize for the winner.

Extension

Pupils to research the requirements for pre-chill germination and present a report.

Homework Suggestion

Pupils to write up the germination practical. Provide lower attaining pupils with a structured worksheet to fill in the required information. Include a pre-formed results table and a conclusion in the form of a cloze passage.

Answers to Reproduction – End of Topic Questions

Answers to know your stuff questions

1
- **a** Cells. [No mark if more than one given.] [1]
- **b** Tail. [1]
- **c** In the testis [or testicle]. [1]
- **d** (i) Carries genes/genetic information/chromosomes (from father). [1]
  (ii) Streamlined shape/able to produce lots of energy/make enzymes (substance/chemical) that breaks down membrane of egg. [1]
- **e** Fertilisation. [No mark if more than one given.] [1]

2
- **a** (i) Any *one* from: [1]
  every month or once a month;
  every four weeks;
  every 28 days. [Accept answers from 26 days to 30 days.]
  (ii) In the oviduct [or fallopian tube]. [1]
  (iii) In the uterus. [1]
- **b** Sperm cannot reach the egg. [1]
- **c** A fertilised egg divides into a tiny ball of cells called an embryo.
  The embryo attaches to the lining of the uterus. Here the embryo grows to become an unborn baby, called a i) **fetus**.
  It takes about ii) **nine** months for a baby to develop inside its mother. [2]
- **d** (i) Any *one* from: [1]
  It cushions the baby;
  It protects the baby (against shocks or bumps);
  It absorbs shocks.
  (ii) The placenta. [1]
- **e**

Substance	Passes from the mother's blood to the fetus's blood	Passes from the fetus's blood to the mother's blood	Does not pass between the mother's blood and the fetus's blood	
Poisons from cigarette smoke	✓			[1]
Oxygen	✓			[1]
Digested food	✓			[1]
Carbon dioxide		✓		[1]

- **f** Antibodies. [1]
- **g** Muscles contract. [Accept 'contractions'.] [1]

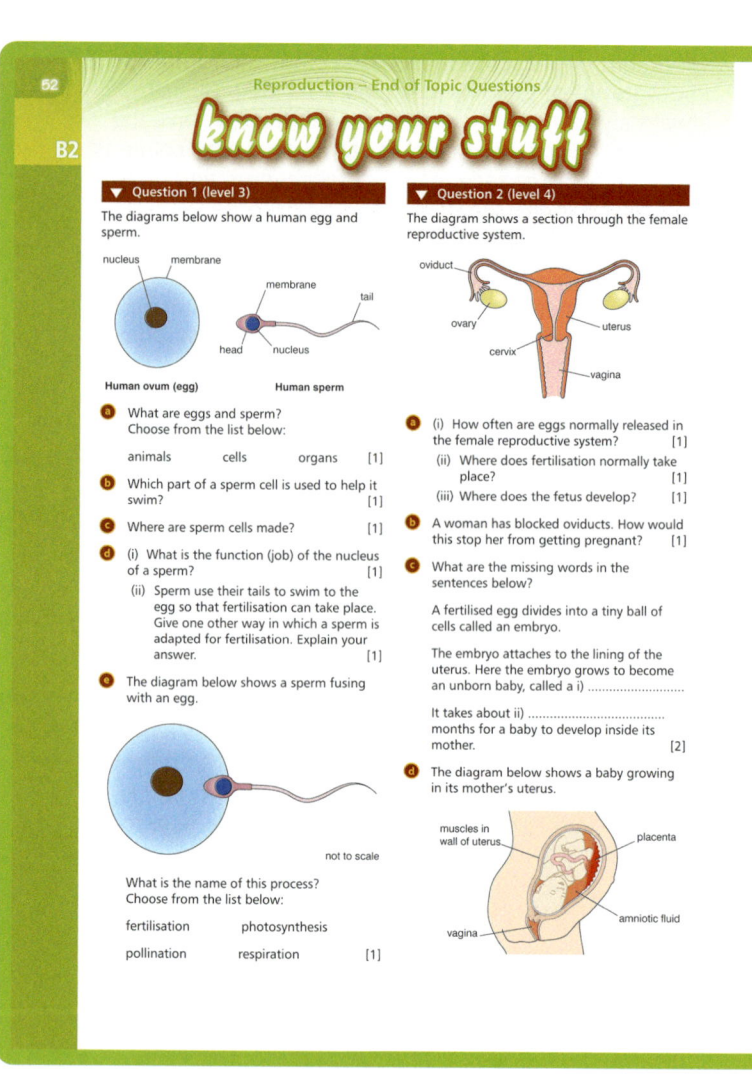

Reproduction – End of Topic Questions

know your stuff

(i) What is the function (job) of the amniotic fluid? [1]

(ii) Some harmful substances, such as nicotine, can pass from the mother's blood to the baby's blood. Through which part does this happen? [1]

e Substances can pass from the mother's blood to the fetus's blood. Other substances can pass from the fetus's blood to the mother's blood.

Which way, if any, do the substances in the table pass? Copy the table and tick one box in each row.

Substance	Passes from the mother's blood to the fetus's blood	Passes from the fetus's blood to the mother's blood	Does not pass between the mother's blood and the fetus's blood
Poisons from cigarette smoke			
Oxygen			
Digested food			
Carbon dioxide			

[4]

f Name one useful substance, other than food and oxygen, which passes from the mother to the fetus. [1]

g How does the wall of the uterus push the baby out when it is born? [1]

▼ **Question 3 (level 6)**

Use words from the list to copy and complete the sentences about the menstrual cycle. [4]

daily   uterus   middle   end
an ovary   weekly
beginning   monthly   vagina

Menstruation is part of a **a**................ cycle.

The cycle begins when the lining of the **b**........................ breaks away.

An ovum (egg) is released from **c**................at about the **d**........................ of each cycle.

▼ **Question 4 (level 7)**

a The diagram shows the male reproductive system.

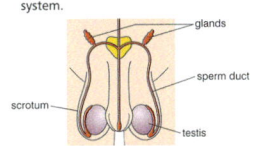

A man's testes are outside the main part of the body. What is the relationship (link) between sperm production and temperature? [1]

b Chemicals, called sex hormones, cause changes in boys' and girls' bodies. They start to be made when people reach puberty.

(i) Where are sex hormone produced in boys? [1]

(ii) Describe two of the changes in boys' bodies and two of the changes in girls' bodies. [4]

c (i) About 200 million sperm are released into the body of a woman during sexual intercourse. Why is it important to release so many sperm? [1]

(ii) Sperm cells are mixed with a fluid to make semen. Semen contains sugar. Explain how and why a sperm makes use of the sugar. [2]

---

3 Menstruation is part of a **a** monthly cycle. [1]

The cycle begins when the lining of the **b** uterus breaks away. [1]

An ovum (egg) is released from **c** an ovary at about the [1]

d middle of each cycle. [1]

4 a The best temperature for making sperm is lower than body temperature. [1]

b (i) In the testes or testis. [1]

(ii) Boys, any *two* from: [2]
body hair *or* pubic hair *or* hairy armpits;
facial hair *or* beard;
breaking *or* lowering of the voice;
growth of the penis or testes;
body becomes more muscular;
sperm production begins;
growth spurt.

Girls, any *two* from: [2]
body hair *or* pubic hair *or* hairy armpits;
growth of the breasts;
hips become wider;
egg production begins;
start periods;
growth spurt.

c (i) Any *one* from: [1]
to increase the chance of one reaching the egg or the oviduct;
most sperm die before reaching the egg or oviduct.

(ii) For respiration. [Accept 'for energy'.] [1]
For movement or for swimming. [1]

C1.1 Reversible and Irreversible Changes

NC links for the topic
- Elements and compounds show characteristic chemical properties and patterns in their behaviour.
- Use a range of scientific methods and techniques to develop and test ideas and explanations.
- Assess risk and work safely in the laboratory, field and workplace.
- Carry out practical and investigative activities, both individually and in groups.
- Obtain, record and analyse data from a wide range of primary and secondary sources, including ICT sources, and use their findings to provide evidence for scientific explanations.
- Evaluate scientific evidence and working methods.
- Use appropriate methods, including ICT, to communicate scientific information and contribute to presentations and discussions about scientific issues.

Level descriptors for the topic
- **AT4 level 4:** Pupils recall simple scientific knowledge and terminology of the properties and classification of materials such as solids. They describe some phenomena and processes, such as gas tests, drawing on scientific knowledge and understanding. They recognise that evidence can support or refute scientific ideas, for example the classification of reactions as reversible and irreversible. They recognise some applications and implications of science, such as the safe use of acids and alkalis.
- They communicate their conclusions using appropriate scientific language. They suggest improvements in their work, giving reasons.
- **AT3 level 5:** Pupils recall straightforward scientific knowledge and terminology of materials and their properties. They describe phenomena and processes, drawing on abstract ideas. They explain processes and phenomena such as combustion in more than one step or using a model. They apply and use knowledge and understanding in familiar contexts, such as identifying changes of state. They recognise that both evidence and creative thinking contribute to the development of scientific ideas, the discovery of oxygen and the development of the fire triangle. They describe applications and implications of science, such as the uses of metals based on their specific properties.

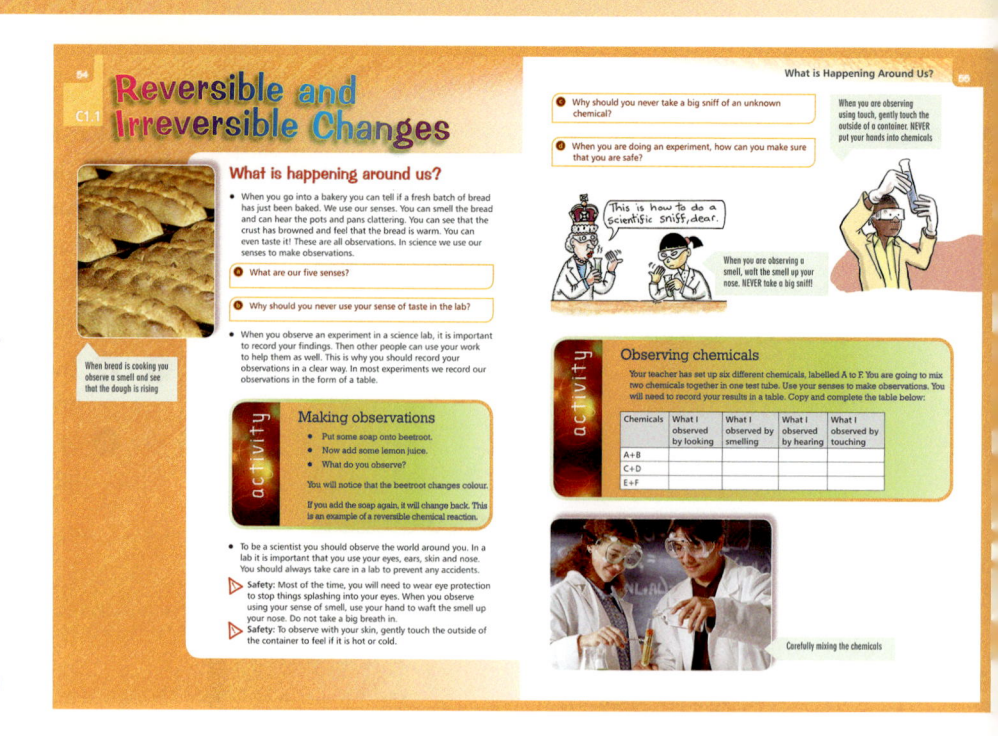

AT3 level 6: Pupils recall detailed scientific knowledge and terminology of properties of materials. They describe phenomena and processes using abstract ideas, such as the idea of molecule rearrangement during combustion. They take account of a number of factors or use abstract ideas or models, such as word equations, in their explanations of phenomena and processes. They apply and use knowledge and understanding, such as relating changes of state to energy transfers, in unfamiliar contexts. They describe some evidence for some accepted scientific ideas, such as the patterns in the reactions of acids with metals and the reactions of a variety of substances with oxygen. They explain the importance of some applications and implications of science, such as the production of new materials with specific desirable properties.

Learning Objectives
Pupils should learn:
- What we mean by 'observation' in science.
- How to describe phenomena.
- How to describe a chemical change.

Learning Outcomes
- All pupils should be able to observe safely.
- Most pupils should be able to record their observations.
- Some pupils should also be able to give examples of chemical changes.

How Science Works
- Describe and record observations and evidence systematically. (1.2d)

Answers to in-text questions

a Sight, smell, touch, taste, hearing.

b Some chemicals can be dangerous if they get into the body.

c Some chemicals can be dangerous if they get into your body. If you take a big sniff then lots of this chemical gets into your body and this could be dangerous.

d Tie any loose clothes and hair back, wear eye protection, wash hands after the activity, never put hands into chemicals.

What is Happening Around Us?

The Lesson

Starter Suggestions

Memory game

Place about 20 everyday items, such as a tennis ball, a pencil, a doll or a toy car on a tray covered with a cloth. Remove the cloth and give the pupils a short time (perhaps 3 mins) to memorise as many of the objects as they can. Once the time is up, cover the tray up again and ask pupils to list all the things they can remember. (10 mins)

What can you see?

Ask pupils to make a list of as many things as they can that can be seen in the room with a particular feature, e.g. all the red things. (5 mins)

Main Lesson

- Ask pupils how we know what is going on around us. Hopefully, they will come up with our five senses. Ask them to list all five: sight, smell, touch, taste and hearing.
- Move on from this to discuss how scientists have found out about the world. Ideally, they will suggest that experiments are used. Lead pupils to realise that in order to find out what is happening in an experiment, we need to use our senses to observe what is happening. Remind them, at this point, that they should never use taste in a science laboratory unless they are specifically told they can.
- Show pupils how to smell something safely, by wafting the smell towards their nose. Explain that they should never put their nose over anything and sniff, as it may be poisonous.
- Ask pupils to carry out a circus of experiments where they need to make careful observations. The emphasis here should not be on describing chemical reactions, but on just observing things as they are using their senses. You could include things such as:
  - Adding baking powder to an acid (e.g. lemon juice) [hear fizzing, see bubbles]
  - Adding spirit vinegar to a chunk of beetroot [colour change]
  - Adding a solution of washing powder to a chunk of beetroot [colour change]
  - Adding a slice of celery to hydrogen peroxide solution (with a few drops of washing-up liquid) [see foaming] (Hydrogen peroxide was the main ingredient in early mouthwashes and often used by people with throat infections. The solution decomposed in the throat, yielding water and oxygen. The oxygen bubbles would push any puss or other material out of the throat and the mild oxidising action would help to kill any bacteria. However, hydrogen peroxide is corrosive!)
- Pupils who make more detailed observations when carrying out the activity, should receive more credit. Tease out from pupils that it is only by making careful observations that scientists can find out how the world works.

Plenary Suggestions

What's happening?

Demonstrate the reaction between sodium and water. There are lots of things to observe here. (5 mins)

It's a what?

Put something into an opaque bag. Ask a volunteer to come to the front. They must put their hand in the bag and feel around and try to guess what is there. You could put science objects in, such as a disconnected Bunsen burner, or something really strange like cold cooked rice. (10–15 mins)

Practical Support

Making observations

Equipment and materials required

Per group: 3 test tubes, spatulas, test-tube rack, 100 cm^3 beaker, thermometer, sodium metabisulfite powder, 30 g crushed ice, 20 g salt, 10 cm^3 lemon juice, 4 g soap flakes, 5 g baking powder, 5 cm^3 spirit vinegar or 1 mol/dm^3 ethanoic acid, 5 cm^3 saturated washing-powder solution, 2 small pieces of raw beetroot (the beetroot must not have been kept in vinegar), 5 cm^3 10 vol. hyrogen peroxide solution, 2–3 drops of washing-up liquid, 1 cm thick slice of celery, dropping pipette, sterilising powder and water.

Safety

Sodium metabisulphite powder: harmful, CLEAPSS Hazcard 92.

Ethanoic acid: CLEAPSS Hazcard 38.

Hydrogen peroxide: CLEAPSS Hazcard 50.

Plenary: What's happening?

Equipment and materials required

A cube of sodium metal (approximately 2–3 mm each side), glass trough (half-filled with water), filter paper, tweezers.

Details

Place the water-filled trough behind a safety screen, ensuring that pupils are looking at the trough through the safety screen and not around the sides. Pick up the potassium using the tweezers and clean any oil from it using the filter paper. Drop the potassium into the water and observe it fizzing and moving around the surface. The hyrdrogen gas evolved should self-ignite, burning with a yellow flame.

Safety

Eye protection must be worn. Use safety screen. Keep pupils well away.

Follow advice on CLEAPSS Hazcard 88 for sodium.

Differentiation

SEN

Lower attaining pupils may only be able to make very simple observations during the practical and may need help in recording them correctly.

Extension

There is an opportunity for higher attaining pupils to lead the plenary 'It's a what?'. You could ask the volunteer who has their hand in the bag to describe what they feel, rather than trying to guess what the item is themselves. Other pupils could then try to guess based on the description.

Homework Suggestion

To test pupils' observation skills further, ask them to describe how the appearance and taste of a squash drink changes as more water is added.

C1.2 What are Reversible and Irreversible Changes?

NC links for the lesson
- Elements and compounds show characteristic chemical properties and patterns in their behaviour.
- Carry out practical and investigative activities, both individually and in groups.
- Evaluate scientific evidence and working methods.

Learning Objectives
Pupils should learn:
- What a reversible change is.
- What an irreversible change is.
- How to decide whether a change is reversible or irreversible.
- One example of each type of change that happens in the home.

Learning Outcomes
- All pupils should be able to recognise a change.
- Most pupils should be able to classify a change as reversible or irreversible.
- Some pupils should also be able to explain why a change is reversible or irreversible

How Science Works
- Describe and record observations and evidence systematically. (1.2d)

Functional Skills Link-up
ICT
- Use appropriate search techniques to locate and select relevant information. (Research reversible and irreversible changes.) (Level 1)

Answers to in-text questions
a) [Any changes to materials.]
b) A change which can easily be reversed.
c) [Any change of state or dissolving.]
d) A change which cannot easily be reversed.
e) [Any example of a chemical reaction, e.g. cooking meat, baking a cake.]
f) Chemical.

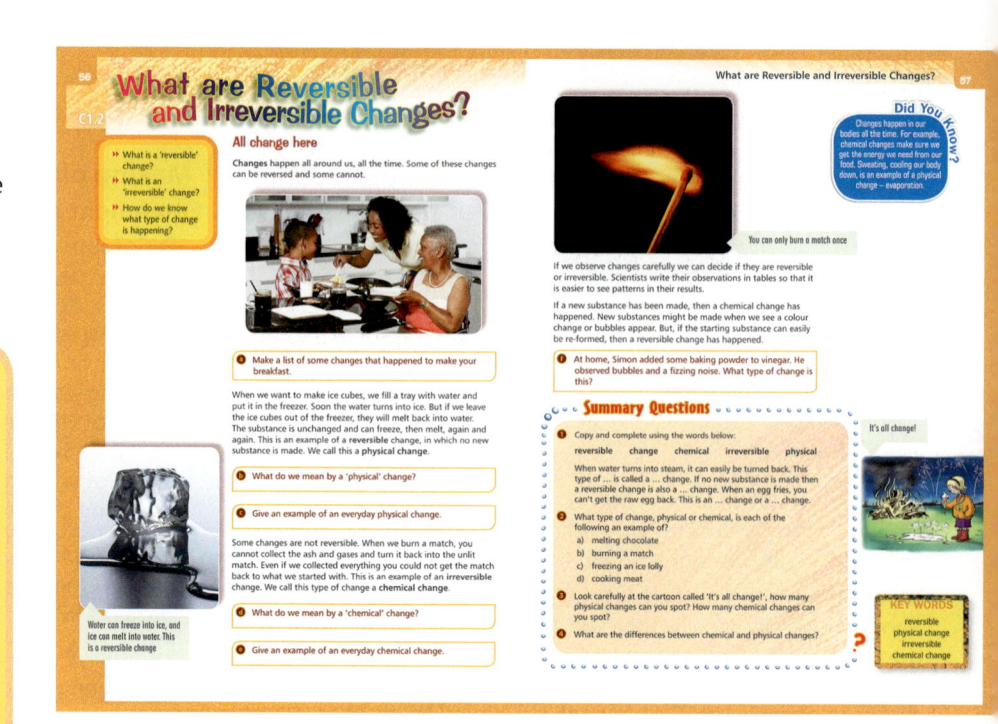

The Lesson

Starter Suggestions

Eggs for breakfast
Recall work on observation from the last lesson. Demonstrate poaching an egg in a beaker. (**Note:** Some pupils may be allergic to eggs.) Ask the pupils to note down what they can observe happening to the egg. Encourage them to explain whether they think the egg can be changed back or not. (10 mins)

Match the word
Present the pupils with the key words for the lesson and, jumbled up, the definitions for those words. Ask them to match the correct definition to each word. (5 mins)

Learning Styles
Visual: Observing physical and chemical changes.
Auditory: Describing observations of changes.
Intrapersonal: Reflecting on the differences between physical and chemical changes.

Answers to summary questions
1. When water turns into steam, it can easily be turned back. This type of **change** is called a **reversible** change. If no new substance is made then a reversible change is also a **physical** change. When an egg fries, you can't get the raw egg back. This is an **irreversible** change or a **chemical** change.
2. a) physical b) chemical c) physical d) chemical
3. Physical – melting ice cream and evaporating water from the puddle.
   Chemical – bonfire, fireworks and glow stick.
4. A chemical change is not easily reversed and a new substance is made. In a physical change no new substance is made and the process is easily reversed.

What are Reversible and Irreversible Changes?

Change – When something becomes different from its previous state/form.

Irreversible – A change which cannot be reversed.

Reversible – A change which can be reversed.

Chemical change – A chemical change is one in which a new substance is formed. Usually irreversible.

Physical change – No new substance is formed and the change can easily be reversed.

Main Lesson

- There are two possible main activities for this lesson, depending upon the facilities you have available. Explain to pupils that changes to materials can generally be placed into two groups: those which are reversible and can be changed back and those which are irreversible. Then select from one of the following options:
- **Circus of observations:** Set up various examples of physical/reversible and chemical/irreversible changes for pupils to try/observe: an ice cube melting [physical], burning a splint [chemical], dissolving copper sulfate in water [physical], boiling water holding a cold watch glass over it to see the steam condense [two physical changes] (**Safety:** steam burns), adding water to sherbet [chemical], melting chocolate (over a water bath) [physical], dropping a piece of magnesium into some acid [chemical]. Pupils should observe each event in turn and record what they observe happening. They should also decide whether they think a reversible, physical change has taken place or an irreversible, chemical one.
- **Cut and stick:** This activity could be carried out individually or in small groups. Pupils to cut out and stick, into books or onto paper, pictures of changes from newspapers and magazines or printed out from the computer which show reversible and irreversible changes occurring or that have happened. Higher attaining pupils should try to justify their groupings. [For example, Reversible: melting ice lolly, butter melting in a pan, a puddle evaporating, washing drying; Irreversible: striking a match, baking a cake, barbecue burning, meat cooking.]
- After completing the task, ask working groups to report back on their findings. This is an ideal opportunity for the pupils to compare their ideas and for any misconceptions to be addressed.

Plenary Suggestions

Match the word – Part 2

Revisit the definitions starter and ask pupils to sort them out again. This time they should get them all right. Ask them to give an example for each one. (10 mins)

Observations

Demonstrate the burning of a small piece of bread in a Bunsen flame. Pupils must explain why it is a chemical change, giving as many pieces of evidence as they can, e.g. 'it goes black', 'smoke can be seen', 'a smell is produced', 'it catches fire'. (5 mins) **Safety:** Wear eye protection.

Practical Support

Starter: Eggs for breakfast

Equipment and materials required

Raw egg, 400 cm^3 beaker, Bunsen burner, tripod, heat-proof mat, gauze, matches.

Main activity: Circus of observations

Equipment and materials required

2–3 ice cubes, splints (1 per pupil), copper sulfate powder (1–2 spatulas full per pupil group), a few watch glasses, bowl of iced water, paper towels, 1 packet of sherbet, tongs, 3–4 squares of chocolate, evaporating basin, 200 cm^3 of 0.5 mol/dm^3 hydrochloric acid, 1 cm long pieces of magnesium (1 per pupil group).

Details

Ice cube in beaker – pupils watch the ice melt.

A few splints and a lit Bunsen burner – pupils burn splints.

Copper sulfate powder with a spatula, a glass rod and some clean water in a 100 cm^3 beaker – add one or two spatulas of copper sulfate to the water and stir.

Bunsen burner with a beaker of water over it – pupils watch the water boil. Take a watch glass which has been chilled in iced water, dry it, hold it over the steam using tongs, and observe the water condense.

Sherbet, small beaker and water – put a small amount (about 50 cm^3) of water in a small beaker and add two spatulas of sherbet.

A few squares of chocolate in an evaporating dish, over a beaker of hot water – fill a beaker nearly full with hot water (water from the hot tap should be hot enough) and rest the evaporating dish containing the chocolate onto it. Ensure the hot water is in contact with the dish but does not overflow.

0.5 mol/dm^3 hydrochloric acid, boiling tube, test-tube rack and a 1 cm piece of magnesium ribbon – place 5 cm^3 of acid into the boiling tube and put in the magnesium.

Plenary: Observations

Hold a piece (3 cm × 3 cm) of white bread in the flame of a Bunsen burner, using tongs. Observe the bread blackening. It may even catch fire.

Safety:

Pupils should wear eye protection during the experiments.

Copper sulfate is harmful: CLEAPSS Hazcard 27C.

Sodium ethanoate is harmful if swallowed. (See 'Extension'.)

Hydrochloric acid is harmful: CLEAPSS Hazcard 47A.

Magnesium: CLEAPSS Hazcard 59A.

Differentiation

SEN

Give pupils cards stating some physical and chemical changes. These could be the changes they have seen during the lesson. Ask pupils to sort them into two groups and then stick them into their books.

Extension

Slowly pour a super-saturated solution of sodium ethanoate onto a sodium acetate seed crystal. A 'stalagmite' of sodium acetate will crystallise out. Challenge pupils to explain this physical change. (**Safety:** sodium ethanoate is harmful if large quantities are swallowed. Wear eye protection.)

You could also get your pupils to try to change the colour of flowers by leaving them in water which has been dyed.

Homework Suggestion

Pupils to identify examples of reversible and irreversible changes around the home. Many examples of irreversible changes exist with respect to cooking food.

C1.3 Are All Acids Dangerous?

NC links for the lesson
- Elements and compounds show characteristic chemical properties and patterns in their behaviour.

Learning Objectives
Pupils should learn:
- How to tell if a chemical is dangerous.
- What acids are.

Learning Outcomes
- All pupils should be able to name household examples of acids.
- Most pupils should be able to recall the hazard symbols.
- Some pupils should also be able to explain why hazard symbols are important.

How Science Works
- Explain how action has been taken to control obvious risk … (1.2c)

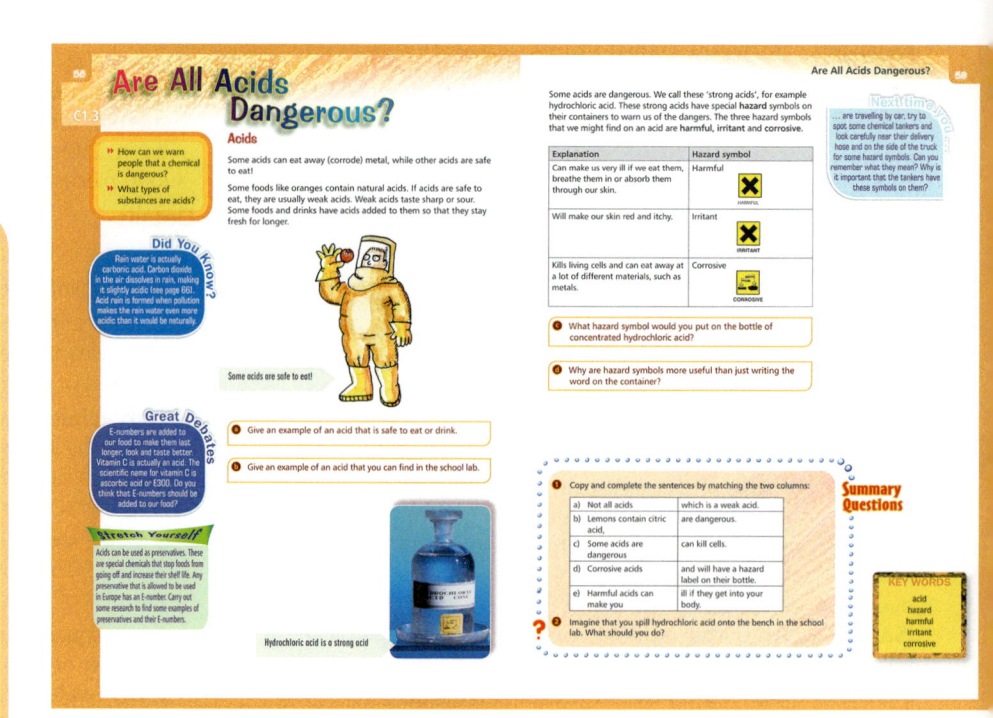

Functional Skills Link-up
ICT
- Obtain, insert, size, crop and position images that are fit for purpose. (Level 2) See Extension work.

Learning Styles
Visual: Studying hazard symbols.
Kinaesthetic: Carrying out practical work.
Intrapersonal: Understanding the idea that warning symbols are a fast way to convey information.

Answers to summary questions
1.
   a) Not all acids are dangerous.
   b) Lemons contain citric acid, which is a weak acid.
   c) Some acids are dangerous and will have a hazard label on their bottle.
   d) Corrosive acids can kill cells.
   e) Harmful acids can make you ill if they get into your body.
2. Tell the teacher. Wash the bench with plenty of water. Wash your skin with plenty of cold water to get rid of the acid.

Are All Acids Dangerous?

The Lesson

Starter Suggestions

What's an acid?
Ask pupils to describe what they think an acid is or what comes to mind when someone uses the word 'acid'. (5 mins)

What does it mean?
Present the pupils with pictures of foreign road and other warning signs. Ask them to guess what the signs mean. Hopefully, they will get many right, which will serve to suggest that picture warning signs are useful because they don't require you to speak the language. (10 mins)

Main Lesson

- Ask pupils whether they think all acids are dangerous. Then show pupils a range of acidic substances including, lemon juice, vinegar, sherbet, hydrochloric acid, sulfuric acid and nitric acid.
- Ask them whether they still think all acids are dangerous (if they did before).
- Show them a bottle of acid with the 'Corrosive' warning symbol on it. Ask pupils to explain what it might mean. They are likely to come up with ideas about burning through things. Explain to them that some acids can damage materials and 'eat' away at them.
- Ask pupils why we need warning signs. Introduce them to the idea that lots of chemicals have warning signs on them. Give them a sorting activity to do where they must match the hazard symbol with its name and its meaning.
- Extend the activity by asking pupils to design their own warning symbol, e.g. for a label for a heavy object which may be difficult to carry, or the edge of a cliff.
- **Note:** CLEAPSS CD-ROM has printable hazard labels and fonts.

Plenary Suggestions

Hazard
Give pupils a recall test by holding up flashcards of hazard symbols and asking them to say what the hazard is and give an explanation. (10 mins)

Acid volcano
Demonstrate just how acid concentration affects the hazard level of an acid by pouring first dilute sulfuric acid, then concentrated acid onto granulated sugar. With the concentrated acid the sugar undergoes dehydration rapidly. (5 mins)

Practical Support

Warning signs

Equipment and materials required
A variety of acidic substances in bottles are needed, including one bottle of laboratory acid which has the corrosive hazard warning symbol on it.

Acids chosen could include: lemon juice, vinegar, sherbet, hydrochloric acid (1 mol/dm^3), sulfuric acid (0.5 mol/dm^3) and nitric acid (0.4 mol/dm)^3).

Plenary: Acid volcano

Equipment and materials required
Two 100 cm^3 beakers, 20 g of white sugar (10 g in each beaker), 25 cm^3 each of concentrated sulfuric acid and 1 mol/dm^3 sulfuric acid, tray to protect the bench/table.

Details
In a fume cabinet, or outdoors, first, pour the dilute acid onto the sugar in one of the beakers. Show that very little happens. Then pour the concentrated acid onto the other sugar. The sugar rapidly turns black and froths up (as carbon and steam are formed).

Safety
Wear eye protection and chemical-resistant gloves.

Hydrochloric acid (CLEAPSS Hazcard 47A), sulfuric acid (CLEAPSS Hazcard 98A), nitric acid (CLEAPSS Hazcard 67) are all irritants.

The main hazard is the concentrated sulfuric acid which can burn skin rapidly as it is corrosive. Wash off well with water if skin contact occurs.

The volcano reaction produces lots of acid-rich steam. Keep well back once the reaction has started and ensure the acid fumes can escape – carry out the reaction in a fume cabinet or outdoors.

Differentiation

SEN
Play a game of hazard warning symbol snap.

Extension
Some pupils can be given the opportunity to design their own hazard symbols.

They could provide a risk assessment for something they consider to be dangerous around the home – operating hair straighteners, boiling a kettle, making a cup of tea, mowing the lawn, etc.

Homework Suggestion

Pupils to find examples of warning symbols, e.g. road signs or those found in the home.

Answers to in-text questions

a) Any citrus fruit, vinegar.

b) Common examples include sulfuric acid, nitric acid, hydrochloric acid.

c) Corrosive.

d) If people cannot read then they can still know what the hazard is. The symbols are the same throughout the world, so you can still recognise the symbol even if you don't speak English. It is quicker to glance at a picture than read a word.

C1.4 Are All Alkalis Dangerous?

NC links for the lesson
- Elements and compounds show characteristic chemical properties and patterns in their behaviour.
- Carry out practical and investigative activities, both individually and in groups.

Learning Objectives

Pupils should learn:
- Which substances are alkalis.
- The difference between an alkali and an acid.

Learning Outcomes
- All pupils should be able to name household examples of alkalis.
- Most pupils should be able to state the difference between an acid and an alkali.
- Some pupils should also be able to explain the difference between alkalis and bases.

How Science Works
- Explain how action has been taken to control obvious risks and how methods are adequate for the task. (1.2c)

Learning Styles
Visual: Recognising colour changes in an indicator.
Kinaesthetic: Testing substances to see if they are alkalis.
Intrapersonal: Understanding that not all alkalis are dangerous.

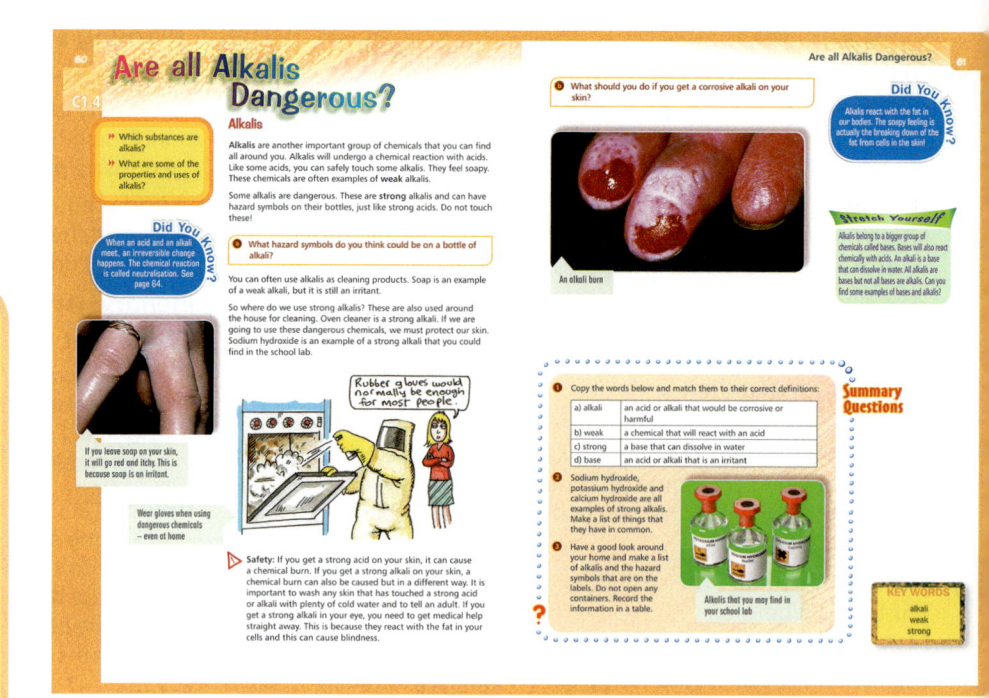

The Lesson

Starter Suggestions

Odd one out

Show pupils four pictures or items. Three should show acids, such as vinegar, lemon juice and hydrochloric acid. Do not tell the pupils they are acids at this stage. The other picture should be of an alkaline substance, such as a bar of soap or some shower gel. The challenge is to work out that the soap is the odd one out as the others are all acids. The pupils should recognise the acids from previous work. (5 mins)

Mix it up?

Challenge pupils to come up with as many words as they can using the letters in the word 'alkali' or 'sodium hydroxide'. To make it harder, only allow words of more than three or four letters. (10 mins)

Main Lesson

- Show pupils a bar of soap. Wet it and ask one of them to touch the soap and then describe how it feels. Explain that soap is made from an alkali which is the chemical opposite of an acid. Most alkalis feel soapy. [Alkalis feel soapy as they react with fats in the skin, turning to a form of soap. Traditionally soap is made by reacting animal fat with 'lye', the traditional name for sodium hydroxide.]
- Demonstrate the reaction between sodium hydroxide and ammonium chloride. Only do this reaction in a well-ventilated area as ammonia is evolved. Pupils could be allowed to smell the ammonia carefully.
- Set pupils the challenge of identifying the alkalis from a range of substances. They can make their own indicator from red cabbage to do this. Use the indicator to test the substances. The indicator will turn green in alkalis and red in acid. You may wish to demonstrate this by dripping some indicator onto the soap shown earlier.
- No explanation of indicators is necessary at this point, as these will be discussed in detail in C1.5.
- After the experiment, check that pupils have correctly identified the alkalis.

Are All Alkalis Dangerous?

Plenary Suggestions

Observing
Mix 5 cm³ of 0.4 mol/dm³ sodium hydroxide and 5 cm³ of 0.5 mol/dm³ copper sulfate in a test tube. A blue precipitate of copper hydroxide will form. Ask pupils whether this represents a chemical or physical change and what evidence there is. [It is a chemical change.] (5 mins)

Alkalis at home
Having seen that soap is an alkali, ask pupils to compile a list of all the alkalis they have at home. Most cleaning products, from shower gel to oven cleaner are alkalis. (10 mins)

Practical Support

Main lesson: Demonstration

Equipment and materials required

10 cm³ of 1 mol/dm³ sodium hydroxide, boiling tube and rack, spatula, ammonium chloride powder.

Details

Pour 10 cm³ of 1 mol/dm³ sodium hydroxide into a boiling tube. Add a spatula of solid ammonium chloride. Only carry this reaction out in a well ventilated area and, preferably, have a fume cabinet available to place the tube in once you have finished it. **Note:** A loose plug of mineral wool will help to contain the gases.

Safety

Eye protection must be worn.
Sodium hydroxide is corrosive: CLEAPSS Hazcard 91.
Ammonium chloride is harmful: CLEAPSS Hazcard 9A.

Main lesson: Find the alkali

Equipment and materials required

Per group: pestle and mortar, a few pieces of chopped red cabbage, 10 cm³ 95% ethanol, disposable pipette, 5 test tubes, test-tube rack, 2 cm³ each of: 0.5 mol/dm³ hydrochloric acid, distilled water, 0.4 mol/dm³ sodium hydroxide, 0.5 mol/dm³ sodium carbonate and limewater.

Details

To make the indicator, each group will need to grind up a few pieces of red cabbage with a pestle and mortar. They should then add to it about 10 cm³ of ethanol and mix to ensure the pigment has dissolved in the ethanol. This is covered in more detail in C1.5.

Next, each group should place about 2 cm³ of each test substance into separate test tubes and add a few drops of their indicator. The indicator can be drawn directly from the pestle with a disposable pipette. Pupils should test 0.5 mol/dm³ hydrochloric acid, distilled water (acidified if necessary to ensure it's not alkaline), 0.4 mol/dm³ sodium hydroxide solution, 0.5 mol/dm³ sodium carbonate solution and limewater. The indicator will turn green in alkalis and red in acid. You may wish to demonstrate this by dripping some indicator onto the soap shown earlier.

Safety

Eye protection must be worn.
Ethanol is highly flammable and harmful: CLEAPSS Hazcard 40A. No naked flames when using ethanol.
Sodium hydroxide is an irritant (at 0.4 mol/dm³): CLEAPSS Hazcard 91.
Limewater is an irritant: CLEAPSS Hazcard 18.

Differentiation

SEN
Allow short words if you are using the starter 'Mix it up'.

Extension
Ask pupils to research the difference between alkalis and bases. Although 'alkali' is the more commonly used term, 'base' is the correct name. Alkalis are bases which are soluble in water.

Ask pupils what might happen if a base and an acid were to react together. This will be covered in C1.6, but they could start to think about it now.

Homework Suggestion

Give pupils some pieces of litmus paper and ask them to identify some alkaline substances they find at home.

Answers to summary questions

1.
   a) Alkali: a base that can dissolve in water.
   b) Weak: an acid or base that is an irritant.
   c) Strong: an acid or alkali that would be corrosive or harmful.
   d) Base: a chemical that will react with an acid.

2. They all contain hydroxide, they are all opposites of acids, they are all strong alkalis, they are all corrosive, they are all liquids, they are all colourless, they are all transparent.

3. Research.

Answers to in-text questions

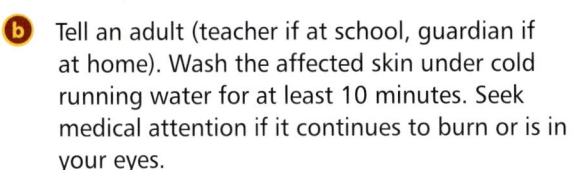

a) Harmful, irritant or corrosive.

b) Tell an adult (teacher if at school, guardian if at home). Wash the affected skin under cold running water for at least 10 minutes. Seek medical attention if it continues to burn or is in your eyes.

C1.5 Indicators

NC links for the lesson
- Elements and compounds show characteristic chemical properties and patterns in their behaviour.
- Use a range of scientific methods and techniques to develop and test ideas and explanations.
- Carry out practical and investigative activities, both individually and in groups.

Learning Objectives

Pupils should learn:
- What an indicator is.
- What the pH scale shows us.
- How we test the pH of a chemical.

Learning Outcomes
- All pupils should be able to test chemicals to classify them as acids or alkalis.
- Most pupils should be able to identify the pH of a chemical.
- Some pupils should also be able to explain why universal indicator is more useful than others such as litmus.

How Science Works
- Describe and record observations and evidence systematically. (1.2d)
- Recognise that the presentation of experimental results through the routine use of tables … makes it easier to see patterns and trends. (1.2d)

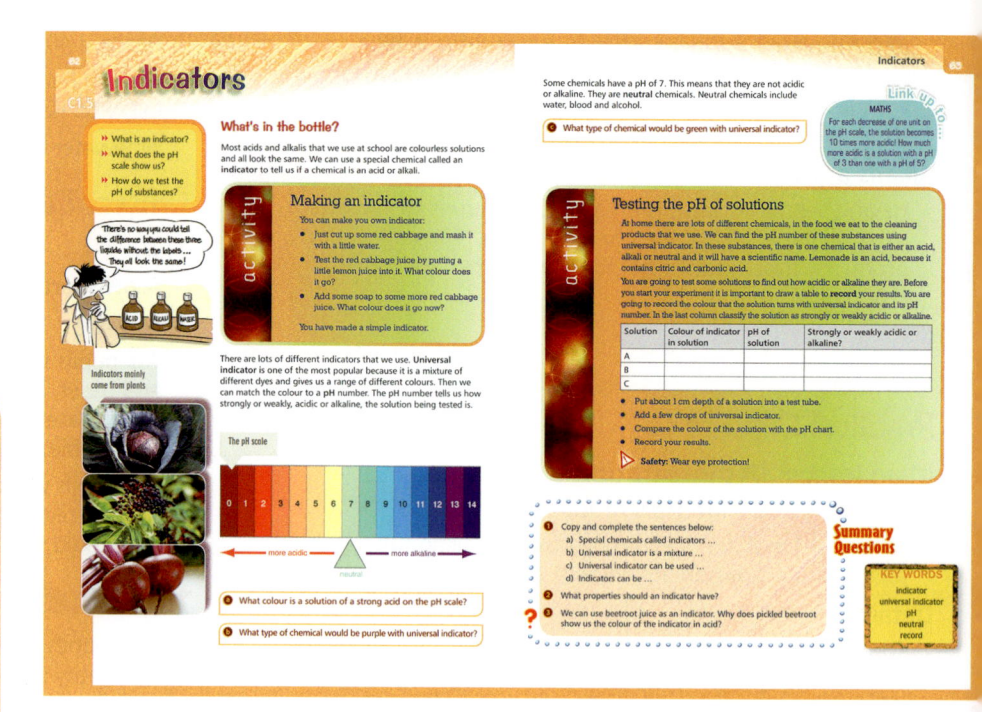

Functional Skills Link-up

Mathematics
- Multiply … whole numbers by 10 and 100 using mental arithmetic. (Level 1) See 'Link up to Maths'.

Learning Styles

Visual: Observing colour changes in indicators.
Auditory: Justifying the decision about pH.
Kinaesthetic: Testing the indicators.
Intrapersonal: Understanding the need for scientists to collaborate.

Answers to summary questions

1.
   a) Special chemicals called indicators can be used to help people work out if a chemical is an acid or an alkali.
   b) Universal indicator is a mixture of dyes and can turn a range of colours.
   c) Universal indicator can be used to find out the pH of a solution and discover if it's strongly or weakly acidic or alkaline.
   d) Indicators can be found as a liquid or as special paper.

2. It should have a different colour in acid and alkali. It should be safe, cheap and easy to use.

3. Vinegar is an acid. So, pickled beetroot would already have changed colour because it is in an acid.

Indicators

The Lesson

Starter Suggestions

Which is which?
Give pupils a list of some of the substances met in the last few lessons and ask them to sort the list into 'acids' and 'alkalis'. Try to include some new substances too and perhaps some that are neither acid nor alkali, such as ethanol. (5 mins)

What's the danger?
Ask pupils to match the hazard symbols to the correct chemical, e.g. concentrated acid = corrosive, concentrated alkali = corrosive, ethanol = flammable. (5 mins)

Main Lesson

- Refer to the previous lessons in which pupils found out how to identify an alkali, and to the work done on acids in which they learned that not all acids are dangerous. It may be useful at this point to demonstrate the use of cabbage indicator, following the instructions for the practical support in C1.4. Establish that the cabbage acts as an indicator, changing colour according to the type of solution. [Red in acid and green in alkali.] You could use litmus paper instead of cabbage indicator.

- Discuss the need for a simple way to tell acids from alkalis and how dangerous they are. Introduce universal indicator as a means of testing how acidic or alkaline a solution is.

- Ask pupils to test a range of substances to find their pH. A suitable table for their results is suggested in the pupil book. [The pH scale is so called as it tells you about the concentration of hydrogen ions (H^+) in a solution. It must be written 'pH', and not PH or Ph, as the letters have a meaning. The H in pH stands for the concentration of H^+, while the 'p' is shorthand for –log (actually from the German word *potenz* meaning 'power'). So, the pH of a substance indicates –log of the concentration of H^+; a pH change of one means a ten fold change in the number of H^+ ions. As it is '–log' the higher the concentration of H^+, the lower the pH number. Water naturally forms some H^+ ions but is considered neutral at pH 7. Anything with a higher concentration of H^+ ions than water is acidic. [A common misconception stemming from work on the pH scale is that acids are red. Acids are not often red. Universal indicator turns red in the presence of acid.]

- Discuss the results of the experiment and allow pupils to share their results. There is often a difference of opinion, which is a good opportunity to discuss the limitations of universal indicator and, perhaps, to get the pupils to consider why it is important that scientists share their research.

Plenary Suggestions

What's the pH?
Give pupils a range of substances and ask them to place them at the correct point on the pH scale. Choose some of the substances seen this lesson and some met in previous lessons. (5 mins)

pH jigsaw
Give pupils a sheet with an outline of the pH scale on it and labels which should go onto it, such as 'strong acid', 'weak alkali'. Ask them to cut the labels out and stick them in the correct places. They could colour in their scale with the colours of universal indicator at each pH. (15 mins)

Practical Support

Testing the pH of solutions

Equipment and materials required
Per group: test-tube rack, 1 test tube per substance to be tested, universal indicator with dropping pipettes, pH scale keys (available from universal indicator suppliers), 2–3 cm³ of each substance to be tested, such as: 0.5 mol/dm³ sulfuric acid, lemon juice, vinegar, distilled water, ethanol, 0.5 mol/dm³ sodium bicarbonate solution, 0.4 mol/dm³ sodium hydroxide, 0.5 mol/dm³ ammonia solution, commercial oven cleaner.

Details
Pour about 2–3 cm³ of the substance to be tested into a test tube and place the tube in a test-tube rack. Add 3–4 drops of universal indicator to the substance and record the colour shown. Convert this to a pH value using a suitable key. (**Notes:** The test tube may need to be gently shaken to mix indicator and test substance. Note that adding too much indicator will result in a dark mixture, the colour of which cannot be ascertained.)

Safety
Eye protection must be worn.

Sulfuric acid: CLEAPSS Hazcard 98A.

Sodium hydroxide: CLEAPSS Hazcard 91.

Ethanol is flammable, so there must be no naked flames: CLEAPSS Hazcard 40A.

Universal indicator usually contains ethanol and is flammable.

Many of the substances suggested are corrosive.

Differentiation

SEN
Give pupils an outline of the pH scale for them to colour in with the colours which universal indicator turns at each pH.

Extension
Ask pupils to explain why universal indicator is a much better indicator than they made in C1.4. [That is, to explain that universal indicator is more useful because it gives more detailed information about a substance.]

Ask pupils to find out how the pH scale was developed. Some higher attaining pupils may wish to research the meaning of 'pH', but this is very advanced (see 'Main lesson' notes).

Homework Suggestion

Pupils to find out what hydrofluoric acid is used for. [It will dissolve glass and has to be stored in Teflon bottles. It is used, in very dilute form, to etch car number plate details onto car windows.]

Answers to in-text questions

a Dark red.

b Strong alkali.

c Neutral.

C1.6 Acid Reactions: Neutralisation

NC links for the lesson
- Elements and compounds show characteristic chemical properties and patterns in their behaviour.
- Assess risk and work safely in the laboratory, field and workplace.

Learning Objectives

Pupils should learn:

- What a neutral chemical is.
- What happens when an acid and alkali are mixed.
- How to measure the volume of a liquid.

Learning Outcomes

- All pupils should be able to measure the volume of a liquid in a measuring cylinder.
- Most pupils should be able to recall that acids and alkali react.
- Some pupils should also be able to explain observations of a neutralisation reaction.

How Science Works

- Recognise that the presentation of experimental results through the routine use of tables ... and simple graphs makes it easier to see patterns and trends. (1.2d)
- Describe patterns and trends in results ... (1.2e)

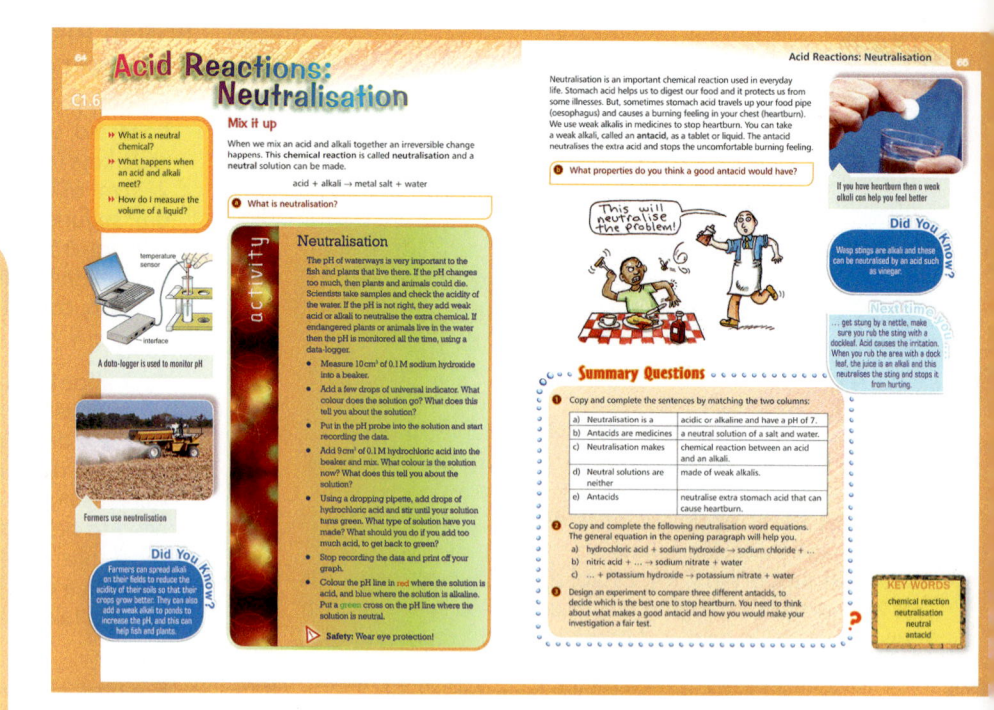

Learning Styles

Visual: Observing the changes in indicator colour as pH changes.

Auditory: Describing and discussing the difficulties in obtaining a neutral solution.

Kinaesthetic: Manipulating the apparatus during neutralisation, which requires good motor control.

Interpersonal: Taking part in discussions about the practical.

Functional Skills Link-up

ICT

- Select and use software applications to meet needs and solve given problems (monitoring neutralisation). (Level 1)

Answers to summary questions

1
- a) Neutralisation is a chemical reaction between an acid and an alkali.
- a) Antacids are medicines made of weak alkalis.
- b) Neutralisation makes a neutral solution of a salt and water.
- c) Neutral solutions are neither acidic or alkaline and have a pH of 7.
- d) Antacids neutralise extra stomach acid that can cause heartburn.

2
- a) Water.
- b) Sodium hydroxide.
- c) Nitric acid.

3 Design.

Acid Reactions: Neutralisation

The Lesson

Starter Suggestions

pH rainbow
Ask pupils to sketch out the pH scale on a piece of paper, *without* checking their exercise or a text book. They should try to colour it in according to the colours shown by universal indicator and to add labels such as 'strong acid', 'weak alkali'. (10 mins)

Chemical clash
Ask pupils to consider what would happen if a chemical of pH 1 were to meet a chemical of pH 14. (5 mins)

Main Lesson

- Remind pupils that a neutral substance is neither acid nor alkaline. Introduce the idea of neutralisation of an acid and ask pupils how they could make an acid less acidic. [Hopefully they will suggest adding an alkali.]
- Ask pupils to carry out the neutralisation reaction between dilute hydrochloric acid and sodium hydroxide solution. It is quite tricky to get the solution to be completely neutral, so challenge them to be the first to successfully complete the task. There is also an excellent opportunity here to get pupils to measure out liquids in a measuring cylinder accurately and the chance to introduce some data-logging.
- Get the class to feedback on any problems they had with the practical and how they tried to solve them.

Plenary Suggestions

pH logging
If the pupils do not have the opportunity to data-log the pH when carrying out the neutralisation experiment, demonstrating this would make a good plenary. It will allow pupils to see the pH change during the process. If they have done the data-logging themselves, demonstrate the effect of an antacid indigestion tablet on 'stomach acid' (HCl). (10 mins)

See-saw
Challenge pupils to explain how neutralisation is like a see-saw. If you add too much acid it will tip one way. Too much alkali and it will tip the other. (5 mins)

Practical Support

Neutralisation

Equipment and materials required

Per group: two $10\,cm^3$ measuring cylinders, $50\,cm^3$ of $0.1\,mol/dm^3$ hydrochloric acid, $50\,cm^3$ of $0.1\,mol/dm^3$ sodium hydroxide, a few drops of universal indicator, two dropping pipettes (one for acid and one for alkali), glass stirring rod, $100\,cm^3$ beaker; optional: data-logger with pH probe and access to a PC to review data.

Details

A suggested method for this experiment is detailed in the pupil book. This practical uses two visually identical solutions and duplicate equipment. There is tremendous scope for pupils to add more and more acid to an already acidic solution, thus getting nowhere fast. Encourage them to keep a close eye on which substance is which. Similarly, they must make sure they do not mix pipettes up and only use one for acid and a separate one for alkali.

The steps which refer to the data-logging can be missed, and the experiment carried out without a pH probe. As the pupils reach the neutralisation point, smaller and smaller amounts of acid should be added. The indicator may show that the solution is acidic for a few seconds before returning to an alkaline colour. If the solution becomes acidic, alkali should be added. Of course, if you have set the challenge to find the first group to achieve a neutral solution, you may not wish to say too much about this.

Safety

Universal indicator usually contains ethanol and is flammable.

Eye protection should be worn to protect from possible acid and alkali splashes.

Watch for pupils squirting pipettes at each other.

Plenary: pH logging

Details

If you are demonstrating the use of data-logging, proceed as per the pupil experiment. It will be very helpful if the data-logger can display live data during the experiment, directly onto a projection screen.

If you are demonstrating the effect of an antacid tablet, set the experiment up as per the pupil experiment, but with some amendments. Use $25\,cm^3$ of $0.1\,mol/dm^3$ hydrochloric acid (which you can call 'stomach acid' as it is present in the stomach). You may wish to use a magnetic stirrer to leave you free to address the class rather than stir. The pH may well become more acidic initially, as many commercial antacids have citric acid in to make them 'fizz'.

Differentiation

SEN
Pupils with poor motor skills may struggle to obtain a neutral solution, as only tiny drops of acid or alkali will be needed at the end point.

Extension
Ask pupils to write a word equation for the reaction. Support for this is available in the pupil book.

Homework Suggestion

Pupils could find out what the acid-neutralising ingredient in an antacid tablet is. [It is usually a carbonate of some sort.]

Answers to in-text questions

a An irreversible chemical change between an acid and alkali. It makes water and a salt.

b A weak alkali, that is safe to eat, cheap, easy to take, tastes good, effective.

C1.7 Acid Reactions: Metals

NC links for the lesson
- Elements and compounds show characteristic chemical properties and patterns in their behaviour.
- Use a range of scientific methods and techniques to develop and test ideas and explanations.
- Assess risk and work safely in the laboratory, field and workplace.
- Carry out practical and investigative activities, both individually and in groups.

Learning Objectives
Pupils should learn:
- What we observe when a metal reacts with an acid.
- How to test for hydrogen gas.

Learning Outcomes
- All pupils should record observations.
- Most pupils should recall the test for hydrogen.
- Some pupils should also complete word equations.

How Science Works
- Describe and record observations and evidence systematically. (1.2d)
- Describe patterns and trends in results ... (1.2e)

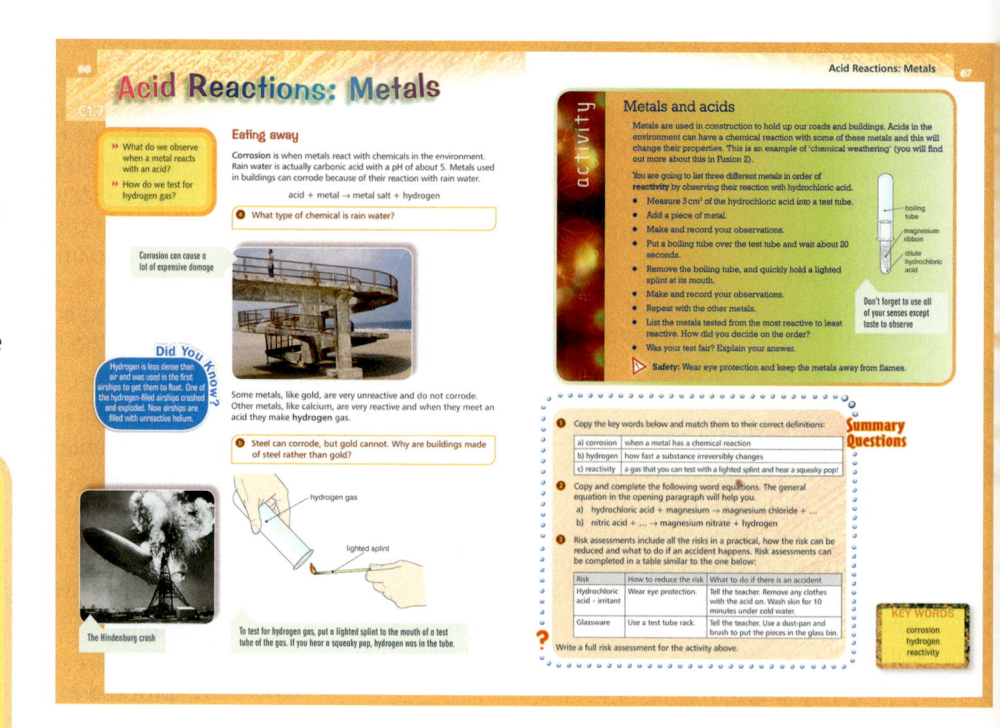

Functional Skills Link-up

English
- Present information in a logical sequence. (Level 1) See Plenary 'Diminishing words'.

Learning Styles

Auditory: Listening to the 'pop' when hydrogen burns.
Kinaesthetic: Collecting hydrogen gas.
Interpersonal: Working with others to collect the gas.
Intrapersonal: Understanding that all acids react with metals in a similar way.

Answers to summary questions

1.
   a) Corrosion: when a metal has a chemical reaction.
   b) Hydrogen: a gas you can test with a lighted splint and hear a squeaky pop!
   c) Reactivity: how fast a substance irreversibly changes.

2.
   a) Hydrogen.
   b) Magnesium.
   c) Hydrochloric acid.

3. Risk assessment.

Acid Reactions: Metals

The Lesson

Starter Suggestions

Metal everywhere

Ask pupils to list as many metals as they can. To make it more difficult, they must give a use for each metal. (5–10 mins)

Catch those bubbles

Show pupils a picture of a bubbling test tube or, by putting some marble chips in 1 mol/dm³ hydrochloric acid, the real thing. Challenge them to design a way to catch the gas coming from the reaction. (10 mins)

Main Lesson

- Remind pupils about what they have seen of acids in the preceding lessons and that acids are quite reactive substances.
- Explain that in this lesson they are going to study what happens when an acid reacts with a metal. In this lesson they will use magnesium, which is a lightweight and reactive metal. It is often alloyed (mixed) with aluminium.
- Show the pupils how to set up the experiment. They are unlikely to have collected a gas before and will need to be shown how to do this.
- Get the pupils to carry out the experiment according to the instructions in the pupil book. At this stage you may not want to tell them that the gas given off is hydrogen. It will give you scope to ask them to guess what gas it might be. They may well have heard of hydrogen.
- Explain to pupils that the gas is hydrogen and demonstrate the test for hydrogen once more. Emphasise that a lighted splint makes a squeaky pop in hydrogen gas.
- Ask pupils if they observed a difference in how well the acids reacted. They should have noticed that magnesium was the most reactive, followed by zinc, then copper.

Plenary Suggestions

Diminishing words

Ask pupils to write down five sentences which summarise the lesson. They must then reduce this to five words and, finally, to just one word. (10 mins)

Will it last forever?

By adding pieces of magnesium ribbon to a test tube of acid, one after the other, demonstrate that the acid will eventually stop reacting. Challenge pupils to explain why. They will have seen in the lesson that the piece of magnesium is 'used up', but may not realise that this also happens to the acid as it will still appear to be there. (10 mins)

Answers to in-text questions

a Carbonic acid, a weak acid.

b Gold is too expensive and soft. Steel can be protected using paint and other methods to reduce the amount of corrosion.

Practical Support

Metals and acids

Equipment and materials required

Per group: three test tubes, 2 cm long piece of magnesium ribbon, 2–3 g of granulated zinc (1 or 2 pieces), one piece of copper, 9 cm³ of 1 mol/dm³ hydrochloric acid, boiling tube, test-tube rack, splints, access to a lit Bunsen Burner nearby.

Details

A suggested method for this experiment is detailed in the pupil book.

Safety

Wear eye protection and keep the metals away from flames.

Magnesium ribbon: CLEAPSS Hazcard 59A.

Demonstration of hydrogen test

The teacher will need: 2 boiling tubes of hydrogen gas. These could be pre-filled from a cylinder or obtained by the method given in the pupil experiment.

Safety

Hydrogen is extremely flammable: CLEAPSS Hazcard 48.

Starter: Catch those bubbles

Equipment and materials required

A boiling tube with 10 cm³ of 1 mol/dm³ hydrochloric acid to which you should add 5–6 large marble chips.

Safety

Hydrochloric acid is an irritant.

Plenary: Will it last forever?

Equipment and materials required

Boiling tube and rack, 3 cm³ of 0.4 mol/dm³ hydrochloric acid, magnesium ribbon (short strips).

Details

Add a 2 cm long piece of magnesium ribbon to the acid. If it all reacts, add another. Repeat this process until the magnesium does not all react and the acid has been used up.

Differentiation

SEN

Some pupils may need extra guidance with the 'Diminishing words' plenary. They could use five sentences provided to them and try summarising into one sentence.

Some may not successfully catch enough hydrogen in order for the test to work. However, the demonstration at the end should cover this aspect.

Extension

Ask pupils to write word equations for the reactions. Support for this is available in the pupil book.

Homework Suggestion

Find out what the 'Hindenburg Disaster' was. [The Hindenburg was an early airship, filled with hydrogen, which exploded. Later airships were filled with the inert gas helium.]

C1.8 Acid Reactions: Metal Carbonates

NC links for the lesson

- Elements and compounds show characteristic chemical properties and patterns in their behaviour.
- Use a range of scientific methods and techniques to develop and test ideas and explanations.
- Assess risk and work safely in the laboratory, field and workplace.
- Carry out practical and investigative activities, both individually and in groups.

Learning Objectives

Pupils should learn:

- What is observed when a carbonate reacts with acid.
- How to test for carbon dioxide.

Learning Outcomes

- All pupils should record observations.
- Most pupils should recall the test for carbon dioxide.
- Some pupils should also be able to complete word equations.

How Science Works

- Explain how action has been taken to control obvious risk and how methods are adequate for the task. (1.2c)

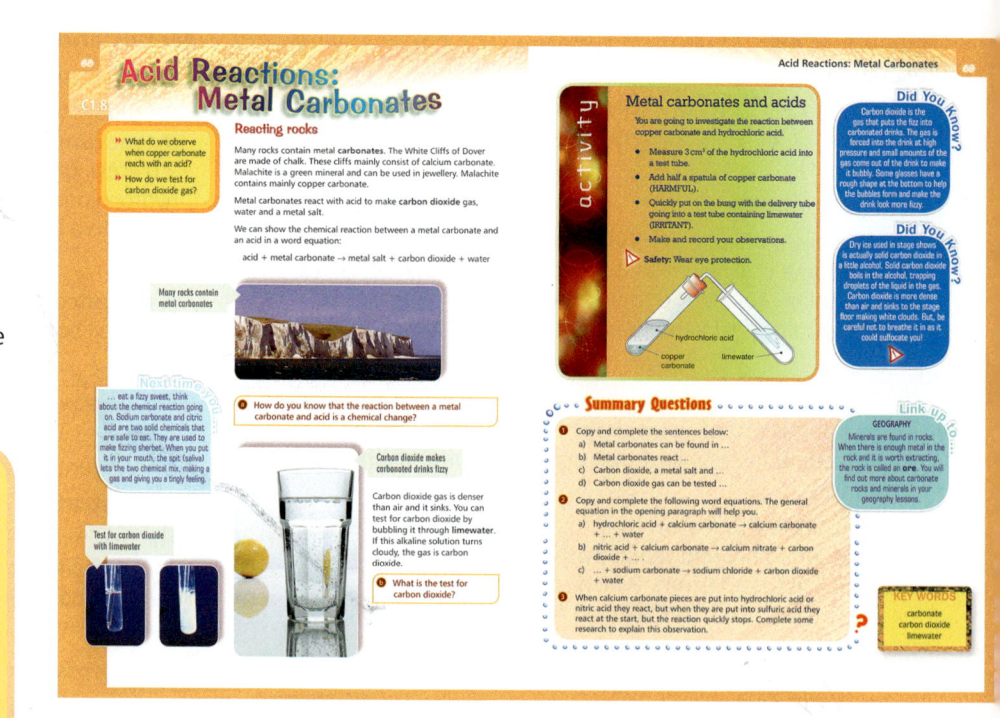

Learning Styles

Visual: Observing the reaction between acids and carbonates.

Auditory: Describing observations of the reactions.

Kinaesthetic: Reacting acids with carbonates.

Interpersonal: Working with others during the practical and discussing ideas with other pupils.

Intrapersonal: Understanding that all acids react with carbonates in a similar way.

Answers to summary questions

1. Metal carbonates can be found in rocks.
   Many metal carbonates react with acids to make a neutral solution.
   Carbon dioxide, a metal salt and water are made when a metal carbonate reacts with an acid.
   Carbon dioxide gas can be tested by making limewater go cloudy.

2. a) Carbon dioxide.
   b) Water.
   c) Hydrochloric acid.

3. The calcium carbonate makes calcium sulfate on the surface of the solid. The calcium sulfate does not dissolve in water and protects the rest of the calcium carbonate from reacting.

Acid Reactions: Metal Carbonates

The Lesson

Starter Suggestions

Observing
Ask pupils to list as many things as they can think of that they observe during a chemical reaction. [Such as fizzing, colour change, light given off, temperature change.] (10 mins)

All of a muddle
Give pupils the steps of the practical suggested for this lesson, but in the wrong order. They must put the steps into the correct order. (5 mins)

Main Lesson

- Remind pupils about what they observed when an acid reacted with a metal and the test for hydrogen gas that they saw in C1.7.
- Introduce metal carbonates as the main mineral in many rocks: calcium carbonate in limestone, copper carbonate in malachite.
- Introduce the practical and explain how to carry it out. A suggested method is given in the pupil book. You may wish to get pupils to collect some of the gas, rather than bubbling it through limewater. They could then test it in the same way as in C1.7 and prove that the gas collected was not hydrogen.
- Discuss with the group the fact that the limewater turning milky is a test for the presence of carbon dioxide gas and that when acids react with carbonates, carbon dioxide is always produced. Carbonates are the basis for many antacid remedies. That's why they can taste chalky; they are often made from chalk. The carbonate reacts with excess stomach acid. Carbon dioxide is released, which is why taking an indigestion remedy can give you wind.

Plenary Suggestions

Sort it out!
Give pupils the key words (carbonate, carbon dioxide and limewater) as anagrams. Ask them to sort the words out and then write a sentence which includes each word. (10 mins)

Is there a pattern?
Repeat the pupil practical but replace the hydrochloric acid with nitric acid. Before doing it ask pupils what they think will happen – will there be any differences? [No, there is no difference in the observation as all acids behave similarly. The salt produced is copper nitrate.] (10 mins)

Answers to in-text questions

a A new product (a gas) is made.

b Limewater (calcium hydroxide solution) changes from colourless to cloudy when the gas mixes with it.

Practical Support

Metal carbonates and acids

Equipment and materials required

Per group: 2 test tubes, 1–2 spatulas of copper carbonate powder, 10 cm^3 measuring cylinder, 3 cm^3 of 0.4 mol/dm^3 hydrochloric acid,

5 cm^3 of limewater (calcium hydroxide solution), test-tube rack, bung attached to delivery tube to fit test tubes used.

Details
A suggested method for this experiment is detailed in the pupil book.

Pupils may include the fact that the limewater bubbled as evidence of a chemical reaction. It, of course, is not. It is merely the gas from the acid/carbonate reaction passing through it. Limewater is calcium hydroxide solution which, when it reacts with carbon dioxide, forms calcium carbonate. It is the reverse of the reaction between an acid and a carbonate taking place in the other test tube. The 'limestone' produced is insoluble in water and forms tiny particles of white solid precipitate which make the solution appear milky or cloudy.

Safety
Wear eye protection to protect from acid spills and from copper carbonate which is harmful.

Copper carbonate powder is harmful: CLEAPSS Hazcard 26.

Limewater is an irritant: CLEAPSS Hazcard 18.

Plenary: Is there a pattern?

Equipment and materials required

As per 'Metal carbonates and acids' above, except: 3 cm^3 of 0.4 mol/dm^3 nitric acid in place of the hydrochloric acid.

Safety
Nitric acid is an irritant: CLEAPSS Hazcard 67.

Differentiation

SEN
Some pupils may struggle to understand that the limewater 'bubbles' because of the carbon dioxide passing through it and not because it is reacting (see 'Practical Support').

Extension
Ask pupils to write word equations for the reactions. Support for this is available in the pupil book.

Homework Suggestion

Pupils to find out what carbon dioxide is used for. [Certain fire extinguishers, the fizz in 'fizzy' drinks, a packaging gas for some foods which slows oxidation, the gas given off by yeast which makes bread rise.]

C1.9 Is It a Metal?

NC links for the lesson
- Elements and compounds show characteristic chemical properties and patterns in their behaviour.
- Use a range of scientific methods and techniques to develop and test ideas and explanations.
- Evaluate scientific evidence and working methods.

Learning Objectives
Pupils should learn:
- What a metal is.
- What a non-metal is.
- How to decide if a substance is a metal or non-metal.

Learning Outcomes
- All pupils should be able to group some metals and non-metals.
- Most pupils should be able to recall the physical properties of metals and non-metals.
- Some pupils should also be able to explain why a material is a metal or non-metal.

How Science Works
- Describe and record observations and evidence systematically. (1.2d)

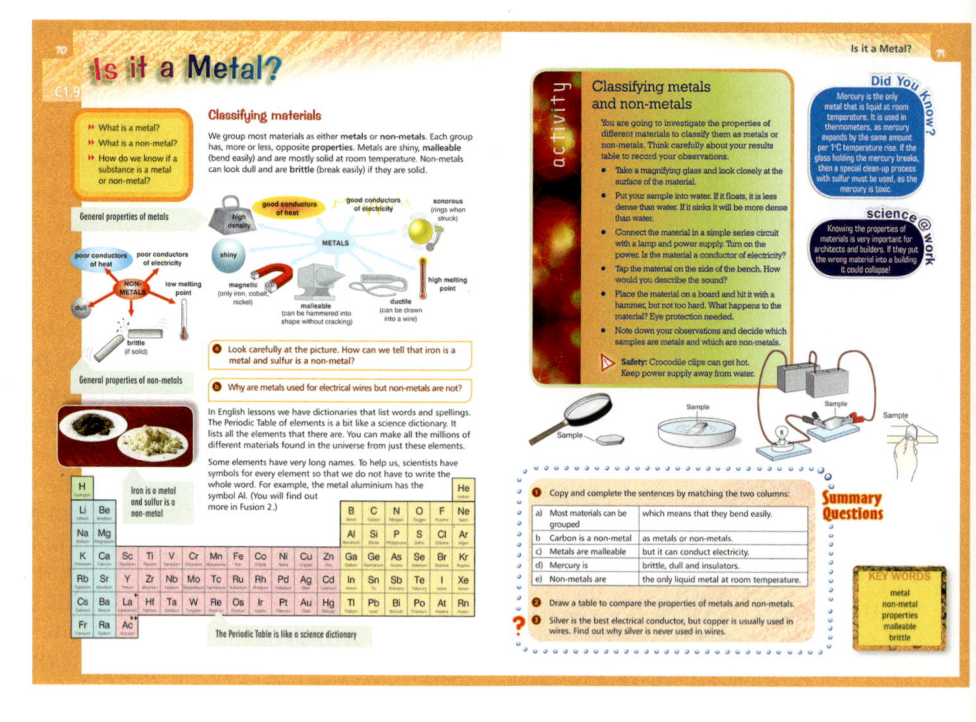

Learning Styles
Visual: Observing the behaviour of metals.
Kinaesthetic: Testing the properties of metals.
Interpersonal: Working with others during practical.
Intrapersonal: Understanding that some substances, such as graphite, are not easily classed as metals or non-metals.

The Lesson

Starter Suggestions

Is it a metal?
Give pupils a list of materials and ask them to divide them up into 'metallic' and 'non-metallic'. Ask them to give a reason why they put each one into a particular group. (5 mins)

Make it work
Ask pupils to design an electrical circuit to decide whether a material conducts electricity or not. You may wish to suggest that they use a cell, a lamp, wires and crocodile clips. (10 mins)

Answers to summary questions

1.
   a) Most materials can be grouped as metals or non-metals.
   b) Carbon is a non-metal but it can conduct electricity.
   c) Metals are malleable which means that they bend easily.
   d) Mercury is the only liquid metal at room temperature.
   e) Non-metals are brittle, dull, and insulators.

2.

Metals	Non-metals
conductor	insulator
malleable	brittle
ductile	
shiny	dull
sonorous	
high melting point	low melting point

3. Silver reacts with oxygen in the air to make a non-conducting coating. This happens quite quickly. Also silver is very expensive compared to copper and less abundant.

Is It a Metal?

Main Lesson

- Show pupils a piece of metal and a piece of wood. Ask them to suggest differences between them.
- Show the class a Periodic Table (see pupil book, page 70) and ask them to pick out the names of elements which they know to be metals.
- Explain that there are lots of metals on the Periodic Table and that they must come up with a set of 'rules' which describe what a metal is, while carrying out the main activity.
- Ask pupils to carry out the practical 'Classifying metals and non-metals'. A method for this is suggested in the pupil book. [Many of the materials pupils meet in the practical are not pure metals and non-metals in the elemental sense; they do not appear on the Periodic Table. However, the aim of this lesson is to convey typical metallic and non-metallic properties and the materials for the practical work have been chosen to be easy for the pupils to use. Most non-metal elements are gaseous at room temperature. A common misconception is that steel is a metal. Strictly speaking it is an alloy, a mixture of metals. Aluminium often has a dull appearance as it has a thin layer of aluminium oxide coating it. Graphite is a non-metal but, when carbon is in this form, some electrons are freed allowing it to conduct electricity.]
- Demonstrate the typical difference in melting points between metals and non-metals by heating, first a piece of copper and then a lump of sulfur.

Plenary Suggestions

That can't be right?
Show that a piece of graphite will conduct electricity even though it is a form of the non-metal carbon. Challenge pupils to say why it is probably still a non-metal. [Dull appearance, not sonorous, brittle, other forms of carbon, such as diamond, do not conduct electricity.] (5 mins)

Metal or non-metal?
Give pupils a list of the typical properties of:

Metals: shiny, conduct electricity, conduct heat, sonorous, malleable, ductile, high melting point, high density.

Non-metals: dull, insulator, brittle, low melting point, low density.

Give them the list mixed-up. The challenge is to sort the two groups of properties out. (10 mins)

Practical Support

Classifying metals and non-metals
This practical is designed to be carried out as a circus of short activities.

Equipment and materials required
Per station: a selection of metallic and non-metallic materials such as thick copper foil, thick zinc foil, iron nail, aluminium foil, rubber tubing, wood, sugar cube, sulfur flowers (lumps); 2–3 magnifying glasses, bowl (a dog's water bowl or a washing-up bowl will be adequate) half-filled with water, paper towels to dry materials; lamps (up to 6V), 3 wires, power supply (low voltage) to match lamps, 2 crocodile clips; board to protect bench, small hammer.

Details
Pupils should take a magnifying glass and look closely at the surface of the material.

They take their sample and put it into water. (You may wish to exclude sugar here as it will dissolve.) If it floats it is less dense than water, if it sinks it will be denser than water. [Metals will sink and non-metals should float.]

Pupils should then connect the material in a simple series circuit with a lamp and power supply. Turn on the power. Is the material a conductor of electricity? [Metals will conduct electricity, non-metals will not.]

They should place the material on a board and hit it with a hammer, but not too hard. What happens to the material?

Pupils should note down their observations and decide which samples are metals and which are non-metals.

Safety
Keep electrical conductivity test away from floating test. Pupils should wear eye protection when testing malleability.

Melting point demonstration

Equipment and materials required
Fume cupboard, iron nail, tongs, tin lid, piece of sulfur (if fume cabinet available), sugar cube (if no fume cabinet available), Bunsen burner, heat mat, tripod, gauze and matches.

Details
Holding the nail in the tongs, show that it does not melt in the flame of the Bunsen burner.

Now place either sulfur or sugar in the tin lid and show that it does melt. Do not heat for longer than necessary as both materials catch fire easily.

Safety
When sulfur burns it produces sulfur dioxide which is an irritant if inhaled. Carry out the heating of sulfur in a fume cupboard.

Sulfur: CLEAPSS Hazcard 96.

Plenary: That can't be right

Equipment and materials required
As per pupil practical for testing electrical conductivity except: 1 graphite electrode stick.

Details
Demonstrate that the graphite will conduct electricity.

Differentiation

SEN
There are many new key words and terms used in this lesson which pupils with poor literacy skills may need support with.

Extension
Challenge pupils to explain what a 'semi-metal' is. A good element for them to research here is silicon.

Answers to in-text questions

a Iron is shiny but sulfur is dull.

b Metals can conduct electricity whereas non-metals can't. Metals can be easily made into wires (ductile) without breaking (malleable), but non-metals would break (brittle).

C1.10 Burning

NC links for the lesson
- Elements and compounds show characteristic chemical properties and patterns in their behaviour.
- Assess risk and work safely in the laboratory, field and workplace.
- Use appropriate methods, including ICT, to communicate scientific information and contribute to presentations and discussions about scientific issues.

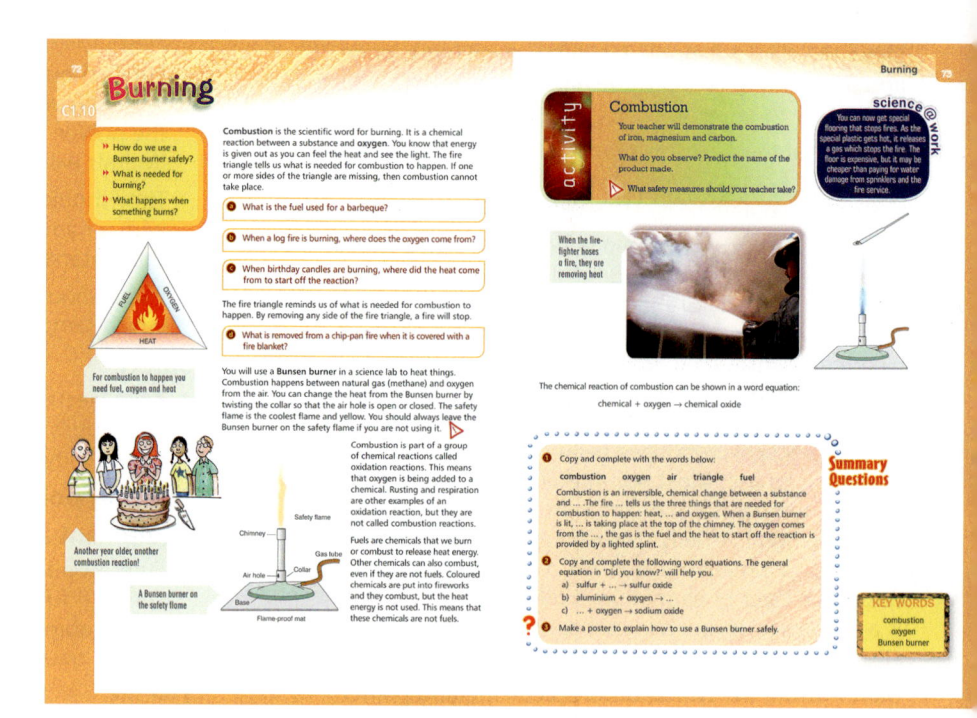

Answers to summary questions

1. Combustion is an irreversible chemical change between a substance and **oxygen**. The fire **triangle** tells us the three things that are needed for combustion to happen: heat, **fuel** and oxygen. When a Bunsen burner is lit, **combustion** is taking place at the top of the chimney. The oxygen comes from the **air**, the gas is the fuel and the heat to start off the reaction is provided by a lighted splint.

2. a) Oxygen.
   b) Aluminium oxide.
   c) Sodium.

3. Pupils should produce a poster to explain how to use a Bunsen burner safely.

Learning Objectives
Pupils should learn:
- How to use a Bunsen burner safely.
- What is needed for burning.
- What happens when something burns.

Learning Outcomes
- All pupils should be able to set up a Bunsen burner safely.
- Most pupils should be able to explain the laboratory safety rules.
- Some pupils should also be able to write word equations for the reactions they have seen.

How Science Works
- Explain how action has been taken to control obvious risk and how methods are adequate for the task. (1.2c)

Functional Skills Link-up

ICT
- Access, navigate and search internet sources of information purposefully and effectively. (Level 1) See Starter 'Who was he?'

English
- Present information in a logical sequence. (Level 1) See Plenary 'Bunsen's rule!'

Learning Styles
Auditory: Observing differences between Bunsen flames.
Kinaesthetic: Operating a Bunsen burner safely.
Interpersonal: Working in a way which keeps others safe.
Intrapersonal: Understanding the need to work safely.

Burning

The Lesson

Starter Suggestions

Who was he?
If Internet connection is available, ask pupils to find out who Robert Wilhelm Bunsen, who is credited with the invention of the Bunsen burner, was. Pupils who complete this quickly could try to think how a Bunsen burner might work. (10–15 mins)

Bunsens' rule!
Explain that Bonfire Night can be a dangerous evening if people don't think about the possible risks and how to avoid them happening. Ask pupils to write a set of safety rules that a family should follow when having a bonfire party on Bonfire Night. (5–10 mins)

Main Lesson

- Remind pupils about the general laboratory safety rules, especially those relating to experiments. They may have had access to or seen a Bunsen burner in earlier lessons, but the focus here is on getting the pupils to use one correctly.
- Ask them if they have heard of the fire triangle – some may have. If anyone knows, ask them to explain what it means. It may be useful here to have a lit candle, Bunsen burner or spirit burner in front of the class as a visual prompt. [Your local fire service may be willing to visit the school to talk to pupils about fire safety and even show a demonstration of fire extinguishers and chip-pan fires. This would link very well with work on the fire triangle.]
- There are instructions for setting up a Bunsen burner for the pupils to follow in the practical support section. You may wish to give them extra safety advice, such as the need to return to a yellow safety flame when not using the burner for a short time, and any extra local safety rules. It may be best to demonstrate all of this before allowing the pupils access to the apparatus.
- Explain to pupils that opening the air hole allows air to mix with the fuel (gas) and makes the flame hotter. The role of oxygen will be dealt with next lesson.
- Demonstrate the activity, ask the pupils to share their observations.

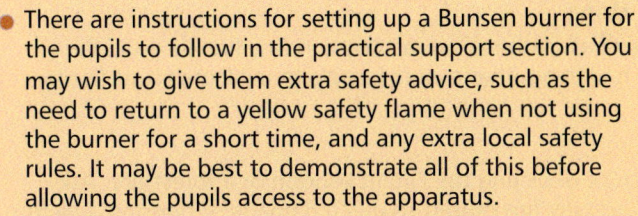

Plenary Suggestions

Act it out!
If you asked pupils to research who Robert Wilhelm Bunsen was at the start of the lesson, they could use their research to prepare and act out a short sketch about it. If your class are not dramatically inclined, you could divide them into two teams and get them to ask each other questions about him. (10–15 mins)

[The Bunsen Burner was not, in fact, invented by Robert Wilhelm Bunsen. Rather, it is the work of his assistant Peter Desaga and was completed in 1855. Desaga called his burner a 'Tirrill' burner, which was an improvement upon a burner designed by Michael Faraday. Most Bunsen burners are, in fact, 'Tirrill' burners.]

Bunsen's rule!
Ask pupils to write a set of instructions to allow other Year 7 pupils to use a Bunsen burner safely. Their instructions should cover setting up and lighting the burner, and how and when to use the safety flame. (5–10 mins)

Practical Support

Combustion demonstrations

Equipment and materials required
Heat mat, Bunsen burner, splints or matches, half a spatula of carbon (charcoal) powder, half a spatula of fine iron filings, half a spatula of magnesium powder.

Details
A suggested method for this experiment is:

Place the Bunsen burner on the centre of a heat-proof mat, away from the edge of the bench.

Put the gas tube onto the gas tap.

Make sure that the air hole is closed.

Get a lighted splint.

Turn on the gas tap.

Move the splint over the chimney of the Bunsen burner to light it.

Turn the collar so that the air hole is open and the flame is blue.

Take a small amount of carbon on the end of a spatula. Then sprinkle it gently into the flame. What do you observe? Predict the name of the product made.

Safety
Make sure anything that can burn is moved away from the Bunsen burner.

Tie long hair and clothes back so that they do not go into the flame.

Wear eye protection.

Iron filings are highly flammable: CLEAPSS Hazcard 55A.

Magnesium powder is highly flammable: CLEAPSS Hazcard 59A.

Differentiation

SEN
Ask pupils to match the safety rules in a laboratory with the reasons for the rule.

Extension
Ask pupils to write word equations for the reactions. Support for this is available in the pupil book.

Homework Suggestion

Pupils to find out what rules are in place at petrol stations to try to prevent fires.

Answers to in-text questions

a Charcoal.

b The air.

c A lighted match.

d Oxygen.

C1.11 Fuels and Oxygen

NC links for the lesson
- Elements and compounds show characteristic chemical properties and patterns in their behaviour.
- Use a range of scientific methods and techniques to develop and test ideas and explanations.
- Obtain, record and analyse data from a wide range of primary and secondary sources, including ICT sources, and use their findings to provide evidence for scientific explanations.
- Evaluate scientific evidence and working methods.
- Use appropriate methods, including ICT, to communicate scientific information and contribute to presentations and discussions about scientific issues.

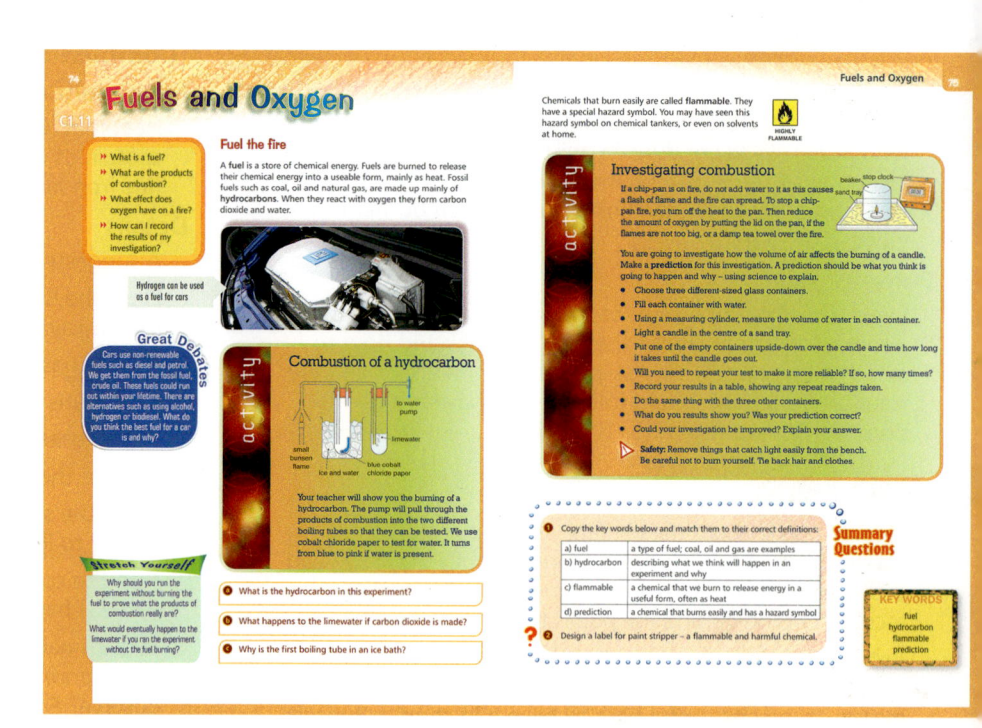

Learning Objectives
Pupils should learn:
- What a fuel is.
- The products of combustion.
- What effect oxygen has on a fire.
- How to record the results of an investigation.

Learning Outcomes
- All pupils will recall that oxygen is needed for burning and the fire triangle.
- Most pupils will recall that length of burning is related to amount of oxygen available.
- Some pupils will also draw a graph of their results.

How Science Works
- Describe patterns and trends in results and link this evidence to any prediction made. (1.2e)

Functional Skills Link-up
Mathematics
- Find mean and range. (Level 1)
- Collect and represent discrete and continuous data, using ICT where appropriate. (Level 2)

The Lesson

Starter Suggestions

Good thing / bad thing
Ask pupils to think of as many reasons as they can why fire is a good thing and, sometimes a bad thing. They should be able to think of at least five for each. (5 mins)

Fire of London
Show pupils a picture depicting the Fire of London or a forest fire. Ask them to think about why fire caused so much damage. [Choosing a picture that shows the buildings or trees close together may hint that the fire could move easily and that there was plenty of fuel available.] (5–10 mins)

Learning Styles
Visual: Observing the burning candles.
Auditory: Describing how to carry out the investigation.
Kinaesthetic: Carrying out the investigation into burning.
Interpersonal: Working with others during practical work.
Intrapersonal: Deciding how to plot a graph of results.

Answers to summary questions

1.
   a) Fuel: a chemical that burns easily and has a hazard symbol.
   b) Hydrocarbon: a type of fuel; coal, oil and gas are examples.
   c) Flammable: a chemical that we burn to release energy in a useful form, often as heat.
   d) Prediction: describing what we think will happen in an experiment and why.

2. Pupils should design a label for paint stripper.

Fuels and Oxygen

Main Lesson

- Remind pupils of the safety rules they learned in C1.10.
- Remind pupils of the fire triangle studied last lesson. Ask them to consider if a flame needs all the gases in the air or just some of them. [You may not wish to tell them that only oxygen is required until after the demonstration.]
- Demonstrate the products of burning by drawing the waste gases from a candle through cooled tube and limewater. Explain that this shows that both carbon dioxide and water (hydrogen oxide) are formed. They should recall the test for carbon dioxide from earlier lessons. Demonstrate that water is made by testing with cobalt chloride paper which changes from blue to pink if water is present.
- Establish that, as oxides are formed, oxygen is required for burning. [It is a common misconception that oxygen burns. Burning is generally an oxidation reaction; that is a substance may burn when it reacts with oxygen. Oxygen cannot react with oxygen and so does not burn. For burning to take place, a fuel (such as petrol) must react with oxygen. The reaction is fast enough for us to feel heat and see light being given off.]
- Explain that they are going to investigate whether the amount of air available affects how long a candle will burn.
- Get pupils to carry out 'Investigating combustion' described in the pupil book. You could, at this point, ask pupils to plan the investigation themselves, including a table for their results, if you have the time available.
- Ask pupils to plot a graph of their results, plotting jar size against candle burn time. If you want pupils to plot a line graph, they will need to know the volumes of the jars used. Establish the pattern that the greater the volume of the jar, the longer the candle burns. Ask pupils to say why they think this is the case [more oxygen in the larger jars than the smaller jars].
- Relate the experiment back to the fire triangle and explain that removing any part of the triangle puts the fire out.

Plenary Suggestions

Put it out!
Give pupils different ways of putting out a fire and ask them to explain why it works. [For example, spraying water on a fire cools it (takes away the heat), putting a fire break in a forest means the fuel will run out, spraying CO_2 foam restricts the oxygen supply.] (5–10 mins)

Safety first
Ask pupils to produce a fire safety leaflet for householders. They could include things such as dealing with chip-pan fires and being careful with cigarettes. (15 mins +)

Practical Support

Combustion of a hydrocarbon

Equipment and materials required
Candle or spirit burner filled with ethanol, glass funnel, two glass delivery tubes in 'U' shape, boiling tube with piece of blue cobalt chloride paper or 1 spatula of anhydrous copper sulfate, boiling tube one-third filled with limewater, rubber tubing, water suction pump.

Details
For detailed set-up, please refer to pupil book diagram. Turn on the water or hand pump to start sucking air through the system. Show pupils that this is happening by referring to the bubbling limewater as evidence. Light the flame and place under the funnel. Do not have the funnel too low or the flame will go out. Extinguish the flame as soon as the water and carbon dioxide tests have occurred.

Safety
Wear eye protection.
Cobalt chloride is toxic: CLEAPSS Hazcard 25.
Copper sulfate is harmful: CLEAPSS Hazcard 27C.
Limewater is an irritant: CLEAPSS Hazcard 18.

Investigating combustion

Equipment and materials required
2–4 different-sized glass containers: glass beakers will be fine, measuring cylinder, tray of sand, candle (about 2 cm tall), splints or matches, stop-watch.

Details
A suggested method for this experiment is detailed in the pupil book.

Safety
Wear eye protection.
Remove things that catch light easily from the bench.
Tie back hair and loose clothing.
Avoid skin contact with cobalt chloride paper.

Differentiation

SEN
If plotting line graphs many pupils in Year 7 will need support in preparing the axes. It may be better just to ask them to identify the pattern that 'the larger the jar, the longer the candle burns for' and then to explain why this is.

Homework Suggestion

Pupils to find out how long the world's oil reserves are predicted to last. [Answers will vary wildly, as oil company optimism changes regularly, but the important point to establish is that oil is a finite resource.]

Answers to in-text questions

a Natural gas (methane).
b Turns from colourless to cloudy.
c To make the water vapour condense.

C1.12 Making Oxygen

NC links for the lesson
- Elements and compounds show characteristic chemical properties and patterns in their behaviour.
- Use a range of scientific methods and techniques to develop and test ideas and explanations.
- Assess risk and work safely in the laboratory, field and workplace.
- Carry out practical and investigative activities, both individually and in groups.

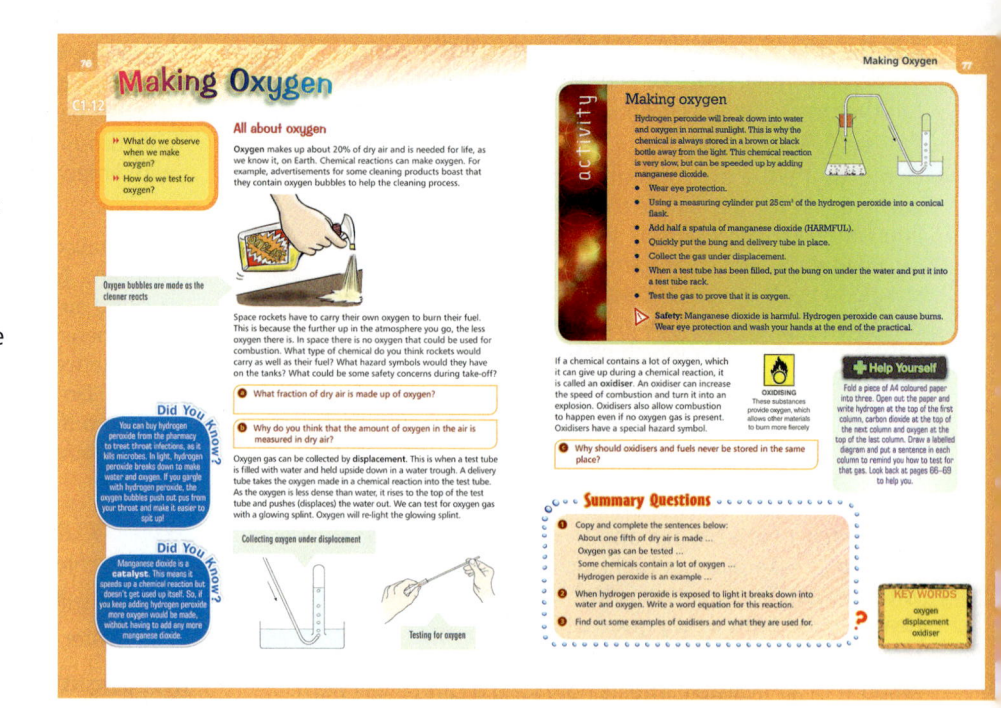

Learning Objectives

Pupils should learn:
- What we observe when hydrogen peroxide reacts with manganese dioxide.
- How we test for oxygen.

Learning Outcomes
- All pupils should record observations and be able to collect gas by displacement.
- Most pupils should recall the test for oxygen.
- Some pupils should also be able to write word equations.

How Science Works
- Explain how action has been taken to control obvious risk and how methods are adequate for the task. (1.2c)

Functional Skills Link-up

English
- Make relevant contributions to discussions, responding appropriately to others. (Level 1) See Plenary 'Ask the expert'.

Learning Styles

Auditory: Asking or answering questions in the 'Ask the expert' plenary.

Kinaesthetic: Collecting oxygen.

Interpersonal: Taking part in class discussion in the 'Ask the expert' plenary.

Intrapersonal: Understanding that oxygen had to be discovered and that all the gases in our atmosphere are not the same.

Making Oxygen

The Lesson

Starter Suggestions

Fire, fire!
Ask pupils to draw the fire triangle from recall, which they should remember from C1.10 and C1.11. (5 mins)

The stuff of life
Ask pupils to make a list of all the things we need oxygen for and some unwanted things it does. [Car engine, bonfire, Bunsen burner, respiration, to help things rot, food going off, ageing our skin, rusting, corrosion of metal, welding.] (5–10 mins)

Main Lesson

- Remind pupils about combustion and the rest of the work covered in C1.10 and C1.11.
- Remind pupils how important oxygen is to many processes on Earth, including respiration.
- Demonstrate to pupils how to collect a gas by displacement, as they are unlikely to have done this before. It is quite tricky, so be sure to emphasise to make sure that the boiling tube is completely full of water before they start collecting the gas. Place a bung in while the tube is still submerged under the water.
- Ask them to carry out the decomposition of hydrogen peroxide, collect the gas produced and test for oxygen. At this level, most pupils do not need to know that the hydrogen peroxide decomposes in the presence of the manganese(IV) oxide catalyst. They can simply observe it as a chemical change.
- Once they have collected two or three test tubes of oxygen, show them how to test for oxygen.
- **Issues / Key concepts in pupil book:** The hazard symbol on a rocket's tank which contains the oxygen supply would be 'Oxidant'. Oxygen is usually carried as a liquid compound of oxygen rather than the element. The rocket fuel, which is usually hydrazine (N_2H_4), would need to carry the hazard symbol for 'Highly flammable'. The main risk on take-off is of explosion, which is exactly what happened to the NASA space shuttle 'Challenger' in the late 1980s.

Plenary Suggestions

It's a gas!
Ask pupils to match the name of a gas (carbon dioxide, hydrogen or oxygen) to the correct gas test and the correct test result. (5–10 mins)

Ask the expert
Invite a panel of three pupils to the front. Choosing at least one high attaining pupil might be a good idea. The rest of the class must then think of questions about this topic. The person who asks the question has to decide if they were given the correct answer or not. (10–15 mins)

Practical Support

Making oxygen

Equipment and materials required
Per group: conical flask, 25 cm³ of 10 vol. hydrogen peroxide solution, bung with single hole attached to rubber delivery tube, 2–3 boiling tubes for gas collection with bungs, test-tube rack, bowl, half-filled with water (a dog water bowl is ideal), spatula, manganese (IV) oxide powder, splints and access to a lit Bunsen burner.

Details
A suggested method for this experiment is detailed in the pupil book. Pupils need to ensure that the boiling tube they use to collect oxygen in is brim full with water before they invert it. They need to check that there is no air inside before they start to fill it with gas. It is advisable to get pupils to collect more than one tube of gas as the first tube often contains air from inside the apparatus.

Safety
Wear eye protection.
Hydrogen peroxide solution: CLEAPSS Hazcard 50.
Manganese(IV) oxide powder is harmful: CLEAPSS Hazcard 60.

Differentiation

SEN
Some pupils may struggle to collect enough gas to test. You may wish to have a few tubes of oxygen from a cylinder to cover for this eventuality.

Extension
Ask pupils to find out where they might come across hydrogen peroxide in everyday life. (It is used by hairdressers to bleach hair, hence the term 'peroxide blonde').

Answers to in-text questions

a One fifth.

b Normal air contains water and the amount of this changers with the weather conditions. The percentage of oxygen would vary if the amount of water varied, but if we calculate it for dry air it remains constant.

c If they get hot, they could explode.

Answers to summary questions

1 About one fifth of dry air is made up of oxygen, the rest is mainly nitrogen gas.
Oxygen gas can be tested by relighting a glowing splint.
Some chemicals contain a lot of oxygen that they easily give away in a chemical reaction. Hydrogen peroxide is an example of an oxidiser which breaks down into water and oxygen.

2 hydrogen peroxide → water + oxygen

3 Pupils should find out some examples of oxidisers and what they are used for.

Answers to Reversible and Irreversible Changes – End of Topic Questions

Answers to know your stuff questions

1 a)

IRRITANT — toxic
TOXIC — flammable
FLAMMABLE — irritant   [3]

b) Irritant.   [1]

c) Either: wear eye protection or wash hands after use.   [1]

2 a)

Chemical	Colour	pH
Water	green	7
Soap	blue/purple	10
Stomach acid	red/pink	1
Lemon juice	yellow	3 5
Sodium hydroxide	purple	13 14

[5]

b) Stomach acid and lemon juice.   [2]

c) Either: a new substance had been made or a colour change observed.   [1]

d) Neutralisation.   [1]

3 a) Irreversible *or* chemical.   [1]

b) One of: hear fizzing, see bubbles, effervescence, see foam.   [1]

c) Hydrogen.   [1]

d) Most reactive calcium
    magnesium
    zinc
Least reactive copper   [2]

4 a) Combustion. [Accept burning.]   [1]

b) methane + oxygen → water + carbon dioxide   [1]

c) Pass gas through limewater;   [1]
and it will change from colourless to cloudy.   [1]

d) More air/oxygen or better mixing of gases.   [1]

Reversible and Irreversible Changes – End of Topic Questions

How Science Works

▼ Question 1 (level 4)

Adam investigated how the amount of air in a jar affects the time a candle burns for.

a Which piece of apparatus would he use to measure the time? Choose from the list below:

  measuring cylinder   thermometer
  stop-watch [1]

b What is the independent variable in Adam's experiment? (This is the variable which Adam has chosen to change in each test.) [1]

c What is the dependent variable in Adam's experiment? (This is the variable that Adam used to judge the effect of varying the independent variable.) [1]

d Give one control variable in Adam's experiment. [1]

▼ Question 2 (level 5)

Sundeep investigated the reaction between metals and hydrochloric acid. He measured the volume of gas that three metals gave off in one minute. He found out that silver released no gas, zinc gave off 1 cm³ and 5 cm³ was made by magnesium.

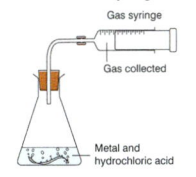

a Copy and complete Sundeep's results table:

Metal	Volume of gas
Silver	0
	1
Magnesium	

[2]

b How could Sundeep best display his results? Choose from the list below:

  bar chart   line graph   pie chart [1]

c How could Sundeep make his work more reliable? [2]

▼ Question 3 (level 6)

Emma investigated the volume of gas given off when calcium carbonate was added to hydrochloric acid. She recorded her results in the following table:

Time (s)	Volume of gas (cm³)
0	0
10	15
20	28
30	17
40	40
50	42
60	43

a Copy and complete the graph below. Include the missing point and the labels on each axis. [3]

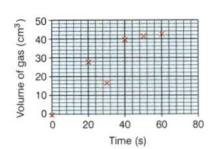

b Draw a line of best fit and circle the point that does not fit the pattern. [2]

Answers to How Science Works questions

1
  a Stop-watch. [1]
  b Time. [1]
  c Volume of air. [1]
  d Any relevant answer, e.g. same candle, same length of wick, same shapes of jar. [1]

2
  a

Metal	Volume of gas (cm³)
Silver	0
Zinc	1
Magnesium	5

[2]

  b Bar chart. [1]
  c Repeat each experiment; [1]
  and take an average of the gas volumes. [1]
  [Also accept checking their work against the data collected by other people.]

3
  a [Marks for missing point and axes labels.] [3]
  b [Marks for line of best fit and circled point.] [2]

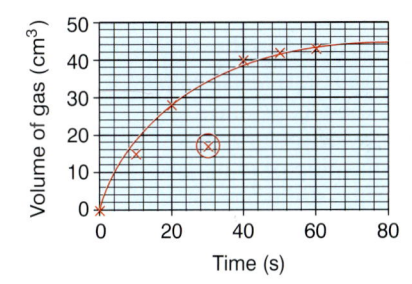

C2.1 Particles in Action

NC links for the topic
- The particle model provides explanations for the different physical properties and behaviour of matter.
- Using ideas and models to explain phenomena and developing them to generate and test theories.
- Critically analysing and evaluating evidence from observations and experiments.
- Use a range of scientific methods and techniques to develop and test ideas and explanations.
- Assess risk and work safely in the laboratory, field and workplace.
- Carry out practical and investigative activities, both individually and in groups.
- Obtain, record and analyse data from a wide range of primary and secondary sources, including ICT sources, and use their findings to provide evidence for scientific explanations.
- Evaluate scientific evidence and working methods.
- Use appropriate methods, including ICT, to communicate scientific information and contribute to presentations and discussions about scientific issues.

Level descriptors for the topic
- **AT3 level 4:** Pupils recall simple scientific knowledge and terminology of the properties and classification of materials. They describe some phenomena and processes, such as separation methods, drawing on scientific knowledge and understanding. They recognise that evidence can support or refute scientific ideas, for example the classification of solids, liquids and gases. They recognise some applications and implications of science, such as methods for separating mixtures.
- **AT3 level 5:** Pupils recall straightforward scientific knowledge and terminology of materials and their properties. They describe phenomena, drawing on abstract ideas, such as the properties of solids. They apply and use knowledge and understanding in familiar contexts, such as identifying changes of state. They recognise that both evidence and creative thinking contribute to the development of scientific ideas, such as basing separation methods for mixtures on physical and chemical properties. They describe applications and implications of science, such as methods for separating mixtures.
- **AT3 level 6:** Pupils recall detailed scientific knowledge and terminology of properties of materials. They describe phenomena and processes using abstract ideas, such as the particle model applied to solids, liquids and gases.

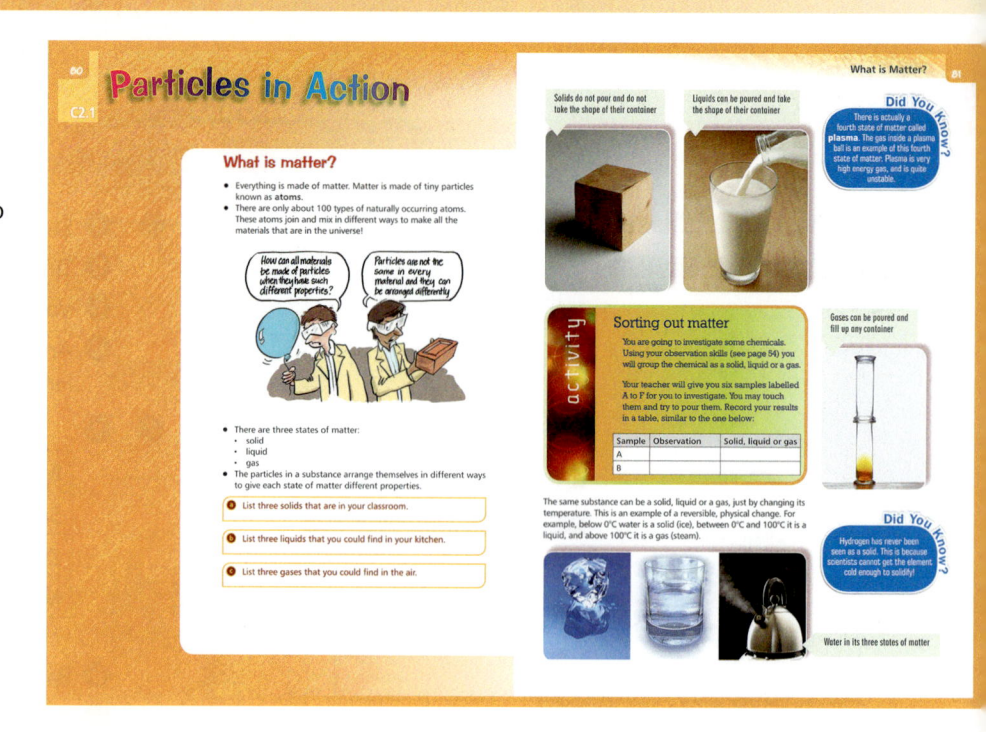

Learning Objectives
Pupils should learn:
- What matter is.
- How matter can be classified.

Learning Outcomes
- All pupils should be able to classify matter.
- Most pupils should be able to recall that everything is made of matter.
- Some pupils should also be able to explain why a sample belongs to a particular grouping.

How Science Works
- Describe and record observations and evidence systematically. (1.2d)

Functional Skills Link-up
English
- Write clearly and coherently including an appropriate level of detail. (Level 1) (Description of observations.)

Learning Styles
Visual: Making observations of the behaviour of materials.
Auditory: Describing their observations of materials.
Kinaesthetic: Manipulating solids, liquids and gases.
Interpersonal: Sharing ideas with other pupils.
Intrapersonal: Understanding that not all substances are easy to classify as solids, liquids or gases.

They take account of a number of factors or use abstract ideas or models, in their explanations of phenomena and processes. They apply and use knowledge and understanding, such as relating changes of state to energy transfers, in unfamiliar contexts. They explain the importance of some applications and implications of science, such as the design of separation techniques.

The Lesson

Starter Suggestions

Odd one out
Show pupils four pictures: a coin, a log, a rock and a stream (water). Ask them to choose the odd one out, giving a reason. Allow open responses, but eventually guide them to considering the way the materials behave. [Water is the odd one out, as it is a liquid and the picture shows that it flows.] (5 mins)

What is it?
Place some items into separate opaque bags. Ask a pupil to feel inside the bag and describe what it feels like, not what they think it is. Choose items such as: a metal block, a piece of wood, a tennis ball or some golden syrup sealed inside a freezer bag. (10 mins)

Main Lesson

- Ask pupils whether something obvious in the room, such as a table or a wall, is a solid a liquid or a gas. Ask them to try to explain why they think so, in order to see if they can explain their ideas.
- Introduce the practical activity 'Sorting out matter', described in the pupil book. Say to pupils that they must decide whether the objects and substances they are given are solids, liquids or gases. In the 'Observation' column they should write down what they saw that helped them to decide.
- Elicit pupils' opinions about the substances they have seen and establish the following broad descriptions:
Solids: do not pour and do not take the shape of their container.
Liquids: can be poured and take the shape of their container.
Gases: can be poured and fill up any container

Plenary Suggestions

Solid, liquid or gas?
Show pupils a sponge and ask them whether it is a solid, a liquid or a gas. Ask them to explain their reasons. [If left on the side it doesn't change shape: solid; if pushed into a beaker it will take its shape: liquid. A sponge is not a true solid, but a foam, i.e. a mixture of a solid and a gas.] (5mins)

What's the matter?
Ask pupils to write a description of a solid, a liquid and a gas in their own words. (10 mins)

Practical Support

Sorting out matter

Equipment and materials required
Per group: 100 cm^3 beaker with water in [liquid], 100 cm^3 beaker containing golden syrup or runny honey in liquid, a modelling balloon inflated and labelled to show it contains air in gas, a 'dry ice' smoke machine or a video clip of 'dry-ice' clouds at a disco or concert [gas], a small block of metal such as a 1 kg mass [solid], a block of wood [solid].

Details
Ask pupils to handle the materials and to record their observations of the way they behave. Gases are difficult to observe as most are colourless. The balloon can be squeezed to show that air can flow and fills the whole balloon. Dry ice 'smoke' shows a gas flowing and moving freely.

Some of the substances met in this lesson are not true solids, liquids or gases. However, the emphasis here is on learning the properties of these classes of matter rather than the names of particular substances. It may be best to operate this activity as a 'circus' rather than providing duplicate equipment for each pupil group.

Safety
If using a real dry-ice smoke machine, check room is well ventilated. The fumes may affect asthmatics. Dry ice can cause burns.

Solid, liquid or gas plenary

Equipment and materials required
A piece of sponge, e.g. car cleaning sponge, a large beaker.

Details
Refer to plenary description: 'Solid, liquid or gas?'

Differentiation

SEN
Lower attaining pupils may only be able to make very simple observations during the practical and may need help in recording them correctly. Emphasise sorting materials into solids, liquids and gases above the reasons for the choice.

Extension
Show pupils some tomato ketchup and ask them to think about why it could be considered to be a solid [doesn't appear to flow] and a liquid [does flow very slowly].

Answers to in-text questions

a Any suitable answer, e.g. wood, paper, steel.
b Any suitable answer, e.g. milk, water, squash.
c Three of: oxygen, nitrogen, carbon dioxide, argon.

C2.2 Solids

NC links for the lesson
- The particle model provides explanations for the different physical properties and behaviour of matter.
- Use a range of scientific methods and techniques to develop and test ideas and explanations.
- Assess risk and work safely in the laboratory, field and workplace.
- Carry out practical and investigative activities, both individually and in groups.

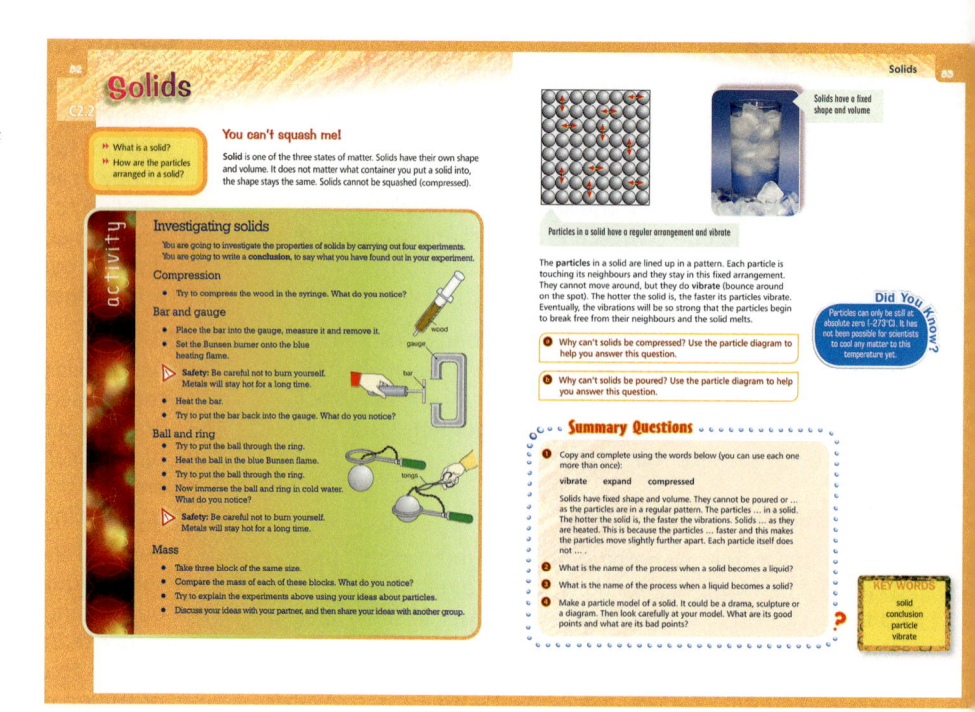

Learning Objectives
Pupils should learn:
- The properties of a solid.
- How the particles in a solid are arranged.

Learning Outcomes
- All pupils should be able to recall the properties of a solid.
- Most pupils should be able to draw the particle diagram for a solid.
- Some pupils should also be able to explain the properties of a solid in terms of the particle diagram.

How Science Works
- Use an existing model or analogy to explain a phenomenon. (1.1a1)
- Recognise that scientific evidence can be used to support or disprove theories. (1.1a3)

Functional Skills Link-up
English
- Use language, format and structure suitable for purpose and audience. (Level 1) See Plenary 'What's it like?'

Learning Styles
Visual: Making observations of the behaviour of solids.
Auditory: Describing how solids behave.
Kinaesthetic: Carrying out practical work on solids.
Interpersonal: Working with others to develop a drama of particle behaviour.
Intrapersonal: Understanding the concept that matter is made of particles too small to see.

The Lesson

Starter Suggestions

Solid as a rock
Pupils must list as many solid materials as they can see in the room. Longest list wins. (5 mins)

True or false?
Give pupils a list of statements that may apply to the way solids behave. They must decide which ones are true. (10 mins)

Main Lesson

- Remind pupils of the work they did last lesson, where they began to look at the differences between solids, liquids and gases [solids have a fixed shape]. Explain that in this lesson they are going to investigate further the properties of solids and to try to explain them.
- Ask pupils to carry out, or demonstrate, the 'Investigating solids' activity described in the pupil book.
- After the practical, gather together the results. [Solids cannot be compressed, when heated solids expand and similar-sized blocks can have a different mass (different density).]
- Introduce pupils to the idea that matter is made of tiny particles. Introduce the word 'atom' but it may be best, especially with lower attaining pupils, to stick to the word 'particles' rather than 'atoms' as, for most substances, the particles are molecules made of several atoms.
- Show pupils a tray that has a layer of marbles covering about two-thirds of its surface. Tilt the tray to one corner slightly and explain that, in solids, the particles are all packed close together. Very gently shake the tray to represent the particles vibrating. Emphasise that the particles can vibrate but not move around and remain touching most of the time.
- Ask pupils if they think they can use the model to explain some of the results of the practical. Solids keep their shape and cannot be compressed as the particles cannot move and are already touching. They cannot be pushed closer together. Raising the temperature causes the particles to vibrate more, meaning they get slightly further apart. This causes the material to expand. **Note:** the particles themselves do not expand as many pupils believe. Solids have different densities because the particles do not pack together as well in some solids as others. The better the packing the higher the density.

Plenary Suggestions

Particle people
Ask the pupils to work in groups of about six to demonstrate how the particles in a solid behave, using themselves as the particles. They should try to represent as many features of solids as possible [non-compressibility, expansion on heating, keeping shape]. (5 mins)

What's it like?
Ask pupils to write a description of a solid for the benefit of Year 6 pupils. Ask some of the class to read their work out. (10 mins)

Practical Support

Investigating solids

Equipment and materials required
Per group: syringe with a piece of wood in it (not sawdust), metal bar and gauge, Bunsen burner, 'ball and ring' expansion apparatus, three metal blocks of identical size, balance.

Details
See pupil book. Ask pupils to note down what they have found and to try to explain why they think has happened.

Safety
Care must be taken when heating the metal bar and ball. The metal remains hot for a considerable time afterwards.

Differentiation

SEN
The idea of particles is highly conceptual and lower attaining pupils may well struggle with the idea. It is important that as many pupils as possible can represent solids using a particle diagram, even if they cannot fully explain it.

Extension
Ask pupils to explain why talc, which is a solid, can be made to behave like a liquid or even a gas. [Although it's a solid it is ground into a powder. The individual pieces of that powder can move separately, allowing the substance to flow like a liquid and, if the container is banged on the desk, to spread out like a gas.]

Homework Suggestion

Pupils to make a model of the particles in a solid.

Answers to in-text questions

a All the particles are touching. So when you push them, they cannot squeeze any closer together.

b All the particles are in a fixed arrangement and cannot move past each other.

Answers to summary questions

1 Solids have fixed shape and volume. They cannot be poured or **compressed** as the particles are in a regular pattern. The particles **vibrate** in a solid. The hotter the solid is, the faster the vibrations. Solids **expand** as they are heated. This is because the particles **vibrate** faster and this makes the particles move slightly further apart. Each particle itself does not **expand**.

2 Melting or fusing.

3 Freezing or solidifying.

4 Pupils should make a particle model of a solid – it could be a drama, a sculpture or a diagram. They should then discuss good and bad points of their model.

C2.3 Liquids

NC links for the lesson
- The particle model provides explanations for the different physical properties and behaviour of matter.
- Use a range of scientific methods and techniques to develop and test ideas and explanations.
- Assess risk and work safely in the laboratory, field and workplace.
- Carry out practical and investigative activities, both individually and in groups.

Learning Objectives

Pupils should learn:
- The properties of a liquid.
- How the particles in a liquid are arranged.

Learning Outcomes
- All pupils should be able to recall the properties of a liquid.
- Most pupils should be able to draw the particle diagram for a liquid.
- Some pupils should also be able to explain the properties of a liquid in terms of the particle diagram.

How Science Works
- Use an existing model or analogy to explain a phenomenon. (1.1a1)

Functional Skills Link-up
English
- Use language, format and structure suitable for purpose and audience. (Level 1) See Plenary 'What's it like?'

Learning Styles
Visual: Making observations of the behaviour of liquids.
Auditory: Describing how liquids behave.
Kinaesthetic: Carrying out practical work on liquids.
Interpersonal: Working with others to develop a drama of particle behaviour.
Intrapersonal: Understanding the concept that matter is made of particles too small to see.

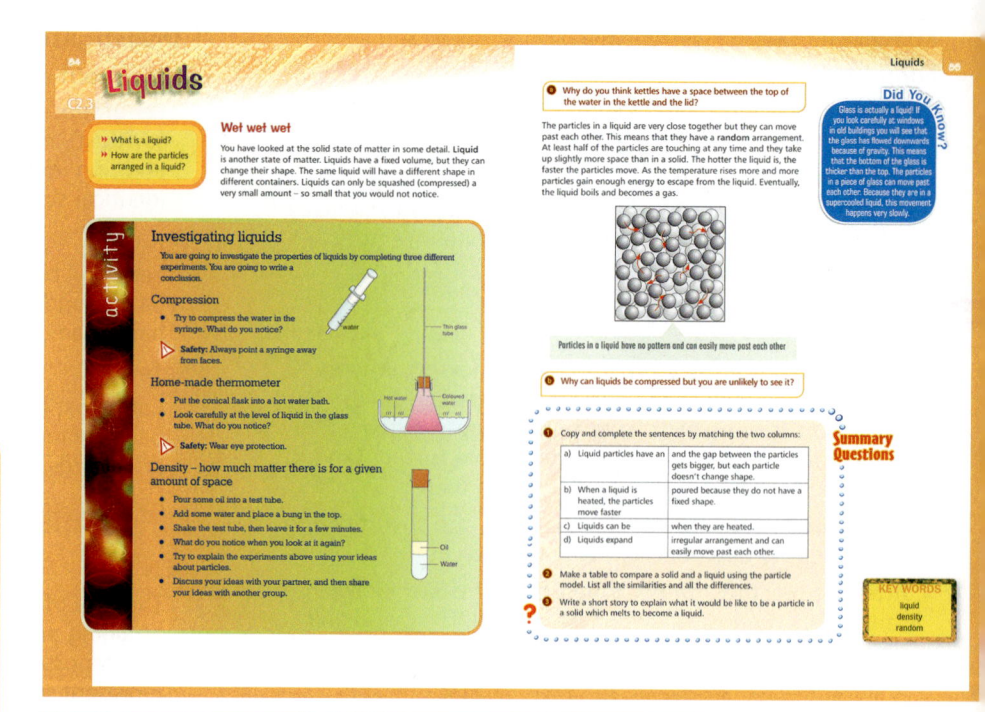

Answers to summary questions

1
a) Liquid particles have an irregular arrangement and can move past each other.
b) When a liquid is heated, the particles move faster and the gap between each particle gets bigger, but each particle doesn't change shape.
c) Liquids can be poured because they do not have a fixed shape.
d) Liquids expand when they are heated.

2

Similarities	Differences
Contains particles	Regular arrangement of particles in solid, irregular in liquid
Particles are not still	Particles can move in a liquid, but vibrate in a solid
Particles touch	In a liquid only 50% of particles touch at any time

3 Pupils should write a short story to explain what it is like to be a particle in a solid which melts to become a liquid.

Answers to in-text questions

a Water will expand as it is heated. This is because the particles are moving further apart. Without this space for expansion, the water would overflow from the kettle.

b Liquid particles occupy slightly more space than solid particles, so they can get closer together. But, the extra space is so small you are unlikely to be able to see it.

The Lesson

Starter Suggestions

Liquid asset
Pupils must list as many liquid materials as they can think of. Longest list wins. (5 mins)

True or false?
Give pupils a list of statements that may apply to the way liquids behave. They must decide which ones are true. (10 mins)

Main Lesson

- Remind pupils of the work they did about solids last lesson. Ask them to describe how liquids are different from solids. [They flow and take the shape of a container.]
- Ask pupils to carry out, or demonstrate, the activity 'Investigating liquids' which is described in the pupil book.
- After the practical gather together the results. [Liquids cannot be visibly compressed, when heated liquids expand (the level rises up the straw) and that they can have a different density (oil floats on water).]
- Refer back to the particle model introduced to pupils when learning about solids. Show pupils a tray which has a layer of marbles covering about two-thirds of its surface. Tilt the tray to one corner slightly and explain that, in liquids, the particles are all packed close together but they can slide past each other. Gently shake the tray to represent the particles vibrating. You will have to shake slightly harder than when trying to represent a solid – a little practice is recommended. Emphasise that the particles can vibrate and slide past each other but remain touching most of the time.
- Ask pupils if they think they can use the model to explain some of the results of the practical. [Particles can slide past each other means that a liquid can change shape and flow. Particles mostly touching means that a liquid cannot be compressed enough to see it. High density liquids have closer packed particles.]

Plenary Suggestions

Particle people
Ask the pupils to work in groups of about six to demonstrate how the particles in a liquid behave, using themselves as the particles. They should try to represent as many features of liquids as possible [non-compressibility, expansion on heating, ability to flow]. (5 mins)

What's it like?
Ask pupils to write a description of a liquid for the benefit of Year 6 pupils. Ask some of the class to read their work out. (10 mins)

Practical Support

Investigating liquids

Equipment and materials required
Per group: syringe filled with water and the end sealed with resin or glue, conical flask filled almost to brim with coloured water (use food colouring), bung to fit conical flask with 20 cm long straight glass delivery tube inserted through it, glass straw, beaker larger than flask half-filled with hot water (hot tap water should be sufficient), test tube and bung, 2 dropping pipettes, 5 cm^3 of cold water, 5 cm^3 of cooking oil.

Details
See pupil book. Get pupils to note down what they have found and to try to explain why they think it has happened.

The end of the syringe needs to be well sealed before the pupils use it. Many of them will try very hard to compress the liquid and if the glue seal fails water will shoot out. The expansion of heated water is most obvious if the water starts (when cold) about one-third of the way up the delivery tube.

Safety
Care should be exercised when using hot water. Pupils should be well controlled.

Crazy custard (Extension)

Equipment and materials required
Per group: small plastic tub (250 g margarine tub or similar), water, cornflour, 2 spatulas (one for stirring and one for spooning out cornflour).

Details
See Extension notes. The mixture needs to be very thick, but not so thick that dry cornflour is visible. If the dish is tipped the mixture will flow like a liquid. A finger can be slowly pushed into the mixture but if it is poked quickly this will not be possible – the mixture becomes hard.

Differentiation

SEN
The idea of particles is highly conceptual and lower attaining pupils may well struggle with the idea. It is important that as many pupils as possible can represent liquids using the particle diagram, even if they cannot fully explain it.

Extension
'Crazy custard' is an example of shear-thickening which is exhibited by many liquids. When a force is applied to a liquid the particles attempt to move away by sliding over each other. If they cannot do this fast enough the mixture appears thicker than it is normally. Water exhibits this behaviour if you 'belly-flop' into a pool. 'Crazy custard' thickens so much it becomes solid.

If you ask pupils to consider whether glass is a solid or a liquid, as suggested in the 'Did you know?', you may wish to provide the follow information to help them. The particles in glass are not as uniformly arranged as in most solids; they share much of the randomness of arrangement that liquids do. Many scientists believe that glass continues to flow even once cooled and cite the fact that many old windows are thicker at the bottom than the top and rippled as evidence. However, it is unlikely that this is true and there are old windows which apparently defy gravity by having the thicker edge at the top. A more probable explanation for this lies in the way sheet glass used to be made. Glass sheets used to be made by spinning semi-molten glass. These were not very flat and slightly thicker at the outside edge. When these sheets were cut the heavier, thicker edge was usually mounted in the frame at the bottom. Modern plate glass is made floating on liquid tin. It may be true that cold glass flows, but the process is too slow to measure reliably.

Homework Suggestion

Pupils could make a model of the particles in a liquid.

C2.4 Gases

NC links for the lesson
- The particle model provides explanations for the different physical properties and behaviour of matter.
- Use a range of scientific methods and techniques to develop and test ideas and explanations.
- Assess risk and work safely in the laboratory, field and workplace.
- Carry out practical and investigative activities, both individually and in groups.

Learning Objectives
Pupils should learn:
- The properties of a gas.
- How the particles in a gas are arranged.

Learning Outcomes
- All pupils should be able to recall the properties of a gas.
- Most pupils should be able to draw the particle diagram for a gas.
- Some pupils should also be able to explain the properties of a gas in terms of the particle diagram.

How Science Works
- Use an existing model or analogy to explain a phenomenon. (1.1a1)
- Recognise that scientific evidence can be used to support or disprove theories. (1.1a3)

Functional Skills Link-up
English
- Use language, format and structure suitable for purpose and audience. (Level 1) See Plenary 'What's it like?'

Learning Styles
Visual: Making observations of the behaviour of gases.
Auditory: Describing how gases behave.
Kinaesthetic: Carrying out practical work on gases.
Interpersonal: Working with others to develop a drama of particle behaviour.
Intrapersonal: Understanding the concept that matter is made of particles too small to see.

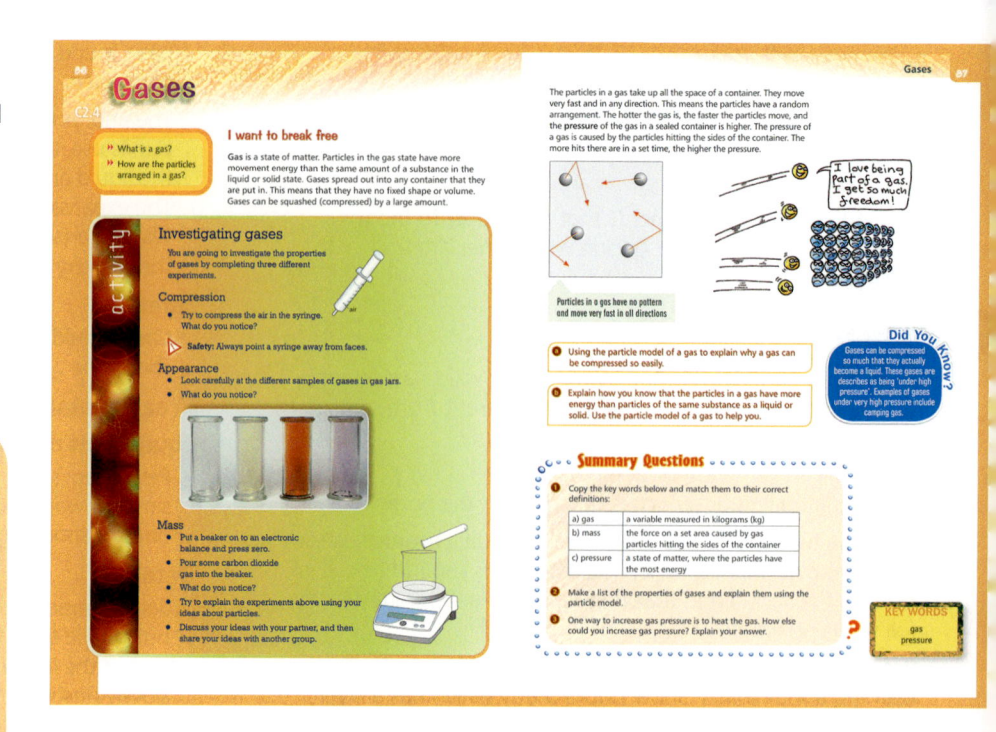

The Lesson

Starter Suggestions

Life's a gas
Pupils must list as many gases as they can think of. Longest list wins. (5 mins)

True or false
Give pupils a list of statements that may apply to the way gases behave. They must decide which ones are true. (10 mins)

Answers to summary questions

1.
   a) Gas: a state of matter, where the particles have the most energy.
   b) Mass: a variable measured in kilograms (kg).
   c) Pressure: the force on a set area caused by gas particles hitting the sides of the container.

2.

Property	Explanation
Pour easily	Particles can move past each other
Compress easily	There is a lot of space between particles
Transparent	There is a lot of space between particles, allowing light to pass through easily
No fixed shape or volume	The particles can move quickly in any direction

3. Compress the gas, this means that there are the same number of particles in a smaller amount of space, and therefore they are more likely to hit the sides of the container and increase pressure. Alternatively, pump more gas into the container, so there are more particles of gas in the same amount of space.

Gases

Main Lesson

- Remind pupils of the work they did about solids and liquids in the last two lessons. Ask them to describe how gases are different from solids and liquids. [They flow, fill the whole container and can move freely.]
- Ask pupils to carry out, or demonstrate, the activity 'Investigating gases' which is described in the pupil book.
- After the practical gather together the results. [Gases can easily be compressed, gases can be seen to fill the whole container and gases have mass.]
- Refer back to the particle model introduced to pupils when learning about solids. Show pupils a tray which has a layer of marbles covering about one-tenth of it's surface. Shake the tray quite hard to represent the particles vibrating. A little practice is recommended in order that you will be able to show effectively that the particles have so much energy that they rarely touch and move around freely. Explain that the particles move in straight lines and change direction when they strike another particle or the walls of the container, like the balls on a snooker table.
- Ask pupils if they think they can use the model to explain some of the results of the practical [Particles not touching each other means that a gas can change shape and flow and that it can be compressed by pushing the particles closer together. That particles can move freely means that a gas will fill the whole of a container.]

Plenary Suggestions

Particle people
Ask the pupils to work in groups of about six to demonstrate how the particles of a gas behave, using themselves as the particles. They should try to represent as many features of gases as possible [compressibility, expansion on heating, ability to flow and fill a container]. (5 mins)

What's it like?
Ask pupils to write a description of a gas for the benefit of Year 6 pupils. Ask some of the class to read their work out. (10 mins)

Practical Support

Investigating gases

Equipment and materials required

Per group: syringe filled with air and with end sealed with resin or glue, sealed gas jar of chlorine gas, sealed gas jar of bromine gas (place a few drops of bromine liquid into a gas jar), sensitive balance, large beaker and a gas jar containing carbon dioxide.

Details
See pupil book.

The carbon dioxide can be poured into the beaker on the balance which will register an increase in mass. If demonstrating, it may be possible to link the balance to a computer and to display the mass to the class via a projector.

Safety
Wear eye protection.

Chlorine is toxic: CLEAPSS Hazcard 22A; bromine is toxic and corrosive: CLEAPSS Hazcard 15A; they should both be kept in a fume cabinet. Wear chemical protective gloves.

Do not let anyone smell the gases.

Ensure technician is aware of the hazards.

Bottle rocket (Extension)

Equipment and materials required

Per group: 2 litre cola bottle, bung with plastic delivery tube to fit bottle, car foot-pump, water, clamp to hold bottle.

Details
Do this outside! Pour a small amount of water into the bottle and push the bung in hard. Attach the other end of the delivery tube to the foot pump. Place the bottle neck into the clamp with the neck pointing down. Do not grip the neck with the clamp. Pump the foot pump to pressurise the bottle. Keep pumping until the bottle flies off.

The amount of water, and how well sealed the bung and delivery tube are, will affect the range. A poor seal anywhere will result in a short flight. Too little water and the flight will be unsteady and short. Too much and the bottle will be too heavy to fly. You may be able to persuade your technology department to fashion a launch ramp from some wire.

Safety
Keep pupils away from the flight path.

Differentiation

SEN
The idea of particles is highly conceptual and lower attaining pupils may well struggle with the idea. It is important that as many pupils as possible can represent gases using the particle diagram, even if they cannot fully explain it.

Extension
Allow pupils to make bottle rockets, as described in 'Practical support'. Challenge pupils to explain what makes the bottle fly and to try to improve the length of the flight. [Pumping the foot pump forces more and more air particles into the bottle until the pressure builds up so much it flies off. The bottle is propelled by the force of the gas inside rushing out as it attempts to expand back to normal pressure.]

Homework Suggestion
Pupils could make a model of the particles in a gas.

Answers to in-text questions

a There is a lot of space between the gas particles. This means that the particles can easily be squashed closer together.

b The particles move fastest in gases. This movement comes from their movement (kinetic) energy being high. Also to become a gas, solids and liquids need to be heated, meaning that energy has been given to the substance.

C2.5 Gases in Action

NC links for the lesson
- The particle model provides explanations for the different physical properties and behaviour of matter.
- Use a range of scientific methods and techniques to develop and test ideas and explanations.
- Assess risk and work safely in the laboratory, field and workplace.
- Carry out practical and investigative activities, both individually and in groups.

Learning Objectives
Pupils should learn:
- How gases spread out.
- What causes an empty can to collapse.

Learning Outcomes
- All pupils should be able to recall what we mean by gas pressure and diffusion.
- Most pupils should be able to explain diffusion using the particle model.
- Some pupils should also be able to explain why a can has collapsed, using the particle model.

How Science Works
- Use an existing model or analogy to explain a phenomenon. (1.1a1)

Learning Styles
Visual: Making observations of how gas pressure can cause things to collapse.
Auditory: Describing how gases diffuse and how the movement of their particles causes pressure.
Kinaesthetic: Investigating pressure in gases.
Interpersonal: Working with others to develop a drama of particle behaviour.
Intrapersonal: Understanding the concept that matter is made of particles too small to see.

The Lesson

Starter Suggestions

Smells good
Spray a can of deodorant in the corner of the room. Ask pupils to put their hand up when they think they can smell it. There should be a wave of hand-raising spreading out from where the can was sprayed. Ask them to think about what might have happened. [The deodorant gas particles gradually spread out.] (5 mins)

Holding up
Show pupils an inflated balloon. Ask them, based on what they saw last lesson, to explain what holds the balloon stretched. [The gas particles inside sometimes hit the sides. As there are so many of them, each little tiny push is sufficient to hold the sides of the balloon out.] (10 mins)

Answers to summary questions

1. Gases spread out in all directions to fill their container.
   Air particles move in all directions and hit our bodies and cause air pressure.
   A model is a simplification of the truth to help us explain and understand the world around us.

2. The gas particles move randomly in all directions, they diffuse. Eventually the two gases meet in the tube and the neutralisation reaction happens. The salt will be closer to the side that contains the heavier gas particles, because they move slower.

3. Pupils should make a pictorial flow chart to explain how the can collapsed in the activity due to air pressure.

Answers to in-text questions

a. Pupil's own diagram, based on particle model.

b. Check the weather forecast; measure it directly with a barometer.

Gases in Action

Main Lesson

- Remind pupils of the work they did last lesson on gases. It may be helpful at this point to review the gas particle model.
- Show pupils the 'Diffusion in Gases' experiment, described in the pupil book. They will be able to see the brown-orange bromine gas diffusing.
- Ask pupils to describe what they can see and to try to explain it using what they know about gas particles. If you used the 'Smells good' starter, link back to this to explain what's happening. [The gas particles are moving in straight lines, frequently bouncing off each other. Slowly, this random movement causes the particles to spread further and further apart. In the gas jar, the colour should spread across the two jars, but be paler than it was when the gas is contained in just one jar. The colour gets paler because the concentration reduces; the same number of bromine particles are spread over a larger volume.]
- Remind pupils that gas particles are constantly moving around. Every time they hit something they give it a little tiny push. The air is doing this to us all the time. [We aren't crushed because there is equal pressure inside us pushing out.] If you used the 'Holding up' starter, refer back to it
- Ask pupils to carry out the 'Air pressure' practical described in the pupil book. [The can collapses because the steam (water gas) inside the can condenses into liquid very quickly when the can is put into cold water. This reduces the pressure inside as liquid takes up much less space than gas. As the open end of the can is sealed with water, the air pressure outside the can is much greater than that inside. The can is crushed by the force of the air particles colliding with it.] This experiment demonstrates the principle behind which Newcomen's first steam engines worked. The engines were used to pump out mines.

Plenary Suggestions

Grub's up
Ask the pupils to write an explanation of why they can smell a chip shop or a curry restaurant from a long distance away. [The smell of the food forms a gas and the particles diffuse through the air.] (5 mins)

Particle people
Ask groups of pupils to prepare a demonstration of gas pressure and diffusion, using themselves as particles. (10 mins)

Practical Support

Diffusion in gases demonstration

Equipment and materials required
1 gas jar with 2 cm^3 of bromine liquid in it and a lid placed on top, further gas jar, same size neck as the first.

Details
Place the gas jar containing the bromine liquid in a fume cabinet. Place the second jar upside-down on top of the first jar. Slide the lid out from between the two jars so both jars are now connected. Observe the orange-brown gas diffusing upwards into the second jar.

Safety
Must be carried out in a fume cabinet.
Bromine is toxic and corrosive: CLEAPSS Hazcard 15A. Wear chemical protective gloves.

Air pressure

Equipment and materials required
Per group: 1 empty 330 cm^3 fizzy drink can, retort stand, boss and clamp, shallow bowl or tray half-filled with water, Bunsen burner.

Details
See pupil book. The pupils will have to proceed quickly but very carefully once the can is hot enough and the burner removed. If they take too long, the can will cool and the experiment won't work.

Safety
Turn the can over using the arm of the clamp. The arm of the clamp near to the burner will get hot.

Diffusion of hydrogen chloride and ammonia (Extension demonstration)

Equipment and materials required
1 m long glass tube, approximately 2–3 cm in diameter, 2 bungs to fit tube, 2–3 cm^3 of concentrated hydrochloric acid, 2–3 cm^3 of concentrated ammonia, mineral wool, 2 pairs tweezers, 2 watch glasses.

Details
Clamp the tube horizontally. Place a small piece of mineral wool on each watch glass. Add the hydrochloric acid to one and the ammonia to the other. Within as short a time as possible use tweezers to place the soaked mineral wool into the glass tube, one at each end. Place bungs to seal the tube. If the two chemicals are not placed in to tube within a short time of each, the other one will have a head start. Place the ammonia in first as this is the lighter molecule and will diffuse faster anyway. Be prepared to defend yourself against cheating and offering unfair advantage though!

Safety
Ensure the area is well ventilated.
Wear eye protection.
Concentrated hydrochloric acid is corrosive: CLEAPSS Hazcard 47A.
Concentrated ammonia is corrosive: CLEAPSS Hazcard 6.
Be aware if any asthmatics are present.

Differentiation

SEN
The idea of particles is highly conceptual and lower attaining pupils may well struggle with the idea. It is important that as many pupils as possible explain the effects of diffusion even if they cannot fully explain it.

Extension
Demonstrate the diffusion of hydrogen chloride gas and ammonia in a tube to these pupils. If the gases start at either end of the tube they will meet closer to the hydrogen chloride, as evidenced by the white cloud of ammonium chloride formed. Challenge pupils to suggest why. [It happens because the ammonia is much lighter and so diffuses faster.]

Homework Suggestion

Pupils to find out who Newcomen was and how his steam pump worked [A piston was pulled up by the weight of the pump hanging on it. Steam was injected into the cylinder behind the pump and then a small quantity of cold water was added. This condensed the steam and the sudden lowering of pressure was enough to make the piston go down.]

C2.6 Changing State

NC links for the lesson
- The particle model provides explanations for the different physical properties and behaviour of matter.
- Use a range of scientific methods and techniques to develop and test ideas and explanations.
- Assess risk and work safely in the laboratory, field and workplace.
- Carry out practical and investigative activities, both individually and in groups.

Learning Objectives

Pupils should learn:
- What happens when we heat a solid or a liquid.
- What happens when we cool a liquid or a gas.

Learning Outcomes
- All pupils should be able to define melting, boiling, condensing and freezing.
- Most pupils should be able to explain the difference between boiling and evaporation.
- Some pupils should also be able to define sublimation and give an example.

How Science Works
- Use an existing model or analogy to explain a phenomenon. (1.1a1)

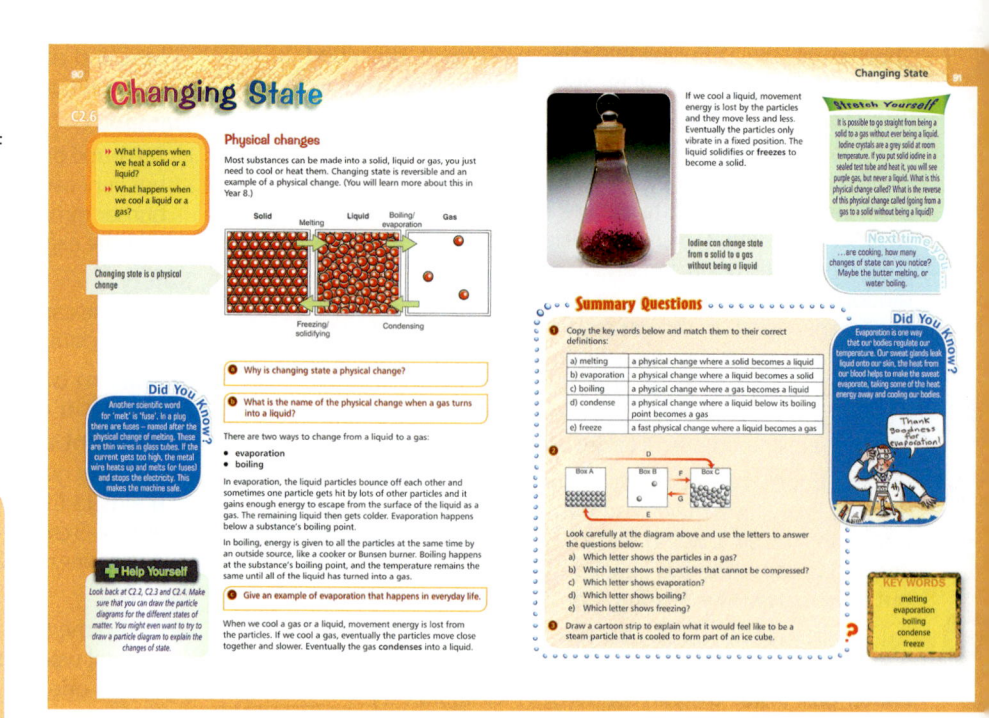

Functional Skills Link-up

Mathematics
- Understand and use whole numbers and recognise negative numbers in practical situations. (Level 1)

Learning Styles

Visual: Observing changes of state.
Auditory: Describing their observations of salol changing state.
Kinaesthetic: Carrying out practical work on changing state.
Interpersonal: Working with others to develop a drama of particle behaviour.
Intrapersonal: Understanding the concept that matter is made of particles too small to see.

Answers to summary questions

1.
   a) Melting: a physical change where a solid becomes a liquid.
   b) Evaporation: a physical change where a liquid below its boiling point becomes a gas.
   c) Boiling: a fast physical change where a liquid becomes a gas.
   d) Condense: a physical change where a gas becomes a liquid.
   e) Freeze: a physical change where a liquid becomes a solid.

2.
   a) B
   b) A
   c) G
   d) G
   e) E

3. Pupils should draw a cartoon strip to explain what it would feel like to be a steam particle that is cooled to form part of an ice cube.

Answers to in-text questions

a) No new substance has been made.

b) Condensation.

c) One of: a puddle, a drink in a glass, sweating, drying washing.

Changing State

The Lesson

Starter Suggestions

How many substances
Give pupils a list of substances and ask them to tell you how many different ones there are. Include: ice, water, steam [all water]; lava, rock [both rocks]; sugar, hot sugar syrup [both sugar]; cooking oil and margarine [both oil]. There are only four substances listed here. (5 mins)

True or false?
Remind pupils of some of the changes they saw in C1.1 and ask them to decide which are reversible (true) and which are irreversible (false). (10 mins)

Main Lesson

- Remind pupils of the work they did in C1.1 regarding reversible and irreversible changes. Remind them that reversible changes can usually be changed back easily by heating or cooling.
- Show pupils some ice cubes and ask them to say what will happen to them if they were left on the side. [They will melt.] Accelerate the process by gently heating the ice in a beaker until it melts.
- Ask the pupils to investigate what happens to salol if it is heated and then cooled. They can observe the salol melting in a test tube and then freezing again. It is important at this stage to establish the meanings of 'melting' [solid becomes liquid] and freezing [liquid becomes a solid]. Many pupils hold the misconception that it has to be zero degrees Celsius for freezing to occur. This is, of course, the freezing point of water. Salol's freezing point is higher. Many metals have a freezing point of several thousand degrees Celsius. Melting and freezing points are the same thing.
- Return to the beaker of melted ice. Ask pupils what will happen if you continue to heat it. Demonstrate this, heating the water to boiling point. Watch the water boil and show that it can be condensed by holding a piece of cold glass over the steam.
- Ask pupils whether they think that the liquid water could turn into a gas if just left. [Yes, the water would slowly evaporate. Although most of the particles do not have enough energy to become gaseous, some do. The water left behind has less energy and becomes cooler. This is how sweating reduces our body temperature.]

Plenary Suggestions

Changing state
Show pupils a flow chart, linking the words solid, liquid and gas. Ask them to add the words, melting, freezing, boiling, condensing, and perhaps even sublimation, to the flow chart. (5 mins)

Particle people
Ask groups of pupils to prepare a demonstration of an ice cube melting and then the water being heated to boiling point, using themselves as the particles. (10 mins)

Practical Support

Melting ice demonstration

Equipment and materials required
5–6 ice cubes in a glass beaker, Bunsen burner, heat mat, tripod and gauze, matches.

Details
After showing pupils the ice, gently heat it to melt it. Later in the lesson, boil the water.

Safety
Equipment will get hot.

Salol (main lesson)

Equipment and materials required
Per group: test tube and grip, 1–2 spatulas full of salol, mineral wool plug, access to hot water (above 50°C), 2 small beakers, access to cold water.

Details
Place the salol in the test tube and then dip the tube into hot water. Observe the salol melting. Ask pupils to record their observations. Then place the tube into cold water and observe the salol freezing. Again, record any observations.

Safety
Eye protection must be worn.
A mineral wool plug will keep fumes in test tube.
Hot water can scald.
Salol is an irritant: CLEAPSS Hazcard 52.

Sublimation of iodine (Extension)

Equipment and materials required
Per group: boiling tube and well-fitted bung, 4–5 iodine crystals, access to hot water.

Details
Refer to pupil book, 'Stretch yourself'. Hot tap water should be sufficient to vaporise the iodine.

Safety
Wear eye protection.
Ensure the bung cannot fall out of the test tube.
Iodine crystals are harmful, avoid skin contact: CLEAPSS Hazcard 54A.

Differentiation

SEN
The idea of particles is highly conceptual and lower attaining pupils may well struggle with the idea of energy changes causing changes of state. It is important that they can name the changes though. You may wish to avoid discussing the melting and boiling points of substances which are gases at room temperature, as this will involve negative numbers.

Extension
Get pupils to carry out the 'Stretch yourself' activity, looking at sublimation of iodine. Substances, like iodine, which change directly from solid to gas are said to 'sublime'. Pupils could research other substances which do this, such as graphite.

Homework Suggestion

Pupils to find out the melting and boiling points of some common substances, such as iron, copper, hydrogen, sugar.

C2.7 Mixtures

NC links for the lesson
- The particle model provides explanations for the different physical properties and behaviour of matter.
- Use a range of scientific methods and techniques to develop and test ideas and explanations.
- Assess risk and work safely in the laboratory, field and workplace.
- Carry out practical and investigative activities, both individually and in groups.

Learning Objectives
Pupils should learn:
- What a mixture is.
- How particles are arranged in a mixture.

Learning Outcomes
- All pupils should be able to recall a definition of 'a mixture' in words.
- Most pupils should be able to define a mixture with a particle diagram.
- Some pupils should also be able to explain why a substance is a mixture and collect reliable data.

How Science Works
- Use an existing model or analogy to explain a phenomenon. (1.1a1)

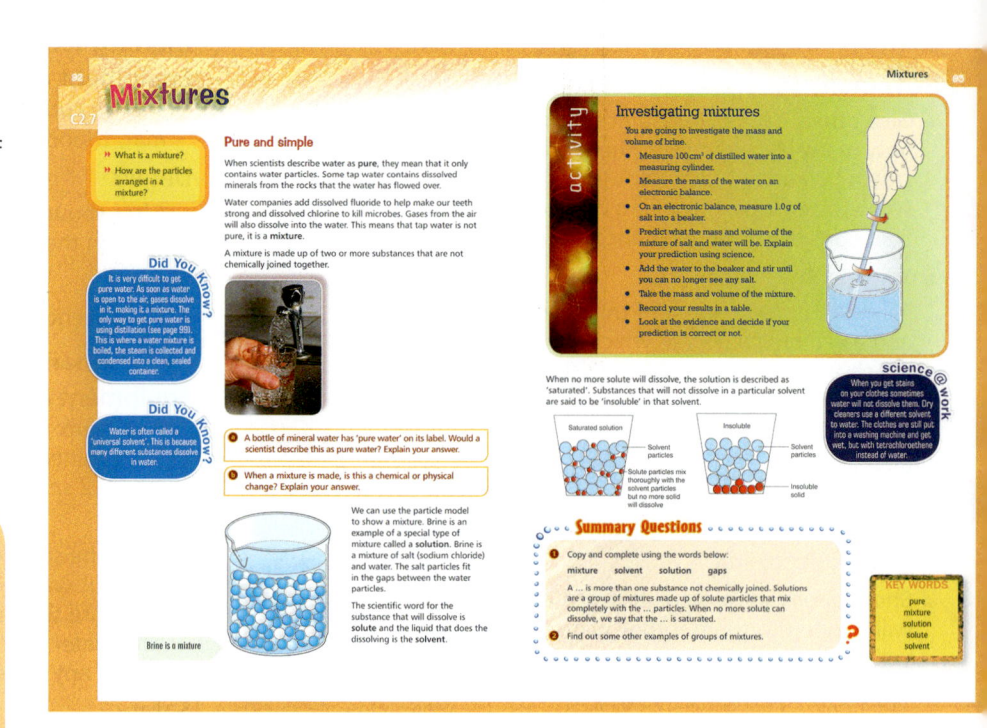

Learning Styles
Visual: Making observations of mixture behaviour.
Auditory: Describing the behaviour of mixtures.
Kinaesthetic: Investigating mixtures.
Interpersonal: Working with others to develop a drama of particle behaviour.
Intrapersonal: Understanding the need to take accurate measurements during the investigation into mixtures.

Answers to summary questions
1. A **mixture** is more than one substance not chemically joined. Solutions are a group of mixtures made up of solute particles that fit in the gaps between the **solvent** particles. When no more solute can dissolve, we say that the **solution** is saturated.
2. Colloids (gel, aerosol, sol, emulsion).

Answers to in-text questions
a. Mineral water contains dissolved minerals that have come from the rocks that the water has flowed over. This means that the water is not scientifically pure.
b. Physical change, as no new substance has been made.

Mixtures

The Lesson

Starter Suggestions

What is pure?
Ask pupils to write a definition for the word 'pure'. Allow open responses. You may wish to tell them afterwards that the chemical meaning is 'to describe a single substance'. (5 mins)

Is it pure?
Show pupils a range of liquids in bottles and ask them to explain whether they think each one is pure or not and why? You could include the following substances: distilled water, ethanol, salt water, saturated sodium carbonate solution (with undissolved solute) and lemon juice. [Only distilled water and ethanol are chemically pure, as they are the only two that contain just one substance.] (10 mins)

Main Lesson

- Remind pupils of some of the elements and compounds they met in C1. Although they may not have been introduced to the term 'element' or 'compound' they met many substances which fall into these categories. Establish that if you have one element or one compound then you have a pure substance. For example, oxygen and copper are both elements, water and carbon dioxide are compounds.
- Explain that when you have more than one substance at a time, you have a mixture. Most materials are mixtures. You could show them a piece of granite at this point; pupils should easily be able to see the different minerals in it. You could also show some food labels; foods are almost always a mixture of many ingredients.
- Explain that, although many mixtures are liquids, it is possible to find solid and gaseous mixtures too. Introduce the solution key words to pupils:
Solution: a liquid mixture.
Solvent: the liquid in which another substance is dissolved, often water.
Solute: the substance which is dissolved in the solvent.
- Ask pupils to carry out the 'Investigating mixtures' activity described in the pupil book. Impress upon them the need to carry out the method carefully or the results could be wrong. Common errors when carrying out this investigation include failing to zero the balance before weighing each time, and stirring the mixture so vigorously they spill some liquid. It is a good opportunity to instil the need for attention to detail when carrying out practical work in order to take accurate measurements. Repeating measurements will improve the reliability of their results.
- Establish that the mass of a solution is the total mass of the solute used and the solvent.
- Ask pupils whether they think an unlimited amount of solute can be dissolved. [No, a saturation point is reached where no more solute will dissolve and any extra solute will settle out.] Add more and more salt to one of the pupils' solutions from the practical to establish that it can't.

Plenary Suggestions

What does it mean?
Ask pupils to match up the solution key words to their meanings. (5 mins)

Particle people
Ask pupils to work in groups to represent the process of dissolving salt in water using themselves as the particles. The 'solute' pupils will need to be dressed differently to the 'solvent' pupils. Perhaps one group could take their jumpers off or wear sports bibs. (10 mins)

Practical Support

Investigating mixtures

Equipment and materials required
Per group: 100 cm^3 measuring cylinder, 100 cm^3 distilled water, 1 g salt, spatula, 250 cm^3 beaker, glass rod, access to a 1 decimal place balance (2 d.p. balance is too precise and is more likely to show a change in mass).

Details
See pupil book. The results should show that the mass of the salt solution made is the mass of the water plus the mass of the salt.

Safety
Clear up spillages immediately.

Solution model (main lesson demonstration)

Equipment and materials required
500 cm^3 beaker, enough rice to half-fill beaker, handful of dried green lentils or similar, spatula.

Details
Place the rice into the beaker and explain to the pupils that this represents the water. Add the lentils, which represents the salt and stir with the spatula. Show that the lentils occupy spaces between the rice grains.

Safety
Ensure pupils do not eat the food.

Ethanol/water mixture (Extension)

Equipment and materials required
Per group: Two 50 cm^3 measuring cylinders, 100 cm^3 measuring cylinder, 50 cm^3 distilled water, 50 cm^3 ethanol.

Details
Measure out 50 cm^3 each of ethanol and distilled water in separate measuring cylinders. Mix the two in the larger measuring cylinder and observe the final volume. [It will be less than the sum of the volumes of the separate solutions.]

Safety
Ethanol is highly flammable and harmful: CLEAPSS Hazcard 40A. No naked flames.

Differentiation

SEN
The idea of particles is highly conceptual and lower attaining pupils may well struggle with the idea of a solute dissolving, believing instead that it simply disappears.

Extension
Get pupils to investigate the properties of a mixture of ethanol and water as described above in 'Practical support'. Mix equal volumes of the two and the final volume will be less that the sum of the volumes of the separate solutions.

Homework Suggestion

Pupils to find substances in the kitchen which are not mixtures. [Any pure substances, such as salt, bicarbonate of soda.]

C2.8 Separating Mixtures: Sieving and Filtering

NC links for the lesson
- The particle model provides explanations for the different physical properties and behaviour of matter.
- Use a range of scientific methods and techniques to develop and test ideas and explanations.
- Assess risk and work safely in the laboratory, field and workplace.
- Carry out practical and investigative activities, both individually and in groups.

Learning Objectives

Pupils should learn:
- How to separate different-sized solids.
- How to separate solids from liquids.

Learning Outcomes
- All pupils should be able to separate a mixture of solids using a sieve.
- Most pupils should be able separate a solid from a liquid by filtering.
- Some pupils should also be able to explain why sieving or filtering is suitable for separating some mixtures.

How Science Works
- Explain how action has been taken to control obvious risk and how methods are adequate for the task. (1.2c)

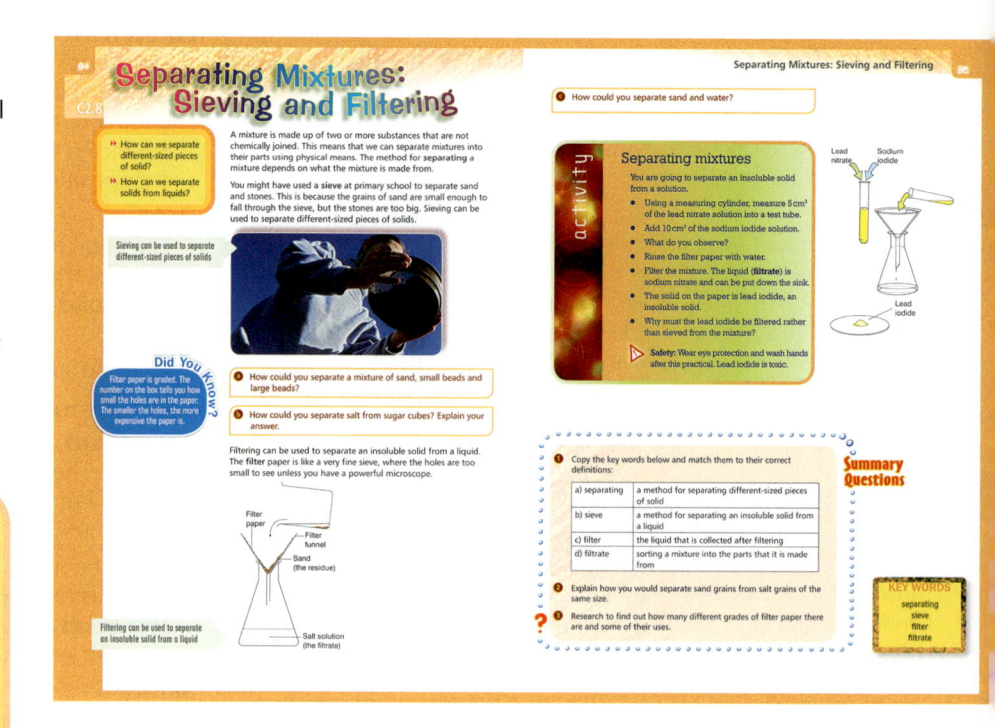

Functional Skills Link-up

ICT
- Access, navigate and search internet sources of information purposefully and effectively. (Level 1) (See Homework Suggestion.)

Learning Styles

Visual: Observing the effects of sieving and filtering.
Auditory: Describing the effects of sieving and filtering.
Kinaesthetic: Carrying out sieving and filtering.
Intrapersonal: Understanding that the particles in a solid are joined together so the solid can't pass through a filter.

Answers to in-text questions

a Use two sizes of sieve to separate the different-sized beads.

b Using a sieve, the salt would go through but the sugar cubes would get stuck in the sieve.

c Filter; the filtrate would be the water but the sand would collect on the filter paper.

Answers to summary questions

1
a) Separating: sorting a mixture into the parts that it is made from.
b) Sieve: a method for separating different-sized pieces of solid.
c) Filter: a method for separating an insoluble solid from a liquid.
d) Filtrate: the liquid that is collected after filtering.

2 Add water, the salt would dissolve and the sand would not. Filter the mixture, the sand is collected on the filter paper.

3 Pupils' own research to find out how many different grades of filter paper there are and some of their uses.

Separating Mixtures: Sieving and Filtering

The Lesson

Starter Suggestions

Sorted

Show pupils some empty bottles and cans. Try to have a range of items: drinks and food cans, plastic and glass bottles. Explain to them that waste like this should be recycled whenever possible. Although in many places, householders put some of these items in a recycle box all together, pupils should understand that these are separated later, prior to recycling. Ask them what they think might happen to these items once they are taken away. Hopefully they will realise that the items need to be sorted out first. Ask them to think about how it could be done. (5 mins)

What's the question?

Give pupils key terms about solutions, such as 'solute', 'solvent' and 'solution'. They met these terms in lesson C2.7. Tell them that these words are the answers, but that they must write the questions. (10 mins)

Main lesson

- Remind pupils of the work they did in C2.7, 'Mixtures'. In particular they should recall that when a mixture is formed, the original materials are still there, even if they can't be seen. A suitable separation technique must be chosen.
- Demonstrate how to separate a mixture of gravel and sand using a sieve, i.e. separating solids. Explain that the sand passes through as the grains are smaller than the holes but the stones of the gravel cannot.
- Ask the pupils to carry out the 'Separating mixtures' practical described in the pupil book. Pupils will probably need to be shown how to fold a filter paper properly. Although they are forming the insoluble solid to filter out using a chemical reaction, stress that this method is suitable for all separations of a solid from a liquid. It may be worth explaining to pupils that filtering is often slow, as the trapped solid blocks the path of the liquid through the filter. Prodding the filter paper will only result in ripping it. The liquid will pass through much quicker but, with a large hole, so will the solid!
- After the practical, ask pupils why they think the method works. [Liquid particles can move individually and can pass through the tiny holes in the filter paper. In the lead iodide precipitate the particles are clumped together as it is a solid. The clumps are too big to pass through.]

Plenary Suggestions

Will it work?

Ask pupils to predict what will happen when a non-saturated solution of copper sulfate is filtered. Demonstrate this to them after they have had time to think. [The whole solution will pass through the filter as, being dissolved, the particles of copper sulfate are small enough to pass through the filter. This may help to address a common misconception which many pupils hold; that filters can separate a solvent and a solute.] (5 mins)

It's a 'thingymajig'

Draw diagrams of the equipment used in this lesson and met so far in Year 7. Ask the pupils to label the items. (10 mins)

Practical Support

Separating solids (main lesson demonstration)

Equipment and materials required

About 500 cm^3 of a 50:50 mixture of sand and gravel, tray, sieve with a suitable mesh to let the sand pass through but not the gravel.

Details

Tip the mixture into the sieve. Show that the sand will pass through but that the gravel will not.

Safety

Sand can make the floor slippery if spilt.

Separating mixtures

Equipment and materials required

Per group: 5 m^3 of 0.01 mol/dm^3 lead nitrate, 10 cm^3 of 0.1 mol/dm^3 sodium iodide, boiling tube and rack, filter paper, filter funnel, conical flask.

Details

Mix the two solutions in the boiling tube. Filter the resulting bright yellow precipitate through the paper and funnel into the conical flask.

Safety

Wear eye protection.

Lead iodide is toxic: CLEAPSS Hazcard 57A. Hands must be washed after any contact with it.

Take care with disposal.

Will it work? (Plenary demonstration)

Equipment and materials required

Bottle of 0.1 mol/dm^3 copper sulfate, filter paper, filter funnel, conical flask.

Details

After asking the pupils what they think will happen, filter the solution to show that, as it is still dissolved, the copper sulfate will pass through.

Safety

Copper sulfate is irritant, harmful and dangerous to the environment: CLEAPSS Hazcard 27C. Keep disposal to the minimum.

Differentiation

SEN

Lower attaining pupils may cope better with the 'It's a thingymajig' plenary if suitable labels for the equipment are provided.

Extension

Ask pupils to repeat the 'Separating mixtures' practical, investigating whether or not different ways of folding the filter paper make a difference. [They should find that fluting provides the best combination of fast filtering and good separation.]

Homework Suggestion

Pupils to find out how the automatic sorting machines work. [Many waste management companies use automatic machines to sort recyclable materials. There are even some in supermarket car parks in the UK now. Some work by weighing the items, but more sophisticated machines use X-rays.]

C2.9 Separating Mixtures: Chromatography

NC links for the lesson
- The particle model provides explanations for the different physical properties and behaviour of matter.
- Use a range of scientific methods and techniques to develop and test ideas and explanations.
- Assess risk and work safely in the laboratory, field and workplace.
- Carry out practical and investigative activities, both individually and in groups.

Learning Objectives
Pupils should learn:
- How we can separate inks and dyes.
- How we can use chromatography.

Learning Outcomes
- All pupils should be able to separate a mixture of dyes with a wick.
- Most pupils should be able to separate dyes into a chromatogram.
- Some pupils should also be able to explain how chromatography works.

How Science Works
- Describe and record observations and evidence systematically. (1.2d)

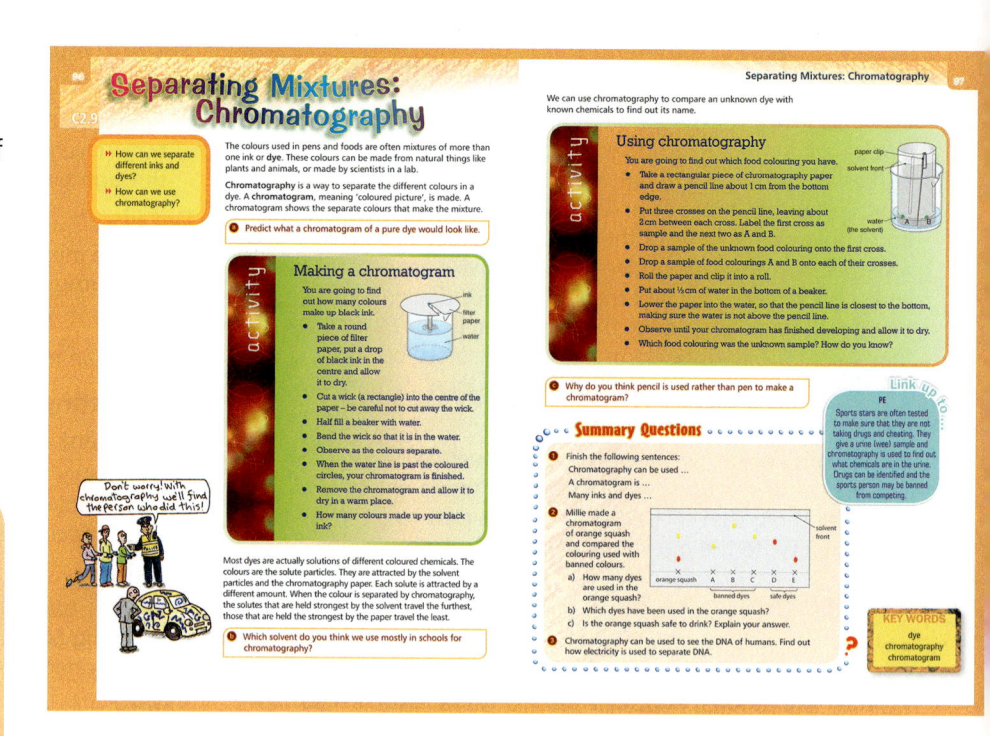

Learning Styles
Visual: Interpreting chromatograms.
Auditory: Describing the process of chromatography.
Kinaesthetic: Carrying out chromatography experiments.
Interpersonal: Working with others during the practical.
Intrapersonal: Understanding that dyes are often made from more than one colour.

Answers to summary questions

1. Chromatography can be used [e.g.] to separate inks and dyes.
   A chromatogram is [e.g.] a coloured picture which shows all the colours that make up an ink or dye.
   Many inks and dyes [e.g.] are mixtures.

2. a) Two.
   b) C and E.
   c) No, as colour C is banned.

3. Research into how electricity is used to separate DNA.

Answers to in-text questions

a) There would not be any colour separation, as the dye is not a mixture.

b) Water.

c) Pencil is insoluble in water, but the pen could be soluble and this would affect the results.

Separating Mixtures: Chromatography

The Lesson

Starter Suggestions

Odd one out
Show pupils four pictures: a bottle of cola, some orange juice, a cup of tea and a glass of water. Ask them to decide which is the odd one out and why. [This is designed to give the pupils an opportunity to provide an open response, but the more scientific answer, in the context of this unit, is that the water is the odd one out as it is not a mixture.] (5 mins)

Mix it up
Ask pupils to explain how they could make different colours of paint from just red, yellow and blue. For example, ask them how to make orange [red and yellow], green [yellow and blue] or what would happen if all three were mixed [brown]. (10 mins)

Main Lesson

- Discuss with pupils how, when they are painting in an art lesson, they can make colours they don't have by mixing others together. Explain that many paints, inks and dyes are actually a mixture of colours. Blacks in particular are rarely, if ever, pure.
- Ask pupils to carry out the 'Making a chromatogram' investigation described in the pupil book.
- After carrying out the experiment, ask pupils to think of any situations where separating colours like this might be useful. [Chromatography is widely used to analyse mixtures to find out what is in them.]
- Ask pupils to carry out the 'Using chromatography' investigation described in the pupil book. This could be turned into a more 'whodunnit'-type approach (see Practical Worksheets in Fusion Online.)
- After the practical establish which food colouring was the same as the unknown one.
- You may wish to ask pupils to set up the 'Evaporation' investigation in advance of next lesson, or you might want to set it up at the end of the lesson. See C2.10 for details.

Plenary Suggestions

Who 'dunnit'?
Show pupils a chromatogram 'prepared by the police' showing the traces produced by two known pens and another one. Set the scene by telling the class that the chromatogram was prepared from samples taken at a murder scene. A note was left in the room and the police have identified two suspects, both of whom were arrested shortly after the incident and pens were found in their pockets. Ask the pupils whether either person could have written the note. [Compare the trace for the known pens and the unknown pen. If the trace matches the unknown pen then the ink is the same.] (5 mins)

Is it pure?
Take a small coloured sweet and a disc of filter paper. Place the sweet in the centre and drop 3–4 drops of water onto it. The dye colours will spread. Ask the pupils which sweets are dyed with a pure dye and which are a mixture. (10 mins)

Practical Support

Making a chromatogram

Equipment and materials required
Per group: 100 cm³ beaker, 50 cm³ water, filter paper disc (approx. 8 cm in diameter), 3–4 drops of black ink or a black, water-based felt pen, dropping pipette if using ink, scissors.

Details
See pupil book. Pupils must be careful not to splash water onto the ink spot.

Safety
Normal laboratory rules.

Using chromatography

Equipment and materials required
Per group: 3–4 drops of green food colouring (which is pure green, not a mixture), 3–4 drops of manufactured green food colouring (made from yellow and blue), 3–4 drops of an 'unknown' food colouring – one of the first two colourings labelled as 'X', 3 dropping pipettes, 250 cm³ beaker, paper clip, sheet of chromatography paper to fit as a cylinder inside beaker (approx. 10 cm by 15 cm).

Details
See pupil book. It is important that only a small amount of water is present in the beaker. If the water level is above the pencil line, the experiment will not work. The trace produced is much better if more than one dot of the same dye is added to its cross to concentrate it, although the dots should be as small as possible.

Safety
Normal laboratory rules.

Plenary: Is it pure?

Equipment and materials required
Per group: different coloured M&Ms [the natural dyes of Smarties no longer work well in this experiment], disc of filter paper, water.

Details
See Plenary Suggestions.

Safety
Normal laboratory rules.

Differentiation

SEN
The 'Using chromatography' experiment will not work unless the pencil marks and the dye spots are prepared carefully and accurately. Some pupils may need assistance with this.

Extension
Ask pupils to find out how DNA electrophoresis is carried out. [It is a form of chromatography where an applied voltage drives the movement of the components of the mixture, rather than the solvent.]

Homework Suggestion

Pupils could make their own chromatograms at home using inks and dyes and blotting paper.

C2.10 Separating Mixtures: Distillation and Evaporation

NC links for the lesson
- The particle model provides explanations for the different physical properties and behaviour of matter.
- Use a range of scientific methods and techniques to develop and test ideas and explanations.
- Assess risk and work safely in the laboratory, field and workplace.
- Carry out practical and investigative activities, both individually and in groups.

Learning Objectives
Pupils should learn:
- How to separate a solid which is dissolved in a liquid.
- How to separate a mixture of liquids.

Learning Outcomes
- All pupils should be able to separate a solid from a liquid by evaporation.
- Most pupils should be able to separate a mixture by distillation.
- Some pupils should also be able to explain why distillation or evaporation is suitable for separating a mixture.

How Science Works
- Use an existing model or analogy to explain a phenonemon. (1.1a1)

Answers to summary questions

1
- a) Solvents can be separated and collected from a solution using distillation.
- b) In evaporation, only the solute is collected.
- c) In distillation, both the solvent and solute could be collected.
- d) Solutions are a type of mixture made of solute and solvent particles.

2
- a) Salt.
- b) Water.
- c) Water.
- d) To cool the steam and condense it into water.

3 Flowchart to show stages of distillation.

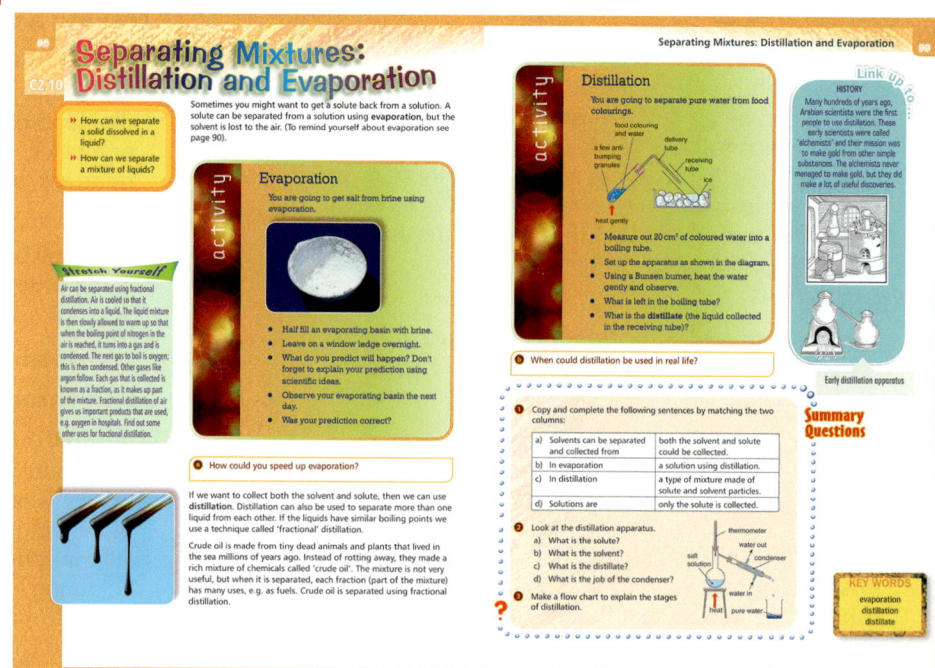

The Lesson

Starter Suggestions

Mixing it

Give pupils a boiling tube containing oil and water. Ask them to shake it up and to observe what happens over a few minutes. Ask them to suggest how the two liquids could be separated. [The oil can, with care, simply be poured off.] (5 mins)

Shipwreck

Ask pupils how they could obtain fresh drinking water from seawater (which also contains some sand, picked up as the water is scooped into a bucket). They have a fire and some basic equipment, such as cloth which can be used as a filter. [Filter the water to remove the sand. Boil the water and collect and condense the steam.] (10 mins)

Main Lesson
- Set up the 'Evaporation' experiment described in the pupil book at least 24 hours in advance.

Learning Styles
Visual: Observing the results of distillation and evaporation.
Auditory: Describing what happens during distillation and evaporation.
Kinaesthetic: Carrying out distillation and evaporation.
Interpersonal: Working with others during practicals.
Intrapersonal: Understanding that dissolved substances are still there even if the particles cannot be seen.

Functional Skills Link-up
English
- Present information in a logical sequence. (Level 1) See Starter and Plenary 'Shipwreck'.

Separating Mixtures: Distillation and Evaporation

- Remind pupils of the work they did on separating an insoluble solid from a liquid by filtering. You may wish to demonstrate that filtering does not work if the solid is dissolved. Try filtering a coloured solution, such as copper sulfate so it's obvious that the dissolved solid passes through.
- Look at the results of the 'Evaporation' experiment. Invite pupils to try to explain what has happened. [The water has evaporated and left the salt behind.]
- Ask pupils to suggest how the process could be speeded up. [Heat the evaporating dish.]
- Take some clean water and 'contaminate it' with some food colouring or ink. Ask pupils to think about how we could get the water back out of it again. Running through the separation methods they have met already should lead to the conclusion that a different method is needed. Refer to the 'Evaporation' experiment where the salt was left behind. Ask pupils to suggest how we could keep the water too. [Cool it down to condense it.]
- Get pupils to carry out the 'Distillation' experiment described in the pupil book.
- After the experiment you may wish to show them a Liebig condenser and ask them to suggest why this is an improvement upon the apparatus they used. [It is continually cooled and provides a large condensing surface.]
- After the practical, establish that only the water transfers from the test tube. Any impurities are left behind.

Plenary Suggestions

What would happen?
Invite pupils to describe what they would observe if copper sulfate solution were distilled. You could demonstrate this if you have time, using the equipment from the pupil 'Distillation' experiment. [Pure water will transfer. The colour of the remaining copper sulfate will deepen initially, then crystals may start to appear.] (5 mins)

Shipwreck 2
Invite pupils to re-plan their method of gaining fresh water from seawater which also has sand in it, based on what they have learned from the lesson. Again, they must not use laboratory equipment but can use things which they might find on a ship. (10 mins)

Practical Support

Evaporation
Equipment and materials required
Per group: 20 cm^3 saturated brine solution, evaporating dish.

Details
See pupil book. This needs to be set up before this lesson but could be done by the pupils in an earlier lesson. The process can be speeded-up by heating the evaporating dish over a water bath. Crystals of salt will form on the sides of the dish.

Safety
If heating, do not heat the dish directly. Wear eye protection.
If salt starts to spit, stop heating.

Copper sulfate (main lesson and plenary: 'What would happen?')
Equipment and materials required
Bottle of copper sulfate solution (2 mol/dm^3), funnel, filter paper, conical flask.
Equipment as for pupil 'Distillation' experiment.

Details
You will need to show that the solution passes through the filter paper at the start of the lesson. You could show what happens if copper sulfate is distilled at the end of the lesson.

Safety
Copper sulfate is harmful: CLEAPSS Hazcard 27.

Distillation
Equipment and materials required
Per group: 20 cm^3 water, coloured, in front of the class, with ink or food dye, two boiling tubes, glass delivery tube with 90° bend, holed bung to attach delivery tube to top of one boiling tube, Petri dish, ice, Bunsen burner and heat-proof mat, matches.

Details
See pupil book. Do not allow the pupils to heat the coloured water too strongly as steam may shoot out of the tube. The equipment may well get too hot to allow any water to condense within a short space of time. The pupils need only collect a few drops of water to show that what appears to be pure water collects.

Safety
Wear eye protection.
Pupils must not drink the distilled water. Do not heat too strongly (see above).

Differentiation

SEN
The idea of particles is highly conceptual and lower attaining pupils may well struggle with the idea that a substance is still there when it is dissolved, even though it cannot always be seen.

Extension
Ask pupils to find out how fractional distillation is carried out and why it is used, using books or the Internet. [Fractional distillation is needed when separating mixtures of liquids with similar boiling points. A fractionating column is placed above the flask where the liquid is being heated. As the temperature drops when the vapour moves higher in the fractionating column, only the liquid with the lowest boiling point will reach the top.]

Homework Suggestion

Pupils to find out how spirits, such as whisky are made.

Answers to in-text questions

a Heat the evaporating basin.

b Any suitable answer, e.g. to make spirits, to make fresh water on a boat.

C2.11 Grouping Chemicals

NC links for the lesson
- The particle model provides explanations for the different physical properties and behaviour of matter.
- Use a range of scientific methods and techniques to develop and test ideas and explanations.
- Assess risk and work safely in the laboratory, field and workplace.
- Carry out practical and investigative activities, both individually and in groups.

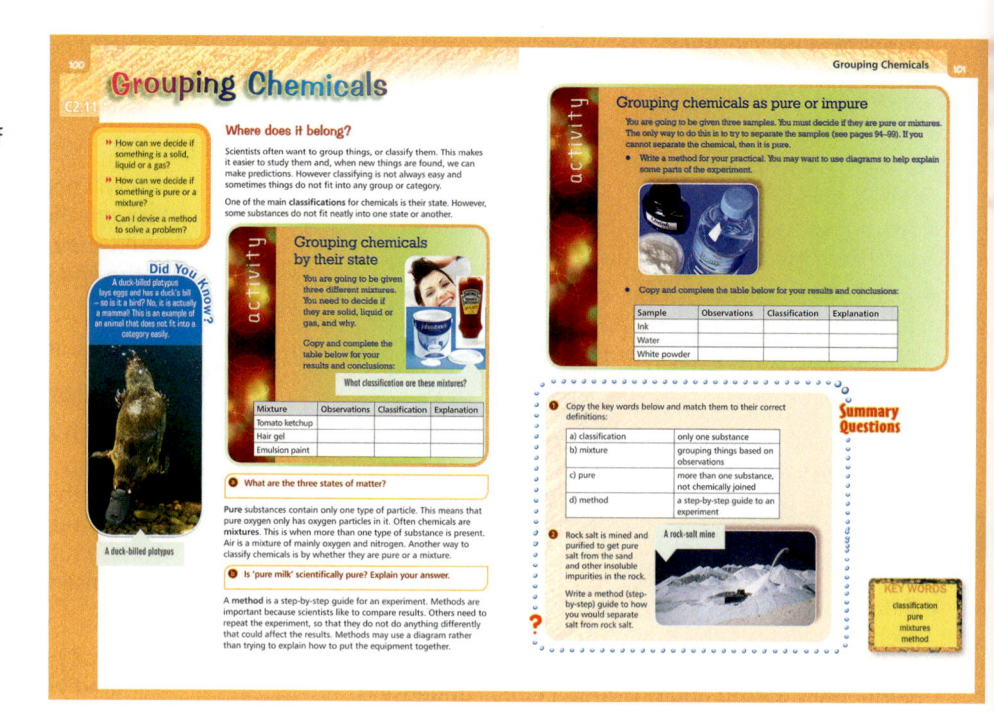

Learning Objectives
Pupils should learn:
- How to decide if something is a solid, a liquid or a gas.
- How to devise a method to decide if something is pure or a mixture.

Learning Outcomes
- All pupils should be able to recognise a solid, a liquid and a gas.
- Most pupils should be able to explain why something is a solid, a liquid or a gas.
- Some pupils should also be able to distinguish between mixtures and pure substances by devising a method independently.

How Science Works
- Describe an appropriate approach to answer a scientific question using a limited range of information and making relevant observations or measurements. (1.2a)

Functional Skills Link-up
English
- Present information in a logical sequence. (Level 1)

Learning Styles
Visual: Observing the behaviour of materials.

Auditory: Describing whether a substance is a solid, a liquid or a gas, with reasons.

Kinaesthetic: Carrying out practical work to decide if a substance is pure or not.

Intrapersonal: Understanding that the state of a substance is sometimes difficult to define.

The Lesson

Starter Suggestions

Particle party

Show pupils some unlabelled particle diagrams of a solid, a liquid, a gas, a solution and a solid mixture. [Use two or more different colours for the mixture particles.] Ask the pupils to label them. (5 mins)

Word challenge

Ask pupils to come up with as many words as they can, using only letters from the word 'chromatography'. Longest list wins. (10 mins)

Main Lesson

- Remind pupils of the work they have done in this unit, from solids, liquids and gases, through to mixtures.
- You could explain that sometimes it's important to be able to describe what sort of substance something is, using symbols. Explain that pupils may see the following written after substances in books:
  (s) = solid
  (l) = liquid
  (g) = gas
  (aq) = aqueous or dissolved in water
- Get pupils to carry out 'Grouping chemicals by their state'. Details are given in the pupil book. Allow open responses here, as all the substances exhibit properties of more than one state. The important aspect here is the reasoning behind the answers.
- Establish that it is not always easy to decide whether something is a solid, liquid or gas.
- Get the pupils to carry out the 'Grouping chemicals as pure or impure' activity. The main focus of this is on the planning of the experiment. Pupils will need advice on what to include in their method. Many pupils will fail to include enough detail. You may wish not to carry out the practical, depending on the time you have available. If you do, plans must be checked before practical work starts.

Plenary Suggestions

Mixture muddle

Give pupils a list of mixtures which they must describe how to separate. For example, mixed fruit [pick each type of fruit out], mud and water [filter it] and sugar in water [evaporation or distillation]. (5 mins)

I've got the key

Ask pupils to prepare a key to guide someone into deciding whether a substance is a solid, a liquid, a gas or a mixture. [The key could start with the question, 'Does it flow?' No – it's a solid; Yes – next question …] (10 mins)

Answers to in-text questions

a Solid, liquid and gas.

b Milk is a mixture of mainly fat and water (an emulsion) and is therefore not scientifically pure.

Practical Support

Grouping chemicals by their state

Equipment and materials required

Per group: watch glass with some ketchup on it, watch glass with some hair gel on it, watch glass with some emulsion paint on it.

Details

See pupil book. Encourage pupils to consider why each substance can be classified as more than one state. It may be helpful if the emulsion paint has started to dry around the edges.

Safety

Pupils must not eat the ketchup.

Grouping chemicals as pure or impure

Equipment and materials required

Per group: a range of the equipment used for the practicals in lessons C2.7 to C2.10, depending upon what methods the pupils plan, a bottle of ink, a bottle of water (distilled or tap, depending on whether you wish the pupils to find it pure or not), a jar of mixed salt and chalk, labelled 'White powder'; Extension: 20:80 ethanol: water mix, labelled 'Water sample 2'.

Details

Refer to pupil book. The challenge is to decide whether the substances are pure or not. Pupils may guess that the ink is not pure. They may also suggest that the water is pure: if they do this, tell them they cannot be sure if it is or not as something may be dissolved in it.

Safety

Ethanol is highly flammable and harmful: CLEAPSS Hazcard 40A.

Wear eye protection.

Differentiation

SEN

Provide pupils with a jumbled method for the 'Grouping chemicals as pure or impure' activity which they must sort into the correct order.

Extension

Get pupils to extend the practical by giving them a mixture of ethanol and water. They will have to employ fractional distillation to prove that it is a mixture. Safety: ethanol is highly flammable and harmful. Wear eye protection.

Answers to summary questions

1
 a) Classification: grouping things based on observations.
 b) Mixture: more than one substance, not chemically joined.
 c) Pure: only one substance.
 d) Method: a step-by-step guide to an experiment.

2 Pupil's own method to show how they would separate salt from rock salt.

Answers to Particles in Action – End of Topic Questions

Answers to know your stuff questions

1

Property	Solid	Liquid	Gas
Can flow		✓	✓
Cannot be squashed	✓		
Takes the shape of its container		✓	✓

[5]

2
- **a** More than one substance; [1]
  not chemically joined. [1]
- **b** Water. [1]
- **c** Distillation. [1]
- **d** Solvent line (water mark) is above any §colours. [1]
- **e** Three. [1]

3
- **a** Evaporation. [1]
- **b** Diagram A. [1]
- **c** Gas particles move faster than liquid particles. [1]
- **d** They move randomly and in all directions. [1]

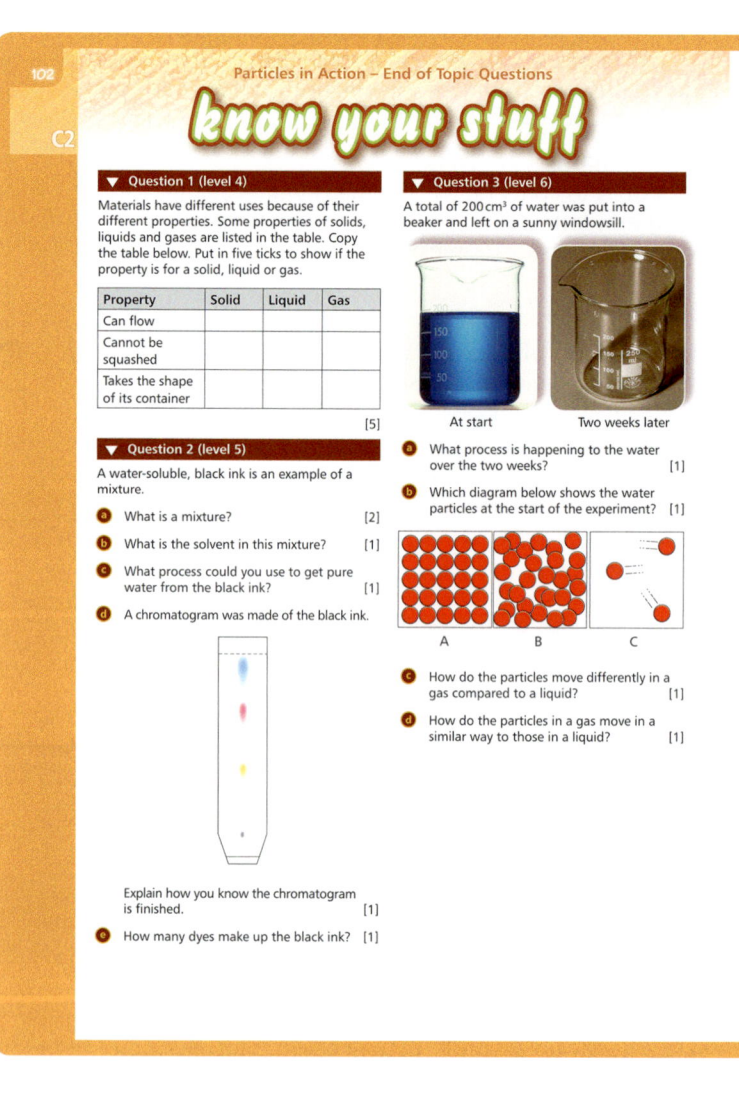

Particles in Action – End of Topic Questions

How Science Works

Question 1 (level 4)

Saffron and Baljit wanted to compare how quickly different-sized pieces of sugar would dissolve in water.

a What is the dependent variable? (This is the variable that Saffron and Baljit used to judge the effect of varying sizes of the pieces of sugar.)

Choose from the list below:

time   particle size   temperature
[1]

b What is the symbol for the unit of the dependent variable? Choose from the list below:

s   cm   °C   [1]

c Saffron and Baljit investigated the solubility of icing sugar, caster sugar and granulated sugar.

Draw a table for them to put their results into. [3]

d Below is a picture of Saffron's stop watch. This is the reading that she saw for the time it took for the granulated sugar to look like it had disappeared.

How many seconds did it take for the granulated sugar to dissolve? Give your answer to the nearest second. [1]

Question 2 (level 5)

An anonymous letter was sent to Bob, from someone in his class. The letter was written in blue ink and only three other people in the class use blue ink.

a What technique could Bob use to separate the dyes in the inks? [1]

b Bob's method is written in the wrong order below. Copy and complete by putting the letters in order from 1 to 7. The first one has been done for you.

1 = G

A Drop a sample of each ink onto each of the crosses.
B Observe until the water level is above all the inks; then allow to dry.
C Roll the paper and clip it.
D Take an rectangular piece of chromatography paper and draw a pencil line about 1 cm from the bottom edge.
E Lower the paper into the water, so that the pencil line is closest to the bottom.
F Put four crosses on the pencil line.
G Put about ½ cm of water in the bottom of a beaker. [6]

Question 3 (level 6)

Lucy decided to investigate how the mass changes when copper sulfate dissolves in water. Below is a label on the bottle of the chemical:

copper sulfate ✗

a Which hazard symbol is on the bottle? [1]

b Give one safety rule that Lucy should follow when using this chemical. [1]

c Lucy measured 100 g of water at 40°C into a beaker. She then measured 1 g of copper sulfate. Predict the mass of the copper sulfate solution. Explain your answer. [2]

d How could Lucy improve the precision of her mass readings? [1]

Answers to How Science Works questions

1 a Time. [1]

b s. [1]

c

Type of sugar	Time(s)
Icing	
Caster	
Granulated	

Correct column heading. [1]
Correct units for time. [1]
Inserting the types of sugar. [1]

d 233 s. [1]

2 a Chromatography. [1]

b G Put about ½ cm of water in the bottom of a beaker.
D Take a rectangular piece of chromatography paper and draw a pencil line about 1 cm from the bottom edge.
F Put four crosses on the pencil line.
A Drop a sample of each ink onto each of the crosses.
C Roll the paper and clip it.
E Lower the paper into the water, so that the pencil line is closest to the bottom.
B Observe until the water level is above all the inks; then allow to dry. [6]

3 a Harmful. [1]

b One of: wear eye protection/wear gloves/wash hands after use/tie loose clothing or hair back [1]

c Mass would be 101 g; [1]
because the water particles and copper sulfate particles are still the only things in the beaker. [1]

d Record the mass to more decimal places (using a more sensitive balance). [1]

P1.1 Electricity and Magnetism

NC links for the topic
- Energy, electricity and forces: forces are interactions between objects and can affect their shape and motion.
- Use a range of scientific methods and techniques to develop and test ideas and explanations.
- Assess risk and work safely in the laboratory, field and workplace.
- Evaluate scientific evidence and working methods.
- Use appropriate methods, including ICT, to communicate scientific information and contribute to presentations and discussions about scientific ideas.

Level descriptors for the topic
- AT1 level 4: Pupils recognise some applications and implications of science, such as the use of electrical components to make electrical devices. They decide on an appropriate approach including using a fair test to answer a question, and select suitable equipment and information from that provided. They record their observations, comparisons and measurements using tables and bar charts and begin to plot points to form simple graphs. They evaluate their working methods to make practical suggestions for improvements.
- AT1 level 5: Pupils decide appropriate approaches to a range of tasks, including selecting sources of information and apparatus. They describe phenomena and processes, such as balanced forces, drawing on abstract ideas (magnetic fields).
- AT1 level 6: Pupils communicate qualitative and quantitative data effectively using scientific language and conventions. (Drawing of circuit diagrams, magnetic field diagrams, force diagrams.)
- AT4 level 6: Pupils describe some evidence for some accepted scientific ideas, such as the transfer of energy by light, sound or electricity, and the refraction and dispersion of light. They explain the importance of some applications and implications of science.
- AT4 level 7: Pupils make links between different areas of science in their explanations, such as between electricity and magnetism. They explain, using abstract ideas where appropriate, the importance of science, such as the uses of electromagnets.

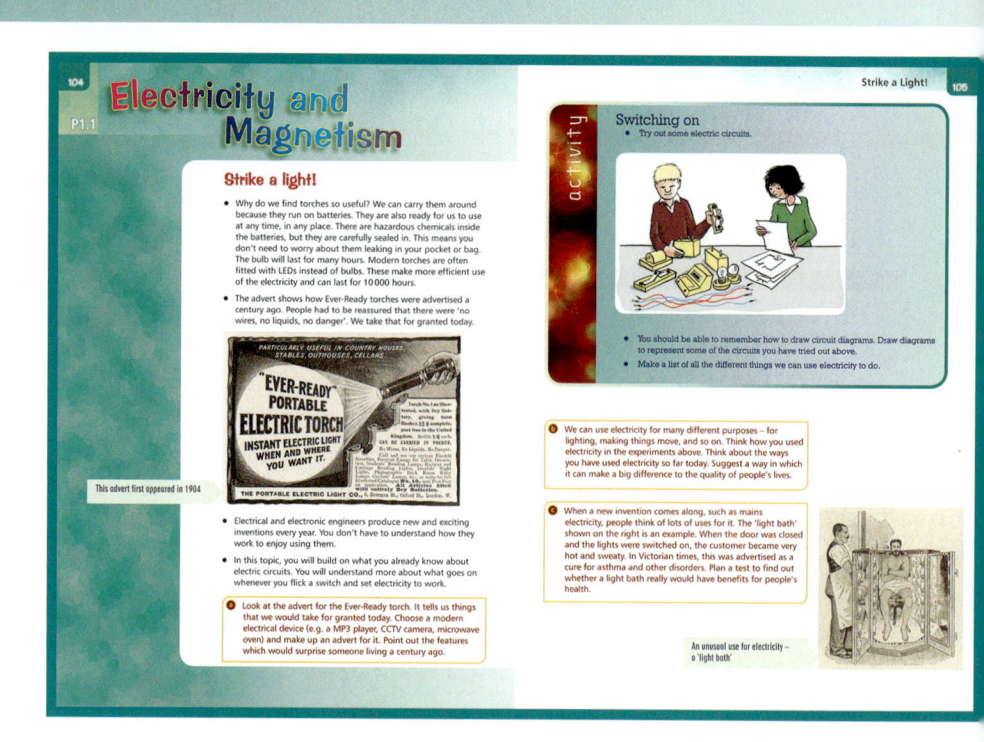

Learning Objectives
Pupils should learn:
- How to make detailed observations about the operation of circuits.
- How to carry out simple experiments safely in a laboratory.
- That electrical circuits can be used for a wide variety of functions.

Learning Outcomes
- All pupils should be able to list a range of battery-operated devices and discuss their usefulness.
- Most pupils should be able to describe what happens when switches are used in particular circuits.
- Some pupils should also be able to draw a circuit diagram for a circuit they have investigated.

How Science Works
- Identify and use the conventions of various genres for different audiences and purposes in scientific writing. (1.1c)

Functional Skills Link-up
English
- Present information/ideas concisely, logically and persuasively. (Level 2)
ICT
- Organise information of different forms or from different sources to achieve a purpose. (Level 2)

Learning Styles
Visual: Making observations about circuits.
Auditory: Explaining verbally what is happening in a circuit.
Kinaesthetic: Manipulating a range of circuits.
Interpersonal: Working in groups to discuss the functions of circuits.

Strike a Light!

The Lesson

Starter Suggestions

Batteries not included
Show the pupils a very large battery and a very small one (from a watch). Ask them to come up with explanations of how they work and why they are different. Encourage them to use the terms 'energy', 'current' and 'voltage'. This will allow you to see if they have previously established a link between the concepts of electricity and energy. (5–10 mins)

One hundred years
Use an archive video clip to show the pupils what life was like at the beginning of the twentieth century. They can discuss how technology, especially electrical devices, has changed lives in the intervening years. (10–15 mins)

Main Lesson

- This is the introductory lesson to the electricity and magnetism topic and its main purpose is to assess the pupils' prior knowledge. This could be very wide-ranging, so it may be necessary to adapt the future lessons to meet the needs of specific groups of individuals.

- When you are discussing torches at the start of the lesson, it is handy to have a range available. Take these apart and show the components to the pupils. You might like to discuss the battery life of some other devices, such as MP3 players or mobile phones; some of which have LED torches built in anyway.

- You can get the pupils to work on a timeline of electrical invention for display during this topic. This can help develop their research skills.

- A significant portion of the lesson should be dedicated to the 'Switching on' practical task. Discuss the function of the circuits with groups of pupils as they test them, so that you can get an impression of their level of understanding. If possible, encourage description of the energy transfers occurring in each of the devices.

- Instead of having each pupil visit each station, you could split them into a number of groups containing six pupils. Allocate each pupil a letter (a to f) and the pupils then go and study that particular circuit. They then reconvene in the original groups and describe and discuss the circuit they have explored. This helps to develop their communication skills.

- It's important that the pupils record their observations clearly using phrases like 'When the switch is pressed the lamp lights up'. Higher attaining pupils should be giving explanations of what they think is happening in the circuit. Check the notes that the pupils make. This will inform you about their knowledge of current and energy, which is essential for the remainder of the topic. The pupils should gain an understanding that circuits have many uses and that electricity is a very convenient way of transferring energy from place to place.

Plenary Suggestions

Battery mismatch
Give the pupils mixed-up photographs of some electrical devices and the batteries that operate them. They need to match them together. You could use real equipment if enough is available. (5–10 mins)

Another hundred years
The pupils should imagine that they are 11-year-olds taking part in a lesson in the year 2100. They should describe how different their lives are from those of the pupils at the start of the twenty-first century. You could show them a 'historical' clip from 2008 to show how primitive technology was back then! (10–15 mins)

Practical Support

Switching On

Equipment and materials required
A set of practical stations with the circuits described below:

a) A simple series circuit with a 3 V battery, 'press to make' switch and 3 V lamp.

b) A series circuit with a 3 V battery, 3 V lamp and 0–100 kΩ variable resistor that can be used to dim the light.

c) A parallel circuit including a 3 V battery and two 3 V lamps controlled by separate switches.

d) A low voltage power supply operated electromagnet (nail with coil) and some magnetic pins. Use a 'push to make' switch in the circuit so that it only remains active when the switch is pressed down.

e) A parallel circuit with two 3 V lamps powered by a 3 V battery pack. Use a two-way switch on one lamp or the other.

f) A battery-powered circuit with a lamp and light-dependent resistor. The lamp turns on when the LDR is covered up by the pupils.

Details
Depending on the size of the class you may need two or three sets of each circuit set up. The pupils need to explore a range of circuits so that they can appreciate the different applications they can have and the ways in which they operate. Set up each of the circuits as a separate station along with instruction cards telling the pupils what to try.

Safety
The circuits should be safe to operate, but test the electromagnet to make sure it does not overheat when in operation. Lock the power supply voltage if possible, so that overheating is less likely.

Answers to activity

a Circuit diagrams should contain appropriate symbols and connections.

Answers to in-text questions

a Pupils produce suitable advertisement.

b Answers related to making life simpler or easier or energy supplies being convenient.

c Test needs to involve some aspect of health that can actually be measured.

P 1.2 Complete Circuits

NC links for the lesson
- Energy, electricity and forces: electricity in circuits can produce a variety of effects (including current and voltage in series and parallel circuits).

Learning Objectives
Pupils should learn:
- That a complete circuit is required for an electrical current.
- How a circuit can be represented by circuit symbols.
- That some materials are good electrical conductors while others are insulators.

Leaning Outcomes
- All pupils should be able to identify the circuit symbols for a battery, bulb and switch.
- Most pupils should be able to construct simple circuits from circuit diagrams.
- Some pupils should also be able to draw accurate circuit diagrams and explain how they work in terms of current.

How Science Works
- Describe and record observations and evidence systematically. (1.2d)

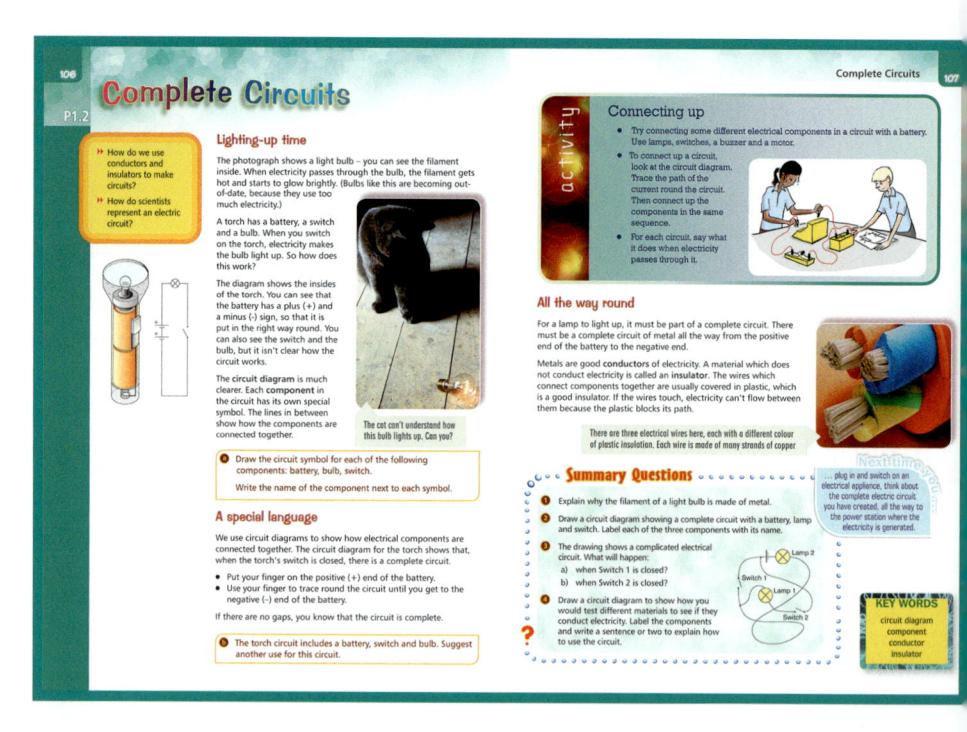

The Lesson

Starter Suggestions

Symbolic

Show the pupils some everyday symbols and ask them to explain what they mean. Start with symbols that give strong visual clues about their meaning (e.g. men working in road) and move onto the more abstract (nuclear radiation). You should include the symbols for a switch, lamp and battery. (5 mins)

A flick of a switch

The pupils must list all of the electrical devices that can be switched on and off in the laboratory. Longest list wins. Are there devices that need more than one switch to turn them on? Are there switches that turn on more than one device at the same time? (10 mins)

Learning Styles
Visual: Analysing circuit diagrams and their relationship to physical circuits.
Auditory: Explaining verbally what is happening in a circuit.
Kinaesthetic: Building and manipulating circuits.
Interpersonal: Working in groups to discuss the function of circuits.
Intrapersonal: Thinking back to their KS2 work on electricity.

Answers to summary questions

1. The filament must conduct electricity if it is to light up.
2. [Circuit diagram showing battery, bulb and switch]
3. a) Lamp 2 lights up.
   b) Nothing happens – lamp 1 does not light.
4. [Circuit diagram with battery, lamp, space for connecting test material.] Connect the material between the two clips. If the material conducts, the lamp will light up.

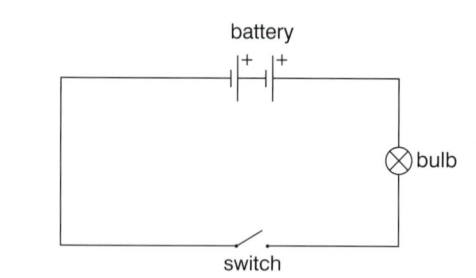

Complete Circuits

Main Lesson

- Pupils have already studied basic circuits at Key Stage 2; they should be familiar with lamps, switches and batteries. Use the symbols for these components in the 'symbolic' starter activity to check this.
- Some may have used the older 'bump in a circle' symbol for a lamp. This should be discouraged; the 'cross in a circle' is much easier to draw, especially when it is on a vertical line in the circuit. The pupil book uses the newer symbol, so all pupils need to be aware of it.
- Real circuits will not often look like their circuit diagrams but many pupils think that they should do. Explain to them that it's only important what is connected to what. Show them this by building a circuit from a diagram connection by connection. Make sure that the resulting circuit looks a bit of a mess but still works.
- It is vital that the pupils can follow the current around the circuit; all other understanding is based around this idea. Trace the current in diagrams and your real circuit. In each device, mention the important energy transfers taking place, for example electrical energy → light and heat in a lamp.
- Pupils should not be told about the flow of electrons at this stage. This would lead to some of confusion about what is happening as the current is traced from positive to negative; just get the idea of a *flow of electricity* across to them. The electrons will be introduced next lesson.
- Pupils can now try to build circuits using a range of components in the 'Connecting up' activity. The goal is to get them to construct the circuit correctly and then simply describe what it does. If some components are not available, then just miss out the circuit.
- Pupils need to be shown how to build the circuits component by component, the same way that they trace the current. Start with the battery and add one component at a time until the connections go back to the battery again. Most problems that pupils have in assembling circuits can be solved using this approach.
- Pupils should be familiar with conductors and insulators, but it is worth demonstrating some materials like plastic strips, copper and graphite rods. Pupils could carry out these tests if time permits.
- It's worth being very fussy about how the pupils must draw circuit diagrams. Don't allow *any* gaps at all, point out that the circuit would be incomplete; using little 'blobs' to show connections is a good idea. Straight lines are important too, so encourage the use of a ruler.

Plenary Suggestions

Any bright ideas?
Show the pupils a full-size mains bulb. Ask them to describe which parts conduct and which don't. Get them to look closely at the filament. Show them the internal parts of other components too, a motor for example. (10 mins)

A magic lamp!
Demonstrate how to light up a fluorescent tube without connecting it with wires. Use a Van De Graaff generator and hold the tube close to it. A small current will pass through you and light the tube. Challenge the higher attaining pupils to explain this. Test this idea out first and keep pupils well back from the VDG. (5 mins)

Safety: VDG: CLEAPSS handbook/CD-ROM section 12.9.1. Be aware of damage to computers, mobile phones, watches, etc. Check pupils' health before using one.

Practical Support

Connecting up

Equipment and materials required

Per group: a battery pack (3 V), two 3 V bulbs, two switches (press to close), six connecting leads, a buzzer, a small electric motor (optional).

Details

The pupils should construct the circuits one at a time and then describe what they do. These descriptions should include what happens when individual switches are pressed. Try to get the pupils to connect the idea of current and energy being provided to components and then being transferred in the components. They should be tracing this current, especially through the parallel circuits they make. Many pupils struggle with assembling circuits; pair lower attaining pupils up with higher attaining ones.

Differentiation

SEN
For lower attaining pupils, you may wish to use photographs of circuits alongside the circuit diagrams so that the pupils can make connections between them. Locktronic type boards can also make the relationship between diagram and circuit construction easier but they are unreliable when rusty or dirty.

Extension
Higher attaining pupils can add a greater range of components in their circuits including an LED. This should be connected in series with a 1 kΩ protective resistor and to a 4.5 V power supply. Ask them to describe what happens when this is placed facing one direction compared to another. They could also try to build a circuit that can turn a light on and off from two separate switches, like those on landings controlled from upstairs and downstairs.

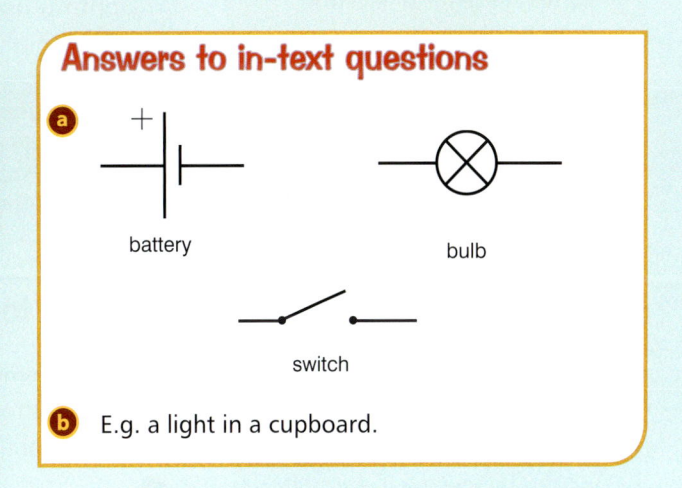

Answers to in-text questions

a battery, bulb, switch

b E.g. a light in a cupboard.

P1.3 Electric Current

NC links for the lesson
- Energy, electricity and forces: electricity in circuits can produce a variety of effects (including current and voltage in series and parallel circuits).

Learning Objectives
Pupils should learn:
- That an electric current is a flow of electrons in metal wires.
- How to measure the current in a circuit with an ammeter.
- How adding components, such as bulbs, affects the current in a circuit.

Leaning Outcomes
- All pupils should be able to measure an electric current using an ammeter.
- Most pupils should be able to describe how an electric current can be increased.
- Some pupils should also be able to describe an electric current in terms of electron movement.

How Science Works
- Use an existing model or analogy to explain a phenomenon. (1.1a1)

Learning Styles
Visual: Analysing circuit diagrams and their relationship to physical circuits.

Auditory: Explaining verbally what is happening in a circuit.

Kinaesthetic: Building and manipulating circuits.

Interpersonal: Working in groups to build curcuits.

Intrapersonal: Appreciating that electrons are not used up when they travel around a circuit.

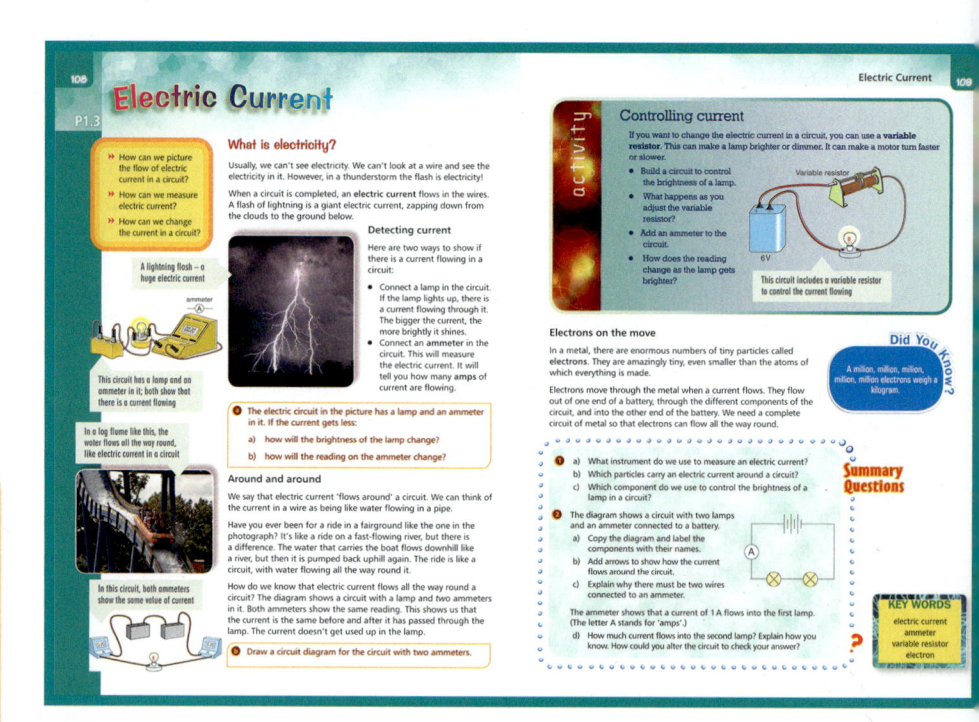

The Lesson

Starter Suggestions

Zzzapp

Use a Van de Graaff generator to demonstrate the flow of electricity. Generate sparks, linking this with the lightning mentioned in the pupil book. Emphasise the flow; talk about how the electricity moves from one place to another. This leads to the idea of a current. (10 mins)

Safety: VDG: CLEAPSS handbook/CD-ROM section 12.9.1. Be aware of damage to computers, mobile phones, watches, etc. Check pupils' health before using one.

Lighting up

Challenge the pupils to build a circuit that lights up a lamp and is controlled by a simple switch. (5–10 mins)

A river runs through it

Show the pupils a video clip about the flow of a river from its source into the oceans and perhaps the rest of the water cycle. Concentrate on the flow of the water particles and the word 'current'. (10–15 mins)

Answers to summary questions

1
a) An ammeter.
b) Electrons.
c) A variable resistor.

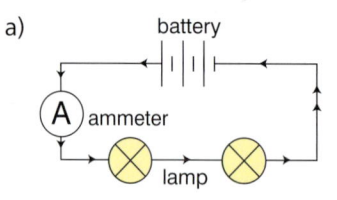

2
a) [circuit diagram showing battery, ammeter, and lamp]

b) Arrows to show current from positive to negative terminal.
c) The current has to flow through the ammeter, in *and* out.
d) 1A; you could place the ammeter after the lamp.

Electric Current

Main Lesson

- Pupils should have experienced building very basic circuits during their Key Stage 2 course. They shouldn't have much trouble when building a circuit with a lamp and battery.
- When they add the ammeter, it is best to keep the lamp in place so that the pupils still have a visual representation of the current. You'll have to introduce the unit of current; the ampere or amp as it's usually called.
- Sometimes the ammeter is connected the wrong way around and gives a negative value; this confuses some pupils so get them to switch the leads to the meter around.
- The pupils should now adapt the circuit by adding a variable resistor to control the current. They should easily see how the brightness of the lamp is related to the current, but check that they can state this relationship to you. As an alternative, the pupils can use a set of bulbs and measure the current when there is one bulb, then two, and finally three in series.
- The idea of an invisible current in the wires is something many pupils will struggle with, and it is essential to get them to develop a model of the process. This is the most difficult aspect of the lesson for the pupils and you will need to take some time to discuss the ideas.
- The model used in the pupil book is a water flume, where the water represents the electrons and a pump represents the battery. Take great care that the pupils understand that you are attempting to describe what the current is like, not what it actually is. The water current does not get used up as it goes around the flume and similarly the electrons in the circuit are not used up when they travel. This is a point very often misunderstood by pupils with a majority believing that electrons are used up when they light up the lamp. Some pupils may point out that some water escapes. This is a limitation with the model and you may wish to explain that all science models have some limits – an excellent opportunity to reinforce 'How Science Works'.
- An alternative model uses a loop of rope to represent the current. The loop is held by a group of pupils, these represent components. One of the pupils acts as the battery and pushes the rope around causing the 'current' to pass through the components. The Institute of Physics has resources to support this model.
- There are various computer simulations showing current in a metal wire. Some will be at an appropriate level for the pupils. Most simulations correctly show that the electrons move from the negative terminal to the positive, while the current is in the opposite direction. This can lead to quite a lot of confusion for the pupils.
- Finally, check that the pupils have the correct picture of electrons moving around the circuit carrying energy to the components as they go.

Plenary Suggestions

Model
The pupils should compare their model of a current, the water flume, with the real thing. What does each part represent? (10–15 mins)

Electron journeys
Ask the pupils to imagine they are an electron on a journey around a circuit that has a cell, two bulbs and a variable resistor. Ask them to describe this journey using the key words: current, energy, cell, bulb, heat and light. Some pupils may like to do this as a comic strip. (10–15 mins)

Practical Support

Controlling current

Equipment and materials required

Per group: a 12 V power supply, a 10 W bulb (or three), a variable resistor (1 kΩ), an ammeter, four connecting leads.

Details

The pupils connect up the components in a simple series circuit and investigate the effect of changing the resistance on the current. Depending on the type of variable resistor used, you will need to explain how to control the resistance to the pupils. As an alternative, the pupils can measure the current when different numbers of bulbs are placed in series. This can give a relationship that is a bit easier to understand as long as the bulbs are identical.

The experiment can be carried out with battery packs at lower operating voltages, but the current will be smaller and milli-ammeters will need to be used.

Differentiation

SEN
Pupils may need some help setting up the circuits. As in the previous lesson the pupils could be given photographs of what the completed circuit should look like. Locktronic type boards are also an option.

Extension
With higher attaining pupils you should discuss energy in the circuit and log flume in more detail. [The battery provides the electrons with energy and they lose this energy as they travel around the circuit. In the log flume the pump lifts up water and provides it with energy that is consequently loses as it travels back around the loop.]

You could ask the pupils to try to come up with their own model to describe an electric circuit. This is rather a difficult task, but they could be lead towards a rollercoaster type model or even a central heating version.

Homework Suggestion
The 'electron journeys' plenary makes a good homework task. The pupils can read out some of their descriptions next lesson and you can make sure that they use the correct concepts.

Answers to in-text questions

a) Decreasing the current will:
   a) Make the light dimmer.
   b) Reduce the reading on the ammeter.

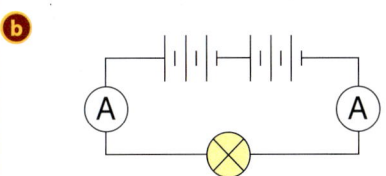

b)

P1.4 Cells and Batteries

NC links for the lesson
- Energy, electricity and forces: electricity in circuits can produce a variety of effects (including current and voltage in series and parallel circuits).

Learning Objectives
Pupils should learn:
- That cells/batteries produce a voltage that causes an electric current in a complete circuit.
- The size of a voltage depends on the number, and orientation, of the cells.
- How to use a voltmeter to measure the voltage in a circuit.

Leaning Outcomes
- All pupils should be able to describe what happens to the voltage of cells when they are combined in a battery.
- Most pupils should be able to describe what happens to the current in a circuit when the voltage is increased.
- Some pupils will also be able to measure the voltage of a battery using a voltmeter.

How Science Works
- Recognise the range of variables involved in an investigation and decide which to control. (1.2b)

Learning Styles
Visual: Designing an advertising campaign.
Auditory: Discussing the uses and limitations of batteries.
Kinaesthetic: Testing different fruits in a practical task.
Interpersonal: Working in groups during experiments.
Intrapersonal: Making conclusions about which fruit would make the best battery.

Answers to in-text questions
a. Battery-powered devices, e.g. remote control, calculator, clock.

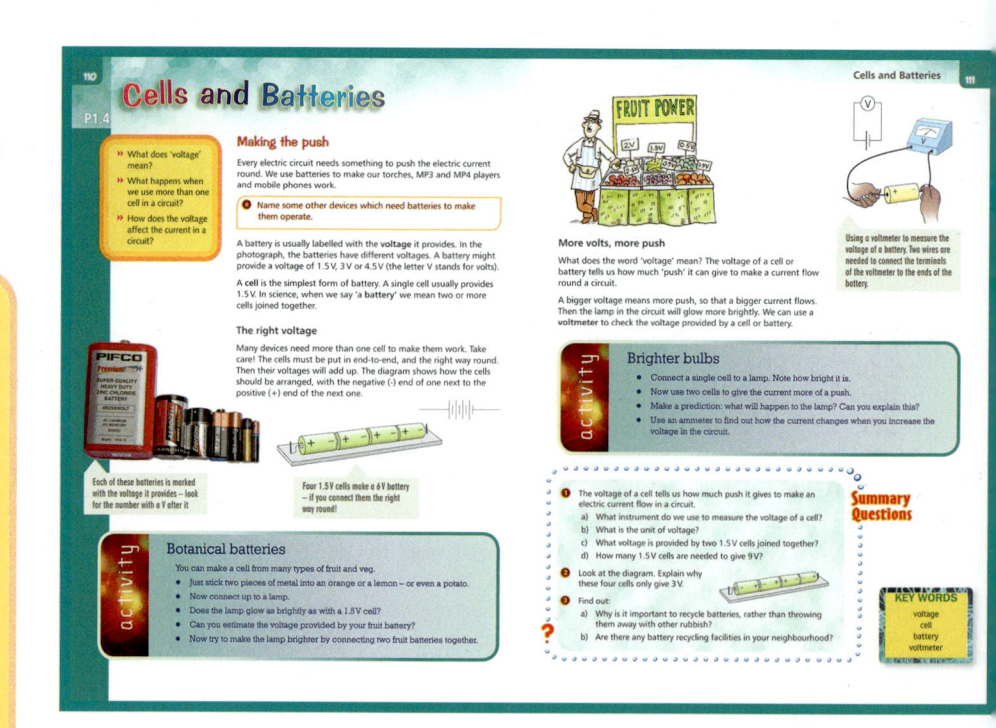

The Lesson

Starter Suggestions

Potato clock
Show the pupils a clock that operates using potato power. These are available in various gadget shops. Ask them to explain how they think it works. (10–15 mins)

Battery power
Pupils list devices that operate with batteries. They place items in the list in order of which device consumes the most energy to which consumes the least [e.g. radio-controlled model plane, portable TV, portable radio, mobile phone, personal music player.] Why can't all devices operate on battery power? (5–10 mins)

Main Lesson
- Show a wide range of batteries to the pupils including the typical AA batteries they will be most familiar with and some they may not know about. Introduce square batteries, rechargeable batteries, a photograph of a car battery and especially batteries that are usually integrated into devices, like a mobile phone. The pupils need to understand that, whatever they look like, the batteries have positive and negative terminals and a voltage rating.
- For the demonstration involving batteries, its best to have single battery holders (not the paired holders that are more common). This gives you a lot of flexibility in the way you connect the batteries.
- Demonstrate the effect of using a single 1.5 V battery on a 6 V bulb; it won't light up. Add three more batteries to the circuit, one at a time, until the lamp is fully lit. You can point out that each battery is providing the electrons

Cells and Batteries

with more energy as they travel, so they can provide more energy to the lamp. Later in the lesson, the pupils will look at the effect on the current of adding more cells so don't have an ammeter in the circuit.

- You can show what happens when some of batteries are connected the wrong way by just reversing the connections. The bulb won't be harmed, but it is worth telling the pupils that some devices can be damaged if batteries are connected the wrong way around in them.
- The main practical activity, 'Botanical batteries' can take up a quite a bit of time but is well worth carrying out. With the higher attaining pupils you may wish to introduce the use of a voltmeter to measure voltage produced by the fruits.
- The results from the battery experiment can be varied, so get the groups to compare results with each other until they reach an appropriate conclusion about which fruit provides the highest voltage (usually kiwi). Talk about the fairness of comparing results across groups as an opportunity to introduce the importance of controlling variables (How Science Works).
- After the practical is complete, you can show the pupils the inside of a simple battery to show that these depend on a chemical reaction to provide their voltage too. A zinc–carbon 'D' (or 'R20') sized cell can be sawn in half in advance of the lesson to show the graphite rod, zinc case and ammonium chloride and manganese oxide pastes.
- Discuss the energy transfer taking place inside the cell; chemical energy is transferred to electrical energy (and thermal energy warming up the cell). A battery 'dies' when all of the chemicals have reacted together. The website 'www.energizer.com' has a useful animation of the parts and processes occurring in a battery.
- Take the opportunity to discuss the environmental impact of battery disposal. Many contain heavy metals that are highly toxic and these metals leak out if the batteries are simply dumped along with normal rubbish. These can poison wildlife or leak into human water supplies.
- You could now get the pupils to carry out the 'Brighter bulbs' activity from the pupil book.
- Round off the lesson by reminding pupils that a battery is just a device where a chemical reaction takes place. This reaction provides the electrons with the energy they give out as they travel around a circuit.

Plenary Suggestions

Do not dispose of in fire
Batteries should not be disposed on in general household waste. The pupils should design a battery disposal point for the UK to be situated in a supermarket. They could also produce a leaflet to encourage people to dispose of batteries properly. (10–15 mins)

Extra-Super-Ultra-Mega Long Life (Plus)
Many batteries make claims about how long they will last. The pupils should design a series of tests that would be able to check these claims. They should remember it would be a bit dull watching a lamp for a few hours. (5–10 mins)

Practical Support

Botanical batteries

Equipment and materials required
Per group: a range of citrus fruits (lemon, orange, kiwi, grapefruit) quartered, a 1.5 V bulb, a voltmeter and or milli-ammeter, a copper and a zinc electrode (just strips of the metal that won't bend too much), connecting leads, crocodile clips, a tray.

Details
It's important to test this practical out beforehand to see if the fruit will provide enough current to light even a low-powered lamp. If not, then use the voltmeters or a milli-ammeter to compare the fruit instead.

The pupils need to place one of both types of electrode into the fruit and then connect these through a lamp. Make sure that the pupils use two different electrodes. The voltmeter can be placed in parallel with the lamp if you want the pupils to measure the voltage produced by the fruit. A single piece of fruit is unlikely to provide a large enough current to light the lamp, but the pupils can place several fruits in series.

The practical tends to get a bit messy, lots of fruit juice on the leads and benches, so make sure you allocate enough time for a good clean up. To reduce the mess get the pupils to carry out the work in a tray.

Differentiation

SEN
Lower attaining pupils will need quite a bit of support in building their circuits. You may want to limit each group to one type of fruit, and then they can investigate the effect of increasing the number of fruits without changing the type of fruit. The results can then be shared with other groups.

Extension
Challenge higher attaining pupils to design a device that operates on 'fruit power'. They can even work on a marketing campaign for their product. Remember, fruit is renewable.

Homework Suggestion

The pupils could make a plan to test the claims about how long a rechargeable battery in a portable music player actually lasts. Can they really play music for 24 hours before needing to be recharged?

Answers to summary questions

1 a) A voltmeter.   b) Volts (V).
   c) 3 V   d) 6

2 One cell is the wrong way round.

3 Information about battery recycling; mention hazardous/polluting chemicals that should not be allowed to enter groundwater.

P1.5 Shocking Stuff

NC links for the lesson
- Energy, electricity and forces: electricity in circuits can produce a variety of effects (including current and voltage in series and parallel circuits).

Learning Objectives
Pupils should learn:
- That mains electricity is at a high voltage and that it can force a current through a person.
- That the current can cause burns or even kill.
- That a fuse is a device designed to melt if the current is too large.

Leaning Outcomes
- All pupils should be able to describe the action of a fuse.
- Most pupils should be able to explain why mains electricity is dangerous.
- Some pupils will also be able to state the UK mains voltage and to link this with the level of danger.

How Science Works
- Explain how action has been taken to control obvious risk and how methods are adequate for the task. (1.2c)

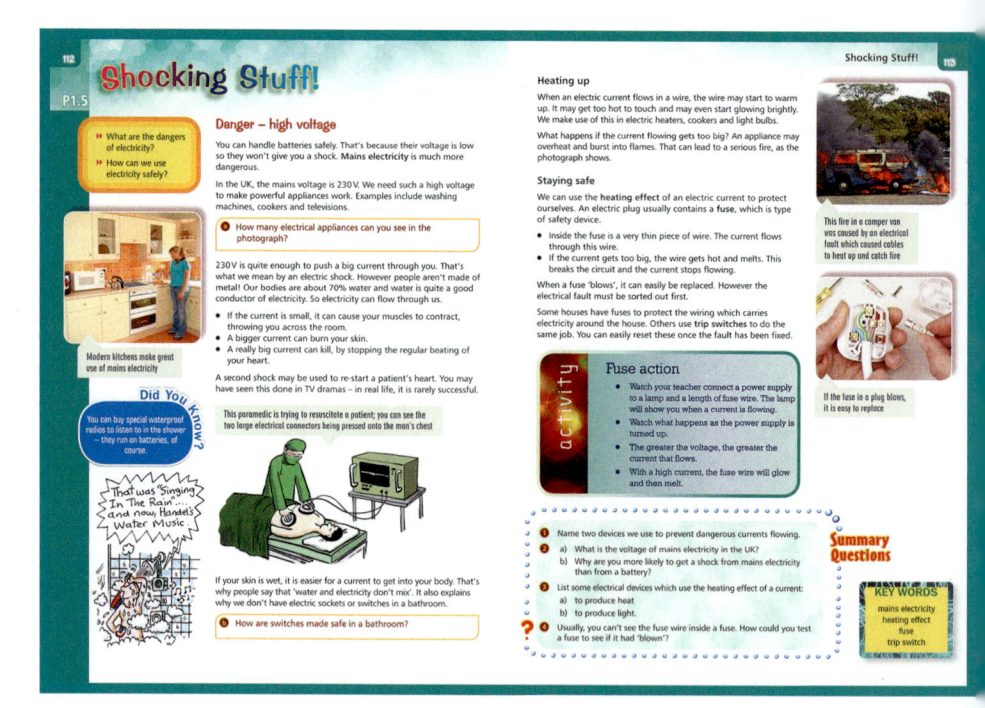

The Lesson

Starter Suggestions

Hot stuff

Ask the pupils to list as many devices that use electricity to produce heat as they can. Then they should list all of the other electrical devices that produce heat as a side effect [almost everything]. (5–10 mins)

Is it safe?

The pupils should give an explanation about why they think mains electricity is dangerous but batteries aren't. This will allow you to gather their misconceptions about the dangers and safety precautions. Ask them how big a voltage is needed to push a dangerous current through you? 1 V, 10 V, 100 V or 1000 V. Remind them that the Van de Graaff from an earlier lesson operated at several thousands volts but was not particularly dangerous. This leads to the idea that it is the power (amount of energy each second) that is transferred that is important. (10–15 mins)

Learning Styles
Visual: Watching various demonstrations.
Auditory: Listening to, and giving, explanations about why mains electricity is dangerous.
Kinaesthetic: Examining a plug.
Interpersonal: Discussing the dangers of mains electricity in groups.

Answers to in-text questions
a) Oven, TV, kettle, microwave oven, food processor (= 5).
b) Switches in bathroom operated by cord, which is a good insulator.

Answers to summary questions
1. Fuses and circuit breakers.
2. a) 230 V
   b) The voltage is larger and can push a current through you more easily.
3. a) An electric fire, a kettle, an iron, etc. produce heat.
   b) Light is produced by a light bulb.
4. Connect the fuse in a series circuit with a lamp and battery – if the lamp lights, the fuse has not blown.

Shocking Stuff

Main Lesson

- Due to the danger of mains electricity, there are a number of demonstrations in this lesson instead of a major practical activity for the pupils. The pupils should leave the lesson understanding the dangers of using mains electricity inappropriately, but they should not be afraid of its safe use. Let them make safety suggestions through the lesson. This will develop their 'How Science Works' skills.
- You can start off with a demonstration of electrical conduction through water. It is fairly difficult to push a current through pure water but a small about of salt changes this. Try the 'Water conducts' demonstration (see 'Practical Support'). Remind them that you have used low voltages because mixing water with mains electricity is dangerous; mains electricity would push a much bigger current through the water.
- Pupils will know that electricity is used to produce heat. Most won't be aware that an electric current always produces thermal energy. You can show that lamps produce heat by letting some low voltage lamps heat up a bit. Ask the pupils why you shouldn't take out a mains lamp when it has just been switched off.
- After this, check that the pupils understand that an electric current always causes heating. With higher attaining pupils you could link the heating effect to resistance (see Extension).
- A few pupils will be expecting a fuse to explode when it 'blows', so they will be a little disappointed when the circuit simply cuts off. The 'fire starter' demonstration (see 'Practical Support') should make up for the disappointment if you start a real fire.
- As another quick demonstration, you can place some wire wool (on a heat-resistant mat) across the terminals of a 1.5 V battery and it will ignite, each strand with a small orange glow. Be very careful that you don't burn your fingers. This is a handy way of starting a fire when you have been trapped in the jungle and it shows that even low voltages can cause fires.
- Bathrooms needs to have electric lights and sockets for electric razors. Discuss how these are made safe in the bathroom [pull cords and extra earthing].
- At the end of the lesson, remind the pupils that mains electricity is perfectly safe as long as it is used correctly.

Plenary Suggestions

Clear!
Show a video clip of a patient being shocked to restart the heart. The doctor always shouts 'Clear!' Ask the pupils to explain why this is important. What would happen to anybody touching the patient? What could happen to any electronic equipment? (5–10 mins)

A quick plug
Show the pupils a mains plug. Ask them to describe all of the components and their function. For example, why are the pins metal but the case is plastic? Make sure that there is no chance that a pupil could plug in an unwired mains plug into a socket. The pupils should not be asked to wire up the plug; merely explain what they think the parts are for. (10–15 mins)

Practical Support

Water conducts (demonstration)

Equipment and materials required
A 9 V battery (or low voltage d.c. power supply), a 500 cm^3 beaker, distilled water, salt, a stirrer, a 3 V lamp, connecting leads.

Details
Set up a series circuit with the lamp and battery so that there is a gap between two leads. Place the two leads in a beaker of distilled water and the lamp will not light, as 9 V is not sufficient to push a current through the water. Make sure that the pupils understand that you are using a low voltage and you would never try this with mains electricity. Gradually add salt to the water (you might need to stir a bit) and the lamp will light as the current passes through the solution. In our bodies the water contains many different salts and so conducts.

Fire starter (demonstration)
This is a simple demonstration of how a current can cause a fire and how a fuse can eliminate the risk.

Equipment and materials required
A heat-proof mat, a d.c. power supply, a 10 cm length of thin constantan or Nichrome wire coiled, connecting leads, four crocodile clips, a 1 A fuse, preferably in a clear glass casing.

Details
Set up a simple series circuit that consists of the wire sample connected to the power supply by the leads and crocodile clips. Make sure the wire is on a heat-proof mat as it reaches very high temperatures. Turn on the power supply and gradually increase the voltage; the wire will begin to glow red-hot and then white-hot. To show that this can cause a fire you can leave some paper on top of the wire. Watch out that you don't melt the plastic coating on the connecting leads.

Repeat the experiment, but this time add the fuse in series in the circuit. The fuse should melt long before the wire starts to get hot.

Differentiation

SEN
For these pupils concentrate on the safety features used to protect users from mains electricity.

Extension
These pupils should take a look at mains electricity in other countries. They can find out about the supply in the USA. They could take a look at what alternating current is compared to direct current and find out about the mains frequencies used in the UK and USA.

As an alternative, the pupils can look at the connection between resistance and the heating effect of a current. You can go through the model of electrons colliding with ions in the metal to release energy.

Homework Suggestion

The pupils can produce an electrical safety booklet containing a list of what we should and shouldn't do with mains electricity.

P1.6 Series and Parallel

NC links for the lesson
- Energy, electricity and forces
- Electricity in circuits can produce a variety of effects (including current and voltage in series and parallel circuits).

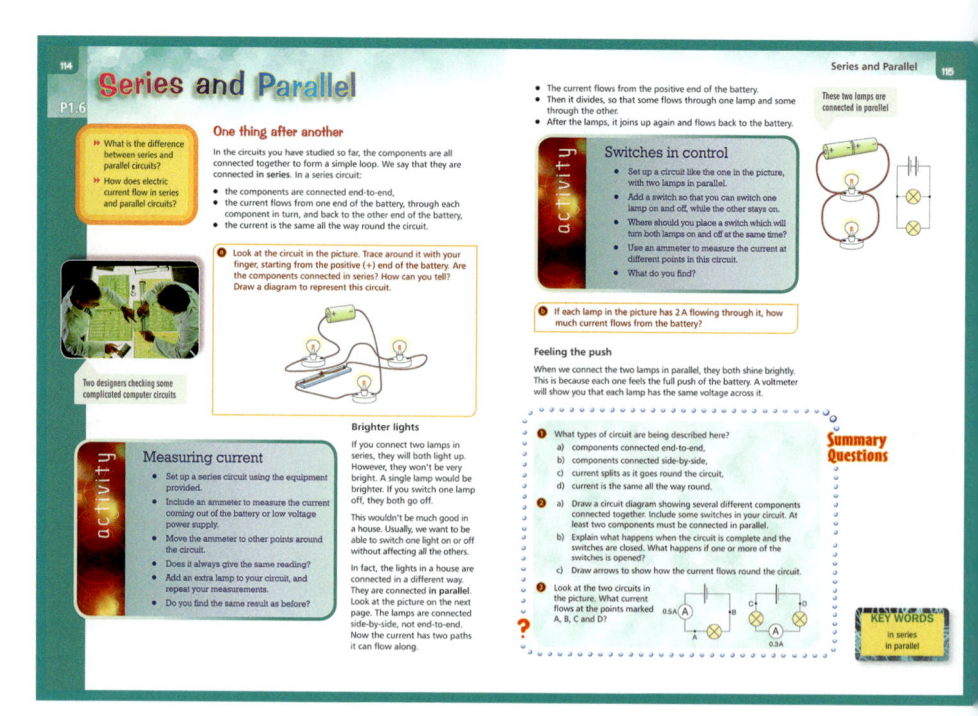

Learning Objectives
Pupils should learn:
- That in a series circuit the current is the same through all devices.
- How the current divides in parallel circuits.
- That the voltage across parallel branches is the same.

Leaning Outcomes
- All pupils will be able to describe the behaviour of the current in a series circuit.
- Most pupils will be able to describe how the current divides in a parallel circuit.
- Some pupils will also be able to state that the voltage across parallel branches in a circuit is the same.

How Science Works
- Describe and record observations and evidence systematically. (1.2d)

Learning Styles
Visual: Solving maze puzzles, picturing electron movement.
Auditory: Describing the flow of current in various circuits.
Kinaesthetic: Constructing circuits.
Interpersonal: Working in groups to set up circuits.
Intrapersonal: Making deductions about the behaviour of current in parallel circuits.

The Lesson

Starter Suggestions

Amazing circuits
Give the pupils a maze worksheet to find their way through. The first maze should have only one route through and the second should have two correct routes. (5–10 mins)

Continuity checking
Check that the pupils have remembered the key words and ideas from the previous lessons by using a crossword. Provide a clue for every one of the key words. (10 mins)

Main Lesson
- In this lesson the pupils are challenged to make more complicated circuits and take measurements of the current through components and the voltage across them.
- Start by making sure that the pupils understand the meaning of the word 'series' as in 'one after another'. It's a little bit like a television series where one episode follows another.
- Once you are sure that the pupils understand the concept of a series circuit they can carry out the 'Measuring current' activity.

Answers to summary questions

1. a) Series. b) Parallel. c) Parallel. d) Series.
2. a) [circuit diagram]
   b) Description of effect of closing switches
   c) Arrows showing current around circuit.
3. A= 0.5A, B= 0.5A, C= 0.3A, D= 0.3A.

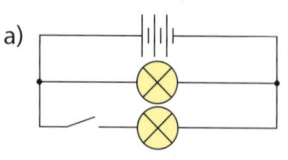

Series and Parallel

- The current measurement may well vary a little bit from point to point in the circuit. This may be a good point to mention the limitations of measuring devices. If the current seems to get less further around the circuit, then the idea of current being 'used up' will be reinforced in the pupils' minds – so watch out for this.
- After the practical you can show the circuit with three separate ammeters in it to confirm that the current is the same at the three different points. Reinforce the idea that the current isn't used up but energy is provided to each of the devices in turn.
- Show the pupils the problem with having bulbs in series. Place three in a series circuit and then unscrew one to show that they all go out. You could use an old-fashioned set of Christmas tree lights to show the same thing; but watch out, most modern ones use parallel bulbs. **Safety:** Old lights can be dangerous; make sure that the lights are safety tested.
- Remind the pupils of the meaning of the word 'parallel'. Use examples like parallel lines and parallel bars; they need to get the idea that the components are alongside each other and current can go both (or more) ways.
- This is a point where the analogy of the water flume stops being useful; flumes don't have parallel paths. You can use the idea of a river splitting and rejoining or you might consider using the idea that a circuit is a bit like a central heating system, the pump is the battery, the radiators are the components and the water is the current. This might help, but remember that many pupils won't really understand how a central heating system is designed.
- Pupils can now do the 'Switches in control' activity; they should attempt to measure the voltages across components in parallel. Measuring the voltage across components in parallel circuits will be particularly difficult for some. Make sure you demonstrate how to connect and move the voltmeter before the pupils start on the task. Check that all of the pupils have the expected results from the practical.
- To sum up the key ideas of the lesson a computer model/animation should be used to look at what is happening to the current in the circuit. Nothing solidifies the idea of a current branching better than 'watching' the electrons move around, split and rejoin.

Plenary Suggestions

Missing measurements

The pupils can be given a worksheet that has circuit diagrams containing ammeters and voltmeters. The pupils need to work out the values that have been missed off the meters using their knowledge of current and voltage. (10 mins)

Connect-up cards

Give the pupils a set of cards containing circuit symbols, including cells, bulbs, meters and connecting wires. The pupils have to place the cards in a way that makes a functioning circuit where all of the readings are correct. (5–10 mins)

Practical Support

Measuring current

Equipment and materials required

Per group: battery packs or low voltage power supply, two 3V lamps, ammeter, connecting leads.

Details

The pupils should set up a series circuit with one bulb. They measure the current leaving the battery and note it down. They then measure the current after the first bulb. They should find that the current is the same at all points in the circuit. After this they repeat the process with two bulbs in the circuit; their conclusion should be the same.

Switches in control

Equipment and materials required

Per group: battery packs or low voltage power supply, two 3V lamps, two switches, ammeter, connecting leads.

Details

The pupils set up the circuit as shown on the worksheet and then explore the effect of adding switches. Many pupils struggle to connect even two components in parallel, so you will have to check each circuit to make sure that the bulbs are in parallel before asking the pupils to try to place switches. The pupils then need to add in an ammeter before each bulb. They should find that the current going through each bulb is half of that coming from (and going back into) the battery. As usual there will be slight variations.

Pupils can then go on to measure the voltage across each of the bulbs when they are on. This should be the same as the voltage across the battery. In practice, they will probably find a slight variation due to different standards of connection or inaccuracy of the meter. Pupils will find it awkward to connect the voltmeter. Sometimes it is simplest to let them just touch the voltmeter leads against the terminals of the bulbs one at a time instead of making a permanent connection.

Differentiation

SEN

Lower attaining pupils will need a lot of support, especially in measuring voltages. If the pupils struggle, then just get them to measure voltages in a series circuit and note that the voltage is 'shared'.

Extension

These pupils can attempt to make measurements in more complex circuits. Ask the pupils to build a circuit that has two lamps in parallel followed by one in series and to investigate the current through and voltages across the bulbs.

Pupils could use their knowledge of circuits to design a circuit for stairs lights that can be switched on and off by two separate switches (one upstairs and one downstairs).

Homework Suggestion

Give the pupils a worksheet showing circuit diagrams with missing measurements. The pupils must use their knowledge of series and parallel circuits to fill in the gaps using the information already present.

Answers to in-text questions

a Yes, components are in series; current flows through each component in turn and back to the battery.

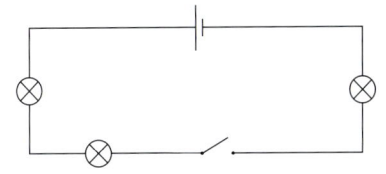

b 4 A.

P1.7 Magnetic forces

NC links for the lesson
- Energy, electricity and forces: forces are interactions between objects and can affect their shape and motion.

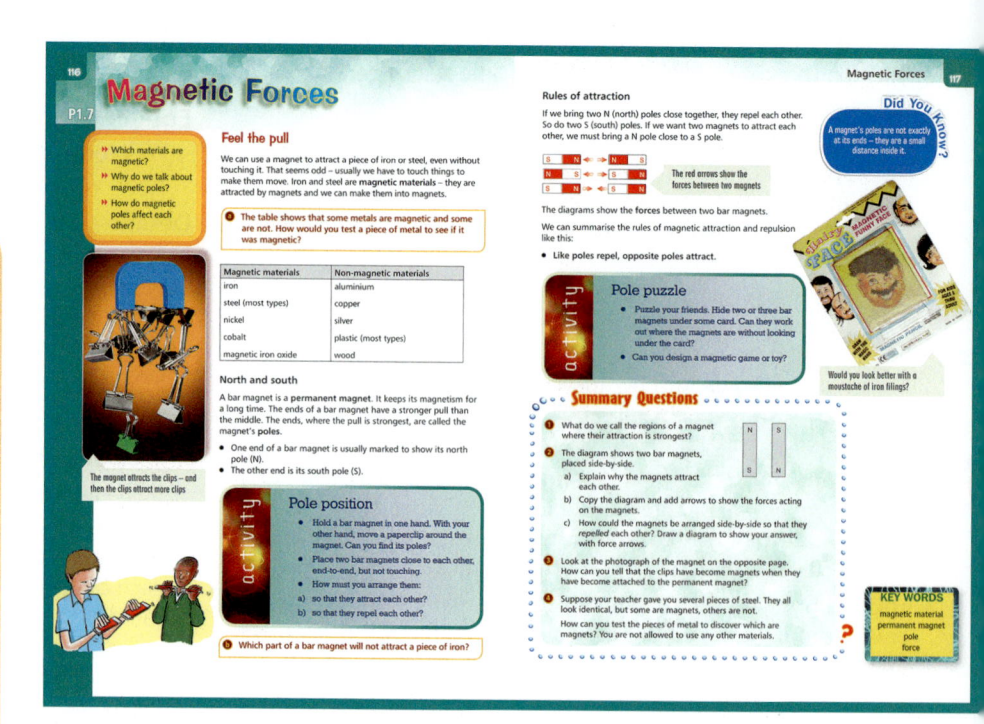

Learning Objectives
Pupils should learn:
- That some materials are magnetic while others are not.
- That magnets have two poles named 'north' and 'south'.
- About the interactions and forces between north and south poles of a magnet.

Learning Outcomes
- All pupils will be able to describe a simple test for magnetic materials.
- Most pupils will be able to describe the interactions between combinations of magnetic poles.
- Some pupils will also be able to describe that when a magnetic material is placed near a magnet it also becomes a magnet.

How Science Works
- Describe an appropriate approach to answer a scientific question using a limited range of information … (1.2a)

Learning Styles
Visual: Using force diagrams to explain forces.
Auditory: Discussing game design.
Kinaesthetic: Experimenting with magnets and constructing magnetic games.
Interpersonal: Discussing the design of magnet-based games.
Intrapersonal: Collaborating with others during game construction.

Answers to summary questions

1. Poles (north and south).

2. a) The opposite poles are near each other so there is an attractive force between them.
   b) [diagram: N → ← S / S → ← N]
   c) One of the magnets must be rotated through 180° so that the like poles are adjacent to each other.
   [diagram: N ← → N / S ← → S]

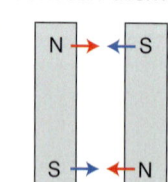

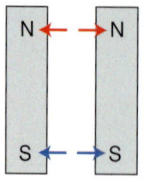

3. A clip which is stuck to the permanent magnet can then attract another clip.

4. Test for magnetisation – must observe repulsion between like poles; an un-magnetised sample will show attraction.

Magnetic forces

The Lesson

Starter Suggestions

Super-magnets
Place two strong ceramic magnets close to each other, but not quite close enough to overcome the friction of the desk. Nudge one towards the other and they will smack into each other and make a noise. Ask the pupils to explain what has happened. (5 mins).

Force facts
Get the pupils to list as many facts about forces as they remember. They should think about the types of force (gravity, friction, etc.) and what effect the forces can have (making things move, bending, squashing, stretching). (5–10 mins)

Main Lesson

- This lesson is a recap and then expansion of material covered in Key Stage 2. Most pupils will have encountered magnets before, as they are very common in children's games, but they will be unclear about the language used to describe them.
- Start by demonstrating the effect of a magnet on a magnetic material and the lack of effect on a non-magnetic one.
- It is a very common for pupils to think that all metals are magnetic; this misconception will have to be challenged again in the lesson. The best way is to let the pupils test as many of the materials mentioned in the pupil book as you have available.
- Pupils may already be aware of the idea of poles and they will know that these are found at the ends of the bar. You could show a horseshoe magnet to show that the position of the poles can be different.
- Bar magnets usually have a small indentation near the north pole to help identify it.
- The 'opposites attract' idea will be commonly known, but some pupils will be confused by the term 'like' so use alternative phrases as well such as 'same poles'.
- The pupils should spend a major portion of the lesson handling magnets, especially during the game construction. You should have some designs in mind or even complete designs to support lower attaining pupils.
- The Earth's magnetic field will be dealt with in P1.9, although some pupils will bring it up now. Answer any basic questions but hold off from the debate about whether the North Pole is a magnetic north pole.

Plenary Suggestions

Levitation
Challenge the pupils to make one magnet float above another. This can partly be achieved by placing one bar magnet on a surface and then lowering the south pole of another slowly onto the north pole of the first. It helps if the surface is rough enough to stop the magnets sliding. (5 mins)

Attract or repel?
Show the pupils a range of diagrams of various combinations of magnets. Ask them to describe what would happen to these. (5 mins)

Practical Support

Pole position
Equipment and materials required
Per pupil: a pair of bar magnets and a steel paper clip.

Details
See pupil book.

Pole puzzle
Equipment and materials required
Per group: three bar magnets, some card.

The exact requirements for the games depend on the designs the pupils come up with, but you should provide them with a range of magnets in different sizes, cardboards, scissors, pens and plastic Petri dishes as starting points.

Details
After the basic task, the pupils can design and build a simple game based around magnetic material. Possibilities include racetracks (dragging paper clips through a sheet of paper) and using iron filings to draw hair on faces (drawn inside Petri dishes).

Safety
If iron filings are used then the pupils will need to wear eye protection. They should also wash their hands afterwards to remove any stray particles.

Differentiation

SEN
You may want to mark the poles of magnets with N and S in permanent marker (or white paint for black magnets), especially if you use unusual magnets.

Provide designs for the games for lower attaining pupils so that they can spend more time constructing and playing them.

Extension
These pupils should investigate magnets other than bar magnets to find the poles. Possibilities include horseshoe magnets and magnets where the poles are on the larger faces, such as the ferrite magnets often used in building model motors. They could also research into which materials can be used to make permanent magnets.

Homework Suggestion

The pupils could make of list of all of the devices they can find that use magnets in their home.

Did You Know?

You can see that a magnet's poles are not exactly at its ends by looking at the alignment of iron filings sprinkled around the magnet. Trace the lines carefully and you can see that they meet inside the magnet. The pupils will be able to see this clearly if you place the magnet on an overhead projector and project the image onto the wall. Iron filings can be contained by using them in a clear plastic folder, sealed with tape or a clear plastic bag or container: CLEAPSS handbook/CD-ROM, section 12.22.

Answers to in-text questions

a E.g. bring permanent magnet close – do they attract each other?

b Middle of the magnet (half-way between poles).

P1.8 Making Magnets

NC links for the lesson
- Energy, electricity and forces: forces are interactions between objects and can affect their shape and motion.

Learning Objectives
Pupils should learn:
- How permanent magnets can be made using strong magnets.
- About methods for testing the strength of a magnet.

Learning Outcomes
- All pupils will be able to make a simple permanent magnet.
- Most pupils will be able to test the strength of a magnet.
- Some pupils will also be also able to evaluate the methods used for testing the strength of a magnet.

How Science Works
- Describe an appropriate approach to answer a scientific question using a limited range of information and making relevant observations or measurements. (1.2a)
- Describe and suggest how planning and implementation could be improved. (1.2e)

Functional Skills Link-up
ITC
- Access, navigate and search internet sources of information purposefully and effectively. (Level 1) See Homework Suggestion.

The Lesson

Starter Suggestions

MAGNET acrostic

Can the pupils come up with an acrostic using the word 'magnet' that is related to how they work? (5–10 mins)

Mine's better than yours

The pupils should design their own test for comparing the strength of magnets, without looking at the techniques shown in the pupil book. They should do this in as much detail as possible. If the technique is workable, then they can use it instead of one of the techniques in the pupil book in later experiments. (10–15 mins)

Learning Styles

Visual: Watching the demonstration of how to make a magnet.
Auditory: Describing their ideas about which test is best.
Kinaesthetic: Testing the strength of magnets.
Interpersonal: Working in groups.
Intrapersonal: Discussing the choice of tests and their outcomes.

Answers to in-text questions

a The end where the stroking magnet leaves the nail will become a N pole.

b Number of clips, end-to-end; the weight which causes the clip to fall; the thickness of cardboard; the distance between clip and magnet; the distance between magnet and compass when the needle turns through, say, 45°; the reading on the balance.

Making Magnets

Main Lesson

- Start the lesson by demonstrating how to make a magnet using a large steel nail as described in the pupil book.
- Make sure that you demonstrate that the nail is not a magnet before you magnetise it. Quite often the nails in science departments are already magnetised because they have been used before.
- After making the magnet, you can try to demonstrate that it will lose some of its magnetic strength if it is banged. Whack it against a solid object a few times and it *should* get weaker. Use this idea to show the pupils it is important to handle their magnets with care or they will get weaker too.
- Magnets can also be made inside solenoids. If you have one available then demonstrate the technique as described in 'Using a solenoid to make a magnet' in the 'Practical Support'. You can explain how it works to higher attaining pupils during P1.11.
- The pupils should now try one of the 'testing magnets' activities. You may want to assign the methods to different groups of pupils or let them decide for themselves. Try to make sure that all of the methods are used by pupils so that they can all be evaluated.
- The second method (suspending weights) is fairly fiddly to set up but it can give numerical data.
- Evaluation is a very difficult, but essential, scientific skill. Many of the pupils will struggle with the ideas. Make the pupils focus on the idea that a comparison of the magnets that gives some sort of numerical value is more useful.

Plenary Suggestions

Make or break

The pupils make a worksheet describing how to make a magnet and how to look after it. They must include an equipment list and diagrams. (10 mins)

Correct me if I'm wrong

Give the pupils a paragraph with many mistakes explaining how to test a magnet's strength. They have to correct the mistakes. (5–10 mins)

Practical Support

Make your own magnet

Equipment and materials required

A permanent bar magnet, an un-magnetised nail or needle, digital electronic balance and block of iron or steel.

Details

See pupil book.

Safety

Needles and nails are sharp. If pupils rub the needle against the magnet they are more likely to stab themselves, so make sure that they move the magnet, not the needle.

Testing magnets

Equipment and materials required

Depending on which tests the pupils choose they will need two bar magnets and one of the following sets: a) paper clips, b) paper clip, cotton, small equal masses (beads are good), c) cardboard, paper clips, d) paper clips, e) a plotting compass or f) a top-pan balance and small iron block.

Details

The idea behind each of the tests is fairly clear from the diagrams. The pupils should discuss the diagrams and then decide how the test works and which ones the want to do. While they are carrying out the tests they should consider how accurate and reliable they are.

Safety

Keep strong magnets away from electronic equipment and data storage systems.

Using a solenoid to make a magnet (demonstration)

Equipment and materials required

A non-magnetised steel nail and a solenoid designed specifically for making magnets (these are available from school electronics suppliers.)

Details

Show that the nail is not magnetic and then place it in the centre of the solenoid. Turn on the current for a few seconds, but make sure that the coil does not become too hot. The nail has become magnetised. You may have to repeat the process a few times to get a useful magnet.

Safety

The solenoid can become very hot if activated for a long time. The pupils must not touch it. If you place a nail that is already magnetised in the coil it can be forced out from the end. It won't be very fast unless you have a very powerful solenoid but watch out for the effect; it is used in nail guns.

Differentiation

SEN

Provide the pupils with more detail about the techniques used to compare magnets. A set of step-by-step instructions would be appropriate.

Extension

Ask the pupils to investigate the breaking of force fields. They should design and carry out an experiment to find out if a material placed between two magnets can affect the strength of the field.

Homework Suggestion

Set the pupils a history lesson task. They must write a short essay on the discovery of magnetism, the compass and how it led to the exploration of the Earth.

Answers to summary questions

1. Magnetised.
2. To magnetise a needle by stroking: stroke one end of a permanent magnet along the length of the needle. Always stroke in the same direction, and with the same pole.
3. A method for comparing strengths of magnets, based on one of the methods shown in the pupil book.

P1.9 A Field of Force

NC links for the lesson
- Energy, electricity and forces: forces are interactions between objects and can affect their shape and motion.

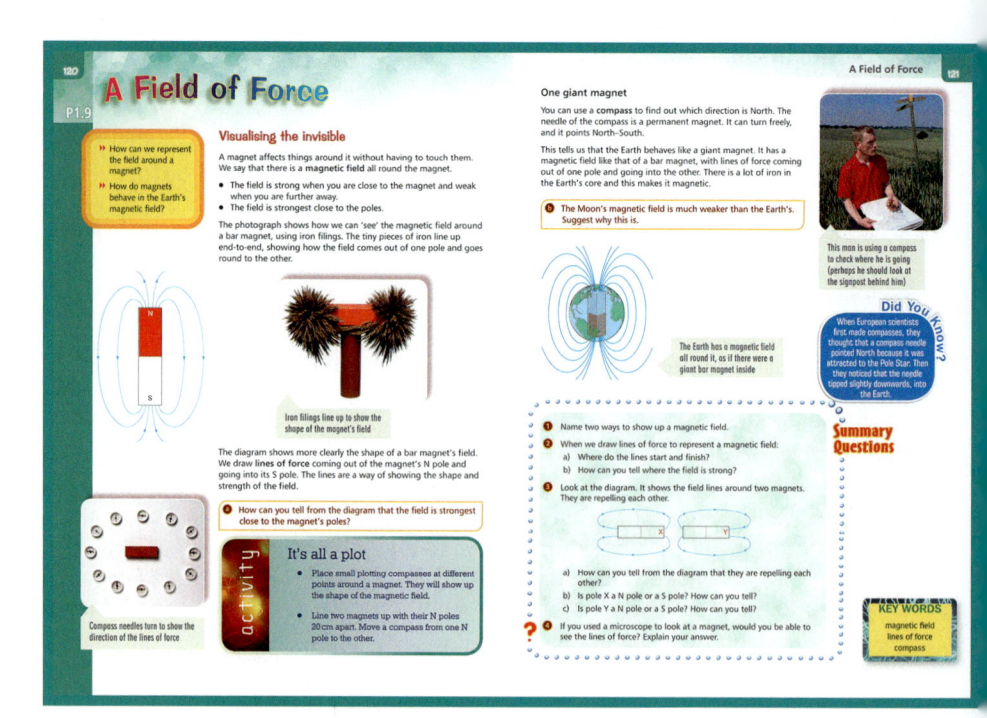

Learning Objectives

Pupils should learn:
- That magnets have a field round them that can be represented in a diagram.
- That magnets interact with each other through these fields.

Learning Outcomes

- All pupils will be aware that magnets, including the Earth, have a field around them.
- Most pupils will be able to detect and draw the shape of the field around a bar magnet.
- Some pupils will also be able to explain how a compass operates in the Earth's magnetic field.

How Science Works

- Describe and record observations and evidence systematically. (1.2d)

Functional Skills Link-up

ICT
- Access, navigate and search internet sources of information purposefully and effectively. (Level 1) See Homework Suggestion.

Answers to in-text questions

a The lines of force are closest together near the poles.

b There is little iron inside the Moon.

Learning Styles

Visual: Drawing and observing magnetic fields.
Auditory: Discussing methods of detecting invisible things.
Kinaesthetic: Plotting magnetic fields.
Intrapersonal: Visualising the structure of the Earth and its field.

A Field of Force

The Lesson

Starter Suggestions

Red alert! Activate force fields!
Show the pupils a short clip from a science fiction film or TV programme where a force field is used. The pupils say whether such a device could exist and how they think it would operate. (5 min)

Is it really there?
The pupils need to make of list of things that they cannot see (e.g. air, gravity). They then need to give explanations of how they could prove that these things exist. (10 mins)

Main Lesson

- At the heart of this lesson lies the idea that there is an invisible field of force around a magnet, and the whole Earth, that affects some things but not others. It's a difficult concept to picture and then accept, so the pupils will need a lot of reinforcement.
- Demonstrate the shape of the field by sprinkling iron filings onto card with a magnet beneath. This makes the concept a bit more real. If you have an overhead projector, place the magnet beneath a transparency, or clear plastic box with lid, and then sprinkle; it's a lot easier for a large class to see.
- The direction of the force lines is important. If pupils ask why they go in that particular direction, then explain that it is the direction a north pole would be pushed if it were placed there.
- The 'It's all a plot' practical is a straightforward way of letting the pupils find the field for themselves. It's a lot less messy than using iron filings.
- If you do want to let the pupils have a go with the iron filings, then make sure the magnets are covered in cling film; this makes it a lot easier to clean the magnets afterwards.
- When discussing the Earth's magnetic field, you should have a globe to make sure the pupils know the locations you are discussing. You can also show them where the bar magnet would have to be to generate the field.
- A pupil may point out that the north pole of a compass points to the north, so the North Pole must be a south pole. This is true. The North magnetic pole is actually a magnetic south pole. It's one of those things that can lead to a lot of confusion so, if nobody mentions it, it isn't worth bringing up. Just to add to the confusion there are a few different 'North Poles' too.
- The Pole star is nearly above the geographic North Pole, so it doesn't appear to move as the Earth rotates. This makes it very useful for guidance; if you can see the Pole star you know which way North is. You could show a picture or video showing the Pole star 'standing still'; there are a few available on the Internet.

Plenary Suggestions

Lost
The pupils have to imagine they are lost deep in the woods next to a huge lump of magnetic rock. They have only what's in their school bags. How could they use the rock to help them find North? Could the rock be a problem? How could they make a compass? (10 mins)

Model Earth
The pupils have to design a model for the Earth that includes its magnetic field. They should draw out their design and list the material they would use. (10 mins)

Practical Support

It's all a plot

Equipment and materials required
A permanent bar magnet, A3 paper, a plotting compass.

Details
The pupils should place the magnet in the centre. They should then draw around it to get a permanent record of where it was and so that they can replace it if they knock it. They should then place the compass at different points around the magnet, working away from one of the poles, and trace the field.

Differentiation

SEN
For the 'It's all a plot' activity the pupils should use a worksheet with the position for the magnet and various positions for the compass already marked on it.

Extension
The pupils could plot the field of a horseshoe magnet. They could also look in more detail at the Earth's magnetic fields and what it does to protect the planet.

Homework Suggestion

Set the pupils a history lesson task. They must write a short essay on the discovery of magnetism, the compass and how it led to the exploration of the Earth.

Did You Know?

The compass was a Chinese invention, a loadstone floating on water, originally used in practices such as feng shui and fortune telling. It took over a thousand years before sailors realised how useful it would be in working out directions. It is unclear if the compass was independently invented in Europe, but Europeans significantly developed the device into what it is today. Of course, satellite navigation has made the compass all but obsolete for navigation at sea.

Answers to summary questions

1. Using a compass or iron filings.

2. a) The lines start at the north pole and end at the south pole.
   b) The closer the lines are together the stronger the field.

3. a) Lines of force pushed apart.
   b) X is a N pole – lines of force coming out.
   c) Y is a S pole – lines of force going in.

4. No, the field lines are always invisible. They are not really there; we just use them to show what a field is 'like'.

P1.10 Electromagnets

NC links for the lesson
- Energy, electricity and forces: forces are interactions between objects and can affect their shape and motion.

Learning Objectives
Pupils should learn:
- That an electric current produces a magnetic field.
- That the strength of the field is increased in a coil.
- That increasing the current, the number of loops in the coil and adding a magnetic core can increase the strength of the magnetic field.

Learning Outcomes
- All pupils will be able to describe how an electromagnet is made.
- Most pupils will be able to describe how the strength of an electromagnet can be increased and a method of testing this.
- Some pupils will also be able to evaluate methods for testing the strength of an electromagnet.

How Science Works
- Recognise the range of variables involved in an investigation and decide which to control. (1.2b)

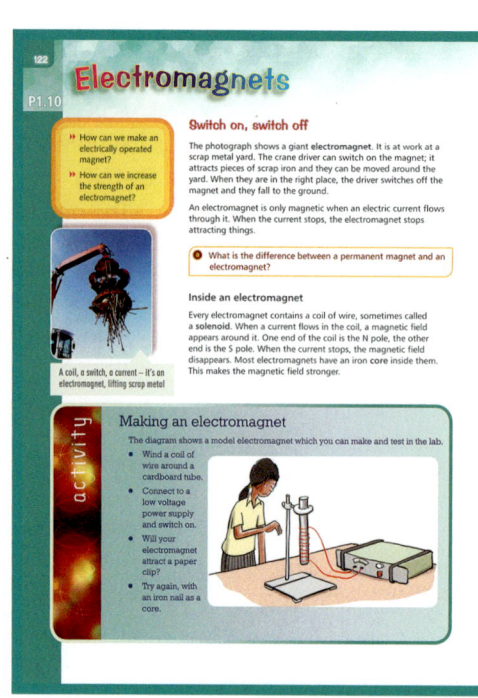

Learning Styles
Visual: Designing the shape of an electromagnet.
Auditory: Discussing how an electromagnet can be made stronger.
Kinaesthetic: Practical work.
Interpersonal: Discussing the factors that increase the strength of an electromagnet.
Intrapersonal: Understanding the advantages and disadvantages of an electromagnet compared to a permanent one.

The Lesson

Starter Suggestions

Anagramania
Give the pupils a set of anagrams of words from the electrical circuits and magnets topic so far, and ask them to solve them. Provide a set of clues after five minutes. (5–10 mins).

Let's check the current situation
Test the pupils' recollection of electric circuits with a quick quiz. (10–15 mins)

Main Lesson
- In this lesson the pupils will link the two concepts of magnetism and electricity together and see how closely connected they are.
- Show the pupils an electromagnet made from a coil of wire. This will look very different from the scrap yard photograph.
- To demonstrate that the field around a solenoid only exists when there is a current, place a set of plotting compasses around it. With the coil off, the

Answers to summary questions

1. Solenoid.
2. Iron is a magnetic material.
3. a) Copper is suitable for a coil as it is a good conductor.
   b) It would be no use for a core as it is non-magnetic.
4. Description of fair test for strength of electromagnet with two values of current, based on ideas from P1.7.

Electromagnets

compasses should all point in the same direction. Turning the current on will cause the needles to align with the field.

- You can show that a simple coil is weak by trying to pick up paper clips; it isn't very effective.
- The pupils should now try to make an electromagnet themselves; see the 'Making an electromagnet' practical for details. It can be quite difficult for pupils to get the coil just right. The pupils should make sure that they think about potential risks associated with the magnets; they should be aware of the heating effect of the electric current.
- Discuss the methods of making the magnet stronger, but point out the disadvantages too. More coils make the magnet larger and heavier, a core makes the magnet heavier and a larger current causes heating and uses more electrical energy.
- The pupils can then test the strength of the electromagnets with the second practical task, 'Testing an electromagnet'.
- There is an opportunity here to discuss some of the implications of using powerful electromagnets (as mentioned in Science@work). Very large electromagnets are very expensive and require a great deal of power to operate. While it may be possible to justify the use of magnets on machines that save lives, is it reasonable to use them to research the nature of the universe? At CERN, massive amounts of energy and billion of pounds are used, but what impact does this have on everyday life? Is it worth the expense and environmental impact? See www.cern.ch for some of the details of the work carried out.
- Finish off by explaining why an electromagnet is often more useful than a permanent magnet. It can be switched on and off and its strength can be precisely controlled.

Plenary Suggestions

Parts

The pupils make a list of all of the parts needed to make an electromagnet along with an explanation of what they do. For example 'the wires are needed to carry the electric current'. They should concentrate on using the correct scientific language. (5–10 mins)

Electromagnetic info

The pupils have to make a summary and comparison of magnets and electromagnets. (10 mins)

Practical Support

Making an electromagnet

Equipment and materials required

Each group will require: a low voltage d.c. power supply, connecting leads, crocodile clips, a long iron nail, a paper, card or plastic tube (thin is better), paper clips and an insulated length of wire to form the coil. The length of wire required will depend on the size of the tube, but it should be long enough to wrap around the tube 20 times. The same length of wire should be used throughout the experiment to limit the current.

Details

The pupils first wrap the wire around the outside of the tube. They connect it to the power supply or battery via the crocodile clips and leads. Without the core the magnet will be weak, at low currents it may not even lift a paper clip. The pupils then add the iron core and concentrate the field. This should improve the lifting power considerably.

Safety

Even at low voltages electromagnets can draw large currents. This can cause them to heat up and cause the circuit breaker in power supplies to trip. Test the circuit before use to make sure that it cannot heat up too much.

Testing an electromagnet

Equipment and materials required

Each group requires the same equipment as before, plus an ammeter and possibly a variable resistor. They may also wish to use the magnet testing equipment from P1.8.

Details

The pupils will have to measure the strength of the magnet at different current settings. They can adjust the current by adjusting the voltage on the power supply. For more precise control they could add a variable resistor into the circuit.

Safety

As before, watch out for overheating wires and tripping power supplies.

Differentiation

SEN

Have some coils with and without a core already prepared, to make the setting up of the practical tasks easier. The pupils can spend more time making measurements.

Extension

Some very powerful electromagnets are used in medical devices such as PET scanners. These magnets carry high currents and have to be cooled to very low temperatures. The pupils could find out why they have to be cooled and what a superconductor is.

Homework Suggestion

'Can Do': the pupils can design a machine that separates out steel cans from the more valuable aluminium ones.

science@work

The operation of a MRI (magnetic resonance imaging) machine is far beyond the scope of a secondary school course, but the pupils may be familiar with them from TV programmes. The magnetic fields involved are very strong and doctors, and the patient, need to make sure that no magnetic materials are brought close to the magnets. More than one patient has been killed by metal objects smashing into the machine. If a patient has metal fragments inside their body they can be ripped out causing nasty injuries

Answers to in-text questions

a A permanent magnet is constantly magnetised; an electromagnet is only magnetised when a current flows.

b Drawings of two electromagnets, one much stronger than the other. Indicate more turns, more current, iron core.

P1.11 Electromagnets at Work

NC links for the lesson
- Energy, electricity and forces: forces are interactions between objects and can affect their shape and motion.

Learning Objectives
Pupils should learn:
- That the shape of a magnetic field around the electromagnet is similar to that around a bar magnet.
- About the applications of an electromagnet.

Learning Outcomes
- All pupils will be able to list some uses of an electromagnet.
- Most pupils will be able to describe the advantages of using electromagnets in comparison to permanent magnets.
- Some pupils will also be able to describe the operation of some electromagnetic devices in detail.

How Science Works
- Describe and record observations and evidence systematically. (1.2d)

Learning Styles
Visual: Examining electromagnetic devices.
Auditory: Describing how a device operates.
Kinaesthetic: Plotting the field of an electromagnet.
Interpersonal: Discussing the operation of electromagnetic devices.
Intrapersonal: Predicting the effect of changing the current on an electromagnet.

The Lesson

Starter Suggestions

Loudspeaker
Demonstrate a large loudspeaker cone connected to a power supply through a switch, so that when the switch is closed the speaker moves outwards; releasing the switch makes it drop back again. Tell the pupils that the device uses an electromagnetic coil and ask them to explain how they think it works. (5–10 mins)

Eye know how
The pupils have to design a device that can remove a metal splinter from the eyeball of a patient. Their designs must be very controllable and easy to operate. A circuit diagram should be included too. (10–15 mins)

Main Lesson
- This lesson consolidates the work on magnets and electromagnets; comparing their fields and looking at their uses.
- It is best to start by showing the shape of the field around a bar magnet again and then comparing this to the field around an electromagnet.
- They both have the same features, field lines going from north to south, a similar shape and more field lines when the magnet is stronger.
- The pupils can then check the comparison using 'The field of an electromagnet' practical. If the field does not seem very strong the pupils can add iron cores to their magnets, if they haven't already done so.
- The lesson them moves on to the applications of electromagnets, starting with a doorbell. It is important to get across to pupils that without electromagnetic devices, many of the things they take for granted would not operate. Every

Functional Skills Link-up
English
- Use a range of different styles of writing for different purposes. (Level 2) See Homework Suggestion.

Electromagnets at Work

- device that produces movement from electrical power needs an electric motor and these use electromagnets.
- The pupils can then investigate other devices, including an electric bell and relay. The exact devices will depend on what is available. See the practical 'How it works' for details.
- It is difficult for some pupils to grasp the way an electric bell works, particularly how the circuit switches off automatically. Once they have completed the tasks it is important to go through the details of how each device works. Computer animations of the operation of the devices are very helpful.
- You could discuss how electromagnetic brakes work; the electromagnet pushes a brake block onto a train's tracks to slow a train. More advanced brakes use the eddy currents caused by moving magnets to cause deceleration without any physical contact.
- The pupils have now completed their topic and you should conclude with a check of what they have learned using one of the plenary tasks.

Plenary Suggestions

Key points
Test the pupils understanding with a range of verbal questions about magnets and electromagnets. These should cover applications of electromagnets too. (5 min)

Crossword
Give the pupils a crossword on magnetism and electromagnetism. Each word is the answer to a question. (10 mins)

Practical Support

Loudspeaker (Starter)

Equipment and materials required
A large loudspeaker connected to a low voltage power supply through a switch.

The field of an electromagnet

Equipment and materials required
Per group: a low voltage d.c. power supply, connecting leads, crocodile clips, a long iron nail, an insulated length of wire to form the coil and several plotting compasses. The length of wire required will depend on the size of the nail.

Details
The pupils should test the shape of the field in the same way as they did for a permanent magnet in lesson P1.9.

Safety
As in previous lessons, watch out for overheating wires and tripping power supplies.

How it works

Equipment and materials required
There are three pieces of equipment to investigate.
a) An electric bell connected to a power supply with a switch.
b) A relay set up so that one circuit turns on another circuit. This will require two power supplies, connecting leads and a bulb.
c) A set of headphones connected to a signal generator.

Details
The pupils investigate each device in turn and try to explain what it does and how it operates.

a) The electric bell should be set so that it vibrates but not too loudly. If you can, limit the voltage on the power supply.
b) The relay should be set so that when one circuit is switched on the relay becomes activated and turns on a separate circuit containing a light bulb.

Safety
Make sure that it is not possible for the pupils to connect any of the devices directly to the mains supply.

Differentiation

SEN
Provide descriptions of how electromagnetic devices work but jumble up the order. The pupils have to sort this order out to get the correct description for each device.

Extension
Pupils could look at how a loudspeaker operates in more detail. They need to understand why an electromagnet and a permanent magnet are used in combination.

Homework Suggestion

Electromagnets are common, but can the pupils come up with a new idea for their use? They can produce an advertisement or instruction manual for their devices.

science@work

Getting a metal splinter in the eye is more common then you'd think. Thousands of injuries occur each year, mainly in the metalworking and construction industries. The splinters may be too small to notice and remain in the eye for many years, but they can be very damaging if you go for an MRI scan (see last lesson)! Having something removed from the eye with a magnet is apparently fairly unpleasant.

Answers to in-text questions

a) There are twice as many lines of force / they are twice as close together.

b) Place iron filings or plotting compasses close to the wire. Do they move when the current is switched on?

Answers to summary questions

1. Electric bell, relay, loudspeaker, etc.
2. 'Proportional' means that twice the current gives twice the field strength and so on.
3. The poles of the electromagnet would reverse, e.g. test using compass.
4. When the current reaches a certain value, the electromagnet is strong enough to attract the switch to its open position, breaking the circuit.

Answers to Electricity and Magnetism – End of Topic Questions

Answers to know your stuff questions

1 **a** A battery or cell. [1]

   b

Bulb	On or off?
A	on
B	off
C	off

   [3]

2 **a** South pole; the north pole of the compass is attracted to it. [2]

   b [2]

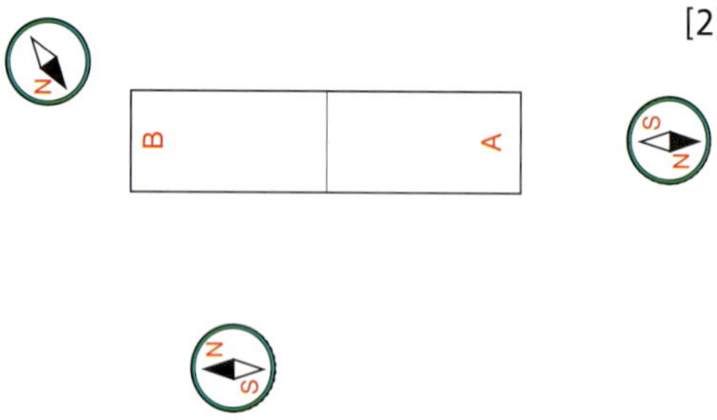

   c A points north; it is a north magnetic pole. [2]

3 **a** Bulb Y. [1]

   b Bulb Z. [1]

   c Parallel. [1]

   d A1: 0.4 A; A2: 0.2 A. [2]

   e 0.6 A. [1]

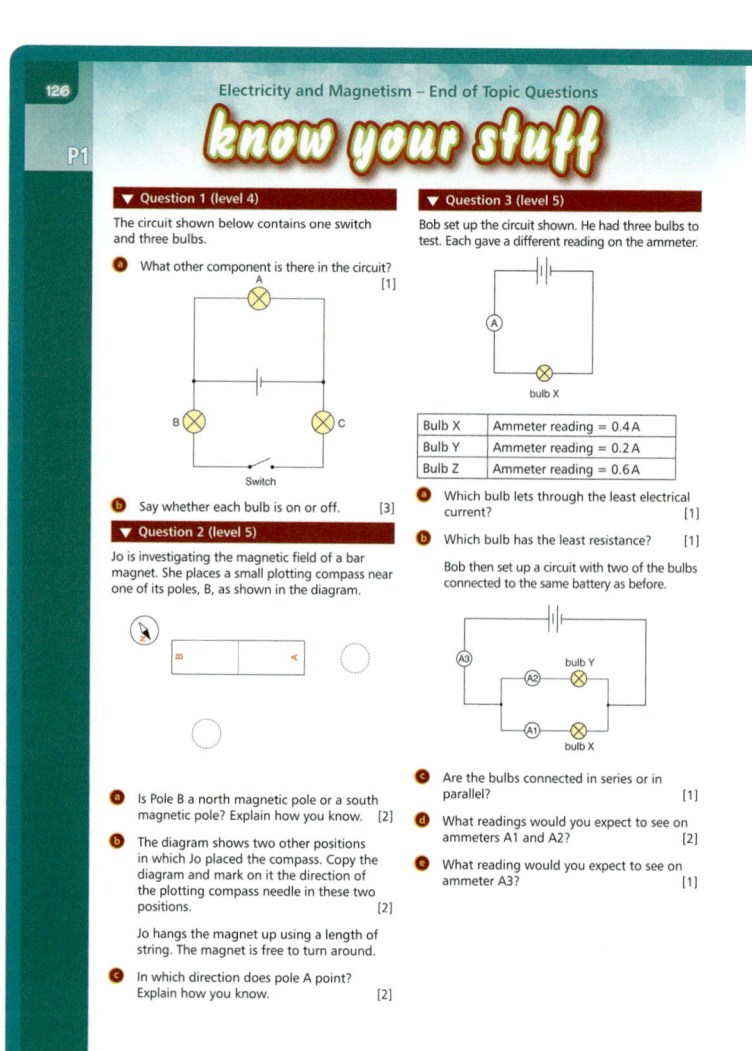

Electricity and Magnetism – End of Topic Questions

How Science Works

▼ Question 1 (level 4)

Mel's teacher asked her to test some batteries. Mel connected each battery in turn to a bulb. She used a light meter to measure the brightness of the bulb.

The table shows her results.

Battery	Reading on light meter
X	0.70
Y	0.95
Z	1.00

a How many batteries did Mel test? [1]

b Which battery made the bulb brightest? [1]

c Draw a bar chart to represent Mel's results. [2]

d Which two things should Mel have done to make her test fair? Give the letters. [2]
- A Use the same bulb each time.
- B Connect each battery the same way round.
- C Keep the distance between the lamp and the light meter the same each time.
- D Keep the bulb on for the same time with each battery.
- E Repeat her measurements with a different bulb.

▼ Question 2 (level 6)

Josh designed a way of comparing two electromagnets. He lined them up, as shown in the picture, with a gap between their ends. He hung a magnet in the gap.

Josh said, 'If one is stronger than the other, the magnet will move towards the stronger one.'

When Josh connected up his circuits, the magnet moved towards electromagnet A. Josh said, 'This shows that the current through A must be bigger than the current through B.'

a Give another reason why electromagnet A might be stronger than electromagnet B. [1]

b Suggest one way in which Josh could redesign his experiment to ensure that the two electromagnets have the same current flowing through them. [2]

▼ Question 3 (level 5)

Pete's teacher gave him an electrical 'black box' to investigate. Pete connected the black box to a cell. He included an ammeter in the circuit to measure the current flowing through the black box.

Pete added more cells, and recorded the current each time. The table shows his results.

Number of cells	Current flowing (A)
1	0.40
2	0.80
3	1.40
4	1.60

a When the teacher looked at Pete's results, she suggested he might have made a mistake with one of them. Which one? [1]

b Draw a graph of Pete's results. Using a ruler, draw a line through his correct results. [2]

c Use your graph to make a prediction: what current would flow if the black box was connected to 5 cells? [1]

Answers to How Science Works questions

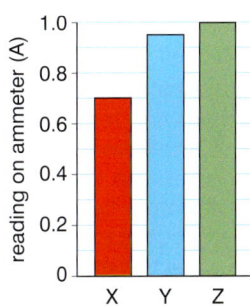

1
  a Three. [1]
  b Battery Z. [1]
  c [2]

  (bar chart: X = 0.70, Y = 0.95, Z = 1.00; reading on ammeter (A))

  d A and C

2
  a A might have more turns than B. [1]
  b Connect the two electromagnets in series to a single battery or add ammeters to both circuits. [2]

3
  a 3 cells. [1]
  b [2]

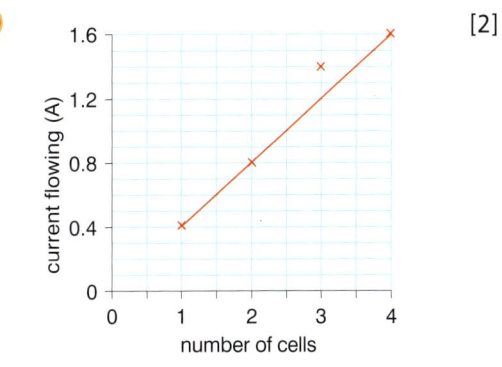

  (graph: current flowing (A) vs number of cells; line through (1, 0.40), (2, 0.80), (4, 1.60); point at (3, 1.40) off the line)

  c 2.00 A. [1]

P2.1 Forces and Energy

NC links for the topic
- Energy, electricity and forces: energy can be transferred usefully, stored, or wasted, but cannot be created or destroyed. Forces are interactions between objects and can affect their shape and motion. The environment, Earth and universe: human activity and natural processes can lead to changes in the environment.
- Key Processes: use a range of scientific methods and techniques to develop and test ideas and explanations. Assess risk and work safely in the laboratory field and workplace. Carry out practical and investigative activities, both individually and in groups.

Level descriptors for the topic
- **AT4 level 4:** They describe some phenomena and processes drawing on scientific knowledge and understanding.
- **AT4 level 5:** They describe phenomena and processes, such as balanced forces, drawing on abstract ideas. They describe applications and implications of science (greenhouse effect).
- **AT4 level 6:** They also use abstract ideas or models, for example sustainable energy resources. They explain the importance of some applications and implications of science, such as the use of unsustainable energy resources.
- **AT4 level 8:** They show they understand the relationship between evidence and scientific ideas and why ideas may need to be changed (development of global warming theory).
- **AT1 level 4:** Pupils communicate their conclusions using appropriate scientific language. (Analysing level 4.)
- **AT1 level 5:** Pupils decide appropriate approaches to a range of tasks, including selecting sources of information and apparatus.
- **AT1 level 5:** Pupils use methods that obtain data systematically and take action to control risks to others as well as themselves.
- **AT1 level 5:** Pupils evaluate their working methods to make practical suggestions for improvements.
- **AT1 level 6:** Pupils recognise a wide range of risks and take action to control them.
- **AT1 level 6:** Pupils may also use methods to collect adequate data for the task, measuring with precision, using instruments with fine scale divisions, and identify the need to repeat measurements and observations.
- **AT1 level 6:** Pupils analyse findings to draw scientific conclusions that are consistent with the evidence.
- **AT1 level 6:** Pupils record data and features effectively, choosing scales for graphs and diagrams.
- **AT1 level 6:** Pupils manipulate numerical data to make valid comparisons and draw valid conclusions.
- **AT1 level 7:** Pupils recognise the need for, and carry out, a simple risk assessment.

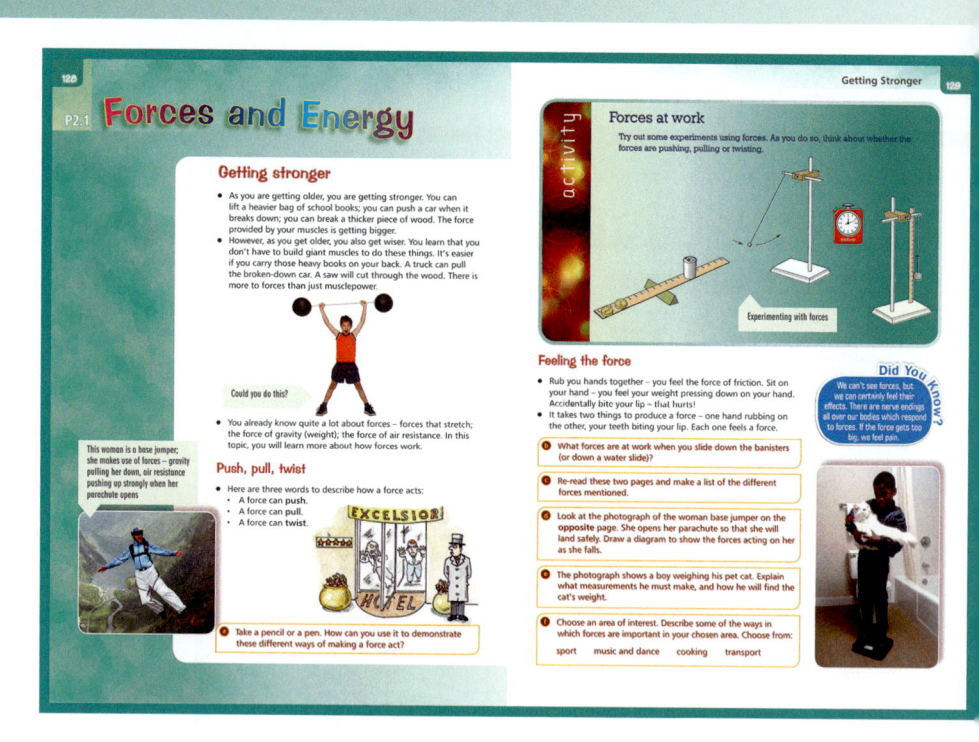

Learning Objectives
Pupils should learn:
- That forces act between objects and can cause changes to them.
- That forces act in pairs that oppose each other.

Learning Outcomes
- All pupils should be able to measure the effect a force has on an object.
- Most pupils should be able to explain how a force can affect the behaviour of an object.
- Some pupils should also be able to present the results of an experiment in the appropriate manner.

How Science Works
- Describe and record observations and evidence systematically. (1.2d)

Answers to in-text questions
a The pen can easily push another object, the clip can be attached to pull something and the nib can be used to twist objects around.

b Sliding downhill involves gravity, friction and air resistance.

c Weight (or gravity), air resistance, friction.

d A diagram showing the weight of the woman's body acting downwards from her centre and air resistance (drag) acting upwards.

e Weigh himself without the cat using accurate bathroom scales, repeat when holding the cat and subtract the two numbers.

f Pupil's own interest.

Getting Stronger

The Lesson

Starter Suggestions

Mind over matter
Demonstrate the use of pulleys or levers in lifting large weights to show that a little wisdom can be more effective than quite a lot of brute force. A pair of pulleys with cord wrapped around twice should be sufficient to show that a small force can be used to lift fairly heavy weights. (5 mins).

Prior knowledge
The pupils could draw out a spider diagram (or mind map) summarising what they already know about forces. This will help you to tailor the following lessons appropriately. (10–15 mins)

Main Lesson

- Use the 'Mind over matter' starter to show forces in action and how we can use simple machines to move objects. You can also introduce the forcemeter in the demonstration.
- Some pupils will struggle with the term 'act' as it is used when describing forces. Check carefully that they understand what you mean when you say a force 'acts' on something; push or pull some objects around and describe the forces acting.
- After the pupils have answered the first question, choose three to demonstrate the ideas to the rest of the class.
- If you discuss the base-jumping photograph you might want to look into the misconception that opening a parachute causes a parachutist to 'shoot upwards'. Use a video clip of a parachute jump (there are many available online) to explain that the illusion is caused because the cameraman continues to fall quickly while the parachutist slows down rapidly.
- The pupils should now try out the 'Forces at work' practical. The emphasis here is carefully to record observations and measurements (How Science Works). If time permits, or as a homework task, you may want the pupils to process the results graphically.
- Even though forces are invisible, you should try to show them acting. There is no simpler demonstration than showing two magnets repelling or attracting. Discuss the force between the magnets; each one pushing or pulling the other.
- Many pupils find it difficult to understand that forces *always* act in pairs; there are many situations where the force is not obvious. Tell them that this is one of the most basic and important rules in all of science. The plenary 'Always two there are …' can be used to emphasise this idea.
- Ask the pupils to note down any situation where they believe that there is only one force acting in their exercise books. Tell them you will give them explanations of these at the next lesson; this gives you the opportunity to choose the most difficult ones and explain to the whole class.

Plenary Suggestions

Use the force loop
Play a question loop game with a set of basic questions about forces and their effects. (5–10 mins)

Always two there are …
Give the pupils a selection of diagrams showing only a single force acting at each point. Ask them to add the other 'missing' forces to the diagrams. Possible diagrams include objects resting on the ground, a ladder leaning against a wall and the attraction between the Sun and Earth. (5–10 mins)

Practical Support

Forces at work

Equipment and materials required
There are five workstations with small experiments for the pupils to observe. Depending on the class size you may wish to have two of each station type available.

Station 1: Set of six 50 g masses with holder, thick elastic band (or fishing pole elastic), stand and 30 cm ruler. Mark the elastic in two places, 5 cm apart, using a permanent marker pen so that the pupils have some easy points to measure from.

Station 2: A stop-watch, a mass holder suspended by string from a stand, a clamp to fix stand to bench, and a set of five 20 g masses. This should act as a simple pendulum.

Station 3: Set of three 100 g masses, 50 cm ruler, and triangular pivot. The ruler should be balanced on the pivot so that the pupils can place masses on the ruler and balance it.

Station 4: A synthetic square sponge, ruler, tray and set of eight 50 g masses.

Station 5: A large wooden block with a forcemeter attached. A range of surfaces (carpet, wood, floor tiles, plastic and possibly glass) that the pupils can drag the block across. The pupils may need some Blu-Tak to keep the surfaces in place.

Station 6: A large wooden block with a forcemeter attached. An adjustable slope to drag the block up.

Safety
The pupils should be warned about the hazards of falling masses. Eye protection should be used at stations 1 and 2 in case the elastic or string snaps.

Differentiation

SEN
Worksheets and results tables should be provided for each of the stations in the practical task.

Extension
Language is important in the description of forces. Encourage the pupils to find out about and use the words 'tension', 'compression', 'torque', 'couple' and 'moments' whenever possible.

The pupils should also consider the energy changes that are occurring during the 'forces at work' practical task.

Homework Suggestion

The pupils should produce charts or graphs of the results of the practical task. They should choose the most appropriate way of showing the information: bar chart, pie chart or scatter graph. This can lead to a discussion of how to present results from experiments (How Science Works).

P2.2 Measuring Forces

NC links for the lesson
- Energy, electricity and forces: forces are interactions between objects and can affect their shape and motion.

Learning Objectives
Pupils should learn:
- That forces act between objects and can cause changes to them.
- That forces are measured in a unit called the 'newton'.
- That forces can be represented by arrows showing the direction, and magnitude, of the force.

Learning Outcomes
- All pupils should be able to draw arrows to represent the forces acting on an object.
- Most pupils should be able to draw a diagram including forces drawn to scale.
- Some pupils should also be able to find the resultant force of a set of forces acting on an object.

How Science Works
- Describe and record observations and evidence systematically. (1.2d)

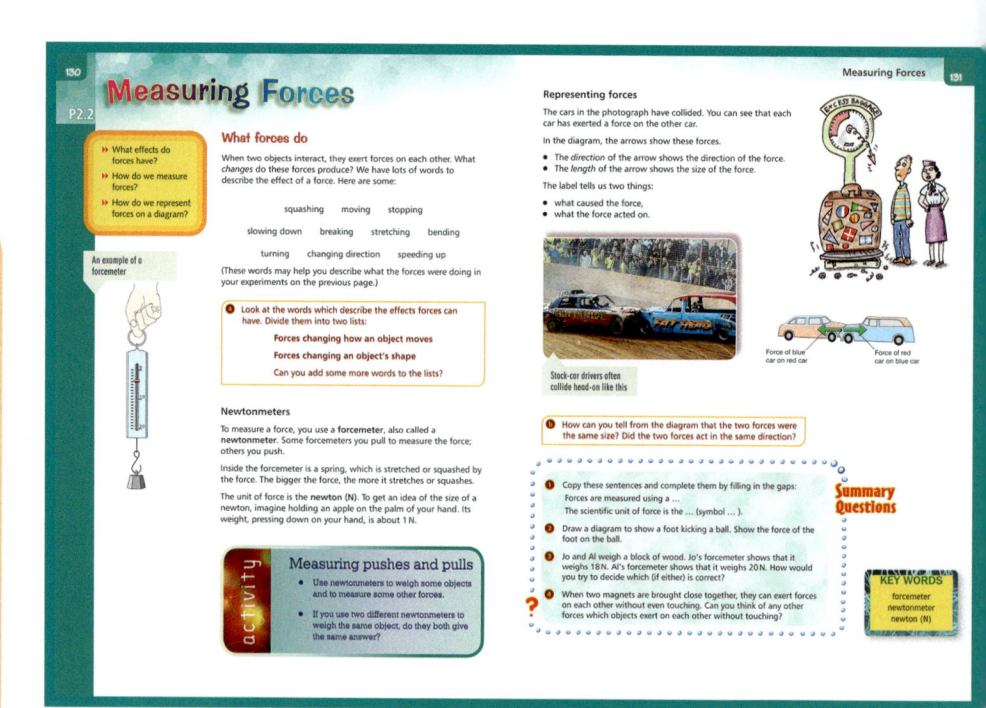

Learning Styles
Visual: Reading scales off measuring instruments.
Auditory: Describing force diagrams.
Kinaesthetic: Measuring forces practical task.
Interpersonal: Discussing the outcome of the experiment.
Intrapersonal: Evaluating the basic experiments and suggesting improvements.

Answers to in-text questions
a) Forces changing how an object moves: stopping, slowing down, turning, changing direction and speeding-up. Forces changing an object's shape: squashing, breaking, stretching and bending.

b) Both arrows are the same size. The forces act in opposite directions.

Answers to summary questions
1. Forces are measured using a **forcemeter**. The scientific unit of force is the **newton, N**.

2. [diagram of foot kicking ball labelled "Force of foot on ball"]

3. Need to test the meters. Measure the same weight several times; are they consistent? Is the difference between them always the same? Need to find a standard weight, or compare with other meters.

4. Static electricity, gravity.

Measuring Forces

The Lesson

Starter Suggestions

The right tool for the job
Show the pupils a range of measuring instruments and get then to explain what each one measures and how it works. (5–10 mins)

Reading scales
Give the pupils a set of diagrams of different measuring instruments in use. The pupils have to read the scales from them and give the appropriate units. Use some analogue and digital devices. (10–15 mins).

Main Lesson

- The pupils should already be familiar with what a force can do, with the possible exceptions of forces causing turning effects and changes in direction. There will also be a few misconceptions about forces, each of which should be tackled during the next few lessons.
- Many pupils struggle with the idea of a 'unit' in science. Take time to ensure that they understand this term and give plenty of other examples of other units, such as the metre and kilogram.
- Use a suitably sized apple as a prop to let the pupils experience the force of 1 N. It is important to try to convey the idea that the object has mass and that, because of this, there is a force called the 'weight' acting on it. There will be more about this next lesson.
- You can also show a 100 g metal mass along with this; it has the same weight but a different volume. The pupils will cover the ideas of density in lesson P2.6.
- Demonstrate the use of a forcemeter and how to attach objects to it. This can be quite tricky depending on the object you are using.
- Then get the pupils to carry out the 'Measuring pushes and pulls' practical task. The emphasis is on measuring the size of the forces carefully and as accurately as possible. The pupils should note down the problems that they have with measuring the sizes of the forces (How Science Works).
- It is important that the pupils gain an understanding of the size of forces in relation to the newton during the practical task. Ask them to estimate, and record, the force they think will be required to lift/move each object before they use the meters. They should then select the appropriate meter for the object.
- Using the correct meter will also give them more precise measurements. Discuss this after the experiment in relation to How Science Works (see page 158).
- The pupils then move on to the idea of representing forces by arrows. This is fairly straightforward, but make sure that they are putting arrowheads on the lines they draw and that the arrows actually point in the right direction.
- The 'Describing forces' plenary should cement the idea in the pupils' minds.
- 'Forcemeter' and 'newtonmeter' are interchangeable terms, but using the term 'forcemeter' will make it certain that the pupils understand what is being measured at all times.

Plenary Suggestions

Describing forces
Show the pupils a set of diagrams or slides with forces represented by arrows and ask them to describe what the diagram is showing in words. They should explain what the forces are doing, what they are acting on and describe the relative sizes of the forces. (10 mins)

Sentence construction
The pupils must write a set of sentences that includes all of the key words or phrases from this lesson. The fewer sentences needed the better. (5–10 mins)

Practical Support

Measuring pushes and pulls

Equipment and materials required
A variety of everyday objects that the pupils can weigh: these can be typical laboratory equipment, furniture or pupil equipment. Avoid fragile objects. Pupils will need a range of forcemeters (1 N, 5 N, 10 N, 25 N and so on) and string to attach objects to the meters.

Details
The pupils use the forcemeters to measure the weight of the object. Depending on the objects chosen, they will probably need to attach the objects with string. To save time, you can make a loop at the end of the string before the experiment. You may also want the pupils to drag objects along and measure the force required; frictional forces will be covered in more detail in P2.4.

Safety
The pupils should be careful if they are lifting large masses or dragging objects around the laboratory.

Differentiation

SEN
Provide the pupils with a worksheet with a results table for the practical task. You may also wish to specify which forcemeter should be used for which object.

Extension
The pupils can find out how a top-pan balance operates. [Some use springs, but others use the electrical properties of materials.]

It is again important the pupils become more familiar with the language of science, so use the terms 'accelerate' and 'decelerate' when possible.

With higher attaining pupils you can move on to the effect of forces that are not acting in the same plane. Can they describe what they think will happen if the forces are at right angles?

Homework Suggestion

The pupils can make a list of all of the devices that can be used to measure forces, and the locations where they are used. They should explain why it is important to measure forces, such as weight, accurately. Examples include electronic bathroom scales, scales at supermarkets, the electronic balances that are used at the checkouts, weighbridges, and check-in scales at airports and so on.

P2.3 Bending, Stretching

NC links for the lesson
- Energy, electricity and forces: forces are interactions between objects and can affect their shape and motion.

Learning Objectives
Pupils should learn:
- That weight is caused by the action of gravity on objects.
- That a spring will extend evenly when the force on it is increased evenly.
- That graphs can be used to find patterns in the behaviour of materials.

Learning Outcomes
- All pupils should be able to state that the weight of an object is caused by gravity.
- Most pupils should be able to describe the connection between the load on a spring and its extension.
- Some pupils should also be able to compare the extension of an elastic material to that of a spring.

How Science Works
- Recognise that the presentation of experimental results through the routine use of tables ... and simple graphs makes it easier to see patterns and trends. (1.2d)
- Describe patterns and trends in results ... (1.2e)

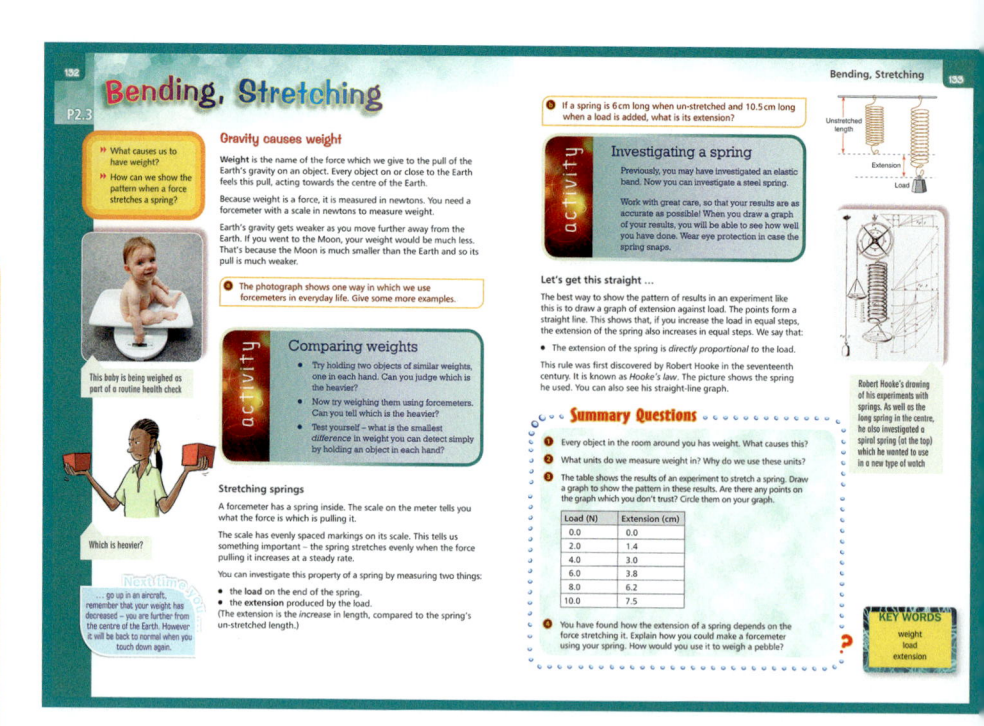

The Lesson

Starter Suggestions

'Bungee boing'
Show a video clip of a bungee jump. The pupils have to draw a set of simple diagrams showing what the forces are doing at each stage of the fall and bounce. (5–10 mins)

Describing patterns from graphs
Give the pupils a set of graphs that show the results of different experiments, e.g. the distance a projectile travels when fired at different angles, the stopping distance of a car. They have to describe the patterns that the graphs show in as much detail as possible. This includes noting the strength of any correlations (How Science Works). (10–15 mins)

Main Lesson
- The difference between 'weight' and 'mass' always causes confusion among pupils. You will have to revisit it constantly throughout the course

Answers to summary questions
1. The pull of Earth's gravity causes weight.
2. Newtons (N) because weight is a force.
3. Load–extension graph, based on table; the extension at load 6.0 N seems incorrect.
4. Need to add a scale and calibrate it.

Functional Skills Link-up
Mathematics
- Collect and represent discrete and continuous data, using ICT where appropriate. (Level 2)

Answers to in-text questions
a. Weighing food, people, cars, etc.
b. The extension is 4.5 cm.

Learning Styles
Visual: Interpreting graphical data.
Auditory: Discussing the difference between weight and mass.
Kinaesthetic: Measuring the extension of a spring.
Interpersonal: Collaborating with others in practical work.
Intrapersonal: Understanding the cause of weight.

whenever weight or mass are mentioned. The mass of an object does not change; it is a measure of the amount of material (stuff, particles, or atoms) in it. The weight depends on the location; the strength of the gravitational field, often referred to as 'the strength of gravity', varies from place to place.

- Many pupils enter Key Stage 3 thinking that there is *no* gravity on the Moon. This misconception must be challenged; show video clips of astronauts on the Moon's surface; they are still pulled downwards but not by as large a force.
- Make sure that the pupils understand the idea of extension before starting the practical task. Answering in-text question b should be enough.
- The emphasis of the 'Investigating a spring' practical should be on making accurate and precise measurements. If there is time, you can ask the pupils to record the extension as the spring is unloaded and calculate the mean extension. These results need to be used to plot an accurate line graph, where the pupils have decided on the appropriate scales and units. This covers a range of How Science Works concepts.
- The experiment should produce a straight-line graph showing that the extension is proportional to the load; Hooke's Law. The pupils can judge the quality of their experiment by how straight their line is.
- Many pupils will have difficulty with the concept of proportionality at this stage of their education. They will revisit the idea many times, so don't let them worry about it too much.
- You can show that all springs behave in this way by showing a set of graphs of extension against load. The steeper the line (higher gradient) the less stiff the spring is. Have more than one set of results on the same set of axes so that you can discuss why this makes it easier to compare the springs.
- This leads to the 'Comparing results' plenary to round off the lesson.

Plenary Suggestions

Comparing results
Give the pupils some sets of results from a spring extension experiment. The pupils must plot graphs and then compare the quality of the results. Which set is the best? Can they explain why? (How Science Works). (10 mins)

Bending
The pupils must design an experiment that will compare the flexibility of different types of ruler. The experiment must be able to produce numerical results (How Science Works). (15 mins)

Practical Support

Comparing weights

Equipment and materials required

A range of objects, including some of very similar weights; sets of masses (50 g, 20 g and 10 g) and holders; forcemeters.

Details

The purpose of this brief experiment is to show that measurement is an important part of science, as it sets a standard test for a property. The pupils should be guided to the conclusion that it is better actually to measure something than it is to guess or to rely on opinion (How Science Works).

The second part of the task is to come up with a method of measuring our sensitivity to forces. The pupils can simply test this out without any planning, or you can extend it into an exercise about coming up with a fair test, possibly a blind test of some kind – an opportunity to discuss how to obtain reliable data. Contrast this problem with the fair test set up in 'Investigating a spring' (How Science Works).

Safety
If larger objects or masses are used, then warn the pupils about the dangers associated with dropping the materials.

Investigating a spring

Equipment and materials required

A spring, 20 g masses with holder, stand, two clamps and a ruler. For more precise measurements, the pupils will need a pin and some Blu-Tak. The spring should have a low enough spring constant to stretch significantly with a load of 100 g placed on it.

Details

The pupils should measure the extension of the spring as it is loaded with the masses. To make the measurement easier, they can measure to the base of the mass holder instead of the spring itself. They must measure the length of the spring when it is only loaded with the holder and then measure the length as each mass is added. From the results, they can calculate the extension and plot a graph. To measure more accurately, the pupils can clamp the ruler alongside the spring and attach a pin to the bottom of the mass holder so that it touches the ruler. This pointer should allow measurement to the nearest millimetre.

As an extension some pupils can investigate the extension of fishing pole elastic. A range is available at all good fishing shops.

Safety
The pupils should again be warned about the risks of objects falling on their feet.

Wear eye protection in case springs snap.

Differentiation

SEN
Use worksheets with results tables and pre-prepared axes for the graph plotting tasks.

Extension
The pupils can compare the extension of a spring to that of elastic. Springs do not always obey Hooke's Law. Pupils can investigate the limit of the law, the idea of an elastic limit or even the concepts of plastic and elastic behaviour. This can be achieved by stretching thick lengths of plastic such as carrier bags, and noting that it does not return to its original shape.

Homework Suggestion

The pupils can find out about gravity on other planets. How much would they weigh on each planet? Is there a connection between the strength of gravity and the size (mass) of the planet? Higher attaining pupils may want to take the diameter into account.

P2.4 Friction

NC links for the lesson
- Energy, electricity and forces: forces are interactions between objects and can affect their shape and motion.

Learning Objectives
Pupils should learn:
- That friction is a force that acts between objects, slowing them or preventing them moving.
- That there are a range of factors that affect the frictional forces between objects.

Learning Outcomes
- All pupils should be able to state that friction is a force that prevents objects moving past each other.
- Most pupils should be able to describe the cause of a frictional force in terms of rough surfaces.
- Some pupils should also be able to list the factors that affect the magnitude of frictional forces.

How Science Works
- Explain how action has been taken to control risk and how methods are adequate for the task. (1.2c)

Learning Styles
Visual: Discussing diagrams, animations and video clips showing the action of friction.
Auditory: Describing the causes of friction.
Kinaesthetic: Practical work on measuring friction.
Interpersonal: Working in small groups.
Intrapersonal: Understanding how lubricants work.

The Lesson

Starter Suggestions

Emergency stop
Show some video clips of cars performing an emergency stop in a range of different road conditions. Video clips can be found on the Internet by searching for the term 'emergency stop'. The pupils should discuss why the cars stop and why the stopping distance is different under different conditions. (5–10 mins)

Get a grip
The pupils make a list of sports/activities where a 'good grip' is essential and explain how this is achieved, for example, putting powder on your hands for weightlifting. The powder absorbs moisture (sweat), which would act as a lubricant. (10 mins)

Main Lesson
- The best way to start the lesson is by using a video to show some dramatic stopping as in the 'Emergency stop' starter. The pupils should be able to explain that the objects stop because of a force and most will know that this is called 'friction'.
- Getting across the idea that the action of friction always opposes motion is fairly straightforward; link the idea that there are pairs of forces.

Answers to summary questions

1. Friction is a force which **opposes** motion when two **surfaces** try to slide over one another.
2. Lubricant; provides a slippery layer so that points on surfaces can slide over each other.
3. Roughness of surface (increases friction); weight of object (increases friction).
4. When surfaces pressed closer together, the bumps on the surfaces interlock more deeply.

Friction

- The concept that the size of the frictional force can grow as you push harder on a stationary object is a bit more difficult. With some pupils you might limit the discussion to moving objects.
- During the 'Measuring friction' practical task, ensure that the pupils are acting with safety in mind as they move around and drag fairly large masses. Get the pupils to write out a quick risk assessment or to choose the possible risks from a list you have already prepared (How Science Works: safety).
- The results are likely to be quite varied, as pupils tend to pull slightly upwards as they drag; you can discuss this when comparing the results of different groups for the same material and mass combination (How Science Works: reliability of data).
- Now move on to the explanation of frictional forces. The pupils may not be used to thinking about objects on a very small scale so use a range of electron micrographs to show the 'roughness' of a range of surfaces including paper, wood and even glass. Images are readily available from the Internet and all of the surfaces show bumps and grooves.
- The idea of surfaces 'catching' on each other is best shown through diagrams and animations. Show rough surfaces like sandpaper or even Velcro. You need to explain that if there is a larger force pressing the objects together (usually the weight) then the surfaces will be 'jammed' more and so friction will be higher.
- Try to move two very flat metal plates across each other; there can be quite high frictional forces. A little oil will make the plates slide much more freely. An animation can be used to show this.
- A wind tunnel video clip can be used to show the flow of air over an object's surface. If the air flows smoothly, then the object is streamlined.
- If time is available, then demonstrate the action of a parachute. You could ask the pupils to make parachutes from a limited range of materials at home for a future competition. Remind them not to climb onto high surfaces to test them though.

Plenary Suggestions

Rough edges
Show some further electron micrographs (or highly magnified optical micrographs) and ask the pupils to guess what the material or object is. A set of decreasing magnifications is best so that you can 'zoom out'. (5 mins)

Slippery when wet
The pupils make a hazard booklet warning of the dangers of slippery surfaces and listing safety precautions (How Science Works: safety). (15 mins)

Practical Support

Measuring friction

Equipment and materials required
Per group: a range of forcemeters, a wooden block, three 1 kg masses, a range of surfaces to pull the block across (carpet, tiles, desktop, etc.).

Details
The pupils will be dragging objects around with the meter and finding the factors that affect friction. The two key factors are the surface conditions; rougher giving higher friction, and the weight of the object being pulled. They should record the force needed to pull the block across each surface and then the force needed to pull the block with a 1 kg mass on it and so on. They should easily discover that rougher surfaces produce larger frictional forces and that the heavier the object the greater the force is.

The most difficult aspect of this practical task is moving the objects at a steady speed. It can be very difficult to read a measurement off the forcemeters when they are moving. Use this problem to explain why it is very important to take repeat readings and calculate averages during the experiment to check the reliability of the data collected (How Science Works).

Safety
The pupils will be moving around the classroom and may be working on the floor. Look out for trip hazards.

Differentiation

SEN
Provide worksheets with instructions about how to take the measurements. The worksheets should have space for recording results and instructions about how to calculate average values.

Extension
During the 'Measuring friction' experiment the pupils could investigate dragging the objects up an adjustable slope to see if the angle affects the size of the force required.

Homework Suggestion

The most important device invented to overcome the problems of friction was the wheel. The pupils can find out about how a wheel works and the history of its development or even the (non-serious) attempt to patent the device in Australia in 2001.

Answers to in-text questions

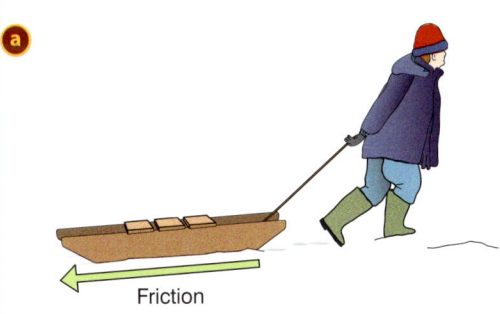

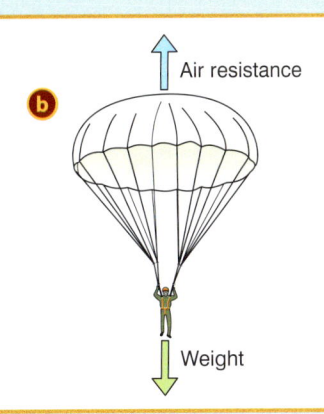

a) Friction

b) Air resistance / Weight

P2.5 Floating and Sinking

NC links for the lesson
- Energy, electricity and forces: forces are interactions between objects and can affect their shape and motion.

Learning Objectives

Pupils should learn:
- That when an object floats its weight is matched by an equal but opposite upthrust force.
- That objects that are more dense than water will sink, while those that are less dense will float.
- That when the weight of an object is greater than the upthrust force it will sink.

Learning Outcomes
- All pupils should be able to draw a diagram showing the forces acting on a floating object.
- Most pupils should be able to use the idea of balanced forces to explain why some objects float while others do not.
- Some pupils should also be able to describe how the forces change on a floating object as it is loaded up and eventually sinks.

How Science Works
- Describe and suggest how … implementation could be improved. (1.2e)
- Explain how action has been taken to control risk … (1.2c)

Functional Skills Link-up

Mathematics
- … Subtract whole numbers using a range of mental methods (Level 1). (See 'Measuring upthrust'.)

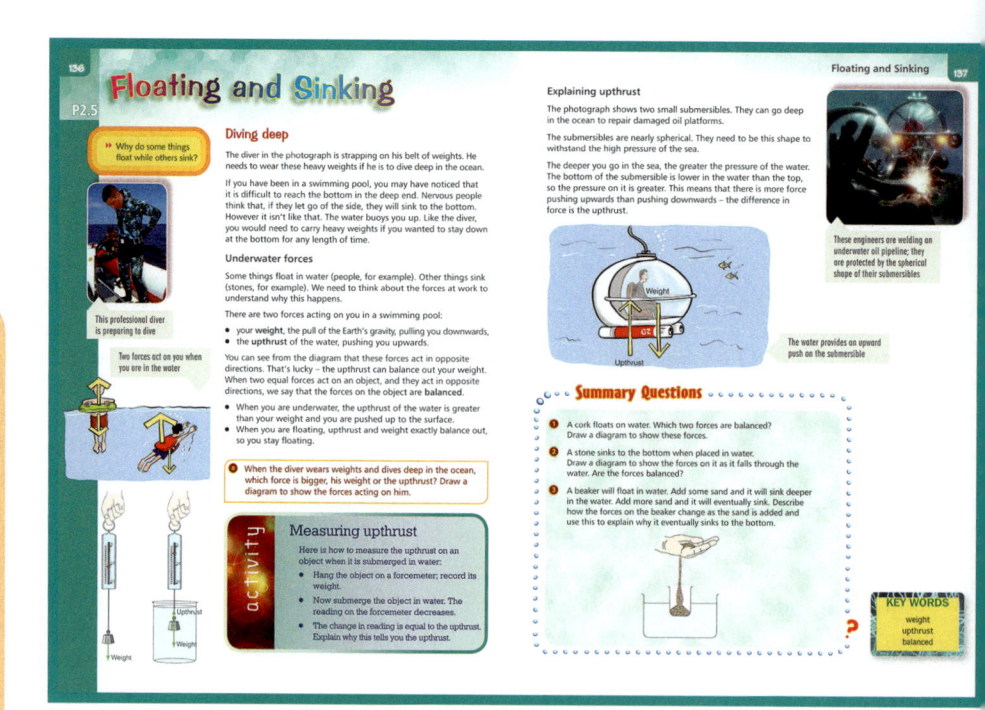

Learning Styles

Visual: Observing the behaviour of floating objects.

Auditory: Talking about how submersibles cope with pressure.

Kinaesthetic: Measuring upthrust.

Interpersonal: Discussing the cause of upthrust.

Intrapersonal: Answering questions in the 'Under pressure' starter quiz.

Answers to summary questions

1. Weight and upthrust are balanced; diagram of cork floating with equal and opposite force arrows.

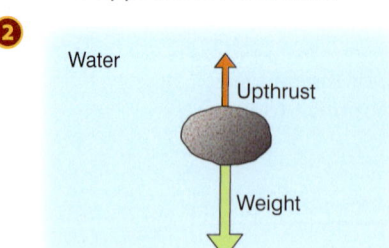

2.
   Water

   Upthrust ↑

   Weight ↓

   The forces are not balanced.

3. As sand is added, the weight increases, causing the beaker to sink further. This increases the upthrust. Eventually, when the water level reaches the top of the beaker, the upthrust can increase no further and the beaker sinks.

Floating and Sinking

The Lesson

Starter Suggestions

Float or sink?
Show the pupils a wide range of objects and get them to vote whether they think each one will float or sink by holding up cards just before you plunge them into a large bucket of water. (5–10 mins)

Under pressure
Use mini-whiteboards to hold a quickfire quiz about forces. The pupils keep their own score and the person that reaches ten points first is the winner. This could also be played as a team game. (10 mins)

Main Lesson

- The pupils may be encountering the word 'upthrust' for the first time here. Explain that a 'thrust' is simply a force and 'up' because it always pushes the object upwards.
- The idea of forces being balanced is very important. Give some extra examples of balanced forces. The pupils should see that whenever an object is not moving the forces are balanced. They will see that objects that are moving can also have balanced forces on them, later in the course.
- Some pupils may be aware that objects under water experience a pressure. Later in the lesson, you can spend a little time discussing this and explaining that this is due to the water pushing inwards on the object.
- The 'Measuring upthrust' practical is a fairly simple one, but it can be a bit messy. Make sure that the pupils are recording the *change* in the forcemeter reading. The pupils should take simple safety precautions and look out for ways of improving the basic method (How Science Works: evaluation).
- Try to get the pupils to see if there is any connection between the size of the upthrust and the shape of the object. This idea can later be linked to the shape of boats.
- Explaining upthrust for an object that is submerged is rather difficult. Make sure that the pupils understand that there are forces (pressure) all around the object. Then they need to be guided to an understanding that the forces on the bottom of the object are larger that the forces on the top and that this produces an overall upwards force.
- Underwater vessels have curved surfaces because these pass on the stresses of the forces and spread them around the ship. You can link this to the shapes of arches, which also distribute large forces.
- The 'Cartesian diver' plenary should round off the lesson nicely.

Plenary Suggestions

Cartesian diver
Place an inverted pen top into a large plastic bottle (1½ or 2 litre) full of water and seal it. The top should have a small bubble of air in it and so should float near the top. Squeeze the bottle and the pen top should sink. Sachets of tomato sauce work too. Can the pupils explain what is happening? [Squeezing the bottle causes the pressure in the bubble to increase and so its volume decreases. This makes it more dense so it sinks.] (5–10 mins)

You've sunk my battleship!
Play a game of battleships on a four by four grid, but you only get to guess a square when you answer a question about forces correctly. (10 mins)

Practical Support

Measuring upthrust

Equipment and materials required
Per group:
A range of forcemeters, a range of objects denser than water (various metal blocks, glass, etc.) and a wooden object less dense than water.

Details
The method is fairly straightforward; the pupils measure the weight of the object with the forcemeter, then measure the weight when the object is submerged in the sink or bucket of water and calculate the difference. The objects will have to have string loops tied around them in order for them to be attached to the forcemeter; this could be done in advance.

Once the pupils have tested all of the objects that sink, get them to calculate the upthrust on the object that floats. The forcemeter should read zero when the object is floating. This means that the upthrust and weight are equal so proving the point from earlier in the lesson.

Safety
Watch out for spilled water hazards.

Differentiation

SEN
Provide a worksheet with a table to help these pupils organise and process their results for the 'Measuring upthrust' activity. Some pupils may need additional help with attaching the objects to the forcemeter.

Extension
The pupils can look into how airships or hot air balloons work. You can demonstrate the lift of a small hydrogen balloon (buy a helium one from a shop) by attaching it to a forcemeter. The pupils have to consider the expansion of air in the hot air balloon in terms of particle behaviour.

Homework Suggestion

The pupils could build their own Cartesian diver at home as mentioned in the plenary.

Answers to in-text questions

a Weight is greater than upthrust; diagram of diver with force arrows: weight downwards longer than upthrust upwards.

P2.6 A Matter of Density

NC links to the lesson
- Energy, electricity and forces: forces are interactions between objects and can affect their shape and motion.

Learning Objectives
Pupils should learn:
- That the mass of an object represents the amount of material (matter) it contains.
- That the volume of an object is the amount of space it occupies.
- That graphs can be used to find patterns in the properties of materials.

Learning Outcomes
- All pupils should be able to compare materials in terms of density.
- Most pupils should be able to decide if a material will float based on the density.
- Some pupils should also be able to measure the density of substances in grams per centimetre cubed (g/cm^3).

How Science Works
- Describe and record observations and evidence systematically. (1.2d)

Functional Skills Link-up
Mathematics
- Carry out calculations with numbers of any size in practical contexts. (Level 2) See 'Measuring density'.

Learning Styles
Visual: Taking measurements using a forcemeter.
Auditory: Describing how mercury feels different to water.
Kinaesthetic: Building boats.
Intrapersonal: Understanding the difference between weight and density.
Interpersonal: Working in groups to measure density.

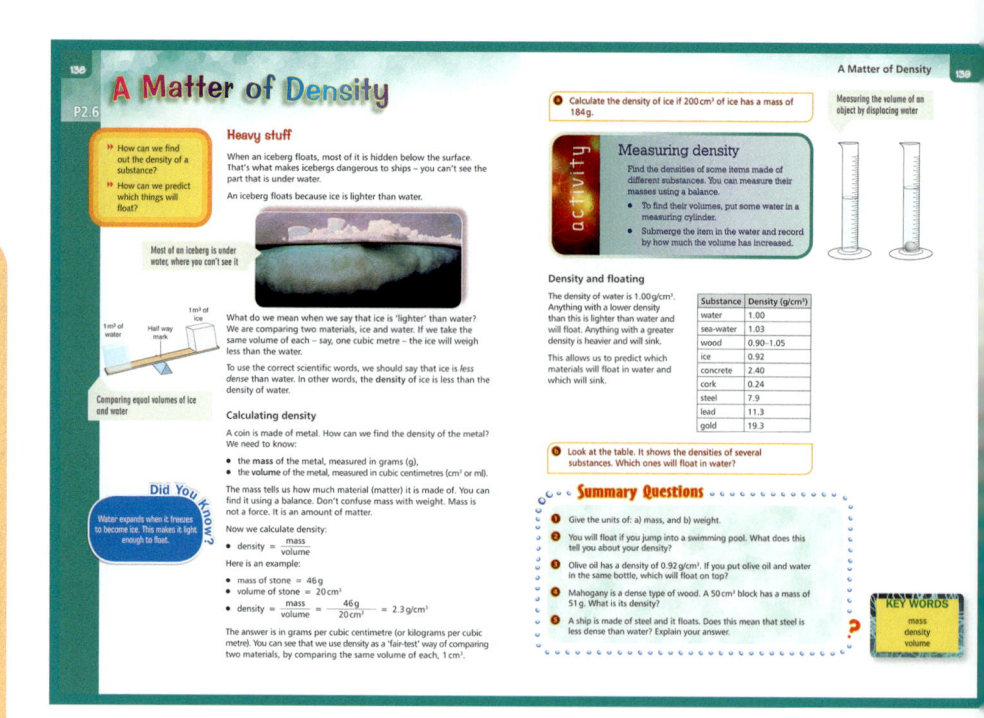

The Lesson

Starter Suggestions

Accident at work?
Spray-paint a block of expanded polystyrene (or foam) to look like a brick, wooden block or chunk of metal. Carry it convincingly in a tray, trip and drop it on your foot. The pupils have to explain why it didn't hurt. (5 mins)

That sinking feeling
Oh dear; the whole school is sinking. The pupils have only ten minutes to design a lifejacket and/or raft from the materials around the laboratory or in their bags. (10–15 mins).

Main Lesson
- In this topic the pupils will be measuring and calculating the density of materials. Some pupils will need assistance with the density calculations, particularly the units used. Take some time to remind the pupils about mass and volume.

Answers to summary questions

1. a) kg
   b) N
2. A person's density is less than that of water.
3. Oil will float on water.
4. 1.02 g/cm^3.
5. Steel is denser than water, but a boat is hollow, so that it is partly steel, partly air. Its overall density is less than that of water, so it floats.

A Matter of Density

- To get a first impression of density, show the pupils a dense metal block and the equivalent mass of water on two top-pan balances. It should be obvious that the metal is much smaller even though it has the same mass (and weight).
- Mercury is a particularly impressive liquid in terms of density. Let the pupils feel the weight of a container with some mercury (10 cm^3 saved from broken thermometers should be enough) compared to an equal volume of water. The mercury is 13.5 times denser than water, so the difference is very noticeable. **Safety:** make sure that the mercury container is sealed, airtight and made from robust plastic, as mercury vapour is toxic. Don't pass the container around; ask some pupils to come to the front and lift it in turn.
- The pupils will be required to perform some calculations of density here; many will not be entirely confident with calculations. Go through a few examples before moving on to the practical task.
- The practical task 'Measuring density' is fairly straightforward, but can have a number of inaccuracies due to the measurement of volume. At the end, the pupils could discuss the problems with accuracy in measuring the volume and share the results for each material to get an average value (How Science Works: improving the reliability of data).
- Some sample materials will not sink in water. You can deliberately use these in the practical task in order to lead to a discussion about how their volume can be measured so that their density can be found.
- To summarise the results, place a series of material samples in order of density so that the pupils can check their results. You can add additional materials to the row, such as polystyrene, wax and even the mercury sample from earlier.
- Pupils will be aware that many ships are made of metal, which is denser than water, and yet they float. You can show the pupils a diagram of a ship and point out all of the air inside it. Its average density is less than water. This can lead onto the 'Boat building' plenary task.

Plenary Suggestions

Iceberg! Dead ahead!
Show the pupils a big, solid, block of ice floating in water inside a large beaker. Many will know that 'you can only see one-tenth of an iceberg above water' but is this statement true? The oceans are salt water, so place a similar-sized block into a saturated salt solution. Is there a difference? You could use a hydrometer to show how the density of the water changes. (5–10 mins)

Boat building
Give each group of pupils a sheet of aluminium foil, measuring approximately 20 cm by 20 cm. They have five minutes to build a boat capable of floating and supporting as many 20 g masses as possible. After the time is up, test the boats to destruction. (15 mins)

Answers to in-text questions

a 0.92 g/cm^3.

b Wood (some types), ice and cork will float in water.

Practical Support

Measuring density

Equipment and materials required
Per group: a range of forcemeters, measuring cylinders large enough to fit the samples into or displacement cans with measuring cylinders. A range of sample materials; these do not need to be regularly shaped but they do need to be denser than water so that they sink. Suitable materials include metal blocks, plastics, ceramics and various rocks. Top-pan balances if available.

Details
The pupils measure the mass of the samples using top-pan balances. If these are not available, forcemeters can be used but the pupils will have to attach the samples using string (they might like to think about how adding the string changes the weight) and then they may have to convert the weight to mass; dividing by 10 is sufficient for this basic experiment. The volume of the samples is then measured. The sample materials need to fit comfortably inside the measuring cylinders, but large measuring cylinders are not very precise. As an improvement, displacement cans can be used but you will have to demonstrate how they operate to the pupils.

Safety
Watch out for water spillage and dropping samples onto feet.

Differentiation

SEN
The pupils should be provided with a template for the calculations of density so that they learn how to lay out these calculations clearly.

Extension
These pupils can look into the density of gases (make sure that they do not think that gases are mass/weightless). Show the pupils a hydrogen-filled balloon and a carbon dioxide-filled one and ask them to explain their behaviour. They could discuss the strange behaviour of water as mentioned in 'Did you know?'

Homework Suggestion

The pupils can research the design of ships to find out how they are made to float. They can also find an explanation of why submarines can float and sink at will.

Did You Know?
Liquid water is at its most dense at 4°C. Lakes freeze from the surface downwards in winter. The layer of ice insulates the water beneath and allows fish to survive in the 4°C zone at the bottom of the lake. Explain to the pupils that if water didn't have this property, then many lakes would freeze completely solid in winter and animals would not be able to survive in them. You wouldn't be able to go ice-skating either.

P2.7 Fuels Alight

NC links for the lesson
- Energy, electricity and forces: energy can be transferred usefully, stored, or wasted, but cannot be created or destroyed.

Learning Objectives

Pupils should learn:
- That fuels are substances that are burned to release useful energy.
- That different fuels release different amounts of useful energy when they are burned.

Learning Outcomes

- All pupils should be able to state that a fuel is a substance that releases heat, light and sometimes sound when burned.
- Most pupils should be able to explain that different fuels release different amounts of energy when burned.
- Some pupils should also be able to describe the products of combustion.

How Science Works

- Describe and suggest how planning and implementation could be improved. (1.2e)

Functional Skills Link-up

Mathematics
- Collect and represent discrete and continuous data, using ICT where appropriate. (Level 2) See 'Comparing fuels'.

Literacy
- The pupils can write a poem.

Answers to in-text questions

a Fuels for cooking: calor gas (propane, butane), coal. Electric oven or microwave don't use fuel.

b E.g. logs crackling in open fire, gas flame 'roaring'.

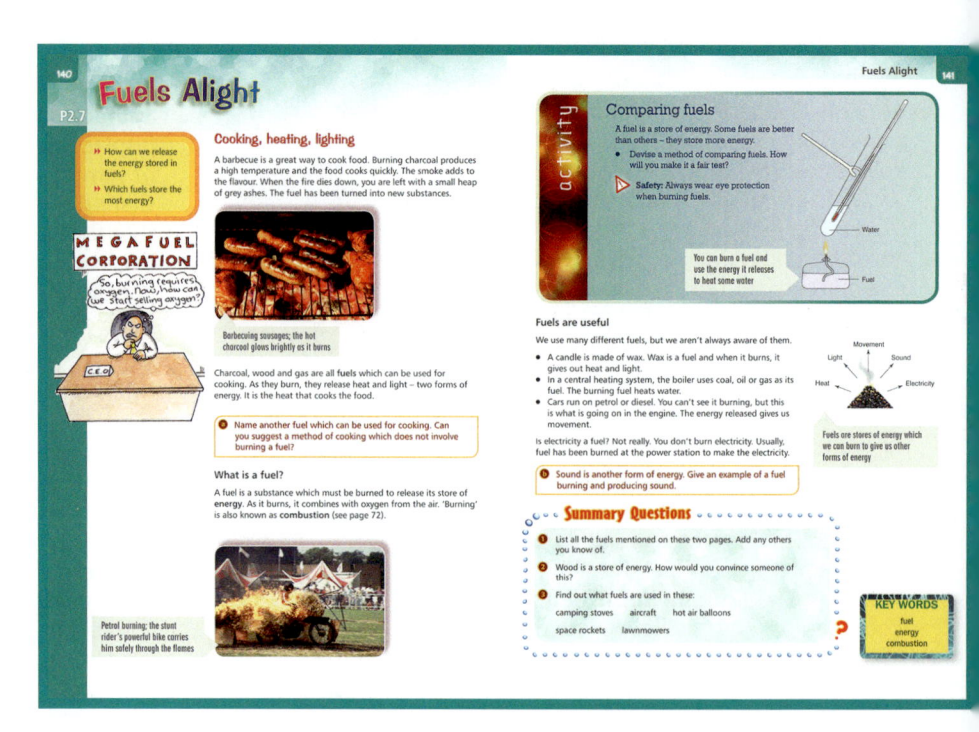

The Lesson

Starter Suggestions

Fire starter

Demonstrate a small fire, such as a watch-glass of ethanol on a heat-resistant mat. As it burns, ask the pupils to describe how it could be put out or why it will eventually go out itself. They should come up with ideas based on the fire triangle. (5–10 mins).

Fuel for a fire

The pupils should give their own definition of a fuel. They should also make a list of all the fuels they know and give an example of how, or where, the fuel is used. (5–10 mins)

Learning Styles

Visual: Watching combustion processes.
Auditory: Reading out poems.
Kinaesthetic: Carrying out the comparison of different fuels.
Intrapersonal: Evaluating experimental procedures.
Interpersonal: Working in groups.

Answers to summary questions

1. Coal, oil, gas, wood, charcoal, wax, petrol, diesel, etc.
2. Burn it and use the heat to do something.
3. Camping stoves: gas (propane, butane). Aircraft: kerosene. Hot air balloons: propane, butane gas. Space rockets: solid fuels which include oxygen (e.g. nitrocellulose and nitroglycerine, or aluminium perchlorate and aluminium powder). Lawnmowers: petrol.

Fuels Alight

Main Lesson

- Start the lesson with the 'Fuel for a fire' starter to establish the pupils' prior knowledge about fuels. They should be aware of the 'fire triangle': fuel + oxygen + heat. This leads to a discussion of how fire fighting techniques work, e.g. removing the oxygen by smothering. This was covered in C1.10.
- Demonstrate the combustion of small samples of charcoal, wood (on a heat-resistant mat) and gas (a Bunsen) to show that they all burn in a similar way: releasing light and heat energy.
- Try to make sure that the pupils do not think that the energy from the fuels is 'used up' when the fuel burns. Just explain that the energy is transferred into heat in the surroundings, so becoming fairly useless.
- In a similar way, it is important that the pupils do not think that the material that made up the fuel is used up; it is converted into carbon dioxide, water and other gases. You could use 'Demonstrating carbon dioxide production' from the next lesson to show some of these combustion products.
- Encourage the pupils to use the term 'combustion' instead of burning throughout the rest of the topic. With higher attaining pupils you could move onto the basic combustion equation for most fuels:

hydrocarbon + oxygen → carbon dioxide + water.

- Once the pupils are comfortable with the definition of a fuel they can move on to comparing them.
- The pupils will enjoy the practical task 'Comparing fuels'. The task presents some new hazards, so there is a good opportunity for the pupils to carry out a risk assessment (How Science Works: safety, see page 157).
- The comparison of the different fuels will not lead to an accurate measurement of how much energy is released but the pupils can move on to look at some of the problems associated with the measurements, such as energy loss to the surroundings (How Science Works: evaluation, see page 161).
- If they have time, the pupils should use a bar chart to show their results. They should be able to explain why a bar chart is the best way of representing this information (How Science Works: presenting data, see page 160–161).
- After the experiment, ask the pupils to list ways that they could improve the practical to be more accurate. They should refer back to these ideas when they test the food sample in P2.11.
- The pupils should now be able to state that as a fuel burns, energy is released and that different fuels store different amounts of energy.

Plenary Suggestions

The right fuel for the job

Give the pupils a list of fuels and a list of tasks that require fuels. They must match up the fuel to the job and give a good reason why that fuel is used. For example, petrol is used in car engines because it releases a lot of energy very quickly. Wax is used for candles because it releases energy fairly slowly. (5 mins)

Tiger, tiger, burning bright

The pupils can write a short poem about fuels and combustion. It can be judged on scientific accuracy or aesthetic beauty. (10–15 mins)

Practical Support

Comparing fuels

Equipment and materials required

Per group: two spirit burners labelled A and B, boiling tubes, a 10 cm^3 measuring cylinder, a thermometer (0.5°C is best), a retort stand and a stop clock. Fuel A is ethanol and fuel B is paraffin. The fuels should be soaked into cotton wool inside the burners to reduce the chance of spillage.

Details

The pupils measure 5 cm^3 of water into a boiling tube and mount it on a clamp. They measure the starting temperature of the water. Then they place a fuel burner underneath the tube at a measured distance (e.g. 2 cm) and light it; allowing the water to be heated for one minute. They record the end temperature and calculate the temperature rise. Finally, they repeat the experiment with the remaining fuel sample.

The simplest method to make the test fair is to allow the fuels to burn for the same period of time. Although this does not compare the amount of energy release per unit mass, it does avoid the need to measure the mass of fuel consumed which is generally very small.

Safety

Eye protection must be worn.

Pupils to tie back hair and clothing.

The pupils will be using only very small quantities of fuels for the practical, but they must be warned about the risk of spillage and combustion.

Spirit burners must not be moved while they are lit.

Ethanol is highly flammable and harmful: CLEAPSS Hazcard 40A.

Paraffin is harmful: CLEAPSS Hazcard 45B.

Differentiation

SEN

A clear step-by-step method should be provided for the practical task so that the pupils can concentrate on taking accurate measurements of changes in temperature.

Extension

Pupils could make, and carry out, a plan to measure the amount of energy released by the consumption of equal masses of a sample fuel. This would involve measuring the mass of the spirit burner before and after the experiment and calculating the amount of energy released (temperature rise in the water) per gram of fuel used (How Science Works: controlling variables).

Homework Suggestion

When fuels burn without enough oxygen, the gas carbon monoxide is formed. The pupils can find out why this is a very dangerous gas and how it can be detected. They could do this as a small advisory booklet.

P2.8 Burning the Past, Wrecking the Future?

NC links for the lesson
- Energy, electricity and forces: energy can be transferred usefully, stored, or wasted, but cannot be created or destroyed.
- The environment, Earth and universe: human activity and natural processes can lead to changes in the environment.

Learning Objectives

Pupils should learn:
- That fossil fuels are the remains of plants and animals that lived millions of years ago.
- That fossil fuels are an important energy resource and are used in the production of electricity and for transport.
- That burning fossil fuels has environmental consequences.

Learning Outcomes
- All pupils will be able to state where fossil fuels come from and that they are a non-renewable resource.
- Most pupils will be able to describe the steps in the formation of fossils fuels.
- Some pupils will also be able to describe the link between the use of fossil fuels and global warming.

How Science Works
- Describe some benefits and drawbacks of scientific developments with which they are familiar. (1.1b)

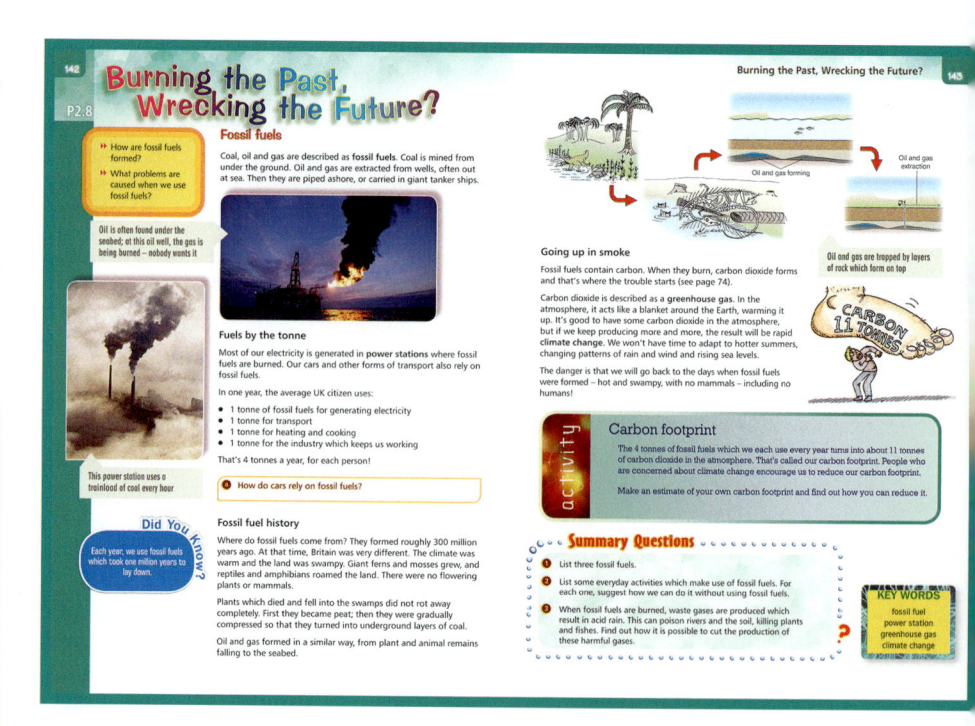

The Lesson

Starter Suggestions

Old fossil

Show the pupils slides of fossils (or the real thing) and ask them what they think they are and where they come from. (5–10 mins)

Really old films

Show the pupils some video clips showing dinosaurs and other prehistoric creatures. Use modern CGI clips plus a few really old 'stop motion' clips. You can discuss what happened to the creatures, especially the plants. (10–15 mins).

Main Lesson

- Have some samples of fossil fuels available for the pupils to see, as many will not be familiar with them. A rough lump of coal, a sealed container of crude oil and a squirt of gas from a gas tap should be sufficient. If you have a set of samples of the fractions made from oil, you can point out the petrol and diesel fuels to show how oil is used in cars too.
- The pupils will have a great deal of trouble imagining the timescales involved in the formation of fossil fuels. It's never going to be easy to show this, but you could try something like the following. Draw a line of 10 cm length on the

Answers to summary questions

1. Coal, oil, gas, peat.
2. For example, cooking – use wood or charcoal; driving – use solar-powered car.
3. Remove harmful gases from power stations, use catalytic converters in car exhaust systems.

Functional Skills Link-up

Mathematics
- Carry out calculations with numbers of any size in practical contexts. (Level 2) See carbon footprint calculation.

Learning Styles

Visual: Using diagrams to show long-term processes.

Auditory: Talking about dinosaurs and the formation of fossil fuels.

Interpersonal: Discussing their personal impact on the environment.

Intrapersonal: Evaluating a carbon footprint.

Burning the Past, Wrecking the Future?

board; this represents *all* of recorded human history, about 10 thousand years. The modern era, 2 thousand years, would only be 2 cm long and a human lifetime would be less than 1 mm long. Going back to the very first humans would be a line 10 m long (one million years). Fossil fuels take about 50 million years to form, so that's a line stretching for 500 m. It takes nearly a million human lifetimes for coal to form, so it's going to be a while before new supplies are available!

- Some of the pupils will have heard of the greenhouse effect, but make sure that they make the connection that the carbon dioxide released from fuels is increasing the levels of the gas in the atmosphere. Use the 'Demonstrating carbon dioxide production' activity if you haven't done so previously. Let the pupils imagine that every fire is releasing the gas, millions of tonnes every day.
- The idea of a carbon footprint is quite a tricky one. Explain that the more fuels you use the bigger your effect on the atmosphere; then move onto the 'carbon footprint' task. This involves making judgements about personal fuel use, if pupils can't make estimates then provide examples on a worksheet (How Science Works: issues).
- Pupils will need support to help them to make their estimates and perform the calculations from the worksheets. Most will require calculators. The manipulation of the data covers an important How Science Works point.
- To round off the lesson the 'Smaller carbon feet' plenary can help the pupils think about how to reduce their impact. Some pupils can get a bit annoyed, because they don't make the choices so they aren't responsible. Remind them that one day they will be.

Plenary Suggestions

Smaller carbon feet
The pupils must list a set of steps that they could take to reduce their carbon footprint. These should be ways to reduce fuel use and to use the fuel more efficiently. The suggestions could be written on cut-out footprints and added to a display board. (10 mins)

Old King Coal
Ask the pupils to imagine that they are an ancient tree that's just fallen down. They must describe the events that happen to them as they turn into coal and eventually end up in the atmosphere after being burnt in a power station. (10–15 mins)

Practical Support

Carbon footprint

Equipment and materials required
The pupils need access to worksheets containing information about carbon footprints and a calculator. The worksheet should contain step-by-step instructions.

Details
To calculate their carbon footprint, the pupils will have to know some of the details of their lifestyles. Provide two sample details (one with a high carbon footprint and one with a low footprint) for the pupils to analyse if they are unclear of their own details.

Pupils will be required to multiply and add to get their total footprint.

Demonstrating carbon dioxide production

Equipment and materials required
Ethanol, a spirit burner, limewater, funnel, boiling tube, stopper with two holes, tubing, a water pump (or hand pump). Optional: a glass U-tube in a tray of crushed ice.

Details
First demonstrate that limewater turns milky when carbon dioxide passes through it. You can do this by blowing into a boiling tube of limewater through a straw; wear eye protection.

Half-fill a boiling tune with limewater. Place the spirit burner underneath an up-turned funnel and connect rubber tubing through the boiling tube, so that the water pump will suck the gases through the limewater. Burn the fuel and pull the gases produced through the limewater using the water pump. The limewater will slowly turn milky, showing the presence of carbon dioxide or carbon monoxide in the fumes.

You might want to add a little black ink colour to the ethanol to make it look a bit 'oily'. You could also show that water is produced during this combustion by making the gasses pass through a U-tube in a tray of crushed ice to condense the water vapour.

Safety
The pupils should wear eye protection.

Pupils to tie back hair and loose clothing.

Be careful of ethanol spillage, it is highly flammable and harmful: CLEAPSS Hazcard 40A.

Limewater is an irritant: CLEAPSS Hazcard 18.

Differentiation

SEN
The carbon footprint task can be quite complex. The pupils should be led through a few examples before completing their own assessment; this should be based on some multiple choice questions such as what type of house they live in, what type of holiday they take, how they travel to school and so on.

Extension
The pupils could find out about peat. This was once a very popular form of fuel but now its use is very restricted.

Homework Suggestion

Where do our fossil fuels come from and how long will supplies last? The pupils can find out information about the sources of the fuels used in our power stations, homes and cars and look at the latest estimates of how long these supplies will be available.

Did You Know?
The current predicted reserves of fossil fuels give average estimates of 45 years for oil, 70 years for natural gas and 250 years for coal, but it is worth discussing the validity of these estimates with the pupils. What actions will make the reserves last longer? You could also discuss old estimates that predicted that oil would run out in the 1990s.

Answers to in-text questions

a. Petrol and diesel fuels are derived from crude oil, a fossil fuel.

P2.9 Renewables – Cleaning up our Act

NC links for the lesson
- Energy, electricity and forces: energy can be transferred usefully, stored, or wasted, but cannot be created or destroyed.
- The environment, Earth and universe: human activity and natural processes can lead to changes in the environment.

Learning Objectives
Pupils should learn:
- There are a range of renewable energy resources that can be used to produce electricity.
- That to maintain a reliable electricity supply and range of different resources, renewable and non-renewable are needed.

Learning Outcomes
- All pupils will be able to name several renewable energy resources.
- Most pupils will be able to describe the advantages and disadvantages of different resources.
- Some pupils will also be able to produce a balanced opinion of the need for different resources.

How Science Works
- Recognise that decisions about the use and application of science and technology are influenced by society and individuals. (1.1b)

Functional Skills Link-up
English
- Present information/points of view clearly and in an appropriate form. (Level 1) Discusssing biofuels.

The Lesson

Starter Suggestions

Start your engines
Demonstrate a small fuel burning engine at work. This can be a model fuel burning motor from a toy car or similar. Show diagrams of how this is scaled-up in a full-sized car engine. (5–10 mins)

Biofuels at work
Show the pupils a video clip showing how biofuels are produced and used. Willow is an important one in the UK and it is easy to understand, as the willow is simply burned (but you could show methane instead). (10–15 mins).

Learning Styles
Visual: Observing energy transfers in different resources.
Auditory: Discussing what makes a resource renewable.
Kinaesthetic: Exploring energy resource models.
Interpersonal: Discussing the 'greenness' of energy companies.
Intrapersonal: Reflecting on the challenge of changing our energy sources.

Answers to summary questions
1. Biofuels (biomass, bio-diesel), hydroelectric, wind power, wave power, solar power.
2. Burn the wood in a power station. It's sustainable.
3. They don't need to carry fuel with them. Sunlight is always available in space (except in the Earth's shadow).
4. Research into existing and future use of renewable resources.

Renewables – Cleaning up our Act

Main Lesson

- Pupils often get confused about the words used to describe energy (occasionally called the forms of energy: 'thermal', 'chemical', etc.) and the energy resources mentioned in this topic. Make sure that you are very clear about the difference when you mention the energy resources.
- Growing biofuels takes quite a lot of land; you may want to discuss whether the land would be better used to grow food crops (How Science Works: issues).
- Pupils usually don't have much difficulty understanding that non-renewable fuels can't be used again. They can have a bit of a problem with biofuels being renewable and they 'disappear' when burnt. It's all a matter of being able to get more; remind them how long it takes for coal to form and point out that a crop can be grown every year.
- The pupils can look at some of the ways of producing electricity with the 'Testing renewable energy' practical tasks. Ask them to try to describe the energy transfers that are happening using correct scientific language. They should also take note of the limitations of the technology; will this work in all areas and in all conditions?
- Show some pictures or video clips of large scale renewable energy resources so that the pupils get a sense of the scale of the structures. You should discuss the problems associated with each of these energy resources in turn. Remember to mention the very high costs of solar energy, but point out that these are falling as the technology becomes more mature.
- In the end, pupils should come to the conclusion that a range of energy resources will be needed to meet the demands of a modern society. They should realise that no one resource can give us a reliable and sustainable supply of electricity.

Plenary Suggestions

Weigh up the pros and cons

Give the pupils a list of renewable and non-renewable energy resources, some advantages and some disadvantages associated with them. They have to match up the resource, advantage and disadvantages. (5–10 mins)

How green is your power?

Give the pupils some advertisements from energy companies, producers and distributors. They have to discuss and decide which company is the 'greenest'. (10 mins)

Practical Support

Testing renewable energy

Equipment and materials required

The pupils will be visiting stations showing how electricity can be generated. If there is enough equipment, two of each station should be set up.

Station 1: Solar power – A solar panel connected to a low power bulb or small motor. A bright lamp if there is no direct sunlight available.

Station 2: Water power – A water turbine connected up to the tap. Ideally the turbine should be enclosed and the water should drain out into the sink.

Station 3: Wind power – A wind turbine connected to a low power lamp or motor. A hairdryer (set on low temperature) to spin the turbine.

Station 4: 'Animal' power – A wind-up radio or torch. A hand-powered turbine connected to a low power lamp or motor would work as an alternative.

Details

The pupils must visit each of the stations and investigate how the apparatus works. Instructions should be placed by each of the stations along with information about how each method can be used on a larger scale.

Safety

Make sure that the hairdryer isn't used on a hot setting as this can cause burns. Make sure it is safety tested.

Differentiation

SEN

Provide explanations of how the electricity generating devices operate. The pupils can then answer a set of questions about each process leading them to realise the limitations of each of the methods. For example, they should find that the solar panel isn't much use at night unless it is connected to a rechargeable battery for energy storage.

Extension

Why don't biofuels contribute to the greenhouse effect even though they are burned? Get the pupils to look into this; they need to find out that the carbon is taken back out of the atmosphere when the plants photosynthesise. They might find that growing crops does have some effect because of the production processes.

Homework Suggestion

The pupils can produce a booklet trying to persuade people to use renewable energy resources instead of fossil fuels.

Answers to in-text questions

a Oats are a renewable supply, because we can grow more oats each year, using the energy of sunlight.

b Solar power relies on today's sunlight, and there will be more tomorrow. Petrol relies on existing stores of oil, a fossil fuel.

Did You Know?

The power from the Sun per square metre of the Earth's surface is around 1 kW but solar panels are usually around 12% efficient at converting this to electricity, and so give a peak power output of 120 W/m^2. The best, and most expensive, designs are reaching towards 40% efficiency. Current designs take around five years to transfer the amount of energy they took to make in the first place when used in sunny locations and quite a bit longer in the UK.

To utilise all of the power output of the Sun we could build a Dyson shell providing an almost limitless supply of energy. Higher attaining pupils might like to look into this.

P2.10 Making More of Energy

NC links for the lesson
- Energy, electricity and forces: energy can be transferred usefully, stored, or wasted, but cannot be created or destroyed.

Learning Objectives
Pupils should learn:
- That the amount of energy we use can be reduced by taking measures to prevent heat loss.
- About the environmental costs of wasting energy.

Learning Outcomes
- All pupils will be able to list measures that can be taken to reduce energy loss.
- Most pupils will be able to describe a simple method to test energy saving techniques.
- Some pupils will also be able to describe the consequences of inefficient use of energy resources in terms of environmental impact and monetary cost.

How Science Works
- Describe an appropriate approach to answer a scientific question using a limited range of information and making relevant observations and measurements. (1.2a)

Answers to summary questions
1. Double glazing, cavity wall insulating, roof insulation, etc.
2. The insulation will reduce how much heat energy enters the house and so keeps it cool.
3. The insulation will pay for its cost after 20 years. This is a bit on the long side.
4. People do not enjoy wearing heavy clothes.

Answers to in-text questions
a. Pupil research.

The Lesson

Starter Suggestions

Wrap up warm
Show the pupils some photographs (or video) of polar explorers and how they have to dress to survive. Now show them some animals that live in the Polar Regions: polar bears, seals, etc. How do these animals manage to survive the very low temperatures? (5–10 mins).

My best suit
The pupils have to write an outline plan that can be used to test which clothing material is the best at keeping you warm. This can be used to inform the plan later in the lesson. (10–15 mins)

Main Lesson
- At the very start of the lesson, pour some boiling water into a thermos flask and seal it. Pour the same amount into an open glass beaker and put to one side. Don't explain why.
- If it is winter, ask the pupils how they dress to keep warm outside. If it's summer, ask them how they keep cool. This leads to the idea of using materials to keep heat in, insulators, or allowing it to escape.
- Show the pupils some of the materials typically used for insulation. This can be clothing or even some materials used in buildings. You should be able to get hold of some foil-backed foam as used in the cavities between brick layers.

Functional Skills Link-up

Mathematics
- Carry out calculations with numbers of any size in practical contexts. (Level 2) Analysing figures for savings made from home insulation measures.

Learning Styles
Visual: Recording thermometer readings.
Auditory: Discussing how thermal energy movement is controlled.
Kinaesthetic: Carrying out investigations into heat loss.
Interpersonal: Discussing the variables associated with cooling.
Intrapersonal: Considering fair tests.

Making More of Energy

Safety: fibreglass materials need to be handled with gloves, and wear eye protection.

- Many insulating materials have layers or bubbles of trapped air. Pupils should be made aware that the air is the reason that these materials are good insulators, but they don't need to worry about conduction or convection yet.
- Two versions of the 'Keeping heat in' practical are provided. The first is fairly basic; the second can be used for a more detailed investigation with higher attaining pupils. Both of the tasks can take quite a bit of time to complete.
- You may wish to take this opportunity to allow the pupils to design their own test to rate the insulating properties of materials by building on the 'My best suit' starter. This will take a lot more time, but it is a good chance to cover some of the planning content of How Science Works.
- To ensure a fair test, the pupils will have to appreciate that two factors must be controlled: the starting temperature of the material and the mass (or volume) of material used.
- After the practical, go back to the water in the thermos flask and beaker. Show the pupils the great difference in temperature: the thermos will have kept the water at over 80°C, while the water in the beaker will be cool. This shows just how effective proper insulation can be.
- Linking the cost of energy to house insulation shows its importance, but the pupils won't be paying the bills.
- If your laboratory has a thermostat, then it can be worth demonstrating it.

Plenary Suggestions

Is it really heat-proof?
Place a small chunk of wax on top of a 'heat-proof' mat resting on the top of a tripod. Heat the mat strongly from below with a Bunsen burner. Does the heat get through? Repeat with a metal plate (not aluminium, it melts). Is there a difference? (5 mins)

Pile up the savings
Give the pupils a table of house insulation measures and the savings that they will make each year. The pupils have to decide which measures they would take and in what order. (5–10 mins)

Practical Support

Keeping heat in

Equipment and materials required
Per group: three boiling tubes, three 100 cm^3 beakers, thermometers, a stop-clock, aluminium foil, a range of insulating materials (cotton wool, thin layers of foam, etc.) and some sticky tape, kettles or another source of hot water. Optional: data-logging equipment with temperature sensors.

Details
The pupils insulate two of the boiling tubes in different ways with the materials provided, while leaving one un-insulated. They can use tape or elastic bands to hold the material in place. Once this is done, the tubes will not fit in normal racks so the pupils stand them in the beakers. They pour hot water into one of the tubes, insert the thermometer, wait for the water to reach 70°C (or 60°C) and then measure how much the temperature falls over a five-minute period. They then repeat the procedure with the other two tubes to compare the effectiveness of the insulation.

Some pupils may want to make aluminium lids to prevent energy escaping through the top of the tubes.

Safety
The pupils will be handling hot water; they must not attempt to hold the boiling tubes while pouring water directly from a kettle into them.

Keeping heat in (alternative)

Equipment and materials required
Per group: metal blocks (aluminium, copper, iron or steel), 250 cm^3 or larger plastic beakers, thermometers, tongs, a blanket of material to wrap the blocks in (old towels or dishcloths cut to the appropriate size are good), a source of hot water. Optional: data-logging equipment with temperature sensors.

Details
This practical is more demanding of the pupils but tends to yield more interesting results.

The metal blocks are traditionally used to measure specific heat capacity; they have a mass of 1 kg or 0.5 kg and have a hole in the centre in which a thermometer or temperature sensor can be inserted. Different metals will have different heat capacities and so will cool at different rates.

The pupils should place their metal block into a beaker of very hot water. They need to let the block rest in the water for about five minutes to warm evenly. They then remove the block carefully using the tongs (it will be fairly hot) by pouring out the water into a sink. The block can them be wrapped in a cloth blanket and a thermometer inserted. When the block reaches a pre-determined starting temperature (60°C) a stop-clock is started and the temperature is recorded every 30 seconds for five minutes. The pupils repeat the experiment using a block without insulation.

You may want to heat the blocks yourself by having a plastic bucket of very hot water on the teacher desk.

Safety
The pupils will be handling hot water.
Do not allow the pupils to drop the metal blocks into a ceramic sink.

Differentiation

SEN
For the 'Keeping heat in' practical have some boiling tubes pre-insulated to save time. The pupils can then concentrate on recording the cooling of the tubes more carefully. If data-logging equipment is used, then the pupils can spend more time looking at the trends in the data during and after the experiment.

Extension
Consider the 'Keeping heat in (alternative)' practical. This can lead to discussions about the ability of different materials to store different amounts of thermal energy. Water is a particularly interesting substance when it comes to specific heat capacity.

You may want the pupils to plot cooling curves. This can lead to the idea that the amount of cooling depends on the temperature difference between the object and the surroundings.

Homework Suggestion

The pupils can bring in labels from food products to be used in the next lesson. Make sure that they know that they will need a large variety of labels.

P2.11 How Much Energy?

NC links for the lesson
- Energy, electricity and forces: energy can be transferred usefully, stored, or wasted, but cannot be created or destroyed.

Learning Objectives
Pupils should learn:
- That energy can be measured in a unit called the joule.
- Larger amounts of energy are measured in kilojoules.
- The amount of energy released by a food can be estimated by burning it, transferring the energy to water and measuring the temperature increase of the water.

Learning Outcomes
- All pupils will be able to describe a simple method for measuring the energy that can be released by burning food samples.
- Most pupils will be able to carry out a procedure to estimate the energy content of a food sample.
- Some pupils will also be able to evaluate and improve on the simple procedure.

How Science Works
- Recognise the range of variables involved in an investigation and decide which to control. (1.2b)
- Describe and suggest how planning and implementation could be improved. (1.2e)

Learning Styles
Visual: Taking temperature measurements.
Auditory: Discussing the improvements that can be made to the experiment.
Kinaesthetic: Sorting cards against the clock.
Interpersonal: Working in teams to test food samples.
Intrapersonal: Interpreting the results of an experiment.

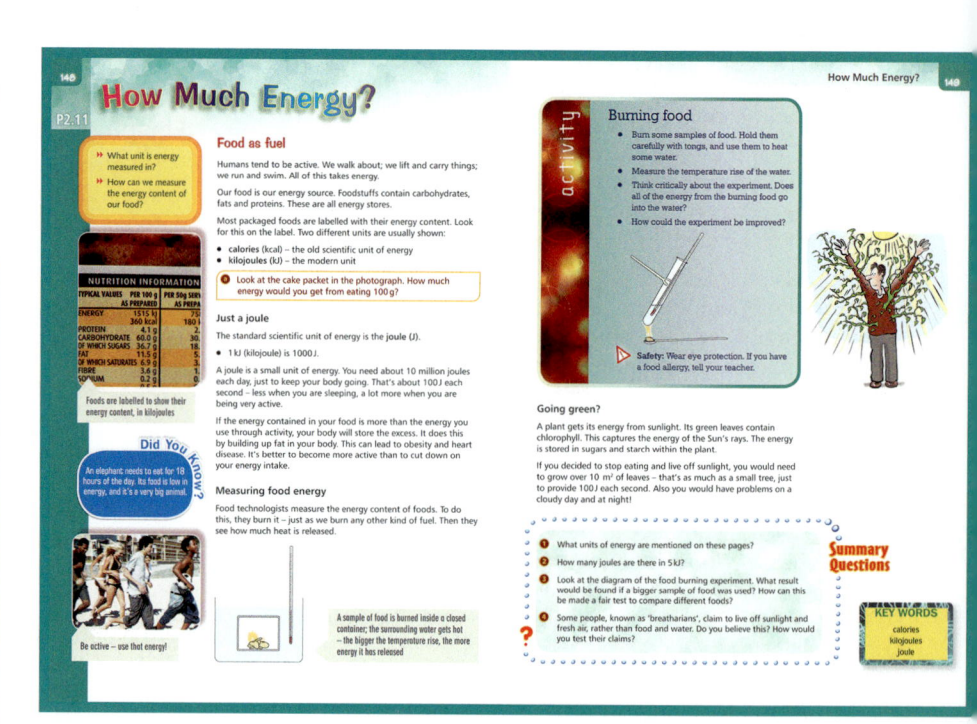

The Lesson

Starter Suggestions

Eat and eat and eat and eat
Show a slideshow showing some animals and discuss how often they need to eat. For example, lions only eat once every few days, while koala bears spend nearly all of their waking life eating. Ask the pupils for their opinions why this is; they should come up with ideas about how much energy is in the food and how active the animals are. (5–10 mins)

Fast food sort
Give the pupils a set of about ten different food labels. Ask them to sort the labels quickly into various orders while you give a one-minute countdown for each sort. Sorting orders should include fat content, salt content, sugar content and finally energy content. Can they see any connections between sugar and fat and the energy value the food has? (10 mins)

Functional Skills Link-up

Mathematics
- Collect and represent discrete and continuous data, using ICT where appropriate. (Level 2) See 'Burning food'.

Answers to summary questions

1. joules (and kJ); calories (kcal).
2. 5000 J.
3. Bigger sample: more energy released so temperature rises higher. Fair test: use the same mass of each.
4. Need to ensure that they did not have access to food and water, but did have sunlight and fresh air; see the Wikipedia article on breatharians for examples of tests.

How Much Energy?

Main Lesson

- Use the starter 'Fast food sort' to check if the pupils have any knowledge of the ways that food energy is measured. Many of them will know about calories already and will be able to sort correctly. Some may not sort fairly; remind them that they should choose values per 100 g for a fair comparison. (How Science Works: fair testing)
- Another scientific unit is introduced in this topic: the joule. As before, remind the pupils of the importance of having standards so that all scientists can make fair comparisons. Check that the pupils still remember the other units they have learned about.
- Pupils should be reminded that it is simplistic to judge a food on energy content alone. Take some time to mention the other values, e.g. salt levels, protein, carbohydrates and vitamins, and their importance.
- You can briefly discuss what the energy is used for in the body [carrying out chemical reactions] and where it ends up [as heat].
- The 'Burning food' practical task does not give very reliable results, but it does give a general indication about which foods types have most energy. Pupils need to link this to the idea that foods with high fat or sugar content have a larger supply of energy.
- The pupils should also be thinking about the limitations of the experiment. Are they using equal masses of food, did they hold the sample the same distance beneath the tube, is all of the energy going into the water, and so on (How Science Works: controlling variables, evaluation). The answers can be compared to those the pupils gave for the 'Comparing fuels' practical task in P2.7
- Food technologists have to be very careful not to let any of the energy of the food escape without being measured.
- You can mention that the process of food production in plants is called 'photosynthesis', but the pupils will look at this in more detail later in the course. Photosynthesis is not particularly efficient, less that 10% of the energy of sunlight is used usefully by plants.

Plenary Suggestions

Food 'Top Trumps'

The pupils can play Top Trumps with the food labels (which has the highest fat?, etc.) or with cards that you have prepared. The winner is the first to win all of the labels. (10 mins)

Unit round-up

The pupils make a mind map or spider diagram of all the information they have learned in this unit. They can re-visit the mind map they made in P2.1 and add to it. (15 mins)

Practical Support

Burning food

Equipment and materials required

Per group: Bunsen burner, tongs, (or a metal spike), thermometer, boiling tube, retort stand with clamp and access to food samples.

Details

The pupils clamp the boiling tubes then measure out 3 cm³ of water into them and place the thermometer so that they can easily take a reading. The starting temperature should be recorded so that a change in temperature can be measured.

A food sample is then lit using a Bunsen burner by holding it in the tongs (or on the end of the spike) and placing it in the flame briefly. Remind the pupils that holding the food in the flame too long will cause some of the energy to be released before it is used to heat the water. The food samples can be held in the tongs beneath the boiling tube so that the flame heats the water. It may be necessary to relight the samples a couple of times.

After the sample is exhausted, the pupils record the end temperature of the water and calculate the change.

Burning the food will produce quite a bit of smoke and a nasty odour so use a well-ventilated room.

Note: Protecting the tubes from draughts will improve the results. Use an empty tin or similar.

Safety

Eye protection must be worn.

Some pupils may be allergic to peanuts or other nuts so do not use them.

Check that there are no other food allergies.

Differentiation

SEN

It is important that the pupils evaluate the limitations of the experiments. Use a question and answer session to lead the pupils to a realisation of the limitations of the measurements that they made, so that they can produce a suitable set of improvements.

Extension

The pupils can find out more details about photosynthesis. What else, besides energy from sunlight, do plants need and what do they produce beside food?

Homework Suggestion

The pupils can find out about the energy requirements of different groups of people, including athletes. How much energy do they require each day?

Answers to in-text questions

a. The energy you would get from eating 100 g of the fruit cake is 1.5 kJ.

Did You Know?

Lions need to eat on average 5–7 kg of meat each day, although they don't eat every day. It might take a while to catch the food but, once caught, it only takes a few minutes for the lions to fulfil their energy requirements. Then they can spend time lying about. A large blue whale has to consume up to 4 tonnes of krill every day to keep itself going; a pretty dull diet. Perhaps the pupils can look into which animals need to consume the least amounts of food.

Answers to Forces and Energy – End of Topic Questions

Answers to know your stuff questions

1 a

Diesel generator	Fossil fuels
Solar cells	Sunlight
Wind turbine	Moving air

[3]

b The Sun does not shine at night, so no light energy is available. [1]

c When the wind stops blowing, the wind turbine stops turning. [1]

d They may need electricity when there is no Sun and no wind. [1]

2 a Gravity. [1]

b Friction *or* contact force. [1]

c Water acts as a lubricant, reducing friction. [1]

3 a Oil, coal, natural gas. [3]

b Three of: geothermal, biomass, moving air, tidal, running water, solar. [3]

c

| D | B | C | E | A |

[4]

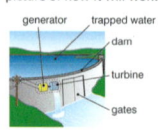

Electricity and Magnetism – End of Topic Questions

How Science Works

▼ Question 1 (level 5)

Mary and John are investigating a small electric heater. They are using it to heat 200 cm³ of water in a beaker. They measure the temperature of the water every minute.

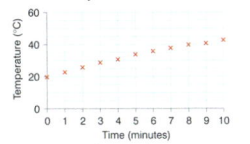

The graph shows their results.

a Explain why Mary stirred the water each time before taking its temperature. [1]

b John wrote this prediction:

'If we wait twice as long, the temperature of the water will go up twice as much.'

Do the results of the experiment support John's prediction? Explain how you know. [2]

c Copy the graph. Add a second line to show the results you would expect if the experiment was repeated with 400 cm³ of water in the beaker. [2]

▼ Question 2 (level 5)

In an experiment to investigate how a spring stretches, Jay and Kay hung weights on the end of the spring and measured its length.

Jay said, 'Every time we increase the weight, the spring will get longer.'

The table shows their results.

Weight (N)	Length of spring (mm)	Increase in length (mm)
0	40	0
1	46	6
2	52	12
3	58	
4	64	
5	70	

a Study Jay's prediction and look at the table of results. Was Jay's prediction supported by the results? [1]

b Copy the table and complete the final column. [1]

c Draw a graph to show the results. [2]

d Use your graph, or the table of results, to find out how much the spring stretched for every newton of load. [1]

e Kay tried to make a better prediction than Jay. She said:

'If we double the weight on the spring, it will get twice as long.'

What Kay said is not quite right. Write down a better conclusion, based on the results they obtained. [2]

▼ Question 3 (level 6)

Emma carried out an experiment to investigate floating and sinking. She had a wooden ruler. She weighed a lump of Plasticine and then attached it to one end of the ruler. Then she floated the ruler in water and recorded the length of the ruler sticking out of the water.

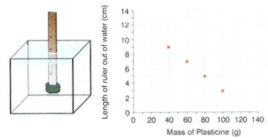

Study the graph of Emma's results.

a Use the graph to predict the mass of Plasticine needed to make the ruler sink. [1]

b If there were no Plasticine, what length of the ruler would stick out of the water? [1]

c Put these materials in order, starting with the most dense: water, wood, Plasticine. [2]

d Emma says, 'As the ruler gets heavier, the upthrust of the water gets less, so eventually the ruler sinks.' Explain why Emma is wrong. [2]

Answers to How Science Works questions

1 a To make sure that all of the water was at the same temperature. [1]

b Yes; the temperature is rising at a steady rate. [2]

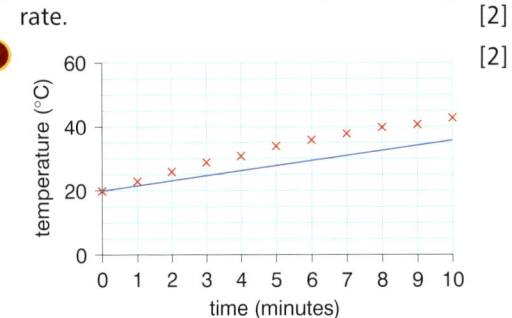

c [2]

2 a Yes. [1]

b

Weight (N)	Length of spring (mm)	Increase in length (mm)
0	40	0
1	46	6
2	52	12
3	58	**18**
4	64	**24**
5	70	**30**

[1]

c [2]

d 6 mm per newton. [1]

e If the weight is doubled, the increase in length is doubled. [2]

3 a 130 g. [1]

b 13 cm. [1]

c Plasticine, water, wood. [2]

d The upthrust increases as the ruler with Plasticine gets heavier. However, eventually the ruler is completely submerged; the upthrust is less than the weight and the ruler sinks. [2]

HSW: Finding the answers to questions (1)

NC links

2 Key processes

- 2.1 Practical and enquiry skills
  Pupils should be able to:
- use a range of scientific methods and techniques to develop and test ideas and explanations.

Level descriptors – How Science Works

- **AT1 level 4:** Pupils decide on an appropriate approach, including using a fair test to answer a question, and select suitable equipment and information from that provided. They select and use methods that are adequate for the task.
- **AT1 level 5:** Pupils decide appropriate approaches to a range of tasks, including selecting sources of information and apparatus. They select and use methods to obtain data systematically.
- **AT1 level 6:** Pupils identify an appropriate approach in investigatory work, selecting and using sources of information, scientific knowledge and understanding. They select and use methods to collect adequate data for the task.

How Science Works

- Recognise that science cannot yet explain everything. (1.1a2)
- Describe an appropriate approach to answer a scientific question using a limited range of information and making relevant observations or measurements. (1.2a)

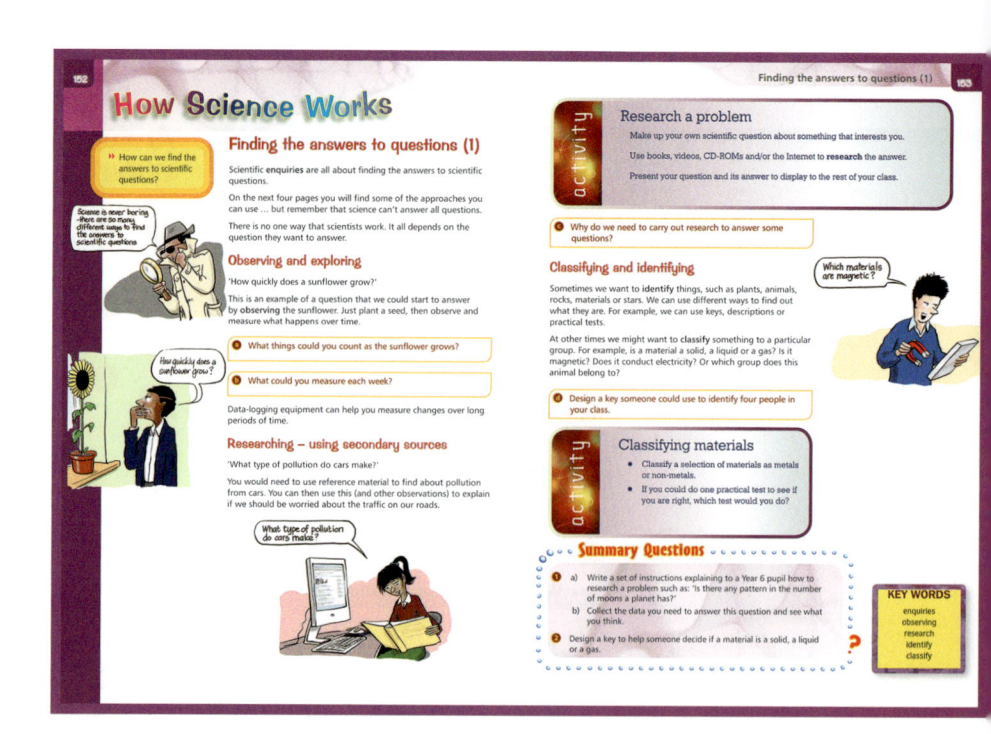

Learning Objectives

Pupils should learn:
- That there are a variety of ways to gather scientific evidence.

Learning Outcomes

- All pupils should be able to list three different ways to collect evidence to answer scientific questions.
- Most pupils should be able to choose a suitable method to gather the data to answer particular scientific questions.
- Some pupils should also be able to identify and carry out different methods to gather data to answer scientific questions.

Learning Styles

Visual: Observing a selection of materials.
Auditory: Listening to the outcomes of the research exercise.
Kinaesthetic: Testing materials in order to classify them.
Interpersonal: Working in groups to research and classify.
Intrapersonal: Thinking back to their Key Stage 2 work on scientific enquiry and how they found the answers to scientific questions.

Functional Skills Link-up

English

- Use appropriate search techniques to locate and select relevant information. (Level 1) See 'Research a problem'.

Finding the answers to questions (1)

The Lesson

Starter Suggestions

Where are we now?
Gather pupils' ideas about what we mean by scientific enquiry / investigation. How have they solved scientific problems in primary school? Some may well be obsessed with 'fair testing', but stress that this is just one of the ways we can carry out scientific enquiries. (5 mins)

How do scientists work?
The pupils can work in groups of four to list all of the ways they know of in which scientists gather data. Start by discussing some jobs in which science plays a role – would they say the role was a major one or is it just a weak link? (10 mins)

Main

- Pupils should have realised from the starter that there is no one way that scientists work to solve problems. At this point you can start to go through some of the approaches that can be used.
- Follow the order of the pupil book and start with general observation and exploration to gather data. The story of Jane Goodall, who studied chimpanzees in Tanzania in the 1950s through to the 1970s, can be used to illustrate how the collection and analysis of large volumes of data can lead to new theories.
- Mention the importance of data-logging equipment in helping scientists observe changes that happen very quickly or over long periods of time. Show some sensors available in your school, perhaps demonstrating their use if time permits.
- Then go on to using secondary sources of information to gather data needed. Pupils will be familiar with this approach, e.g. from their work on the Earth, Moon and Sun in Key Stage 2.
- The activity in the pupil book 'Research a problem' allows pupils to choose an area of interest to delve into and to present their findings to others. Keep it brief here; pupils will have the opportunity for more extensive research later in Key Stage 3.
- Finally look at classifying and identifying as a means of answering scientific questions. The use of keys will have been covered in Key Stage 2, probably in biological enquiries, but extend this to materials in the activity. Depending when you introduce this lesson, you might find it useful to talk briefly about metals and non-metals before tackling 'Classifying materials'.

Plenary Suggestions

Identity parade
Ask for volunteers to try out their keys produced to answer in-text question 4 on the rest of the class. As an extension, they can try out larger numbers of pupils to identify. (10 mins)

States of matter key
Pupils to try Summary question 2 in pairs. Then test out their key on a neighbouring pair to see if it works using some examples from around the room. (5 mins)

Practical Support

Classifying materials
The pupils will be provided with samples of materials to classify. These need not all be metallic and non-metallic elements, e.g. a block of wood.

Equipment and materials required
Per group: blocks of a variety of materials to include some metals (not just iron or steel); magnet, cell, wires, crocodile clips and bulb to test electrical conductivity; plastic beaker (250 cm^3).

Details
The pupils should observe and test materials to see if they have metallic or non-metallic properties. Do not allow pupils to heat the samples of materials. Some might suggest a density test in water which can easily be carried out. Make sure all test the electrical conductivity. Some pupils will also think that all metals are magnetic so have a magnet available to test the metals on display.

Differentiation

SEN
For lower attaining pupils, you may wish to give them practice in framing questions themselves. For example, choose a topic such as the Moon and then get them to ask a question about it using the starting words 'What?', 'Why?', 'How?', 'When?', 'Where?'.

Extension
Higher attaining pupils can suggest investigations in which data-logging equipment could be essential to the work of a scientist.

Answers to in-text questions

a) E.g. number of leaves or petals.

b) E.g. the height of the sunflower.

c) E.g. It might be too difficult / dangerous / impossible to find out the answer by doing an experiment yourself.

d) To check answer, give the key to another group to see if they think it works (See plenary 'Identity parade').

Answers to summary questions

1. a) Pupil list of instructions to search Internet or look up reference book.
   b) E.g. the further away a planet is from the Sun, the more planets it tends to have / the larger the planet, the more moons it tends to have.

2. Pupils should design a key to help someone decide if a material is a solid, a liquid or a gas.

HSW: Finding the answers to questions (2)

NC links

2 Key processes
- 2.1 Practical and enquiry skills
Pupils should be able to:
- use a range of scientific methods and techniques to develop and test ideas and explanations.

Level descriptors – How Science Works
- **AT1 level 4:** Pupils decide on an appropriate approach, including using a fair test to answer a question, and select suitable equipment and information from that provided. They select and use methods that are adequate for the task.
- **AT1 level 5:** Pupils decide appropriate approaches to a range of tasks, including selecting sources of information and apparatus. They select and use methods to obtain data systematically.
- **AT1 level 6:** Pupils identify an appropriate approach in investigatory work, selecting and using sources of information, scientific knowledge and understanding. They select and use methods to collect adequate data for the task.

Learning Objective
Pupils should learn:
- That there are a variety of ways to gather scientific evidence.

Leaning Outcomes
- All pupils should be able to state fair testing, pattern seeking, using models and evaluating techniques as ways of collecting evidence to answer scientific questions.
- Most pupils should be able to choose a suitable method to gather the data to answer particular scientific questions from the range of approaches available.
- Some pupils should also be able to explain why a particular method is chosen to gather data to answer a scientific question.

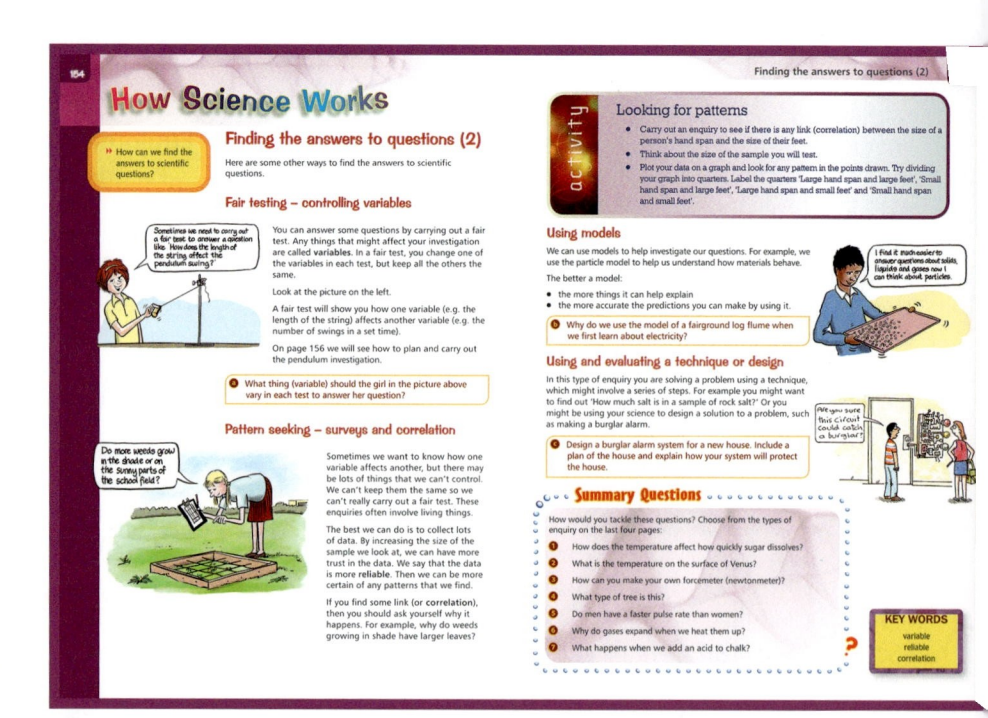

The Lesson

Starter Suggestions
Matching

Ask pupils to identify an approach from the previous lesson to answer each of the following questions:

What type of tree has this leaf come from? [Identifying]

What type of animals live in the deepest oceans? [Research]

How does the temperature in a classroom change over a day? [Observation]

Discuss answers with pupils. (5 mins)

Functional Skills Link-up
ICT
- Create and develop charts and graphs to suit the numerical information, using suitable labels. (Level 2) See 'Looking for patterns'.

Learning Styles
Visual: Looking at points on a scattergram to spot any patterns.
Auditory: Listening to ideas of others about fair testing.
Kinaesthetic: Carrying out the pattern-seeking enquiry.
Interpersonal: Discussing sample sizes.
Intrapersonal: Reflecting on the reliability of data collected.

How Science Works
- Describe an appropriate approach to answer a scientific question using a limited range of information and making relevant observations or measurements. (1.2a)

Fair tests
Ask the pupils to write down five questions that they have investigated using fair tests. Go round the class asking for one question each. (10 mins)

Main Lesson
- Pupils can be asked to define what a fair test is. They might find this difficult without using a specific example and describing how they set up an actual fair test. Introduce the word 'variables'.
- The example of the pendulum given in the pupil book will be used over the next couple of lessons to exemplify the strategy of fair testing, so don't dwell on it here.
- Then introduce the pattern seeking enquiries that rely on data from large sample sizes to improve reliability. These are often biological enquiries which involve elements of fair testing but must be designed with the knowledge that not all variables can be controlled. Therefore to see if there is a connection (correlation) between the two variables under investigation, large sample sizes are important. Discuss reliability in terms of the trust or faith you can put in data collected and therefore in any conclusions drawn from that data.
- Pupils can then try the 'Looking for patterns' enquiry. Data can be gathered as a whole class on a spreadsheet and plotted graphically. Identify any patterns or anomalous data in small groups then discuss as a whole class.
- Ask the class about any models they have used to help explain things in science. Many pupils will have met the particle model already in Year 6, although this is not a requirement of the National Curriculum until Key Stage 3. The second in-text question b prompts them to think about the movement of water as a model for electric current.
- Finally, the pupils are asked to consider solving problems by devising a sequence of steps or designing a system. This has many links with design and technology and this prompt could well stimulate discussion of a richer variety of this type of enquiry.
- Summarise and point out that although we have treated the different approaches separately here, in reality we often use more than one approach to tackle a particular problem. For example, observation can stimulate a fair test which might include elements of research, perhaps to check your data against that produced by other investigators.

Plenary
Heart beat
Ask the class how they would investigate the question 'Do male humans have faster pulse rates than females?' Working in pairs they can jot down key steps in the procedure. Then discuss their ideas as a whole class. Stress the difficulty in controlling all the variables that might affect pulse rate besides male/female, and the need to have a large sample size before you can have any trust in patterns that emerge. (10–15 mins)

Model pupils
In groups of four, ask the class to discuss the behaviour of an elastic band, using themselves as a model for the particles that make up the rubber. Circulate and choose one group to act out their model. (10 mins)

Finding the answers to questions (2)

Practical Support
Looking for patterns
Equipment and materials required
Per group: tape measures, graph paper.

Details
The pupils should use the tape measure to find hand spans. They can use it to measure the length of people's feet or use shoe size for size of feet.

Differentiation
SEN
Help can be given in the plotting of the data on a scatter graph in the 'Looking for patterns' activity.

Extension
Higher attaining pupils can find out how new drugs are developed and tested before being passed as safe for the public to use. A shorter exercise could be to find out and explain the use of a placebo in drug testing.

Answers to in-text questions
a E.g. length of string, mass of bob, method of release.

b E.g. it helps us to understand what happens in an electrical circuit where we can't actually see anything moving.

c To check answer, give the design to another group to see if they think it works.

Answers to summary questions
1. Fair testing.
2. Researching.
3. Using and evaluating a design.
4. Classifying / identifying.
5. Pattern seeking / surveys and correlation.
6. Using models.
7. Observing / exploring.

HSW: The skills of investigation (1)

NC links

2 Key processes
- 2.1 Practical and enquiry skills
Pupils should be able to:
- Assess risk and work safely in the laboratory, field and workplace.
- Plan and carry out practical and investigative activities, both individually and in groups.

Level descriptors – How Science Works
- **AT1 level 4:** Pupils select and use methods that are adequate for the task.

  Following instructions, they take action to control obvious risks to themselves.
- **AT1 level 5:** Pupils select and use methods to obtain data systematically.

  They recognise hazard symbols and make, and act on, simple suggestions to control obvious risks to themselves and others.
- **AT1 level 6:** Pupils select and use methods to collect adequate data for the task.

  They recognise a range of familiar risks and take action to control them.

Learning Objectives
Pupils should learn:
- How to plan a fair test.
- How to plan a safe test.

Leaning Outcomes
- All pupils should be able to fill in a planning framework for a fair test with support and list some hazards associated with an investigation with prompting.
- Most pupils should be able to fill in a planning framework for a fair test and list some hazards associated with an investigation.
- Some pupils should also be able to identify key variables in a simple investigation, classify variables and list hazards associated with an investigation, making suggestions on how to control them.

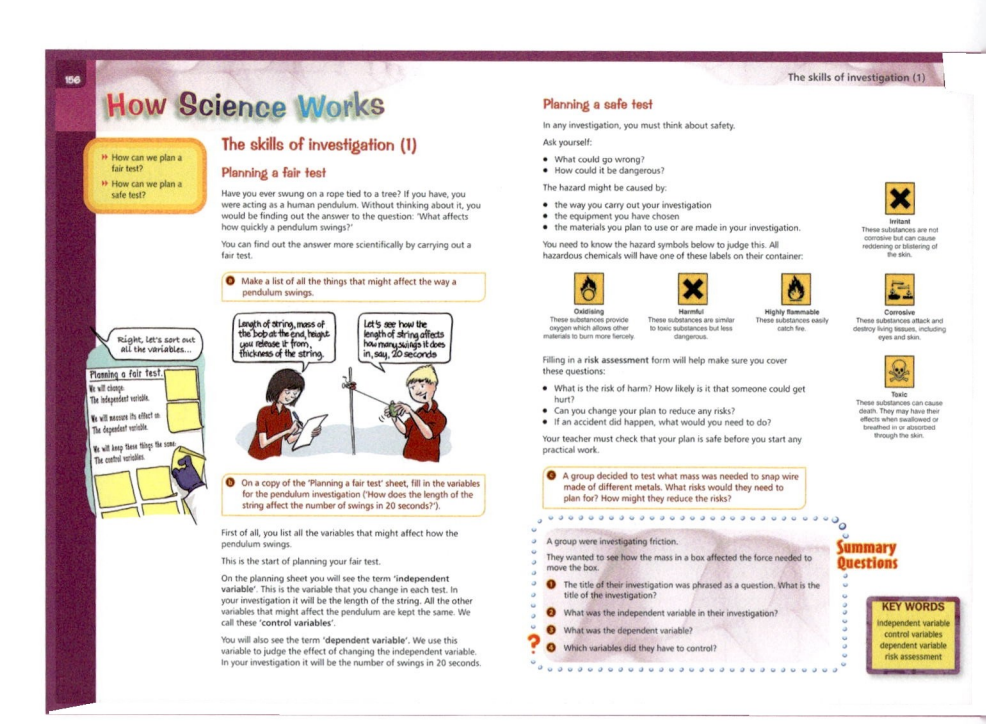

The Lesson

Starter Suggestions

What car?

Gather pupils' ideas about the factors (variables) a consumer takes into account when choosing a new car, and how the decision making process works. Some photos are a good way to stimulate discussion. Link this real-life manipulation of variables to a fair test pupils have done recently. (5 mins)

That's not fair!

You can show the pupils an 'unfair' test and challenge them to identify your mistakes. Which of three balls is the bounciest is a quick and easy starter to demonstrate. Pupils can either list errors spotted individually and feedback at the end, or point out mistakes and discuss how to rectify them as you carry out the test. (10 mins)

How Science Works
- Recognise the range of variables involved in an investigation and decide which to control. (1.2b)
- Explain how action has been taken to control obvious risk and how methods are adequate for the task. (1.2c)

Learning Styles
Visual: Observing the movement of Post-its on the planning frame.
Auditory: Listening to explanations of different types of variable.
Kinaesthetic: Sticking Post-its onto the planning frame.
Interpersonal: Working in groups to identify key variables and hazards.
Intrapersonal: Reflecting on the structure of a fair test in terms of variables.

The skills of investigation (1)

Main Lesson

- Pupils should be familiar with the concept of fair testing from Key Stage 2, although some misconceptions may linger. The use of planning frames is also common in primary schools. The version used here will build on this work and provide a bridge to Key Stage 4 work, introducing the terms 'independent', 'dependent' and 'control variables'.
- The pendulum investigation, which will serve to teach the skills, is 'How does the length of the string affect the number of swings in 20 seconds?'
- The first in-text question can be used to stimulate thinking about the key variables in this investigation.
- Using the planning frame, introduce the terms 'independent variable', 'dependent variable' and 'control variables' and identify them for the pendulum investigation. [The independent variable is length of string, the dependent variable is number of swings in 20 seconds and the control variables are, e.g., mass of the bob, height you release it from.] Note: It is a good idea to have the independent variable and control variables on one colour of Post-it and the dependent variable on a different coloured Post-it. This will help in the following spread when the Post-its are used to explain the presentation of tables, and in the last spread on graphs.
- Discuss the structure of the question with the whole class, i.e. 'How does the [independent variable] affect the [dependent variable]?
- Finish off the spread by introducing safety requirements to consider, including the hazard symbols in the pupil book.
- Show the class a copy of a risk assessment form to fill in for an investigation. You can choose an investigation involving heating, and a chemical with a CLEAPSS Hazcard to model how to fill a form in, if time permits. An example of an appropriate investigation to choose could be the hazards involved in finding out how the solubility of a solid in ethanol is affected by temperature.

Plenary Suggestions

Matching symbols
Ask the class to close their textbooks and then match the hazard symbols to their meanings. Open the books to check their own answers. (5 mins)

Risky business
Go over the answer to in-text question c together as a class, discussing how to control any risks identified. (10 mins)

Practical Support
Per group: the planning frame, six small Post-its, risk assessment form (optional).

Differentiation

SEN
For lower attaining pupils you may wish to use the planning frame to change the independent variable, swapping it with one of the control variables and asking pupils to name the new question being investigated.

Extension
Higher attaining pupils can use the planning frame to devise their own questions to investigate and fill in the appropriate variables.

Answers to in-text questions

a E.g. length of string, mass of the bob at the end, height you release it from.

b E.g. independent variable = length of string; dependent variable = number of swings in 20 seconds; control variables = mass of the bob, height you release it from.

c E.g. the wire springs up when it snaps and hits someone, possibly in the eye. (Wear eye protection.) The masses could fall on someone's foot when the wire snaps (have a bucket containing screwed-up newspapers to catch the masses when they fall).

Answers to summary questions

1. How does the mass affect the force needed to move the box?
2. Mass (in the box).
3. Force (needed to move the box).
4. E.g. surface the box is on, size and mass of box, position of forcemeter.

HSW: The skills of investigation (2)

NC links

2 Key processes

- 2.1 Practical and enquiry skills
  Pupils should be able to:
- plan and carry out practical and investigative activities, both individually and in groups.
- 2.2 Critical understanding of evidence
  Pupils should be able to:
- obtain, record (and analyse – see next spread) data from a wide range of primary … sources, …

Level descriptors – How Science Works

- **AT1 level 4:** They make a series of observations and measurements and vary one factor while keeping others the same. They record their observations, comparisons and measurements using tables.
- **AT1 level 5:** Pupils select and use methods to obtain data systematically. They communicate these using scientific and mathematical conventions and terminology.
- **AT1 level 6:** Pupils select and use methods to collect adequate data for the task, measuring with precision, using instruments with fine scale divisions, and identify the need to repeat measurements and observations. They record data and features effectively. They communicate qualitative and quantitative data effectively, using scientific conventions and terminology.
- **AT1 level 7:** They select and use methods to obtain reliable data, including making systematic observations and measurements with precision.

How Science Works

- Describe and record observations and evidence systematically. (1.2d)
- Recognise that the presentation of experimental results through the routine use of tables … makes it easier to see patterns and trends. (1.2d)

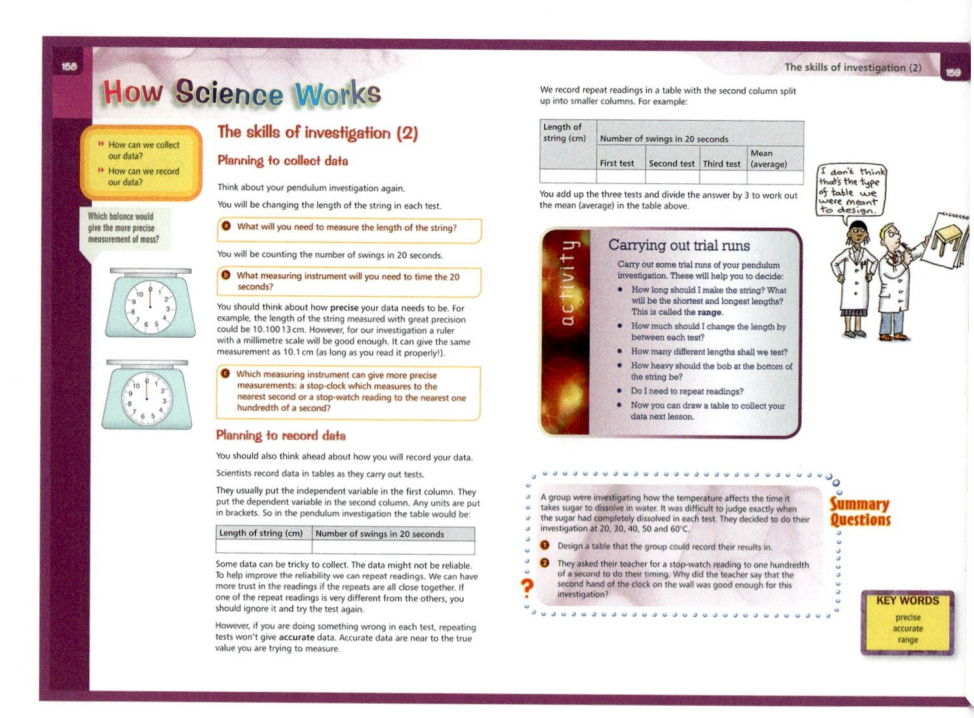

Learning Objectives

Pupils should learn:
- How to obtain data from investigations.
- How to record data from investigations.

Leaning Outcomes

- All pupils should be able to read simple measuring equipment.
- Most pupils should be able to plan a simple table to record data collected from an investigation, carrying out trial runs to decide on a suitable range.
- Some pupils should also be able to design tables to record repeat readings and choose measuring equipment with sufficient precision for the task. They use trial runs to inform their decisions.

Learning Styles

Visual: Observing scales on measuring instruments.
Auditory: Listening to explnations of what we mean by 'reliabilty', 'precision' and 'accuracy'.
Kinaesthetic: Carrying out trial runs of the pendulum investigation.
Interpersonal: Working in groups to design tables.
Intrapersonal: Reflecting on the design of tables to record data from investigations.

The skills of investigation (2)

The Lesson

Starter Suggestions

Reading scales
Give the pupils a sheet showing a variety of scales from analogue measuring instruments. Working individually, ask them to read each one, then quickly give out the answers. Either collect in answers to assess who needs further support, or check during the lesson. (5 mins)

Sort it out
Give the pupils some data that has not been recorded systematically. Ensure that the data show a pattern, and ask them to identify the pattern. Show the same data recorded systematically in a table to illustrate how much easier it is to analyse. (10 mins)

Main Lesson

- Pupils will be familiar with digital and analogue measuring instruments from their work in Key Stage 2. Have a display of a variety of measuring equipment from your school. Talk about the precision possible, perhaps using various sizes of measuring cylinders.
- Discuss the measurements you need to take in the pendulum investigation. What instruments are needed? How precise will measurements need to be?
- Go on to consider how to record their data systematically in a table. Use the planning frame to show how the independent variable usually goes into the first column of your table (with units included in the heading). Physically move the Post-it with 'Length of string' on it into a simple two-column table.
- Then show the dependent variable, 'Number of swings in 20 s' being transferred into the second column.
- Discuss how repeating measurements can improve reliability if they show close agreement, whilst pointing out that this in itself does not guarantee more accurate (true value) data.
- Develop the two-column table into one that can accommodate repeat readings and the mean value by showing pupils how the second column can be divided up.
- Let the pupils carry out some trial runs with the pendulum to help fill in the detail of their planning. The activity 'Carrying out trial runs' introduces the term 'range' which pupils will need to decide on when planning this investigation.

Plenary Suggestions

Table headings
Ask the class to work in pairs to give the table headings to record the results for the investigation 'How does the angle of a ramp affect the speed of a toy car?' Some can be asked to design the table to cater for three repeat readings at each chosen angle. (5 mins)

Working backwards
Give the class some table headings and ask them to write down the title of the investigation (in the form of a question) that each table was designed to record data for. (10 mins)

Practical Support

Carrying out trial runs
Per group: the planning frame, six small Post-its, string, scissors, Plasticine, stop-clock, balance, tape measure/ruler, clamp stand.

Differentiation

SEN
For lower attaining pupils, you may wish to use the planning frame and tables with no headings to practise physically moving relevant Post-its from the planner to the table.

Extension
Higher attaining pupils can devise tables to cater for repeat readings and means.

Answers to in-text questions

a Ruler / tape measure.

b Stop-clock / stop-watch.

c Stop-watch.

Answers to summary questions

1

Temperature (°C)	Time to dissolve (s)
20	
30	
40	
50	
60	

2 Because it is so difficult to judge exactly when the sugar has completely dissolved, it would not be appropriate to give timings to one-hundredth of a second.

HSW: The skills of investigation (3)

NC links

2 Key processes

- 2.1 Practical and enquiry skills
  Pupils should be able to:
- plan and carry out practical and investigative activities, both individually and in groups.
- 2.2 Critical understanding of evidence
  Pupils should be able to:
- obtain, record and analyse data from a wide range of primary … sources, …
- evaluate scientific evidence and working methods.

Level descriptors – How Science Works

- **AT1 level 4:** They begin to relate their conclusions to patterns in data, including graphs, and to scientific knowledge and understanding. They communicate their conclusions using appropriate scientific language. They suggest improvements in their work, giving reasons.
- **AT1 level 5:** They analyse findings to draw scientific conclusions that are consistent with the evidence. They communicate these using scientific and mathematical conventions and terminology. They evaluate their working methods to make practical suggestions for improvements.
- **AT1 level 6:** They analyse findings to draw conclusions that are consistent with the evidence and use scientific knowledge and understanding to explain them and account for any inconsistencies in the evidence. They manipulate numerical data to make valid comparisons and draw valid conclusions. They communicate qualitative and quantitative data effectively, using scientific conventions and terminology. They evaluate evidence, making reasoned suggestions about how their working methods could be improved.

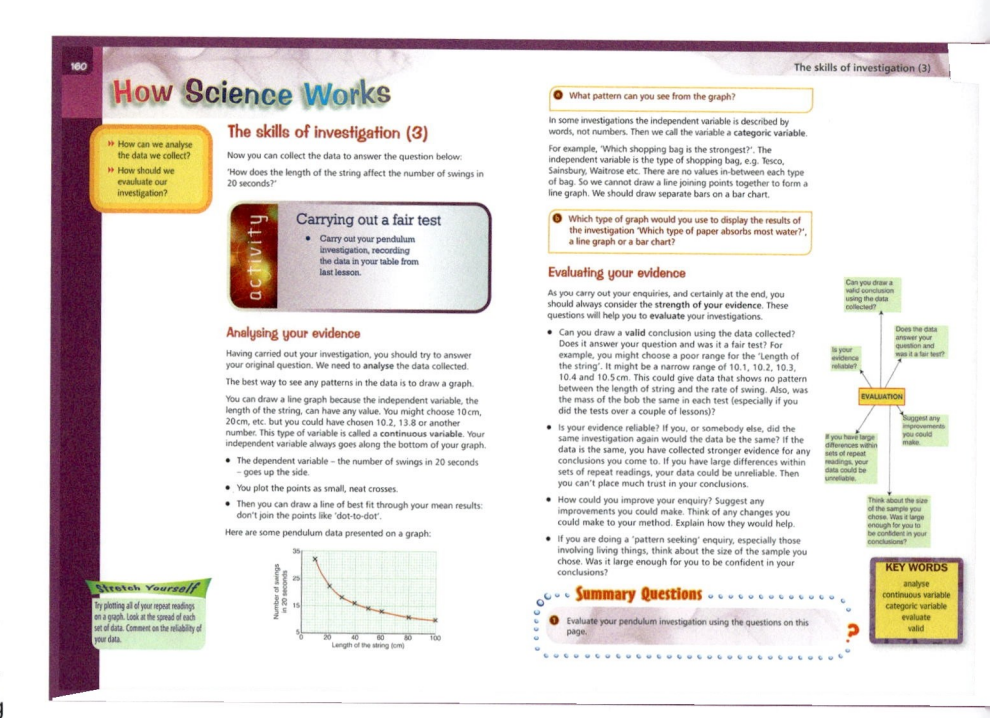

Learning Objectives

Pupils should learn:
- How to present and analyse data graphically.
- How to evaluate investigations.

Learning Outcomes

- All pupils should be able to describe a pattern from a graph and suggest an improvement to an investigation.
- Most pupils should be able to begin to explain the patterns they spot in data and suggest several ways to improve an investigation.
- Some pupils should also be able to explain the patterns they spot in data and suggest several ways to improve an investigation, explaining their reasoning.

Learning Styles

Visual: Looking at different graphs.

Auditory: Listening to others when discussing the patterns shown by a line graph.

Kinaesthetic: Carrying out the pendulum investigation.

Interpersonal: Discussing graphs in pairs.

Intrapersonal: Reflecting on their own investigation, suggesting improvements.

Functional Skills Link-up

Mathematics

- Collect and represent discrete and continual data, using ICT where appropriate. (Level 2)

How Science Works

- Recognise that the presentation of experimental results through the routine use of tables, bar charts and simple graphs makes it easier to see patterns and trends. (1.2d)
- Describe patterns and trends in results … (1.2e)
- Describe and suggest how planning and implementation could be improved. (1.2e)

The skills of investigation (3)

The Lesson

Starter Activities

Name that investigation
Show the pupils a line graph and ask them to discuss, in pairs, which investigation had been carried out to gather the data for the graph. Ask them to phrase the title of the investigation as a question. (5 mins)

Trials
Ask the pupils to look back to the trial runs completed last lesson, and to make a list of all the values they decided on in preparation for the pendulum investigation that is to be completed today. Then they should write a few sentences to persuade a pupil teacher why allowing lesson time for trial runs is a good idea. (10 mins)

Main Lesson

- Pupils have the opportunity to carry out the full pendulum investigation, which should not take too long as values for variables have been decided and the table to record results should have been prepared in the last lesson.
- Stress why some data can be presented on line graphs and others on bar charts. This should involve introducing the terms 'continuous variable' and 'categoric variable'. Some pupils will be able to grasp this new terminology now, but for most these terms and the concepts such as reliability, precision and accuracy will need constant reinforcement throughout the key stage.
- After the data gathering, get pupils to show their data on a line graph, explaining how to use a line of best fit.
- This is a good opportunity to introduce some pupils to the idea of anomalous data and how we can discard it (pupils might initially think this makes their investigation 'unfair').
- Go over the type of things you should consider when evaluating your investigation using the second part of the spread. Stress that although an evaluation is often written down at the end of an investigation, the process is actually on-going and we need to think about the issues raised as soon as we start.
- Ask pupils to do the Summary question and evaluate their pendulum investigation. Ensure that you share the assessment criteria from the Level descriptors with the class. Pupils will raise their level of attainment by explaining why their suggested improvements are needed.

Plenary

Spotting patterns
Show the pupils a series of line graphs and ask them to discuss, in pairs, the patterns shown (if any). Go over the graphs as a whole class. (5 mins)

Carrot cruncher
Ask the class to think about two pupils, each eating a raw carrot. One pupil is a slow eating 'nibbler' and one is a fast eating 'cruncher'. Working in pairs, ask the class to sketch a graph of the length of the carrot against time, showing both pupils' data. Ask a couple of pairs to explain their answers. (10 mins)

Practical Support

Carrying out a fair test
Equipment and materials required
Per group: string, scissors, Plasticine, stop-clock, balance, tape measure/ruler, clamp stand.

Differentiation

SEN
For lower attaining pupils you may wish to use a writing frame to help phrase the relationship between variables, e.g. 'The longer the string, the . . . the pendulum swings.'

Extension
Higher attaining pupils can display all their repeat data on a graph and consider the spread within sets of repeat readings in terms of reliability.

Answers to in-text questions

a The longer the string, the smaller the number of swings in 20 seconds. (The longer the string, the slower the pendulum swings.)

b Bar chart.

Answer to summary question

1 Pupil evaluation: use the Level descriptors to assess quality.

Glossary

accurate Describes data that is near to the true value

acid A chemical that can dissolve in water to make a solution with a pH of less than 7

adapted An animal, plant or cell having specialisations for a certain job

afterbirth The placenta, which is pushed out of the womb after a baby is born

air pressure The force per unit area caused by air particles hitting the sides of a container

air resistance Similar to drag; the force of friction when an object moves through air

alkali A chemical that can dissolve in water to make a solution with a pH of more than 7

ammeter An instrument for measuring electric current

amnion The bag of liquid that surrounds and protects an unborn baby

analyse To examine data collected

antacid A medicine to treat heartburn or acid indigestion

anther The male part of a flower which makes pollen

antibody A chemical produced by white blood cells which helps destroy microbes

aseptic Working in sterile conditions

asexual reproduction A method of reproduction which involves only one parent

bacteria (singular bacterium) A type of microbe

balanced Two or more forces whose effects cancel out

ball and socket joint A type of joint, like that in the shoulder or hip, which gives a wide range of movement

base A chemical that will react with (neutralise) an acid

battery Two or more electrical cells connected together

bio-diesel A fuel for vehicles, made from anything which grows

biomass Living material which can be burned to release energy

biotechnology Using biological methods to make useful products

boiling A physical change where a liquid is heated and becomes a gas

breech birth Where a baby is born bottom first instead of head first

brittle Breaks easily

bulb An adapted leaf bud which some plants use to store food

Bunsen burner A piece of equipment used to heat chemicals in the lab

Caesarean section An emergency form of childbirth, where the mother's uterus is cut open to take the baby out

calorie A unit of energy stored in food

carbon dioxide A gas that forms 0.04% of the air

carbonate Part of a chemical that can react with an acid to form carbon dioxide

carpel The female part of a flower made of the stigma, style and ovary

cartilage A tough elastic material which acts as a shock absorber between bones

categoric variable A variable that is described by words, not numbers

cell A single component that provides a voltage in an electric circuit

cell A small structure that makes up most living organisms

cell membrane A thin layer that surrounds a cell

cell sap The liquid found in the vacuole of plant cells

cell wall A rigid layer around a plant cell, which gives it strength

cellulose The material which cell walls are made of

cervix A narrow tube between the vagina and the uterus

chemical change A difference where new chemicals are made

chemical reaction A change, where new chemicals have been made

chlorophyll A green substance found in plants which traps energy from light for use in photosynthesis

chloroplast The part of a plant cell containing chlorophyll, where photosynthesis takes place

chromatogram The results from a chromatography experiment

chromatography A method for separating inks and dyes

circuit diagram A diagram used to show the arrangement of components in a circuit

circulatory system The parts of the body that carry blood

classification System for sorting things into groups

classify Putting things into groups

climate change Long-term changes in the pattern of our weather

colony A group of millions of bacteria, growing on a Petri dish, which can be seen with the naked eye

combustion A chemical reaction that is also known as burning

compass A device which uses a small magnet to show direction

component Any item used as part of an electric circuit

conclusion What has been found out from an investigation

condense A physical change where a gas becomes a liquid

condom A rubber sheath which stops sperm getting from the penis to the uterus

conductor A material which allows electric current to flow freely

continuous variable A variable that can have numerical values

contraception A method of preventing a woman from getting pregnant

contraceptive pill A tablet containing hormones which stops a woman from getting pregnant

Glossary

contract A muscle contracts when it shortens

contraction When muscles in the wall of the uterus get smaller and squeeze the baby out

control variables These variables are kept constant to make sure an investigation is a fair test

core A piece of magnetic material used to increase the strength of an electromagnet

correlation A link or connection between two variables

corrosion A chemical change between oxygen and metal; rusting is an example of corrosion

corrosive Describes a substance that kills living cells and can eat away at a lot of different materials such as metals

courtship An activity designed to attract a member of the opposite sex

cover slip A thin piece of glass that is placed on top of the specimen on a microscope slide

curd The solid material that is separated from milk in making cheese

cytoplasm The liquid inside a cell where chemical reactions occur

density How heavy something is for its size; it is often measured in grams per centimetre cubed (g/cm^3). Density = mass/volume

dependent variable The variable you use to judge the effect of changing the independent variable

device An item used to perform a task, often run on electricity

diaphragm i) A layer of muscle below the ribs, used in breathing. ii) A rubber disc, used as a contraceptive in women, which stops sperm getting into the uterus

diffusion The spreading out of gas or liquid particles

digestive system The parts of the body used to get nutrients from food

disease Something that stops our body from working properly

dispersal Spreading seeds away from the plant on which they were formed

displacement Movement from one place to another

distillate The liquid collected in the receiving tube in a distillation

distillation A method for separating liquids from each other or solutions

drag The force of friction when an object moves through a liquid or a gas

dye A coloured solution

ejaculation Forcing semen from the penis in sexual intercourse

electric current A flow of electric charge around a circuit

electromagnet A magnet made from a coil of wire, operated by an electric current

electron A tiny charged particle which moves through a metal when a current flows

electron microscope A special kind of microscope, which uses a beam of electrons instead of light and can produce much higher magnifications than a light microscope

embryo The stage in the development of an animal before it has formed most of the main organs

energy What burning fuels release, allowing us to do things

enquiry The way in which we find out the answers to scientific questions

enzyme A protein which controls a chemical reaction in living things

epidermis cells A thin outer layer of cells

epithelial cell A thin layer of cells lining surfaces inside the body, such as lungs, intestines, etc.

erection When a penis becomes larger and stiffer so that sexual intercourse can take place

evaluate To suggest ways of improving an investigation

evaporation A physical change where a liquid becomes a gas below its boiling point

extension Increase in length of a spring or other object

eyepiece A lens in a microscope that you look through

fermentation When microbes use a source of energy and produce a useful product, e.g. beer or wine

fertilisation When the male nucleus joins with a female nucleus

filament A 'stem' which supports an anther

filter A method for separating a solid from a liquid

filtrate The liquid collected after filtration

fixed joint A type of joint, like those in the skull, which does not move

flammable Describes a chemical that burns easily

fetus The stage in the development of an animal after the main organs have been formed

force A push or a pull

forcemeter A device used to measure a force

fossil fuel A fuel formed from materials which were once alive

freeze A physical change where a liquid becomes a solid

friction A force which opposes movement

fruit A structure produced by a plant, which helps the dispersal of seeds

fuel A material burned to release energy in a more useable form

function What something does, its job

fungus (pl. fungi) A type of organism, often microscopic

fuse A component which melts ('blows') when the current flowing through it is too great

gametes Sex cells, such as sperm, egg, ovule and pollen

gas The state of matter in which the particles are spaced out, and move fast in all directions

germination The start of growth of a seed

glands A part of the body which releases a substance, e.g. the liquid added to sperm to make semen

greenhouse gas Any gas (such as carbon dioxide) which contributes to global warming

harmful Harmful chemicals can make you very ill if you eat them, breathe them in or absorb them through your skin

Glossary

hazard Something that can cause an accident

heating effect The increase in temperature caused by an electric current

hinge joint A type of joint, like the elbow, which moves in one direction

hormone A chemical which carries messages to cells, such as those which control puberty and the menstrual cycle

hydrocarbon A chemical that contains only hydrogen and carbon

hydrogen An explosive gas; it can be tested by putting a lighted splint near it when you will hear a squeaky pop

identify Naming things

image What we see when we look through a microscope

in parallel Components connected side-by-side are in parallel

in series Components connected end-to-end are in series

incubate To keep something, such as microbes, in warm conditions so that it grows or develops

independent variable The variable that you choose to change in a fair test

indicator A special chemical that can be used to find out if a liquid is an acid or an alkali

infectious Can spread from organism to organism

inflexible Cannot be easily bent

inoculation The transfer of microbes onto a growth medium

insulation (thermal) Material used to prevent the escape of heat from a building

insulator (electrical) A material which does not allow electric current to flow freely

irreversible Cannot be changed back

irritant Will make your skin red and itchy

IUD Intra-uterine device used as a method of contraception

joule (J) The scientific unit of energy

kilojoule A unit of energy

lactic acid A substance, produced by bacteria, which causes milk to thicken and form yoghurt

ligament Joins bones together at joints

limewater A chemical used to test for carbon dioxide; if the colourless limewater turns milky then carbon dioxide is present

lines of force Used to represent the strength and direction of a magnetic field

liquid A state of matter where the particles are close together and move randomly

load A force which tends to stretch an object

lubricant A substance which reduces friction

magnetic field The area around a magnet where magnetic materials can be affected

magnetic material Any material which is attracted by a magnet

magnetise To turn something into a magnet

magnify To make something look bigger

mains electricity Electricity supplied from a central source such as a power station

malleable Can be hammered into shapes without breaking

mammary glands The parts of a female mammal's body that produce milk

marrow A jelly-like substance inside bones which produces blood cells

mass A measurement of how many particles there are in a material, it is measured in kilograms (kg)

measure Finding the size of a quantity

melting A physical change where a solid becomes a liquid

menstrual cycle The monthly changes in the reproductive organs of a female human

menstruation The part of the menstrual cycle when the uterus lining breaks down

metal A chemical that is shiny, malleable and a conductor; they often have high melting and boiling points and are sonorous (can make a ringing sound)

method A step-by-step guide to completing an experiment.

methylene blue A stain used on microscope slides

microbe A living organism which is too small to be seen

micro-organism Another name for a microbe

microscope A piece of apparatus used to look at very small objects

mixture More than one substance, not chemically joined together

model A simplified way of explaining observations; models have limits but can be used to make predictions

nerve cell A cell which carries electrical impulses between parts of the body as a method of communication

nervous system The brain and nerve cells, which control the body

neutral A chemical with a pH equal to 7

neutralisation A chemical reaction between a base (or alkali) and an acid; this makes a metal salt and water

newton (N) The scientific unit of force

newtonmeter A device used to measure a force; a forcemeter

non-metal A chemical that is dull, brittle and an insulator; they often have low melting and boiling points

non-renewable Describes energy resources which are used up

nucleus The part of a cell which carries genetic information

nutrient agar jelly A substance which is used to grow microbes

objective The lens in a microscope nearest the thing we are looking at

observing Using your senses to gather data

offspring The young or babies of an animal

organ A group of tissues with a particular job

ovary i) The part of the female reproductive system which releases eggs and produces hormones. ii) The part of a flower which makes ovules

oviduct The tube between the ovary and the uterus where fertilisation takes place

Glossary

ovulation The release of an egg from the ovary

ovule The female sex cell in a plant

ovum (plural **ova**) The scientific name for an egg

oxidiser A chemical that gives oxygen to another chemical to help it burn better

oxygen A gas that makes up about 20% of the air

palisade cell A leaf cell containing may chloroplasts; the main site of photosynthesis

particle This is what makes up all matter

pathogen A microbe which causes a disease

penis The male organ which puts sperm inside a female

period Another name for menstruation

permanent magnet A magnet which doesn't require a current to make it work

Petri dish A glass or plastic dish with a lid, often used for growing microbes

pH A measure of how acidic or alkaline

physical change A reversible change that does not make a new chemical

pivot joint A type of joint, such as between the skull and vertebrae

placenta A structure in the uterus where substances pass between the mother's and fetus's blood

pole Where the magnetic force of a magnet is most concentrated

pollen The male sex cell in a plant

pollen tube A tube which grows from the stigma to the ovary and carries the pollen nucleus to the ovules

power station A place where electricity is generated on a large scale

precise Describes measurements taken by an instrument with fine scale divisions, for example, 13.23 cm is more precise than 13 cm

prediction A suggestion about what will happen in an experiment, explaining the reason using science

premature birth A birth more than three weeks before it is expected

pressure A force acting over an area; often measured in newtons per metre squared (N/m^2)

properties A description of how a chemical will look and behave

proportional When one quantity increases in step with another

protozoa (sing. **protozoan**) A type of microbe

puberty The time when we complete the development of our sex organs

pure Contains only one type of substance

random Without a pattern

range The highest and lowest values in a set of data

reactivity A suggestion of how likely a chemical is to undergo a chemical change

record To write down observations and measurements

red blood cell A blood cell which carries oxygen around the body

relax In a muscle, the opposite of contract

reliable Describes data that you can trust

renewable Describes energy resources which will never run out

reproductive system The parts of the body concerned with making babies

research Using sources of information to find out the answers to questions

resistance How much a component opposes the flow of electric current

respiratory system The parts of the body concerned with taking in oxygen and removing carbon dioxide

reversible Can be changed back to what it started as

risk assessment Your judgement of the hazards involved in a task and how to control them

root hair cell A type of plant cell, with a large surface area, adapted to absorb water and minerals

runner A special type of stem which grows across the surface of the soil and on which a new plant starts to grow

scrotum The special bag made of skin which contains the testes

semen A mixture of sperm and liquid

sensitive Able to sense small differences or changes

separating Sort out into pure substances

sex hormones Hormones which control the menstrual cycle and the development of sexual characteristics

sexual reproduction Reproduction involving two parents, male and female

sexually transmitted disease A disease which is passed on in sexual contact

sieve A method for separating different sized pieces of solids

skeleton All of the bones of the body

slide A piece of glass used in preparing microscope specimens

solenoid Another name for the coil of an electromagnet

solid A state of matter where all the particles vibrate and are touching in a regular arrangement

solute A chemical that mixes completely with liquid (solvent) to form a mixture

solution A mixture of a solute in a solvent

solvent A liquid that can dissolve other substances (solutes)

specialised Has a particular job

specimen Something which is looked at through a microscope

sperm cell A male sex cell

sperm tube The tube which carries sperm from the testes to the penis

stain A coloured chemical that makes it easier to see a microscope specimen

stamen The male parts of a flower made of the anther and filament

state symbol A code to explain if a chemical is a solid, liquid, gas or in a solution

Glossary

stigma The female part of a flower which collects pollen

strong A chemical with a high or low pH number

style The part of a flower which supports the stigma

sustainable Can be used far into the future without damaging the environment

synovial fluid A liquid found in joints and acts as lubrication

tendon Connects a muscle to a bone

testis (plural testes) Part of the male reproductive system which makes sperm

thermostat A device for controlling the temperature reached by a heating system

tissue A group of the same types of cell

trip switch An electromagnetic switch, used instead of a fuse

tuber A swollen underground plant stem which acts as a store of food

umbilical cord Carries blood between the placenta and the fetus

universal indicator A special chemical that can be used to find out the pH number of an acid, alkali or neutral chemical

upthrust The upward force on an object in a liquid such as water, or in a gas

uterus The part of the female reproductive system where the baby develops

vacuole A large space in a plant cell containing cell sap

vagina The part of the female reproductive system where sperms are deposited and where the baby comes out

valid Describes a conclusion drawn from data collected in a fair test, which is designed to answer your original question

variable resistor A resistor whose value can be easily changed

variable Factors that might affect an investigation

vibrate Bouncing around a fixed position

virus The smallest type of microbe

voltage A measure of the push of a cell or battery

voltmeter A meter used to measure voltage

volume The amount of space something occupies

weak A chemical with a pH number between 4 and 10, but not 7

weight The force of the Earth's gravity on an object

whey The liquid left when curds are separated from milk in cheese manufacture

white blood cell A type of blood cell which helps fight diseases

Acknowledgements

Alamy 33.5, 44.1, 56.2, 57.3, 68.1, 68.2, 73.4, 74.1, 78.2, 81.2, 81.3, 81.4, 81.5, 81.6, 81.7, 86.1, 92.1, 94.1, 98.2, 100.1, 100.3, 101.6, 102.2, 108.4, 113.4, 114.1, 116.1, 120.1, 120.3, 121.4, 128.1, 128.3, 130, 131.3, 136.1, 140.1, 140.3, 146.1, 147.2, 148.1, 148.2; **Martyn Chillmaid** 60.4, 61, 70, 78.1, 86, 101.5, 112; **Corbis** 56.1, 66.1, 66.2, 132.1, 134.1, 137.4, 142.1, 144.1, 144.2; **Corel 124 (NT)** 18; **Corel 82 (NT)** 22; **Corel 459 (NT)** 23; **Corel 602 (NT)** 29; **Corel 545 (NT)** 42; **Corel 799 (NT)** 142: **Digital Vision 4 (NT)** 33, 108.1; **DK Images** 3.3; **Mary Evans** 104.1, 105.3; **Fotolia** 100.2; **GreenGate Publishing** 110.1; **iStock** 83.1; **Oxford Scientific OSF** 28.2; **Photodisc 72 (NT)** 88; **Photo researchers** 129.5; **David Sang** 117.4; **SATS papers** 26; **Science Photo Library** 3.2, 5.2, 7.2, 8.2, 9.3, 15.2, 16.2, 16.3, 16.4, 18.2, 19.3, 19.4, 20.1, 24.1, 29.3, 29.5, 32.1, 34.1, 34.3, 34.4, 36.3, 37.4, 38.1, 38.2, 41.5, 42.1, 42.2, 43.4, 44.2, 46.2, 47.4, 48.2, 50.1, 50.2, 54.1, 55.3, 60.1, 61.3, 62.2, 62.3, 62.4, 64.2, 65.3, 68.3, 68.4, 70.1, 91.4, 100.4, 102.1,106.107.4, 111, 113.5, 114, 122.1, 123.4, 124.1, 125.5, 133.4, 135.4, 138.1; **Andrew Lambert Photography** 58.2, 88.2, 98.1, 102.1

Picture research by GreenGate Publishing and Kate Lewis.

Every effort has been made to trace all the copyright holders, but if any have been overlooked the publisher will be pleased to make the necessary arrangements at the first opportunity.

Notes

Notes

Notes